D1203453

STAR WARS

HOPE DIES

Jessamine County Public Library
600 South Main Street
Nicholasville, KY 40356
859-885-3523

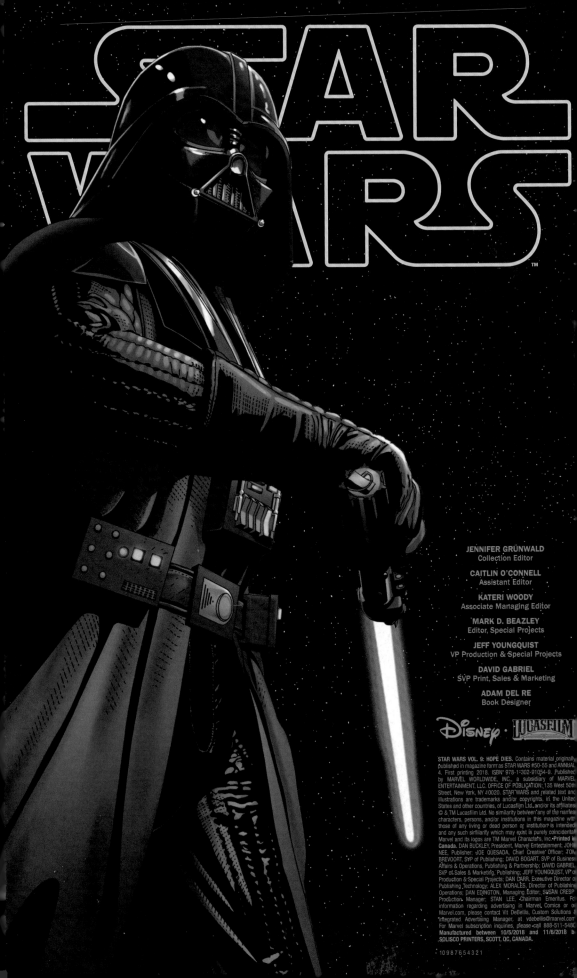

STAR WARS

JENNIFER GRÜNWALD
Collection Editor

CAITLIN O'CONNELL
Assistant Editor

KATERI WOODY
Associate Managing Editor

MARK D. BEAZLEY
Editor, Special Projects

JEFF YOUNGQUIST
VP Production & Special Projects

DAVID GABRIEL
SVP Print, Sales & Marketing

ADAM DEL RE
Book Designer

Disney • LUCASFILM

STAR WARS VOL. 9: HOPE DIES. Contains material originally published in magazine form as STAR WARS #50-55 and ANNUAL 4. First printing 2018. ISBN# 978-1-302-91054-9. Published by MARVEL WORLDWIDE, INC., a subsidiary of MARVEL ENTERTAINMENT, LLC. OFFICE OF PUBLICATION: 135 West 50th Street, New York, NY 10020. STAR WARS and related text and illustrations are trademarks and/or copyrights, in the United States and other countries, of Lucasfilm Ltd. and/or its affiliates. © & TM Lucasfilm Ltd. No similarity between any of the names, characters, persons, and/or institutions in this magazine with those of any living or dead person or institution is intended, and any such similarity which may exist is purely coincidental. Marvel and its logos are TM Marvel Characters, Inc. Printed in Canada. DAN BUCKLEY, President, Marvel Entertainment; JOHN NEE, Publisher; JOE QUESADA, Chief Creative Officer; TOM BREVOORT, SVP of Publishing; DAVID BOGART, SVP of Business Affairs & Operations, Publishing & Partnership; DAVID GABRIEL, SVP of Sales & Marketing, Publishing; JEFF YOUNGQUIST, VP of Production & Special Projects; DAN CARR, Executive Director of Publishing Technology; ALEX MORALES, Director of Publishing Operations; DAN EDINGTON, Managing Editor; SUSAN CRESPI, Production Manager; STAN LEE, Chairman Emeritus. For information regarding advertising in Marvel Comics or on Marvel.com, please contact Vit DeBellis, Custom Solutions & Integrated Advertising Manager, at vdebellis@marvel.com. For Marvel subscription inquiries, please call 888-511-5480. Manufactured between 10/5/2018 and 11/6/2018 by SOLISCO PRINTERS, SCOTT, QC, CANADA.

10 9 8 7 6 5 4 3 2 1

HOPE DIES

ISSUES #50-55

Writer	KIERON GILLEN
Artist	SALVADOR LARROCA
Color Artist	GURU-eFX
Cover Art	TRAVIS CHAREST (#50) & DAVID MARQUEZ (#51-55) WITH JESUS ABURTOV (#51), MARTE GRACIA (#52-53), PAUL MOUNTS (#54) & TAMRA BONVILLAIN (#55)

"SHU-TORUN LIVES"

Writer	KIERON GILLEN
Penciler	GIUSEPPE CAMUNCOLI
Inker	CAM SMITH
Colorist	JAVA TARTAGLIA
Letterer	VC's CLAYTON COWLES
Assistant Editor	TOM GRONEMAN
Editor	MARK PANICCIA

ANNUAL #4

Writer	CULLEN BUNN
Artists	ARIO ANINDITO, ROLAND BOSCHI & MARC LAMING
Color Artists	JORDAN BOYD & ANDRES MOSSA
Letterer	VC's CLAYTON COWLES
Cover Art	TRADD MOORE & MATTHEW WILSON
Assistant Editors	HEATHER ANTOS, TOM GRONEMAN & EMILY NEWCOMEN
Editors	JORDAN D. WHITE WITH MARK PANICCIA

Editor in Chief	C.B. CEBULSKI
Chief Creative Officer	JOE QUESADA
President	DAN BUCKLEY

For Lucasfilm:

Assistant Editor	NICK MARTINO
Senior Editor	ROBERT SIMPSON
Executive Editor	JENNIFER HEDDLE
Creative Director	MICHAEL SIGLAIN
Lucasfilm Story Group	JAMES WAUGH, LELAND CHEE, MATT MARTIN

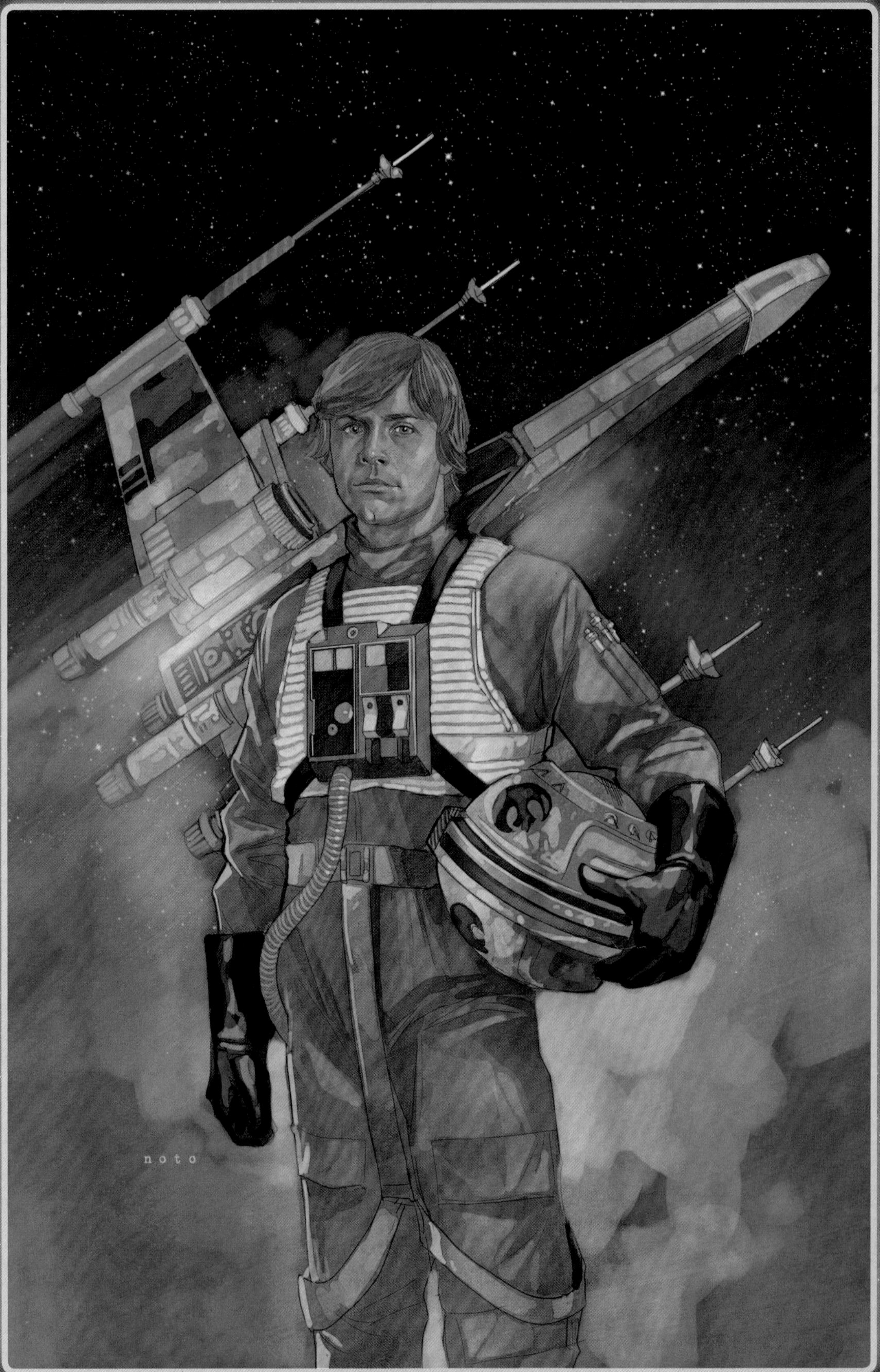
noto

***STAR WARS* 50 Variant by**
PHIL NOTO

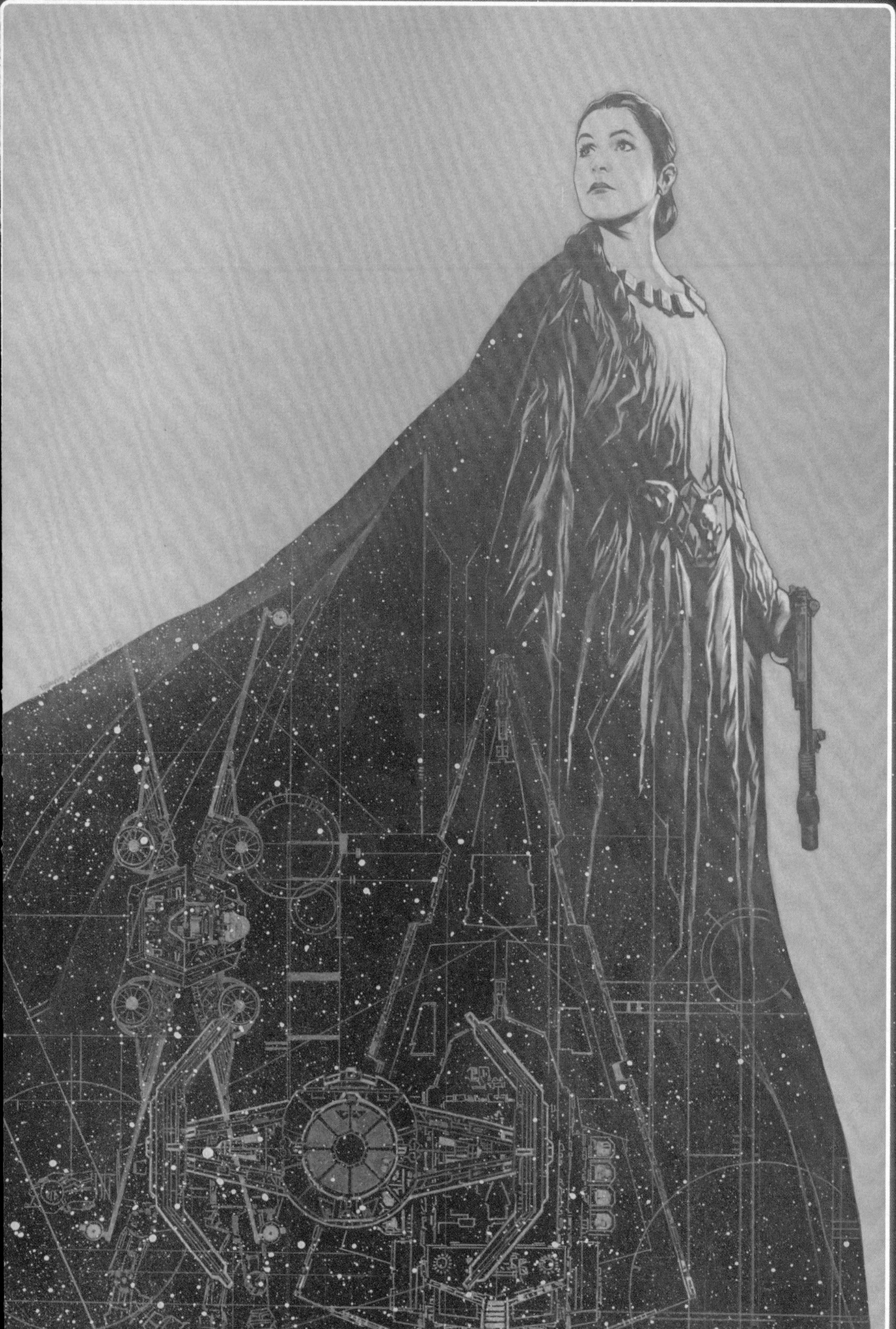

HOPE DIES

The murder of their beloved king at the hands of the evil Empire has inspired open revolt on Mon Cala!

Thanks to a timely counterattack by Admiral Ackbar as well as the heroics of Luke Skywalker, Princess Leia and Han Solo, the Mon Calamari's powerful fleet now stands ready to fight for peace and justice with the Rebel Alliance.

Armed with new ships and new allies, the Rebellion is finally poised to take back the galaxy from the Empire in earnest. But the Rebels also owe their recent victory to Queen Trios of Shu-Torun and her defection to their cause. But Trios may have plans of her own....

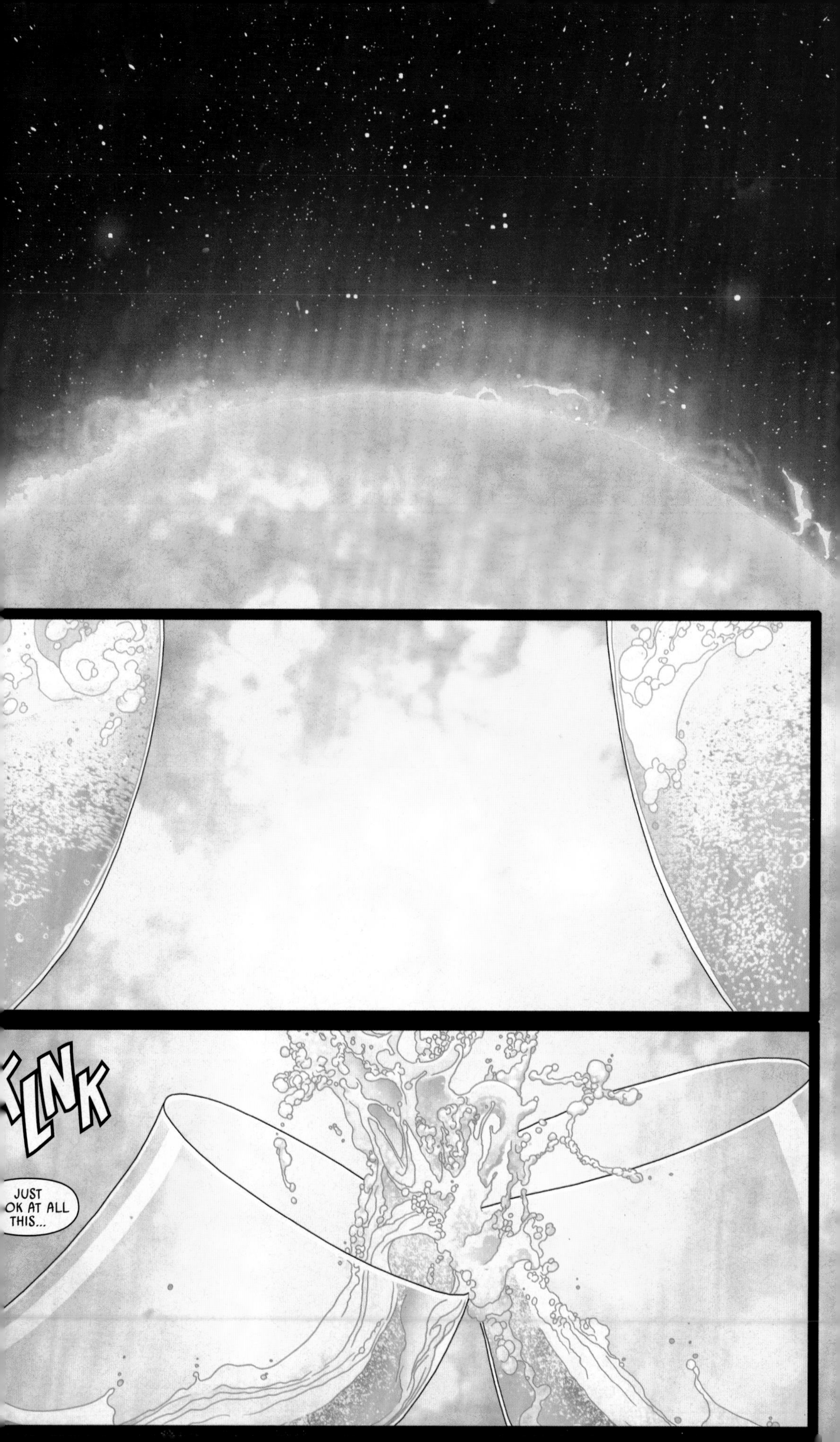

KLNK
JUST
OK AT ALL
THIS...

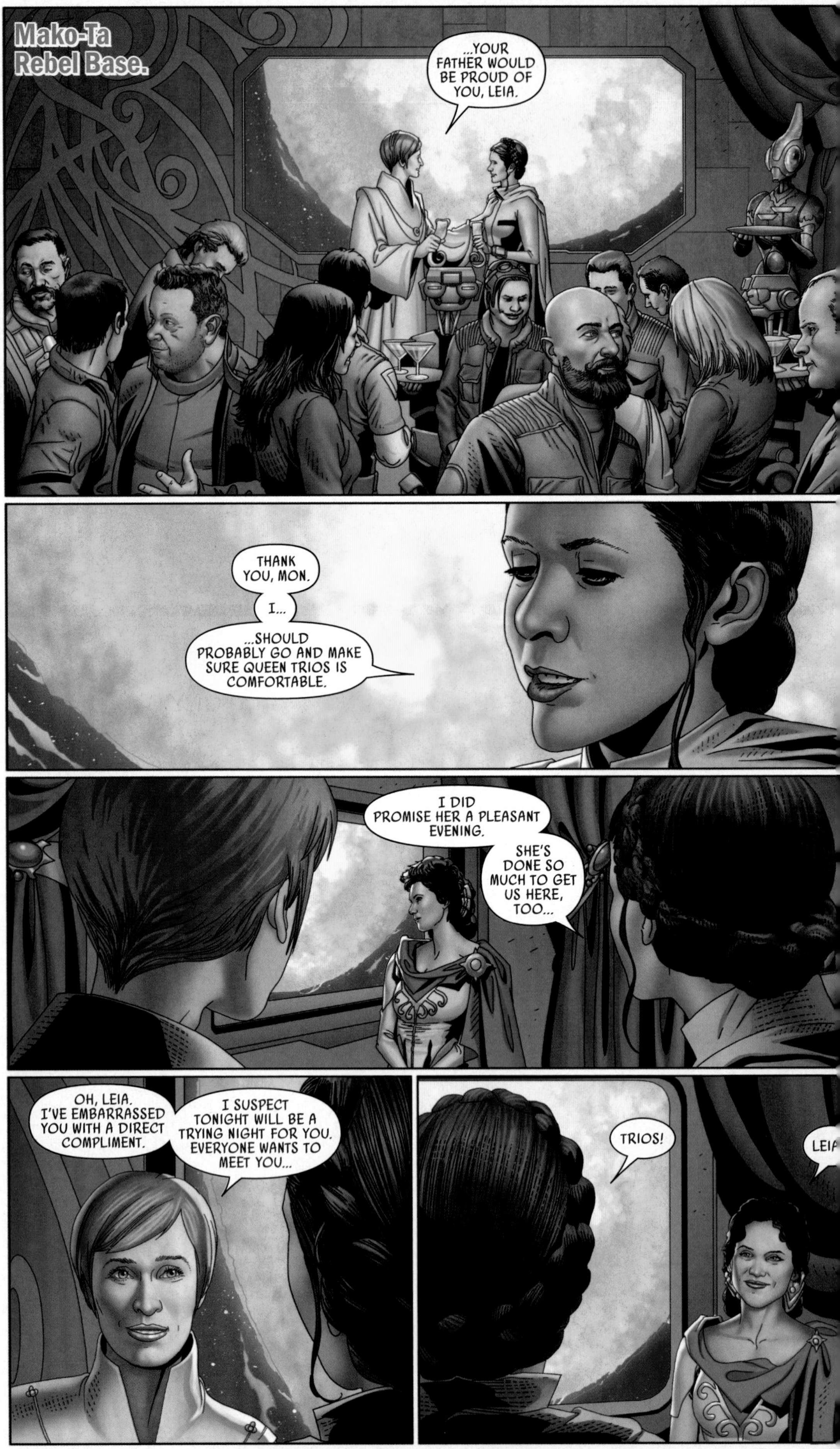
Mako-Ta Rebel Base.
...YOUR FATHER WOULD BE PROUD OF YOU, LEIA.
THANK YOU, MON.
I...
...SHOULD PROBABLY GO AND MAKE SURE QUEEN TRIOS IS COMFORTABLE.
I DID PROMISE HER A PLEASANT EVENING.
SHE'S DONE SO MUCH TO GET US HERE, TOO...
OH, LEIA. I'VE EMBARRASSED YOU WITH A DIRECT COMPLIMENT.
I SUSPECT TONIGHT WILL BE A TRYING NIGHT FOR YOU. EVERYONE WANTS TO MEET YOU...
TRIOS!

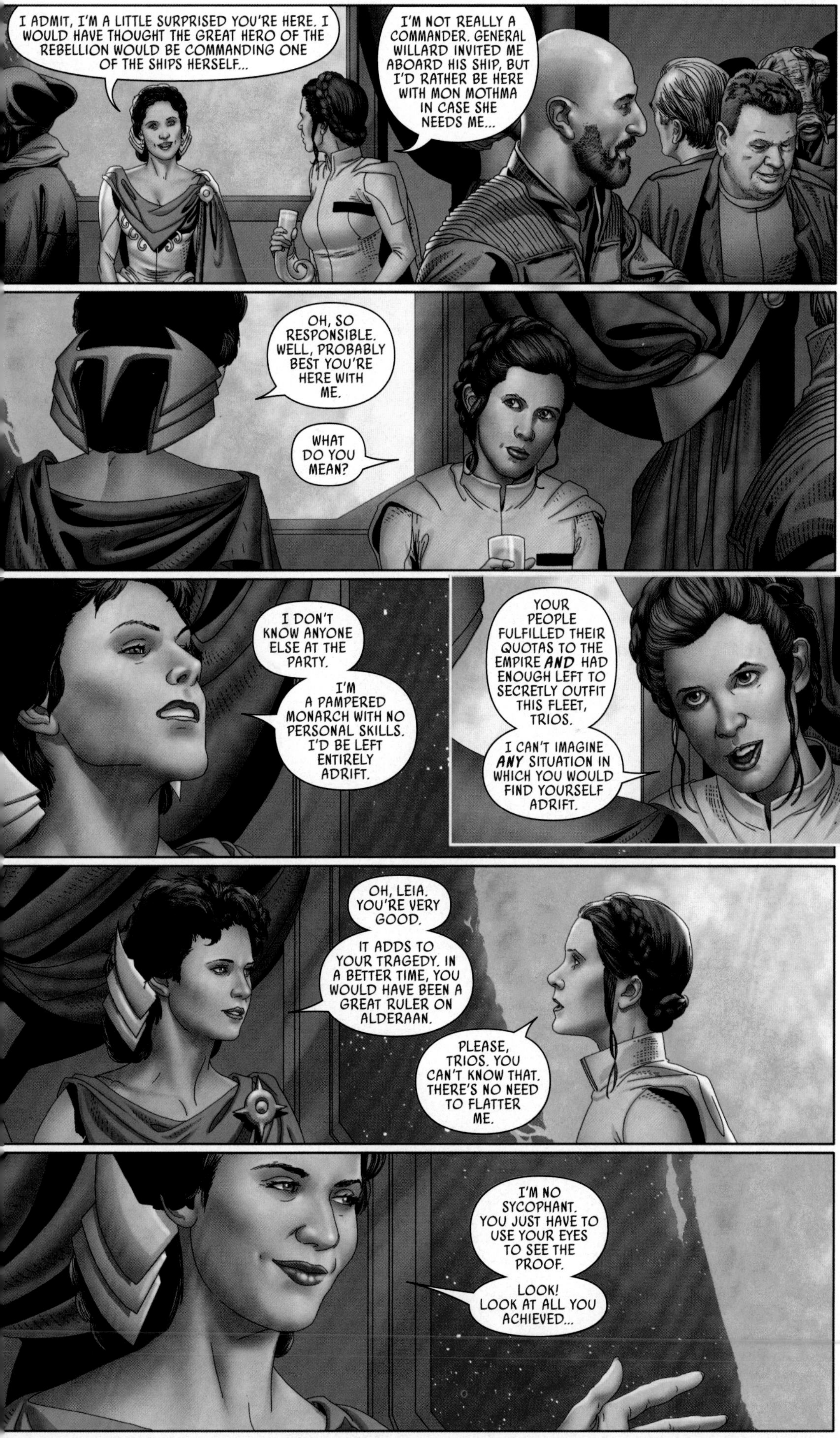
I ADMIT, I'M A LITTLE SURPRISED YOU'RE HERE. I WOULD HAVE THOUGHT THE GREAT HERO OF THE REBELLION WOULD BE COMMANDING ONE OF THE SHIPS HERSELF...
I'M NOT REALLY A COMMANDER. GENERAL WILLARD INVITED ME ABOARD HIS SHIP, BUT I'D RATHER BE HERE WITH MON MOTHMA IN CASE SHE NEEDS ME...
OH, SO RESPONSIBLE. WELL, PROBABLY BEST YOU'RE HERE WITH ME.
WHAT DO YOU MEAN?
I DON'T KNOW ANYONE ELSE AT THE PARTY.
I'M A PAMPERED MONARCH WITH NO PERSONAL SKILLS. I'D BE LEFT ENTIRELY ADRIFT.
YOUR PEOPLE FULFILLED THEIR QUOTAS TO THE EMPIRE ***AND*** HAD ENOUGH LEFT TO SECRETLY OUTFIT THIS FLEET, TRIOS.
I CAN'T IMAGINE ***ANY*** SITUATION IN WHICH YOU WOULD FIND YOURSELF ADRIFT.
OH, LEIA. YOU'RE VERY GOOD.
IT ADDS TO YOUR TRAGEDY. IN A BETTER TIME, YOU WOULD HAVE BEEN A GREAT RULER ON ALDERAAN.
PLEASE, TRIOS. YOU CAN'T KNOW THAT. THERE'S NO NEED TO FLATTER ME.
I'M NO SYCOPHANT. YOU JUST HAVE TO USE YOUR EYES TO SEE THE PROOF.
LOOK! LOOK AT ALL YOU ACHIEVED...

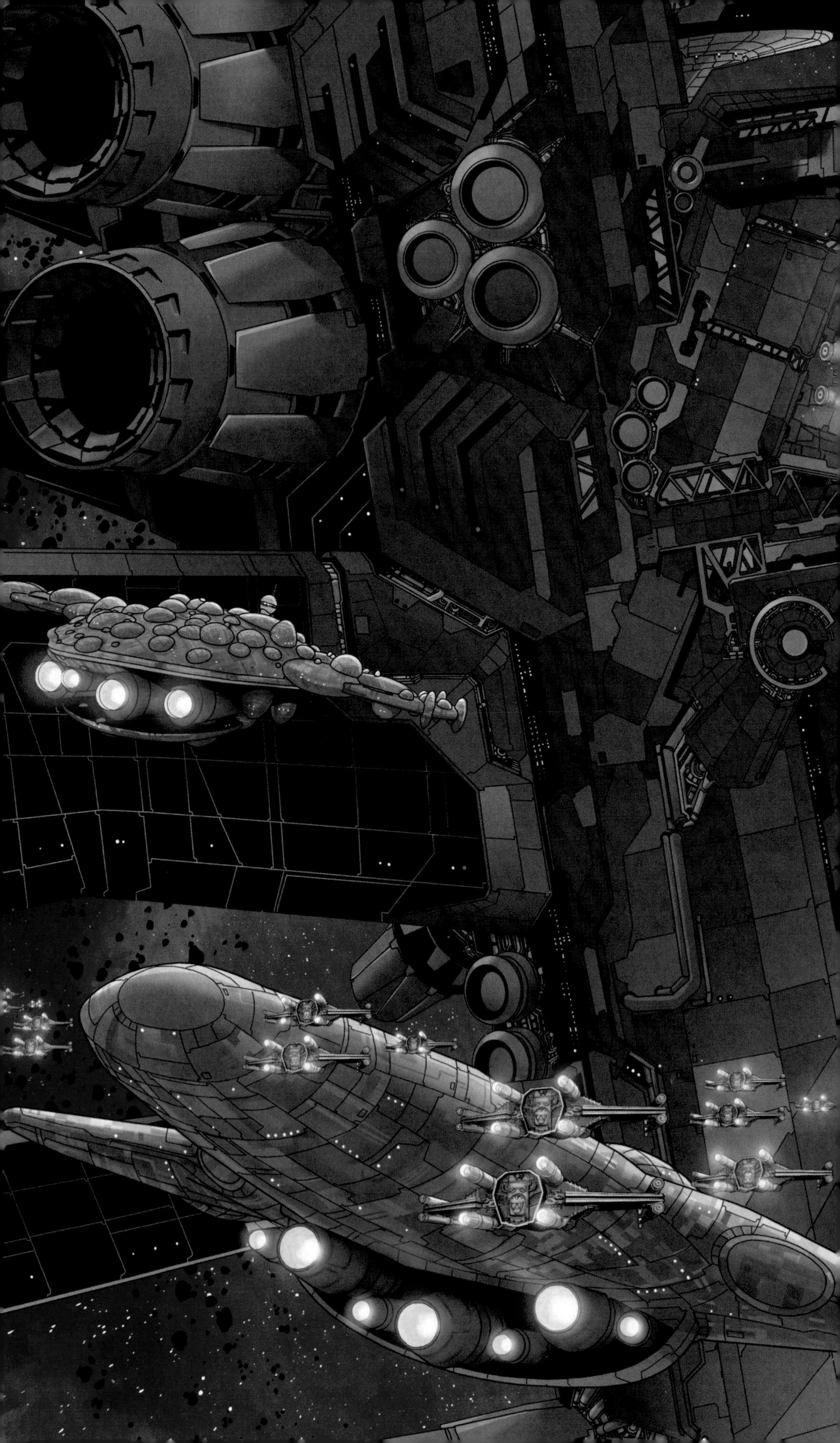

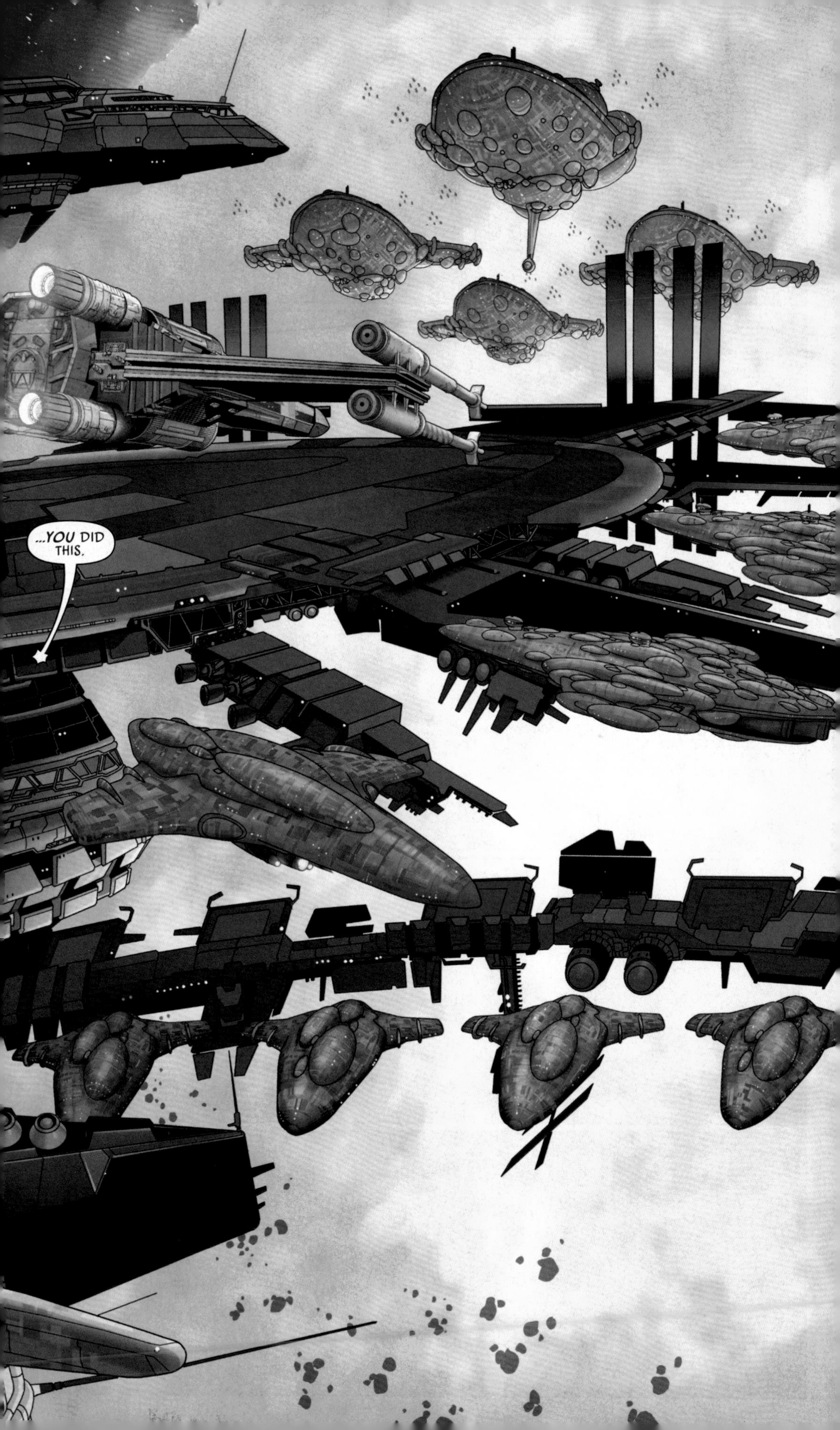
...YOU DID THIS.

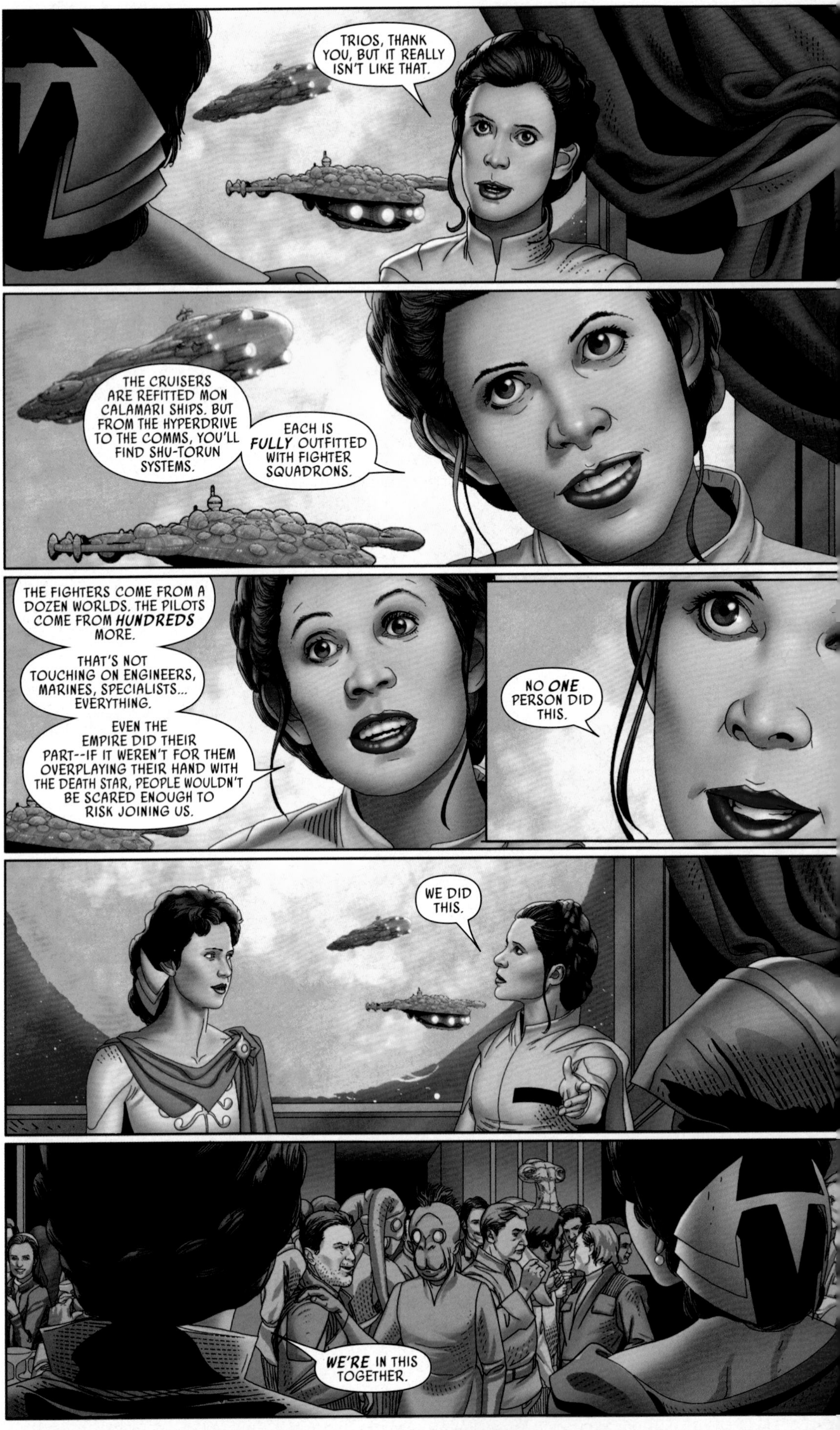

TRIOS, THANK YOU, BUT IT REALLY ISN'T LIKE THAT.
THE CRUISERS ARE REFITTED MON CALAMARI SHIPS. BUT FROM THE HYPERDRIVE TO THE COMMS, YOU'LL FIND SHU-TORUN SYSTEMS.
EACH IS FULLY OUTFITTED WITH FIGHTER SQUADRONS.
THE FIGHTERS COME FROM A DOZEN WORLDS. THE PILOTS COME FROM HUNDREDS MORE.
THAT'S NOT TOUCHING ON ENGINEERS, MARINES, SPECIALISTS... EVERYTHING.
EVEN THE EMPIRE DID THEIR PART--IF IT WEREN'T FOR THEM OVERPLAYING THEIR HAND WITH THE DEATH STAR, PEOPLE WOULDN'T BE SCARED ENOUGH TO RISK JOINING US.
NO ONE PERSON DID THIS.
WE DID THIS.
WE'RE IN THIS TOGETHER.

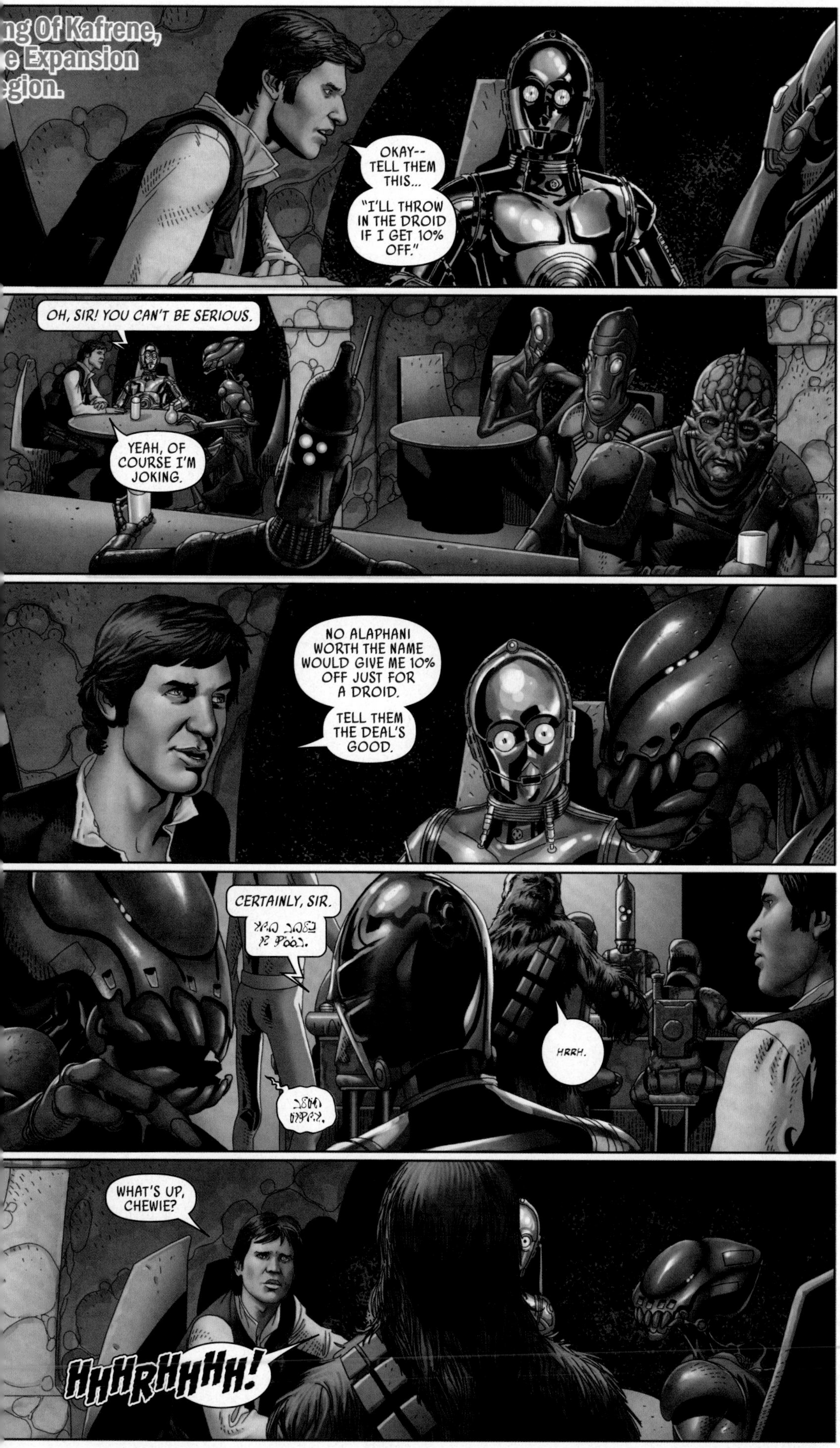

...ng Of Kafrene, ...e Expansion ...egion.
OKAY-- TELL THEM THIS... "I'LL THROW IN THE DROID IF I GET 10% OFF."
OH, SIR! YOU CAN'T BE SERIOUS.
YEAH, OF COURSE I'M JOKING.
NO ALAPHANI WORTH THE NAME WOULD GIVE ME 10% OFF JUST FOR A DROID.
TELL THEM THE DEAL'S GOOD.
CERTAINLY, SIR.
HRRH.
WHAT'S UP, CHEWIE?
HHHRHHHH!

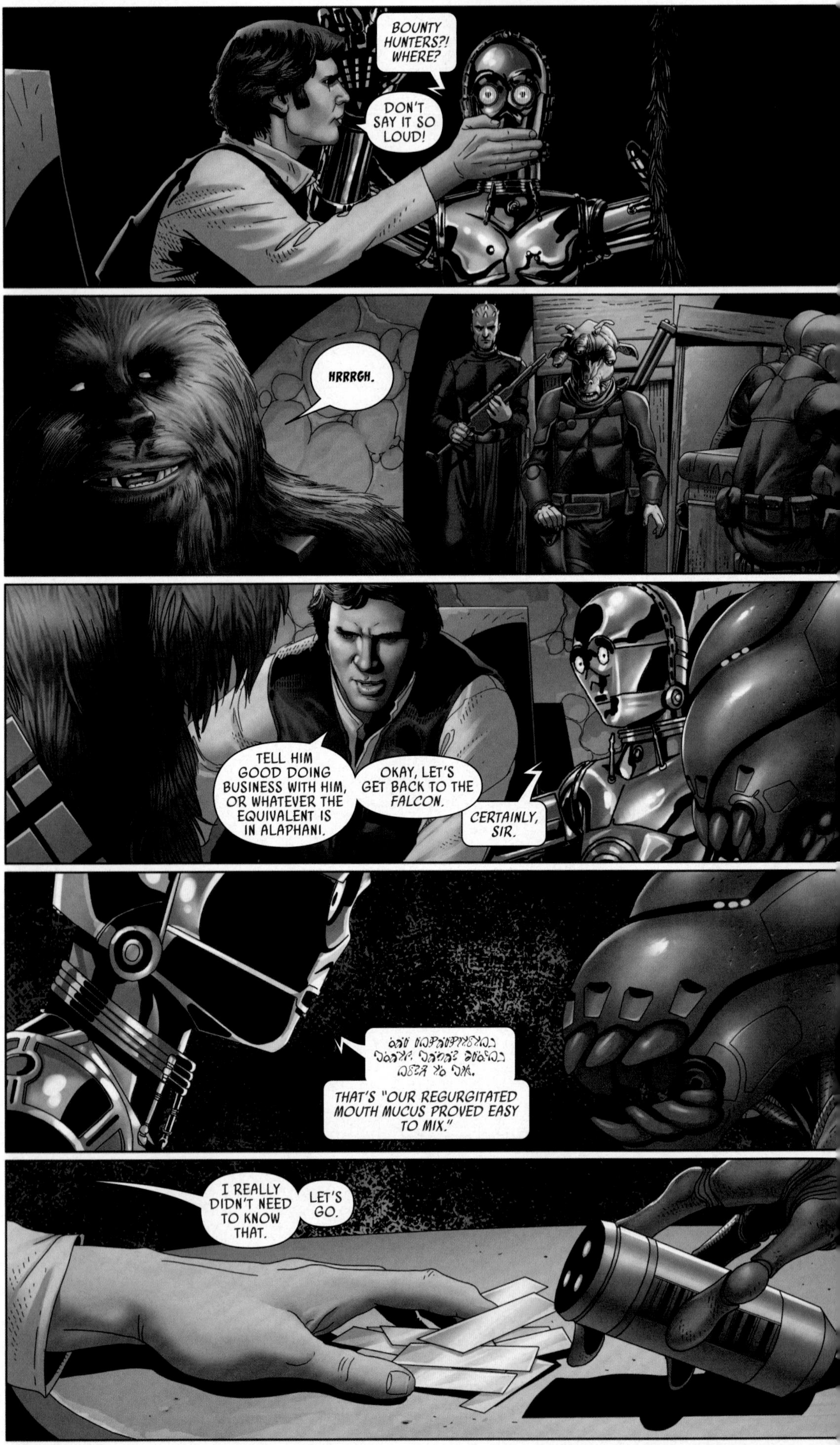
BOUNTY HUNTERS?! WHERE?
DON'T SAY IT SO LOUD!
HRRRGH.
TELL HIM GOOD DOING BUSINESS WITH HIM, OR WHATEVER THE EQUIVALENT IS IN ALAPHANI.
OKAY, LET'S GET BACK TO THE FALCON.
CERTAINLY, SIR.
THAT'S "OUR REGURGITATED MOUTH MUCUS PROVED EASY TO MIX."
I REALLY DIDN'T NEED TO KNOW THAT.
LET'S GO.

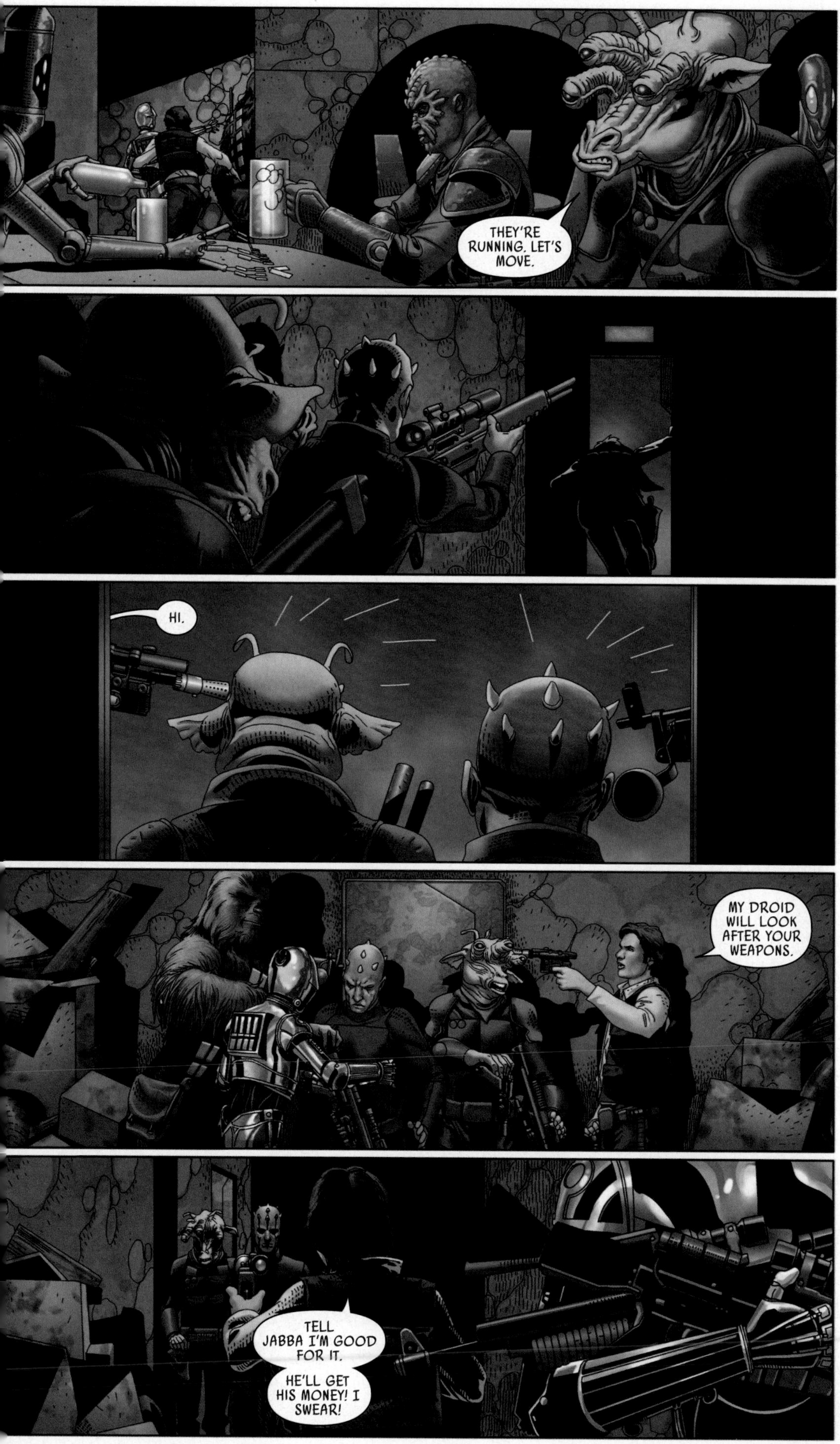
THEY'RE RUNNING. LET'S MOVE.
HI.
MY DROID WILL LOOK AFTER YOUR WEAPONS.
TELL JABBA I'M GOOD FOR IT.
HE'LL GET HIS MONEY! I SWEAR!

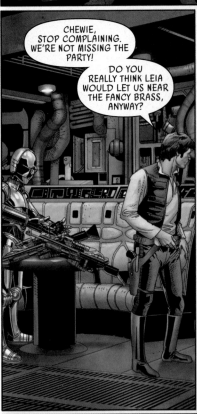

CHEWIE, STOP COMPLAINING. WE'RE NOT MISSING THE PARTY!

DO YOU REALLY THINK LEIA WOULD LET US NEAR THE FANCY BRASS, ANYWAY?

BETTER WE DO WHAT WE'RE GOOD AT--AND I'VE GOT A CONTACT WHO'LL PAY TOP CREDIT FOR THIS PRIME COLLECTION OF FRESH TRANSPONDER CODES.

HHRHRHRHHH!

OH, YEAH, LUKE'S THING...

...YEAH, YOU GOT ME. I'D HAVE LIKED TO HAVE SEEN THAT, TOO.

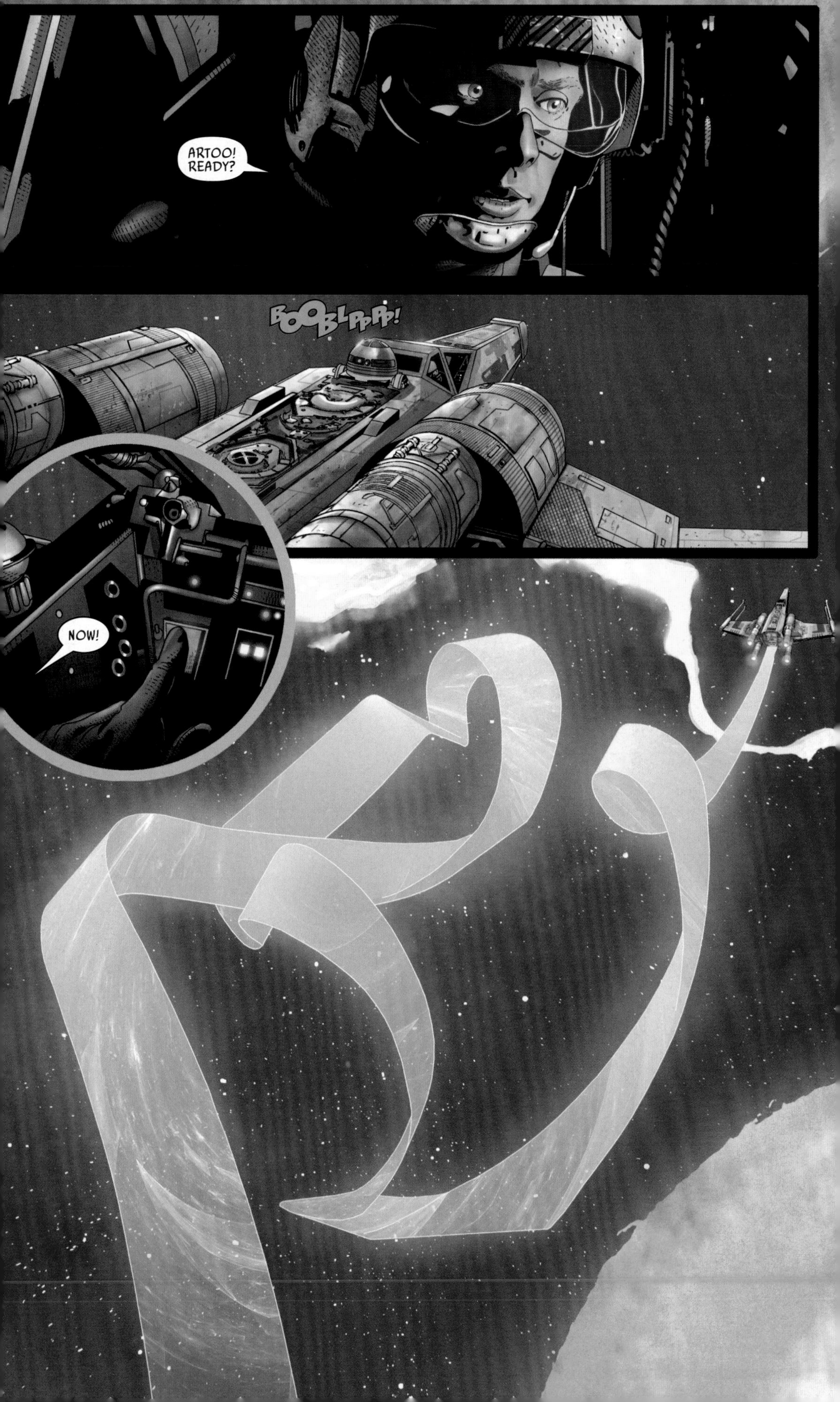
ARTOO! READY?
BOOBLPPP!
NOW!

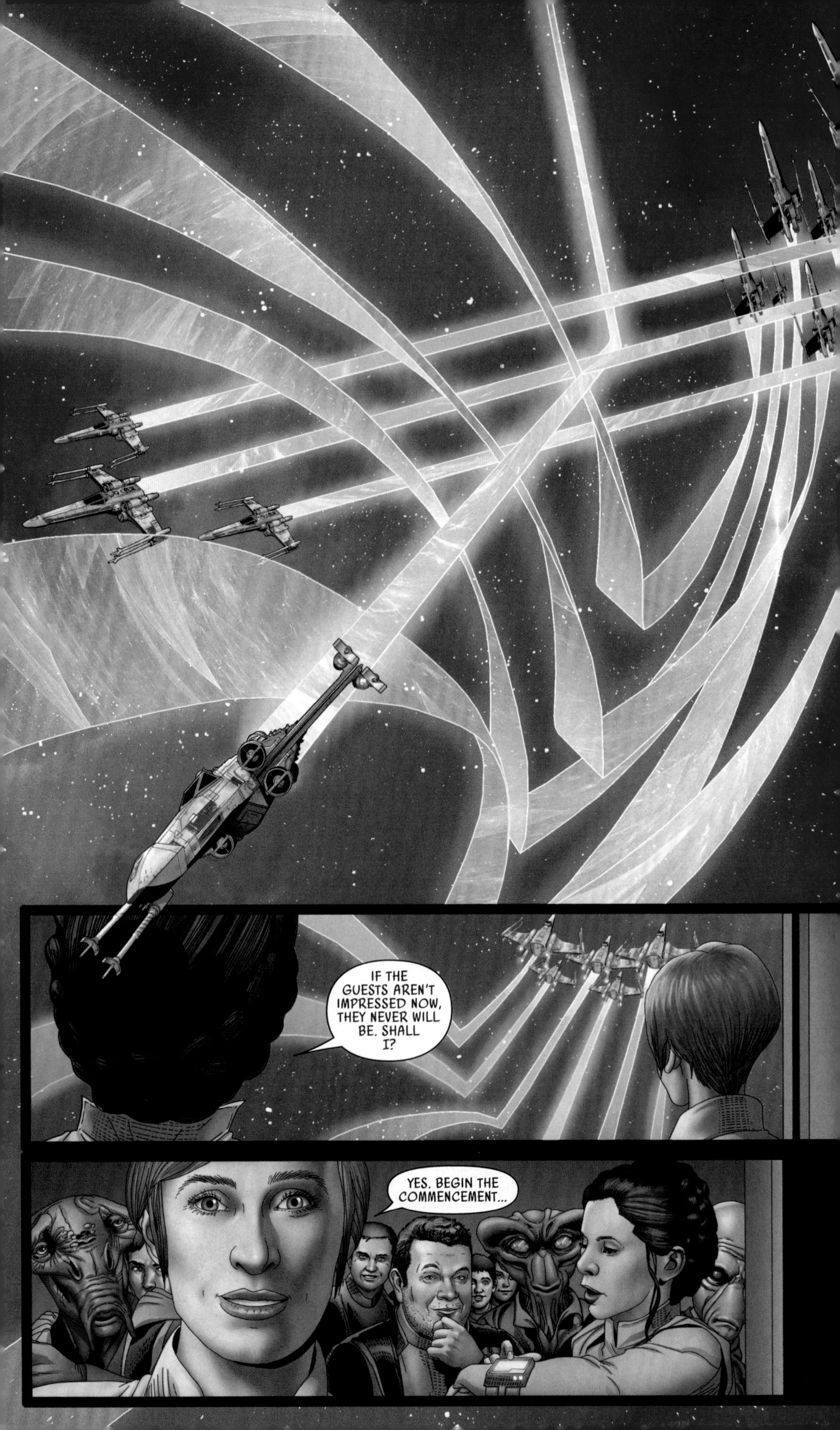
IF THE GUESTS AREN'T IMPRESSED NOW, THEY NEVER WILL BE. SHALL I?
YES. BEGIN THE COMMENCEMENT...

I'VE NEVER SEEN SO MANY REBELS IN ONE PLACE.

THE EMPIRE DOESN'T HAVE A CHANCE!

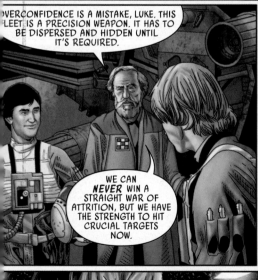

OVERCONFIDENCE IS A MISTAKE, LUKE. THIS FLEET IS A PRECISION WEAPON. IT HAS TO BE DISPERSED AND HIDDEN UNTIL IT'S REQUIRED.

WE CAN *NEVER* WIN A STRAIGHT WAR OF ATTRITION, BUT WE HAVE THE STRENGTH TO HIT CRUCIAL TARGETS NOW.

I UNDERSTAND, SIR.

I'M JUST EXCITED.

YOU ARE FAR FROM ALONE IN THAT SENTIMENT.

GENERAL DODONNA, YOU'RE NEEDED ON THE BRIDGE.

YES, I KNOW. I DID PLAN THIS COMMENCEMENT.

TELL LEIA WE'RE READY WHENEVER THE REST OF THE FLEET IS...

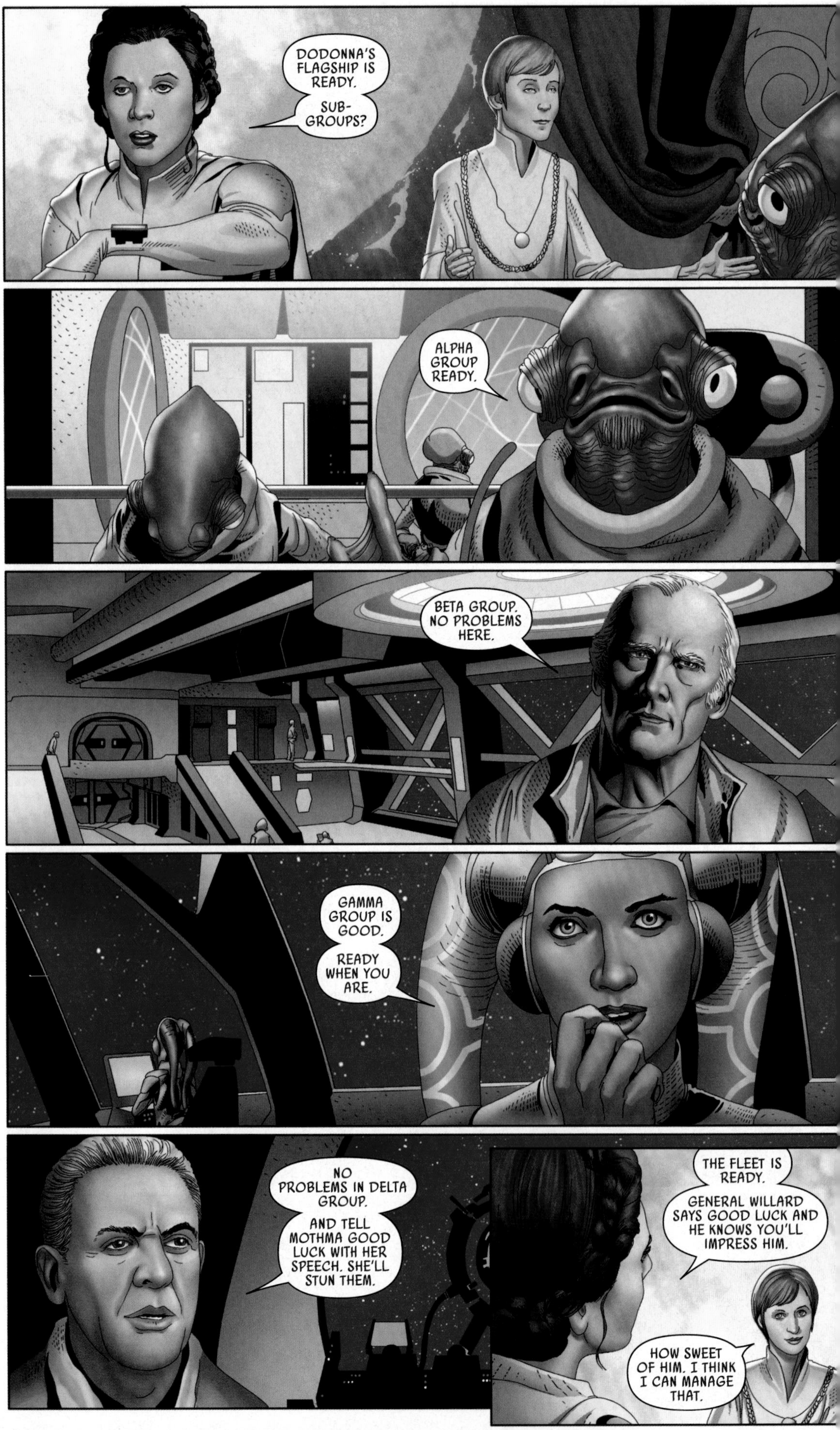
DODONNA'S FLAGSHIP IS READY.
SUB-GROUPS?
ALPHA GROUP READY.
BETA GROUP. NO PROBLEMS HERE.
GAMMA GROUP IS GOOD.
READY WHEN YOU ARE.
NO PROBLEMS IN DELTA GROUP.
AND TELL MOTHMA GOOD LUCK WITH HER SPEECH. SHE'LL STUN THEM.
THE FLEET IS READY.
GENERAL WILLARD SAYS GOOD LUCK AND HE KNOWS YOU'LL IMPRESS HIM.
HOW SWEET OF HIM. I THINK I CAN MANAGE THAT.

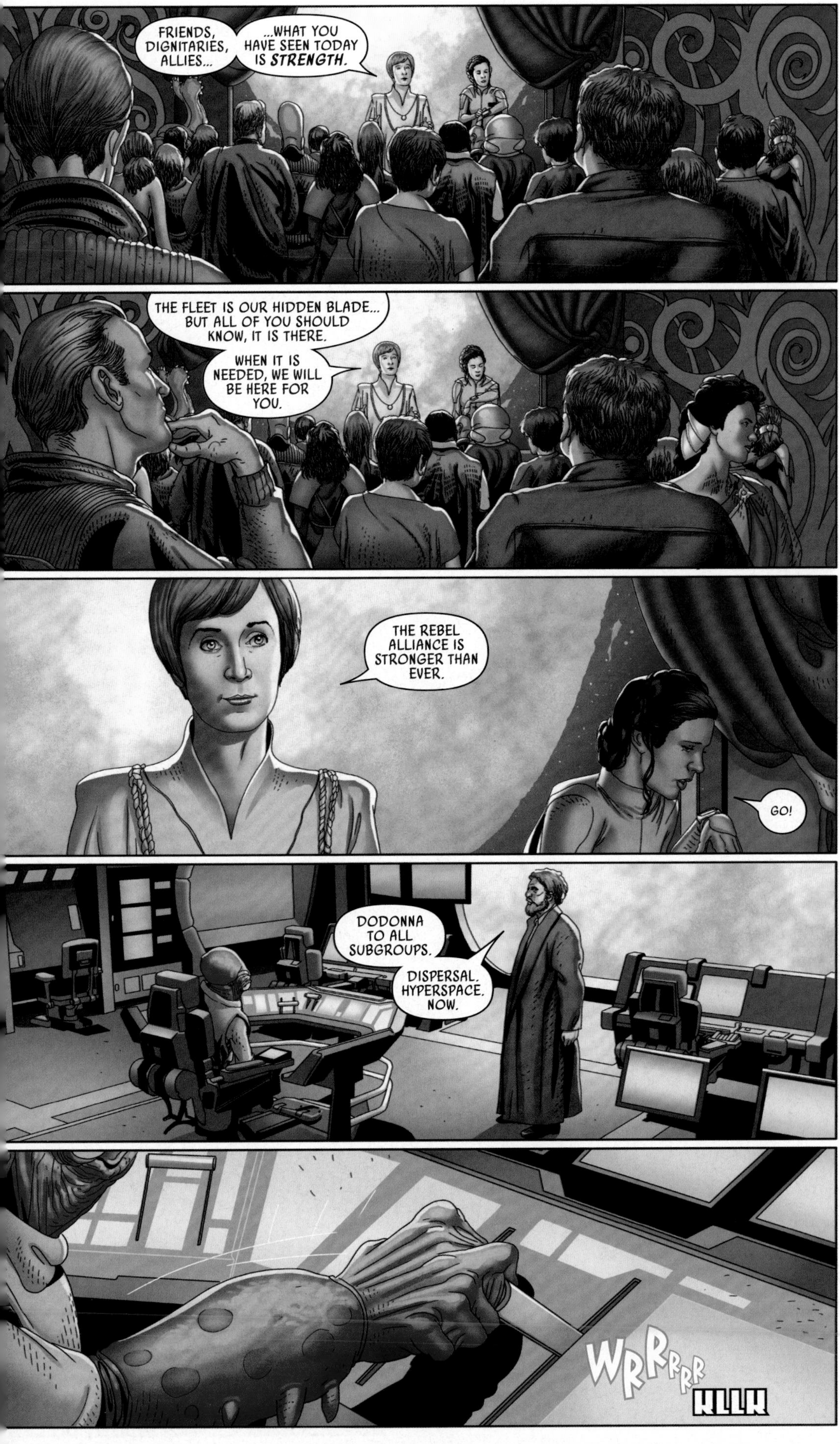
FRIENDS, DIGNITARIES, ALLIES...
...WHAT YOU HAVE SEEN TODAY IS STRENGTH.
THE FLEET IS OUR HIDDEN BLADE... BUT ALL OF YOU SHOULD KNOW, IT IS THERE.
WHEN IT IS NEEDED, WE WILL BE HERE FOR YOU.
THE REBEL ALLIANCE IS STRONGER THAN EVER.
GO!
DODONNA TO ALL SUBGROUPS.
DISPERSAL. HYPERSPACE. NOW.
WRRRRRR
KLLK

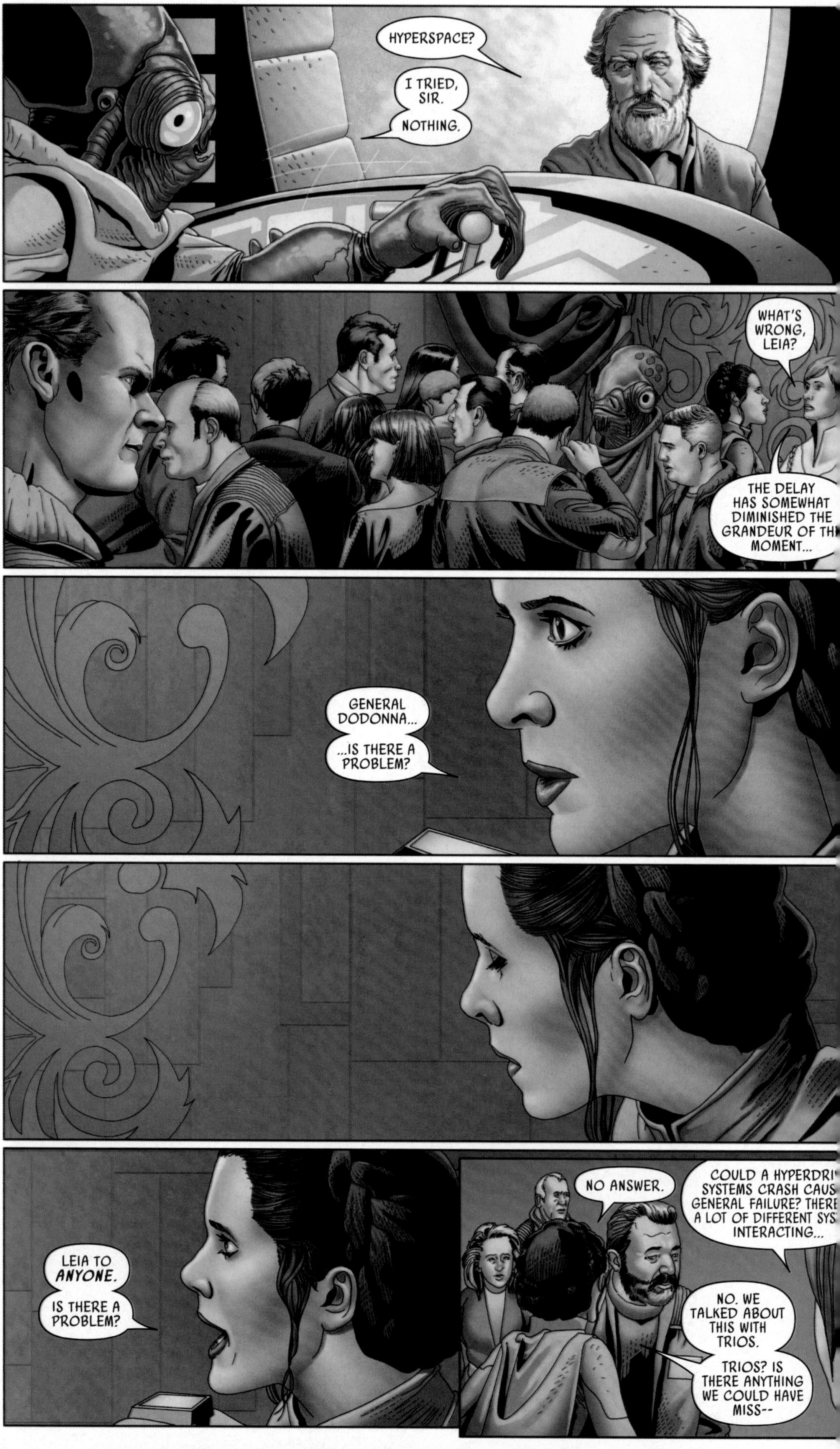
HYPERSPACE?
I TRIED, SIR.
NOTHING.
WHAT'S WRONG, LEIA?
THE DELAY HAS SOMEWHAT DIMINISHED THE GRANDEUR OF TH
MOMENT...
GENERAL DODONNA...
...IS THERE A PROBLEM?
LEIA TO *ANYONE.*
IS THERE A PROBLEM?
NO ANSWER.
COULD A HYPERDRI
SYSTEMS CRASH CAUS
GENERAL FAILURE? THERE
A LOT OF DIFFERENT SYS
INTERACTING...
NO. WE TALKED ABOUT THIS WITH TRIOS.
TRIOS? IS THERE ANYTHING WE COULD HAVE MISS--

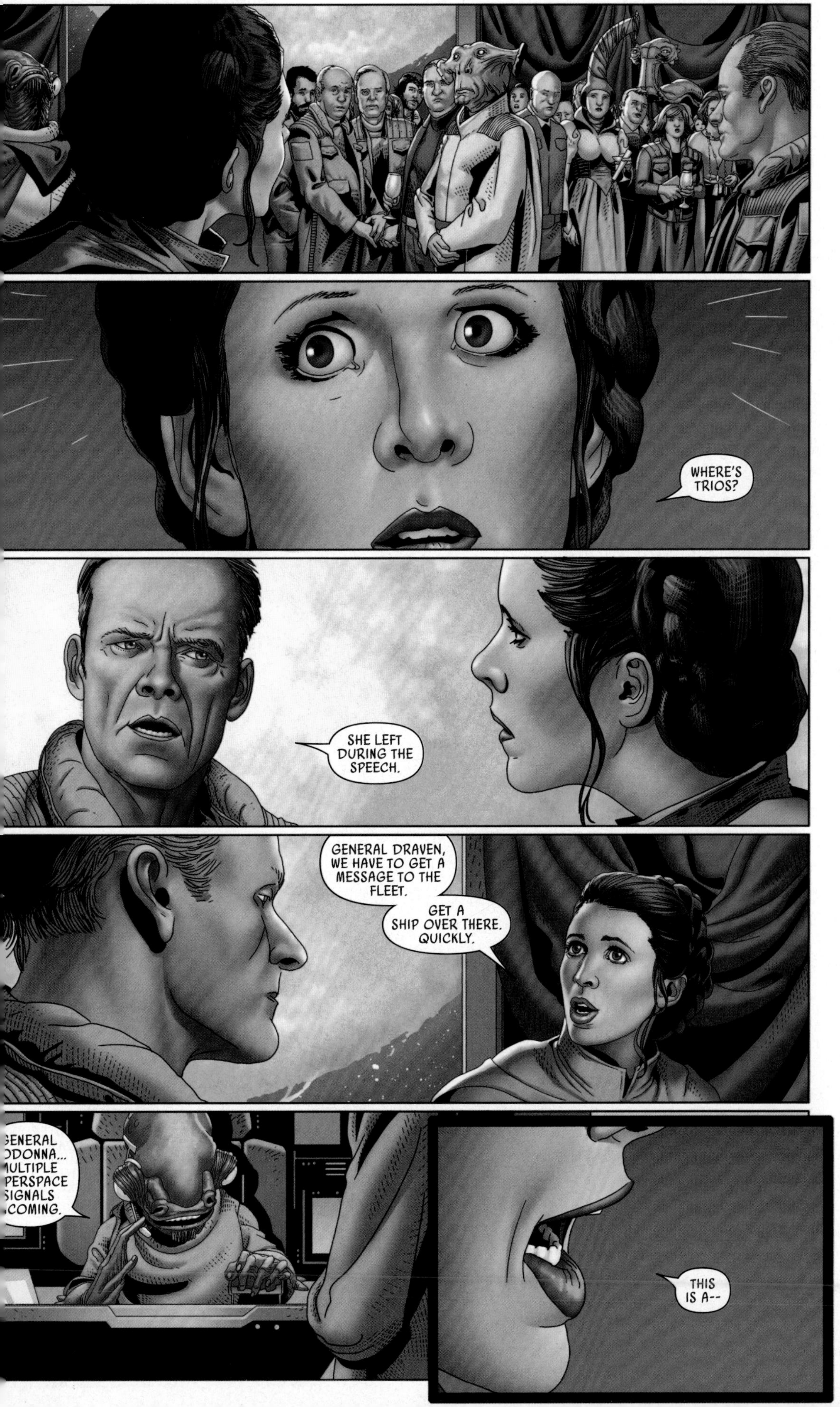
WHERE'S TRIOS?
SHE LEFT DURING THE SPEECH.
GENERAL DRAVEN, WE HAVE TO GET A MESSAGE TO THE FLEET.
GET A SHIP OVER THERE. QUICKLY.
GENERAL ODONNA... MULTIPLE PERSPACE SIGNALS COMING.
THIS IS A--

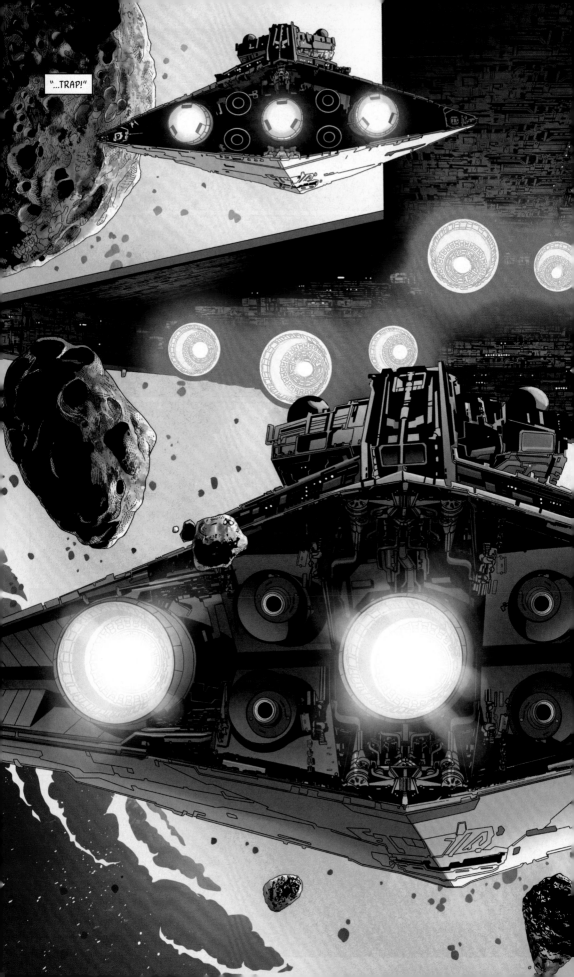
"...TRAP!"

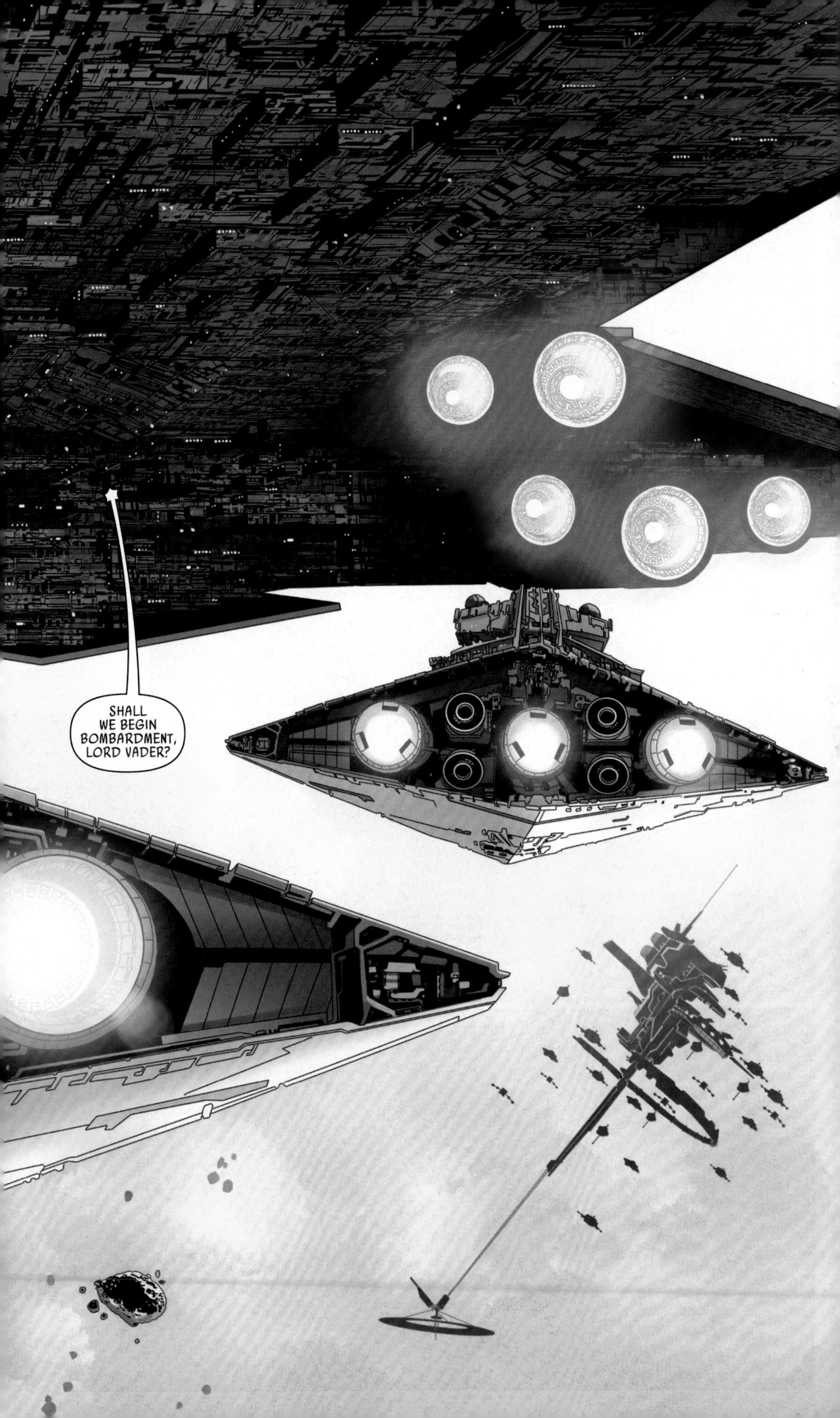
SHALL WE BEGIN BOMBARDMENT, LORD VADER?

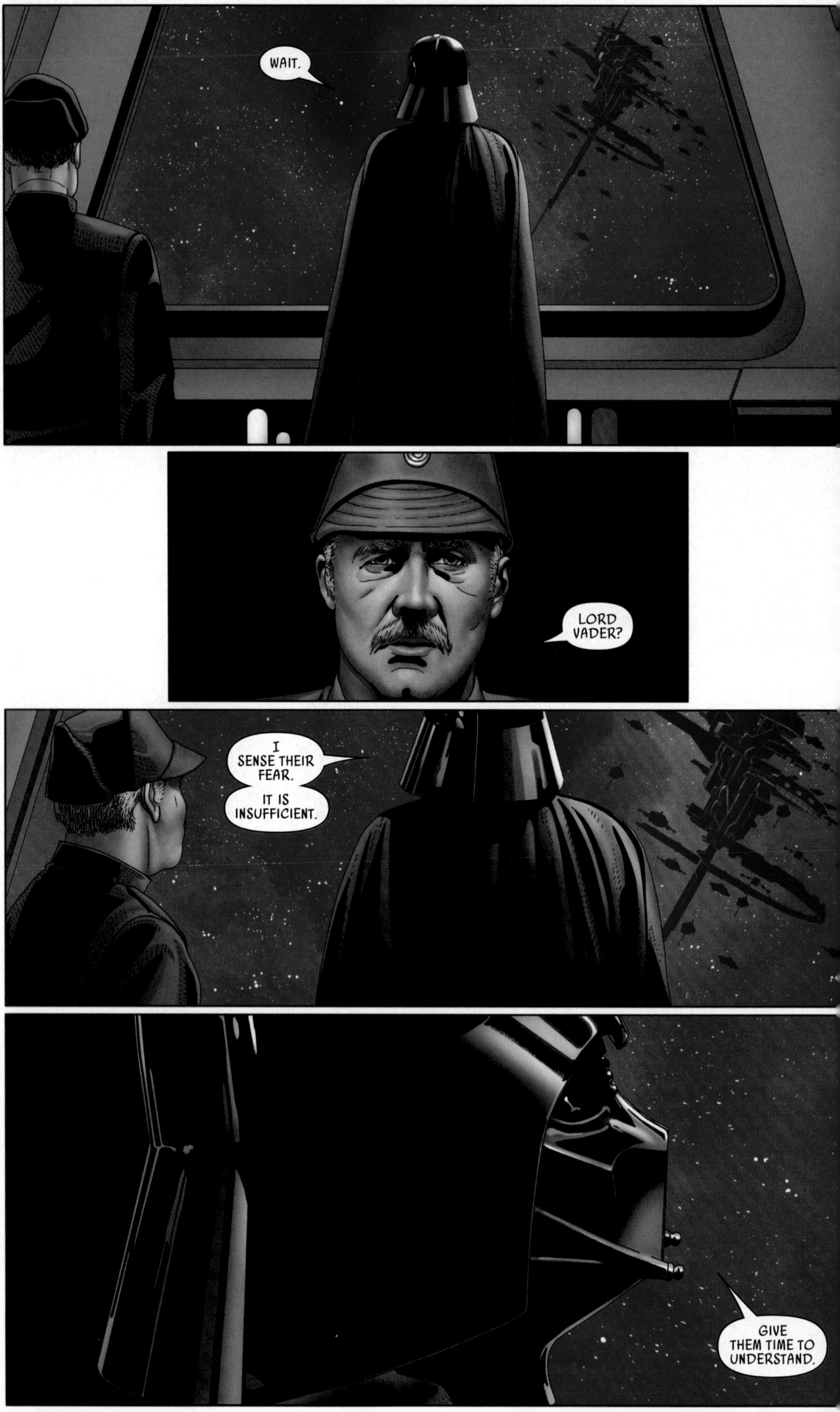
WAIT.
LORD VADER?
I SENSE THEIR FEAR.
IT IS INSUFFICIENT.
GIVE THEM TIME TO UNDERSTAND.

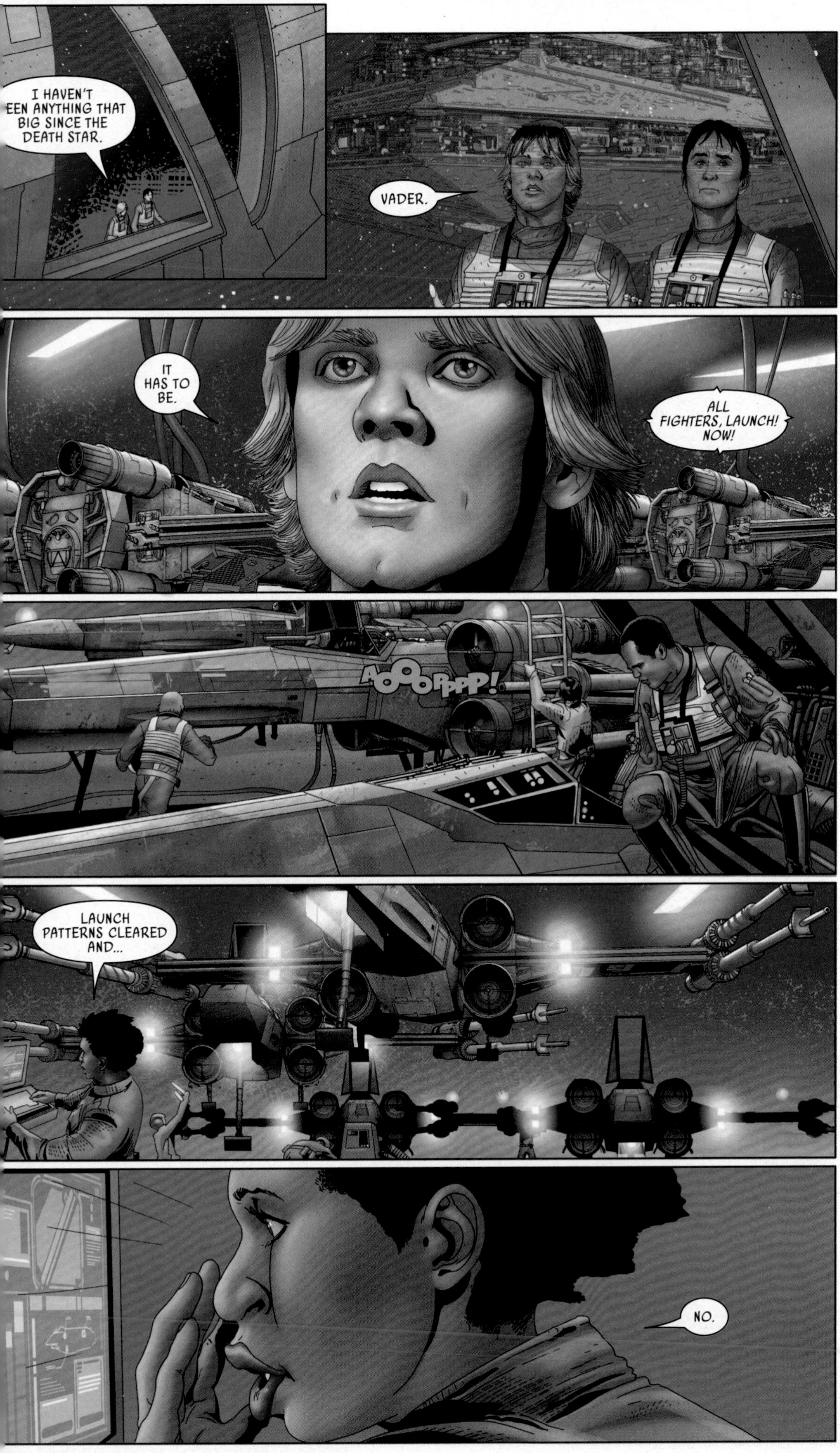

I HAVEN'T
EEN ANYTHING THAT BIG SINCE THE DEATH STAR.
VADER.
IT HAS TO BE.
ALL FIGHTERS, LAUNCH! NOW!
AOOOPPPP!
LAUNCH PATTERNS CLEARED AND...
NO.

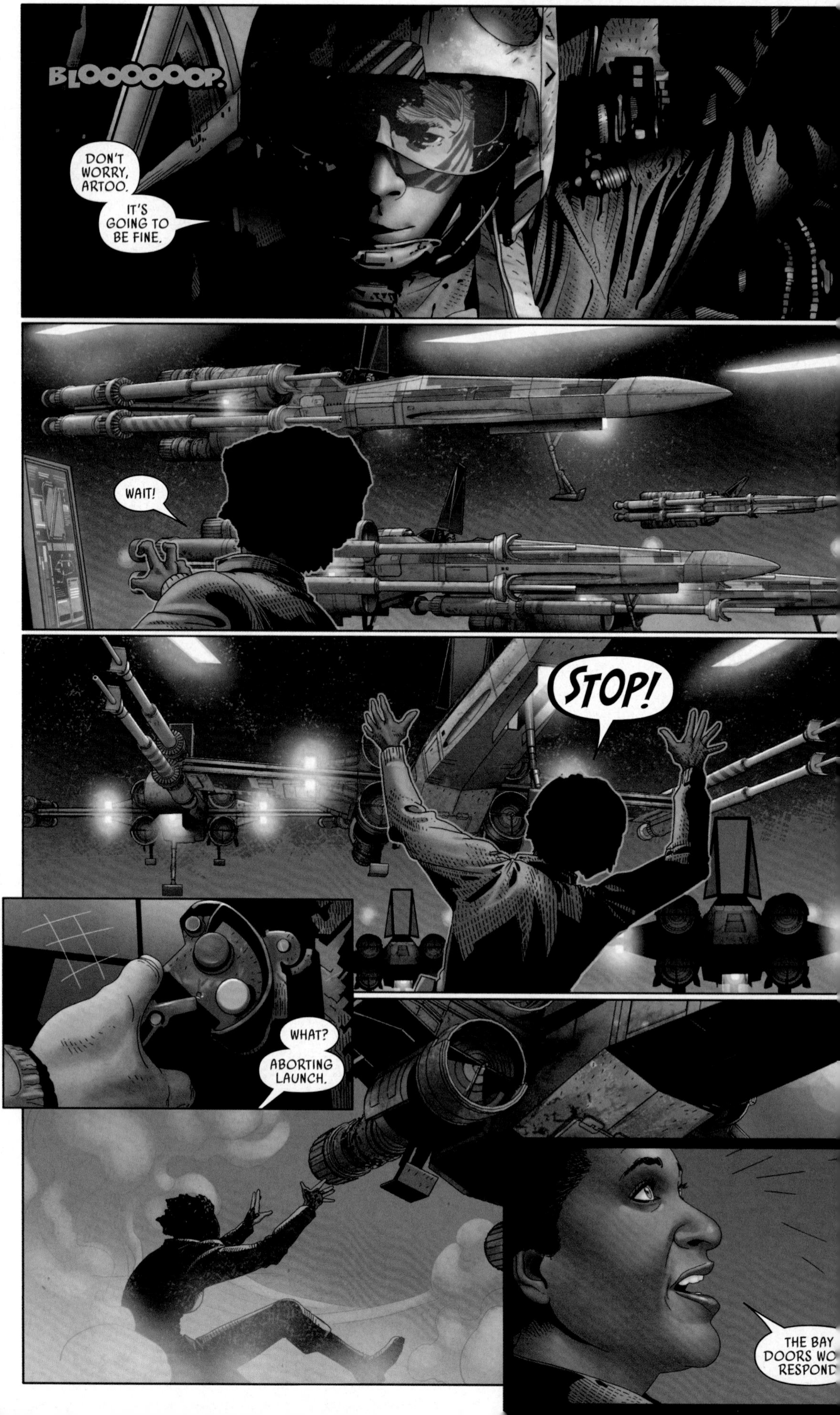
BLOOOOOOP.
DON'T WORRY, ARTOO.
IT'S GOING TO BE FINE.
WAIT!
STOP!
WHAT? ABORTING LAUNCH.
THE BAY DOORS WO
RESPOND

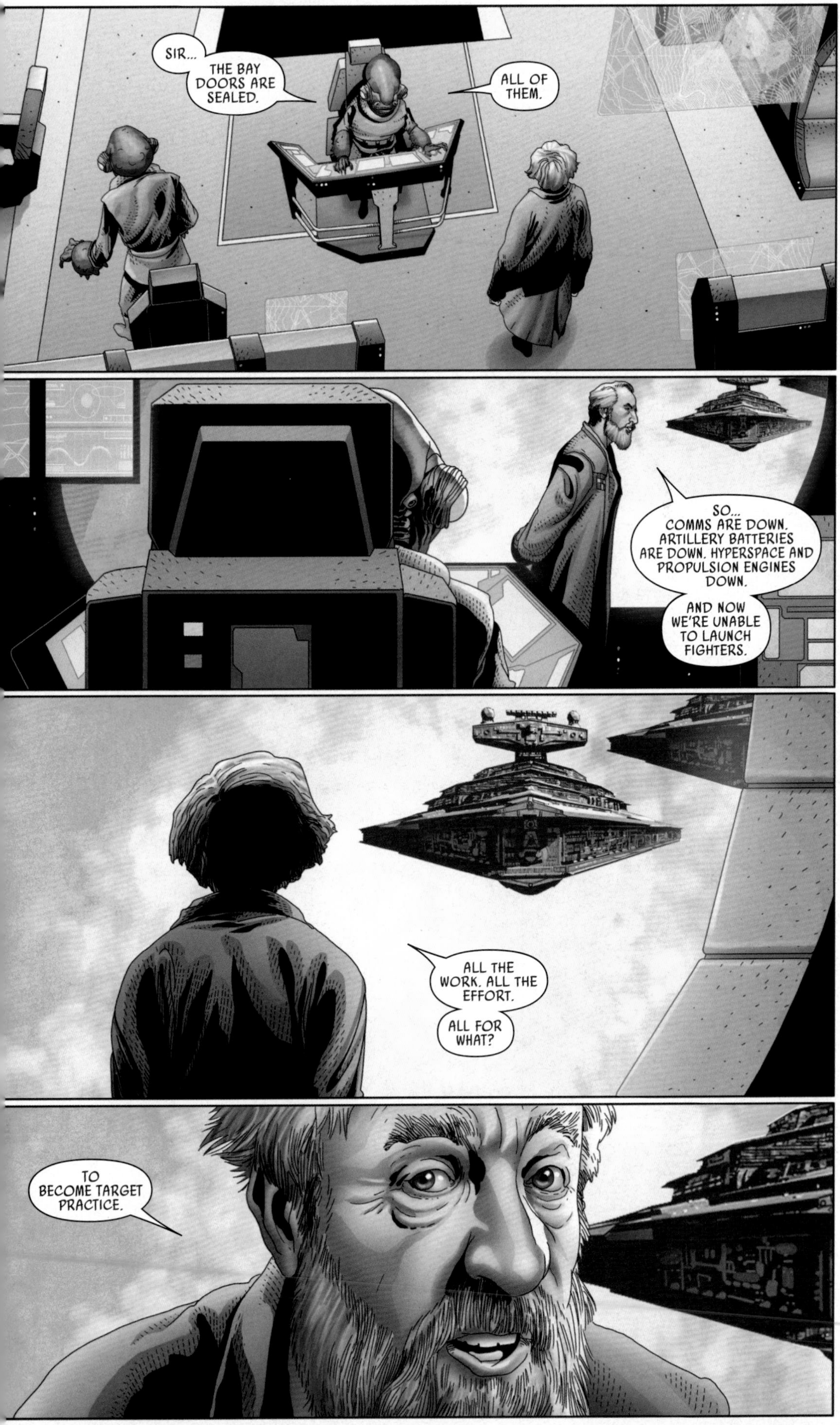
SIR...
THE BAY DOORS ARE SEALED.
ALL OF THEM.
SO... COMMS ARE DOWN. ARTILLERY BATTERIES ARE DOWN. HYPERSPACE AND PROPULSION ENGINES DOWN.
AND NOW WE'RE UNABLE TO LAUNCH FIGHTERS.
ALL THE WORK. ALL THE EFFORT.
ALL FOR WHAT?
TO BECOME TARGET PRACTICE.

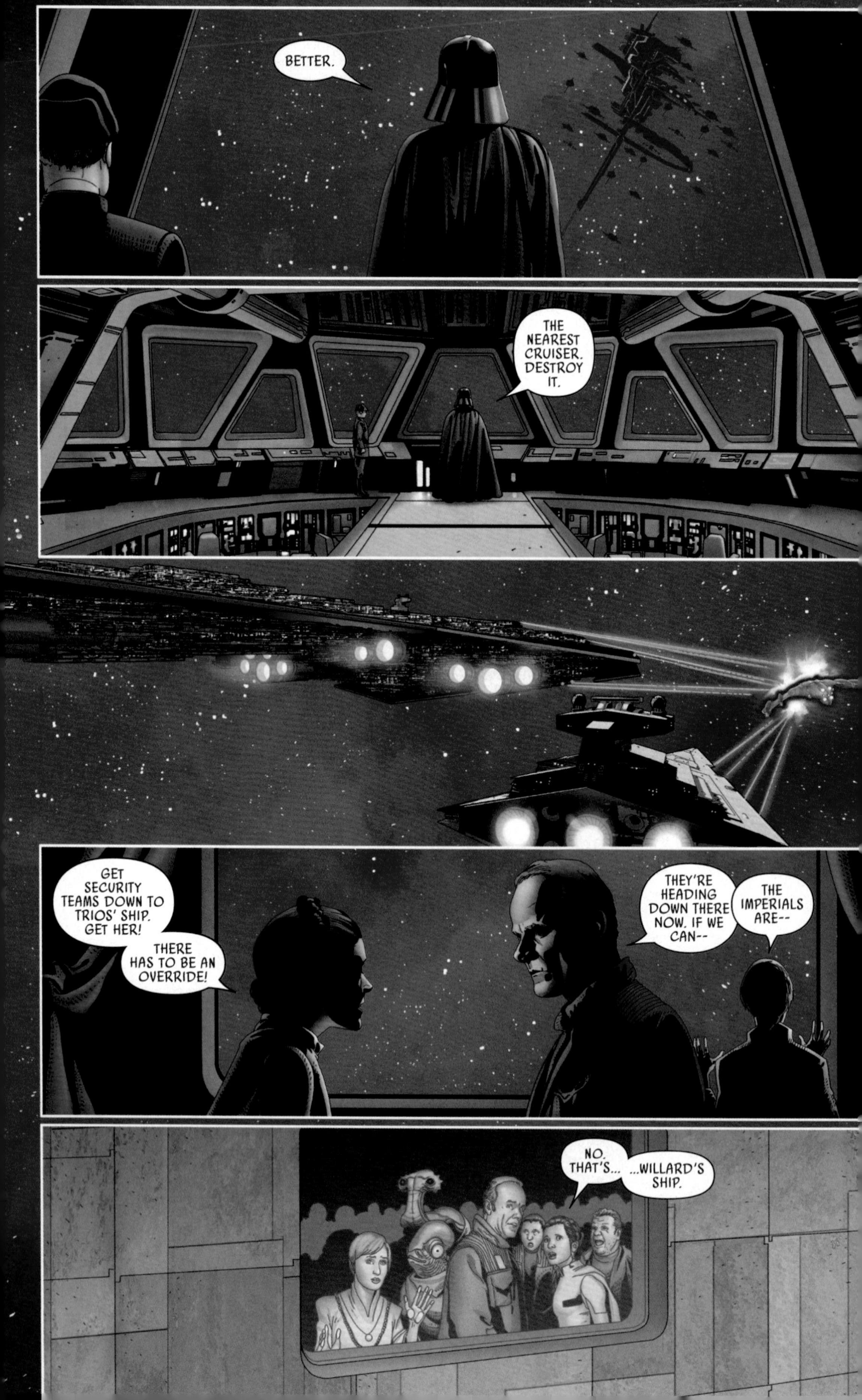
BETTER.
THE NEAREST CRUISER. DESTROY IT.
GET SECURITY TEAMS DOWN TO TRIOS' SHIP. GET HER!
THERE HAS TO BE AN OVERRIDE!
THEY'RE HEADING DOWN THERE NOW. IF WE CAN--
THE IMPERIALS ARE--
NO. THAT'S...
...WILLARD'S SHIP.

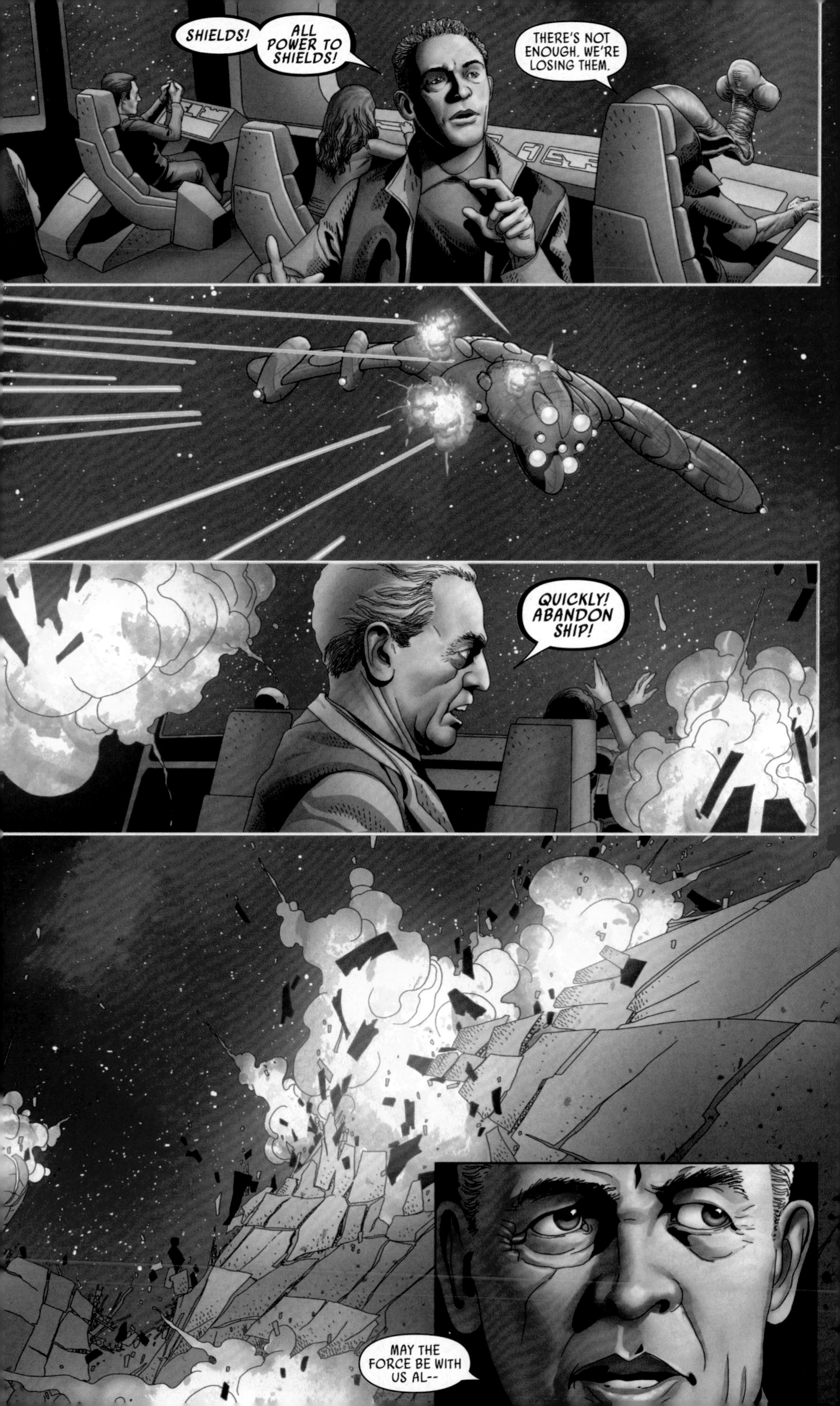
SHIELDS!
ALL POWER TO SHIELDS!
THERE'S NOT ENOUGH. WE'RE LOSING THEM.
QUICKLY! ABANDON SHIP!
MAY THE FORCE BE WITH US AL--

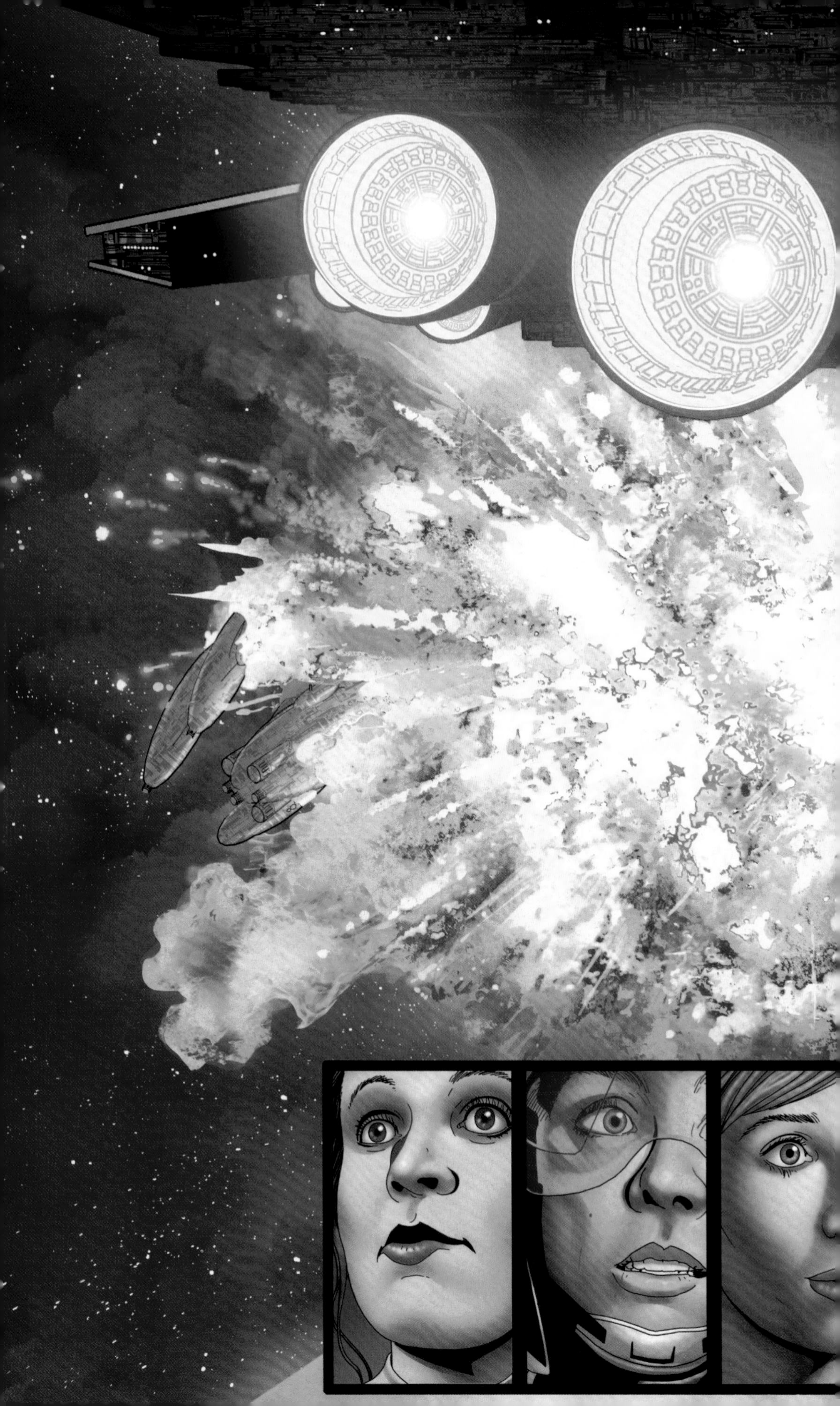

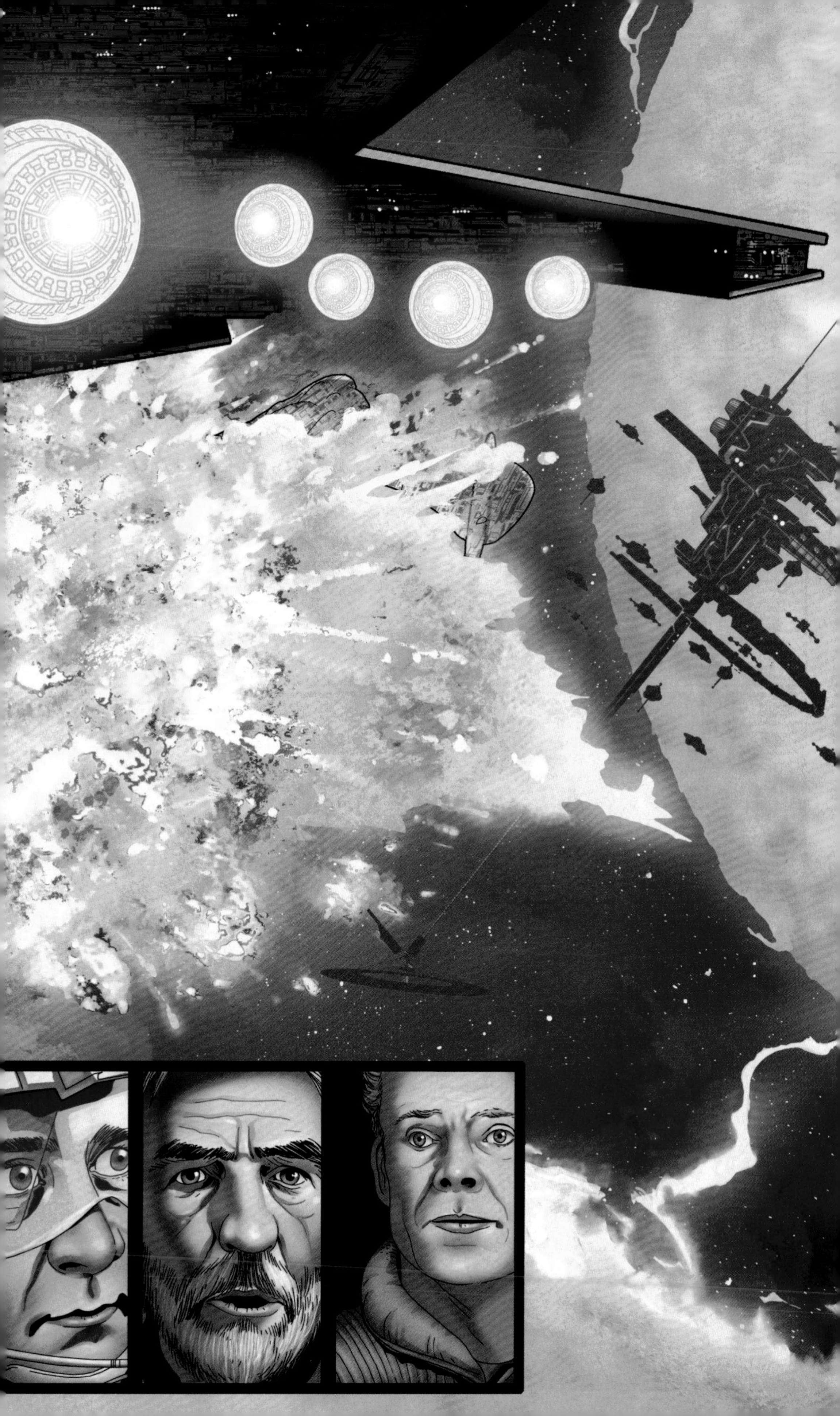

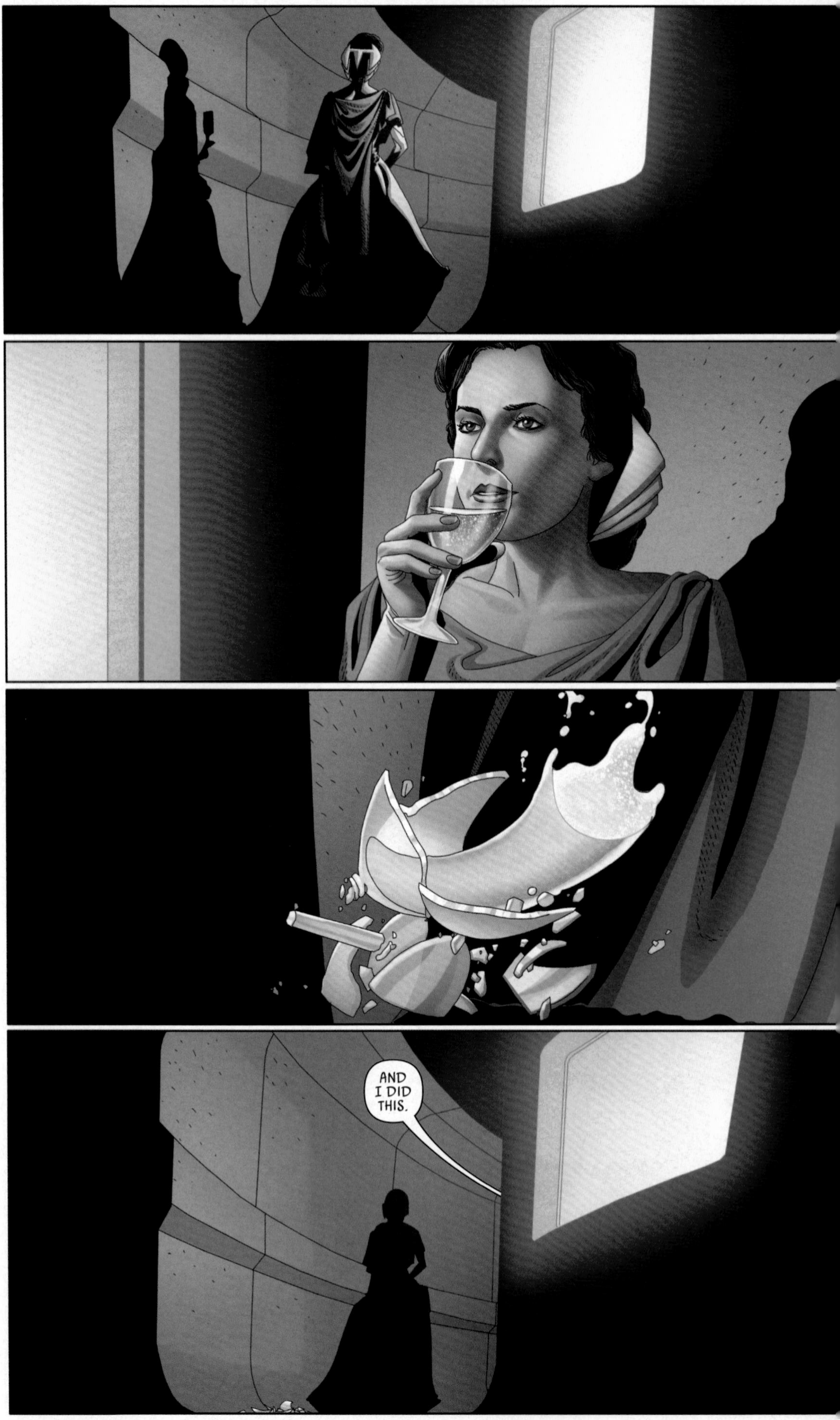
AND I DID THIS.

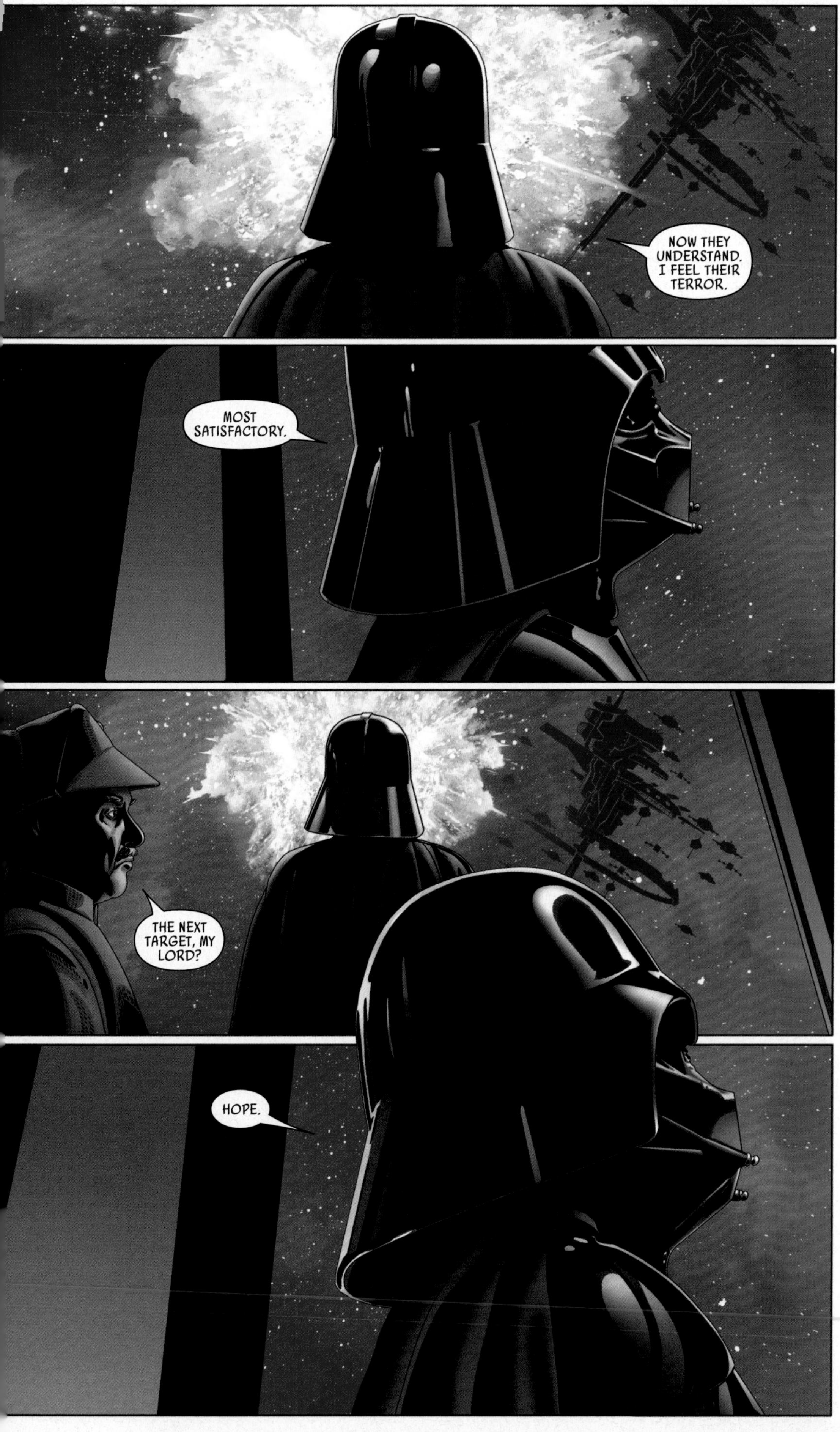
NOW THEY UNDERSTAND. I FEEL THEIR TERROR.
MOST SATISFACTORY.
THE NEXT TARGET, MY LORD?
HOPE.

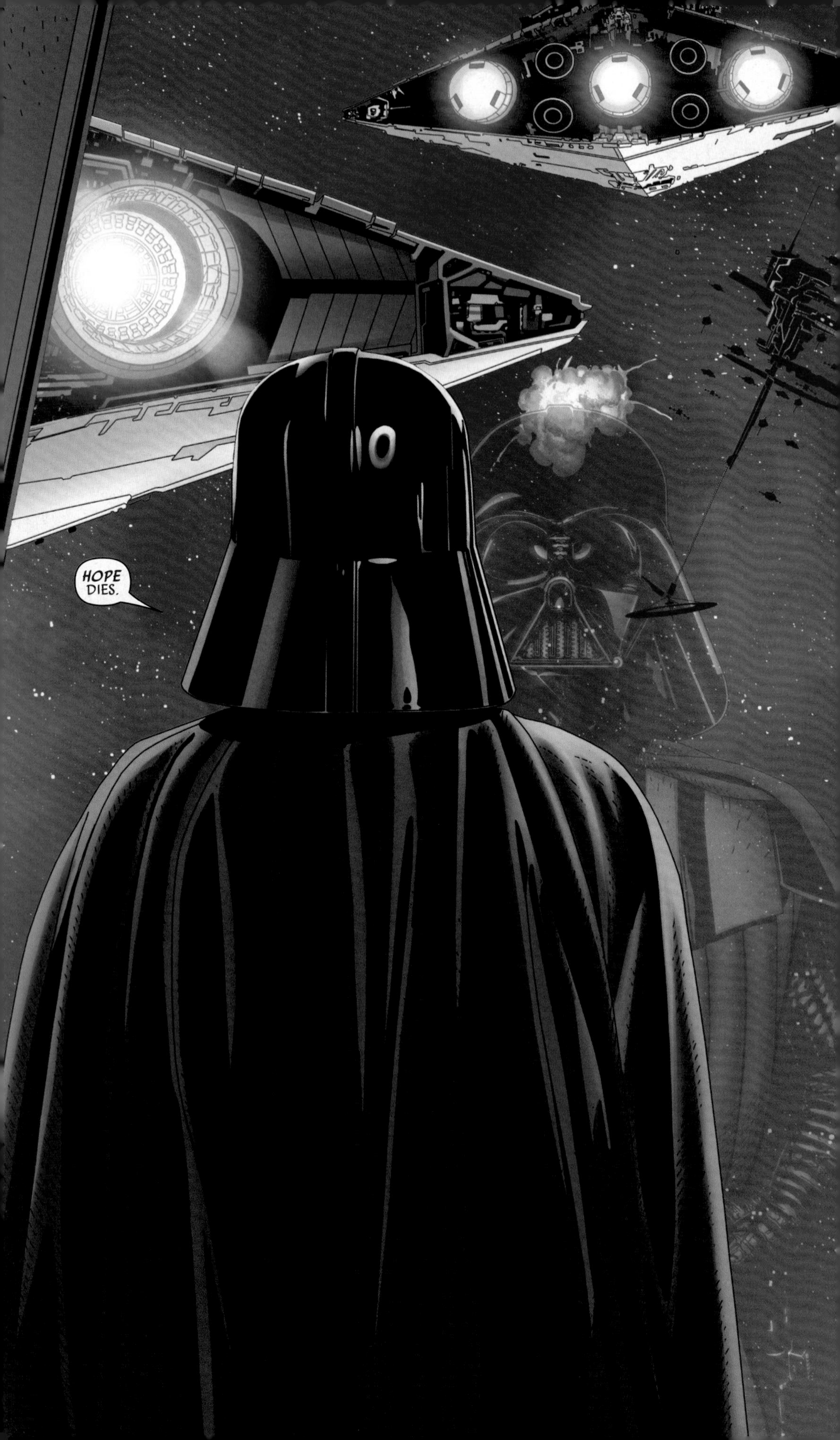
HOPE DIES.

SHU-TORUN LIVES

The dreaded Death Star superweapon is no more, destroyed by Luke Skywalker and the heroic Rebel Alliance.

The evil Galactic Empire's most feared enforcer, Darth Vader, is charged with rooting out the Rebels and restoring order to the galaxy.

But with every victory against Vader and the Imperials, the more dangerous the rebels become....

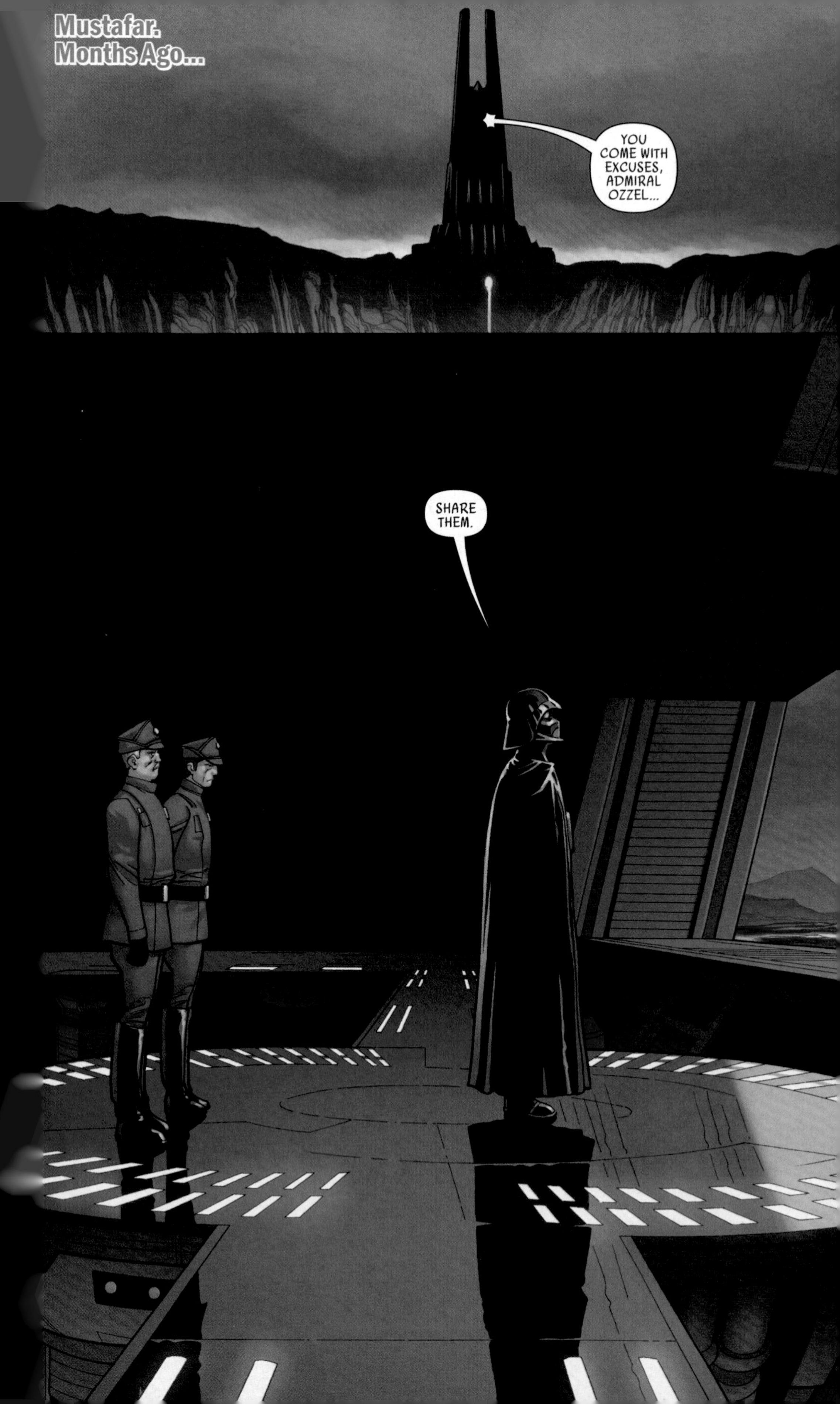
Mustafar.
Months Ago...
YOU COME WITH EXCUSES, ADMIRAL OZZEL...
SHARE THEM.

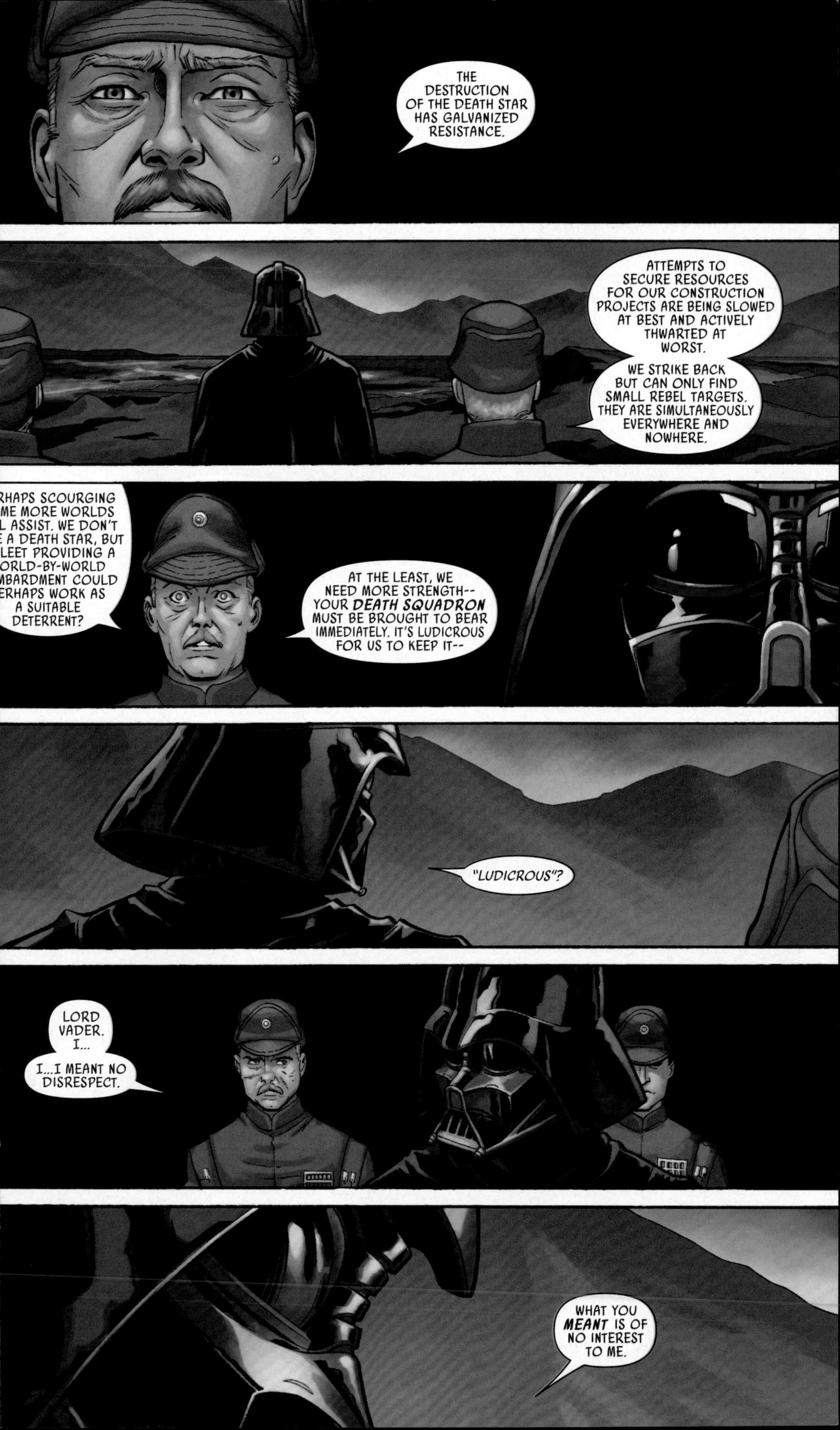
THE DESTRUCTION OF THE DEATH STAR HAS GALVANIZED RESISTANCE.
ATTEMPTS TO SECURE RESOURCES FOR OUR CONSTRUCTION PROJECTS ARE BEING SLOWED AT BEST AND ACTIVELY THWARTED AT WORST.
WE STRIKE BACK BUT CAN ONLY FIND SMALL REBEL TARGETS. THEY ARE SIMULTANEOUSLY EVERYWHERE AND NOWHERE.
RHAPS SCOURGING ME MORE WORLDS L ASSIST. WE DON'T E A DEATH STAR, BUT LEET PROVIDING A ORLD-BY-WORLD MBARDMENT COULD RHAPS WORK AS A SUITABLE DETERRENT?
AT THE LEAST, WE NEED MORE STRENGTH-- YOUR ***DEATH SQUADRON*** MUST BE BROUGHT TO BEAR IMMEDIATELY. IT'S LUDICROUS FOR US TO KEEP IT--
"LUDICROUS"?
LORD VADER. I...
I...I MEANT NO DISRESPECT.
WHAT YOU ***MEANT*** IS OF NO INTEREST TO ME.

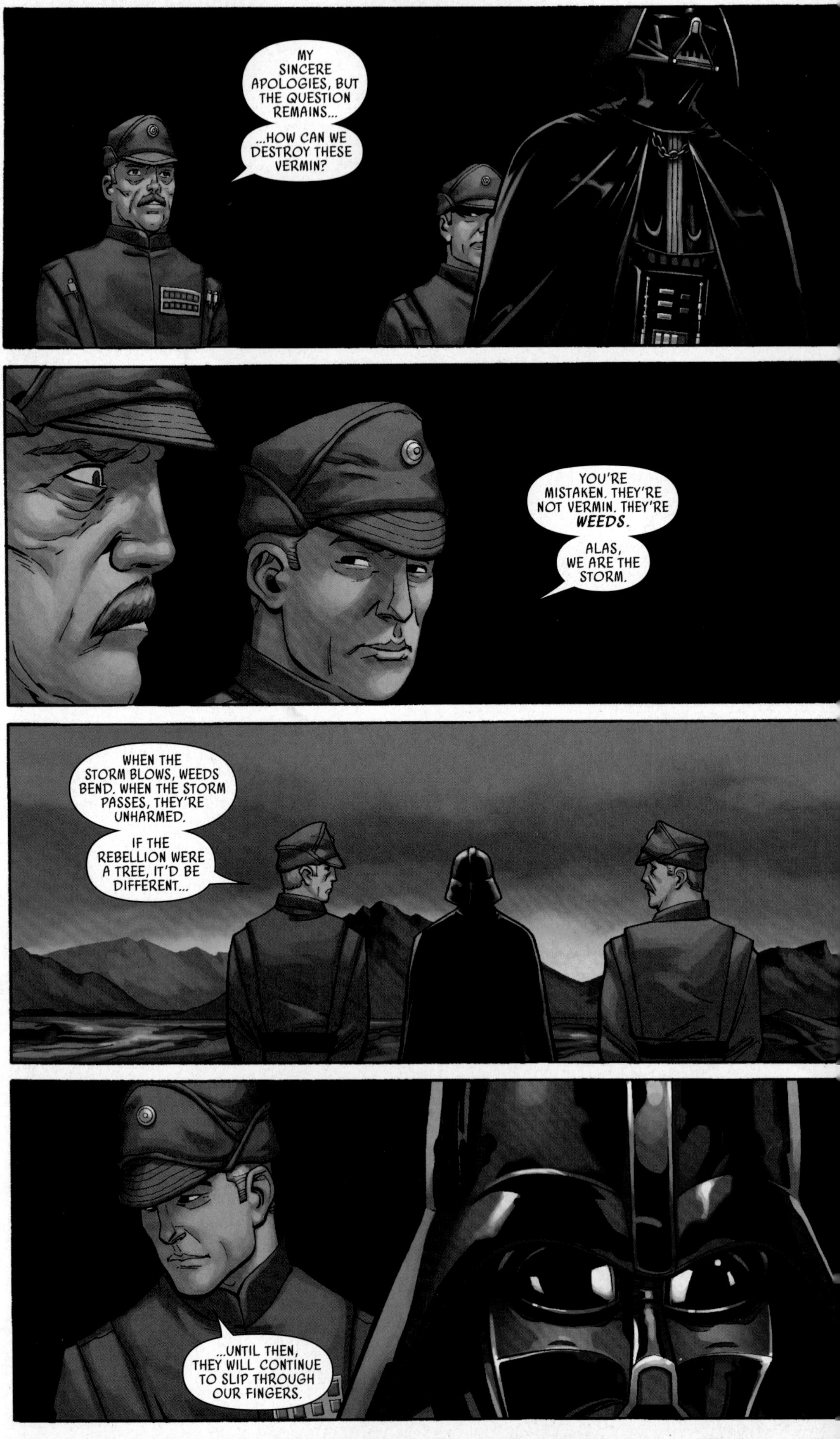
MY SINCERE APOLOGIES, BUT THE QUESTION REMAINS...
...HOW CAN WE DESTROY THESE VERMIN?
YOU'RE MISTAKEN. THEY'RE NOT VERMIN. THEY'RE *WEEDS*.
ALAS, WE ARE THE STORM.
WHEN THE STORM BLOWS, WEEDS BEND. WHEN THE STORM PASSES, THEY'RE UNHARMED.
IF THE REBELLION WERE A TREE, IT'D BE DIFFERENT...
...UNTIL THEN, THEY WILL CONTINUE TO SLIP THROUGH OUR FINGERS.

NO STAR SYSTEM WILL DARE OPPOSE THE EMPEROR NOW.

THE MORE YOU TIGHTEN YOUR GRIP, TARKIN, THE MORE STAR SYSTEMS WILL SLIP THROUGH YOUR FINGERS.

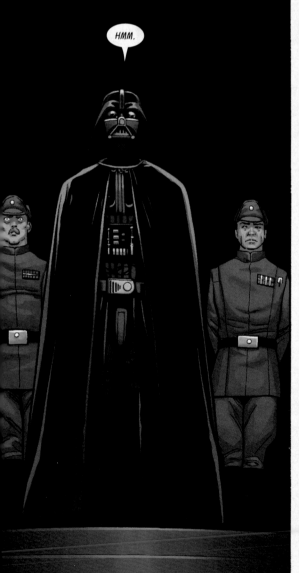

HMM.

LORD VADER?

GENERAL VEERS MAKES AN INTERESTING POINT.

THIS IS WHAT WE SHALL DO.

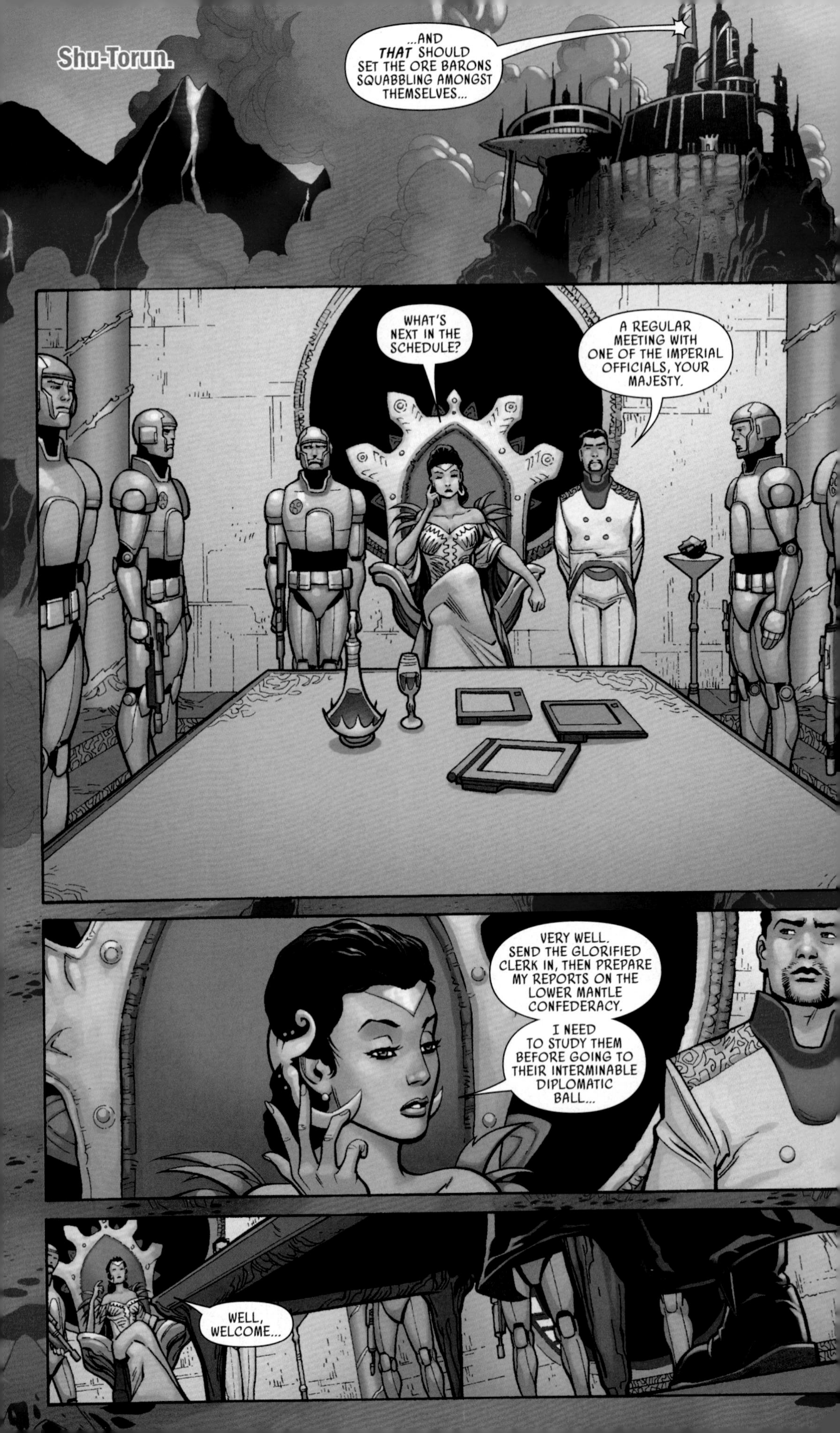
Shu-Torun.
...AND THAT SHOULD SET THE ORE BARONS SQUABBLING AMONGST THEMSELVES...
WHAT'S NEXT IN THE SCHEDULE?
A REGULAR MEETING WITH ONE OF THE IMPERIAL OFFICIALS, YOUR MAJESTY.
VERY WELL. SEND THE GLORIFIED CLERK IN, THEN PREPARE MY REPORTS ON THE LOWER MANTLE CONFEDERACY.
I NEED TO STUDY THEM BEFORE GOING TO THEIR INTERMINABLE DIPLOMATIC BALL...
WELL, WELCOME...

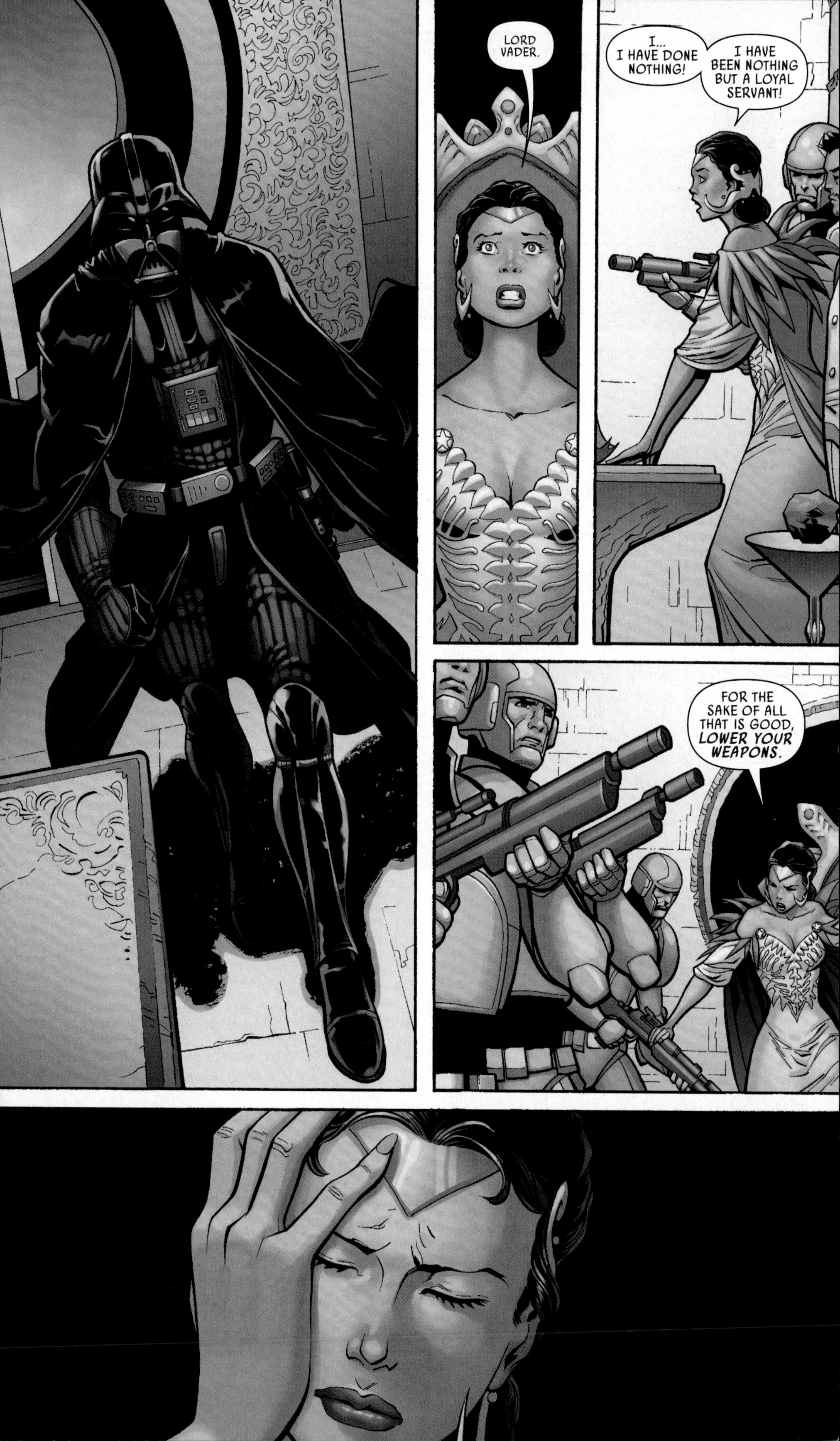
LORD VADER.
I... I HAVE DONE NOTHING!
I HAVE BEEN NOTHING BUT A LOYAL SERVANT!
FOR THE SAKE OF ALL THAT IS GOOD, LOWER YOUR WEAPONS.

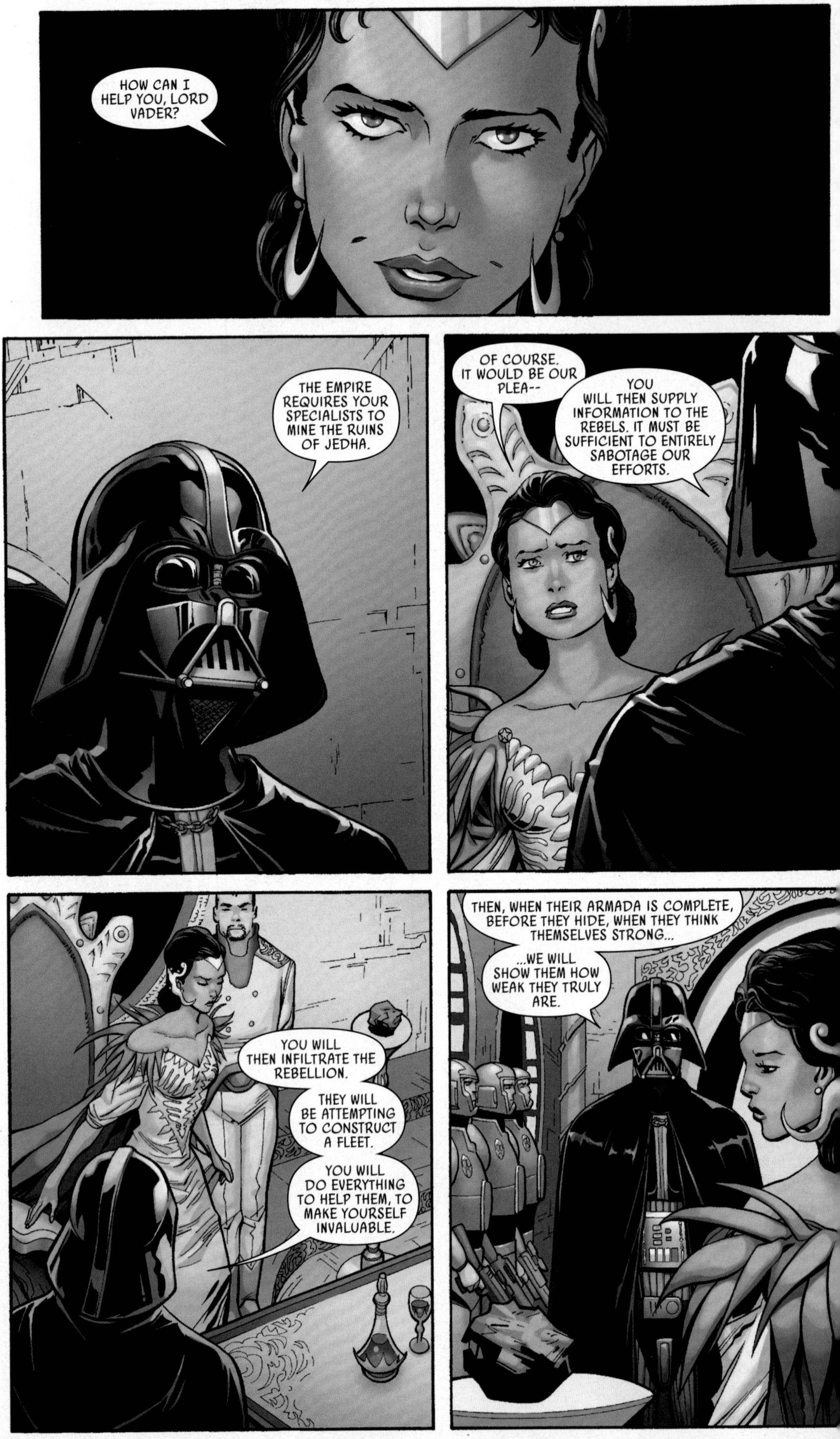
HOW CAN I HELP YOU, LORD VADER?
THE EMPIRE REQUIRES YOUR SPECIALISTS TO MINE THE RUINS OF JEDHA.
OF COURSE. IT WOULD BE OUR PLEA--
YOU WILL THEN SUPPLY INFORMATION TO THE REBELS. IT MUST BE SUFFICIENT TO ENTIRELY SABOTAGE OUR EFFORTS.
YOU WILL THEN INFILTRATE THE REBELLION.
THEY WILL BE ATTEMPTING TO CONSTRUCT A FLEET.
YOU WILL DO EVERYTHING TO HELP THEM, TO MAKE YOURSELF INVALUABLE.
THEN, WHEN THEIR ARMADA IS COMPLETE, BEFORE THEY HIDE, WHEN THEY THINK THEMSELVES STRONG...
...WE WILL SHOW THEM HOW WEAK THEY TRULY ARE.

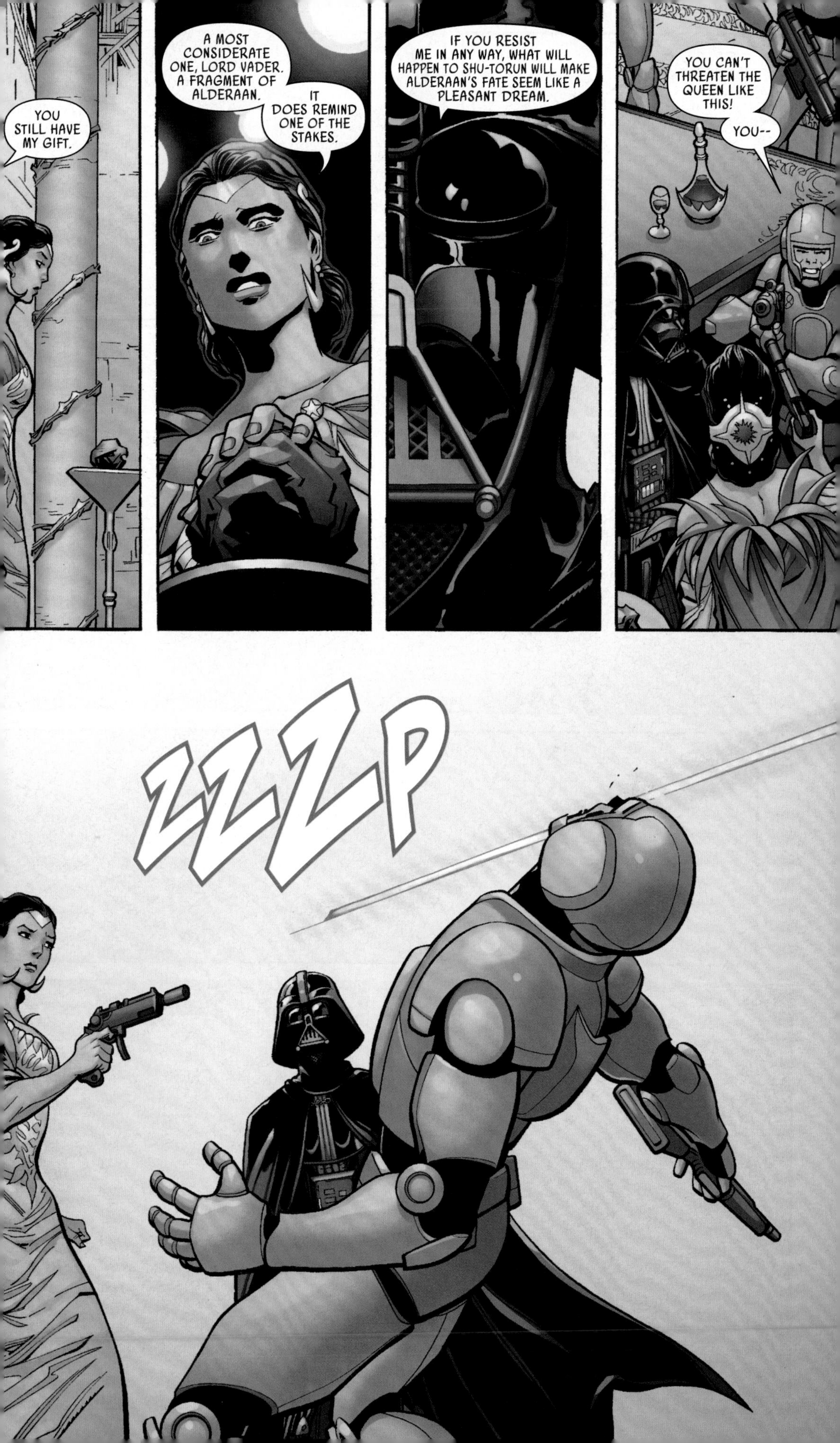
YOU STILL HAVE MY GIFT.
A MOST CONSIDERATE ONE, LORD VADER. A FRAGMENT OF ALDERAAN.
IT DOES REMIND ONE OF THE STAKES.
IF YOU RESIST ME IN ANY WAY, WHAT WILL HAPPEN TO SHU-TORUN WILL MAKE ALDERAAN'S FATE SEEM LIKE A PLEASANT DREAM.
YOU CAN'T THREATEN THE QUEEN LIKE THIS!
YOU--
ZZZP

LORD VADER IS OUR HONORED GUEST.

HE CAN DO ANYTHING HE WISHES.

QUEEN TRIOS. HIS FAMILY WILL BE OUTRAG--

YOU DON[T] UNDERSTA[ND].

VADER WOULD HA[VE] LIKELY KILLE[D] YOU ALL.

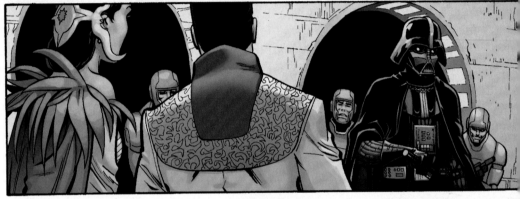

OH, I AM A FOOL.

LORD VADER, PLEASE. BE MY GUEST.

NO WITNESSES, YES?

SSK

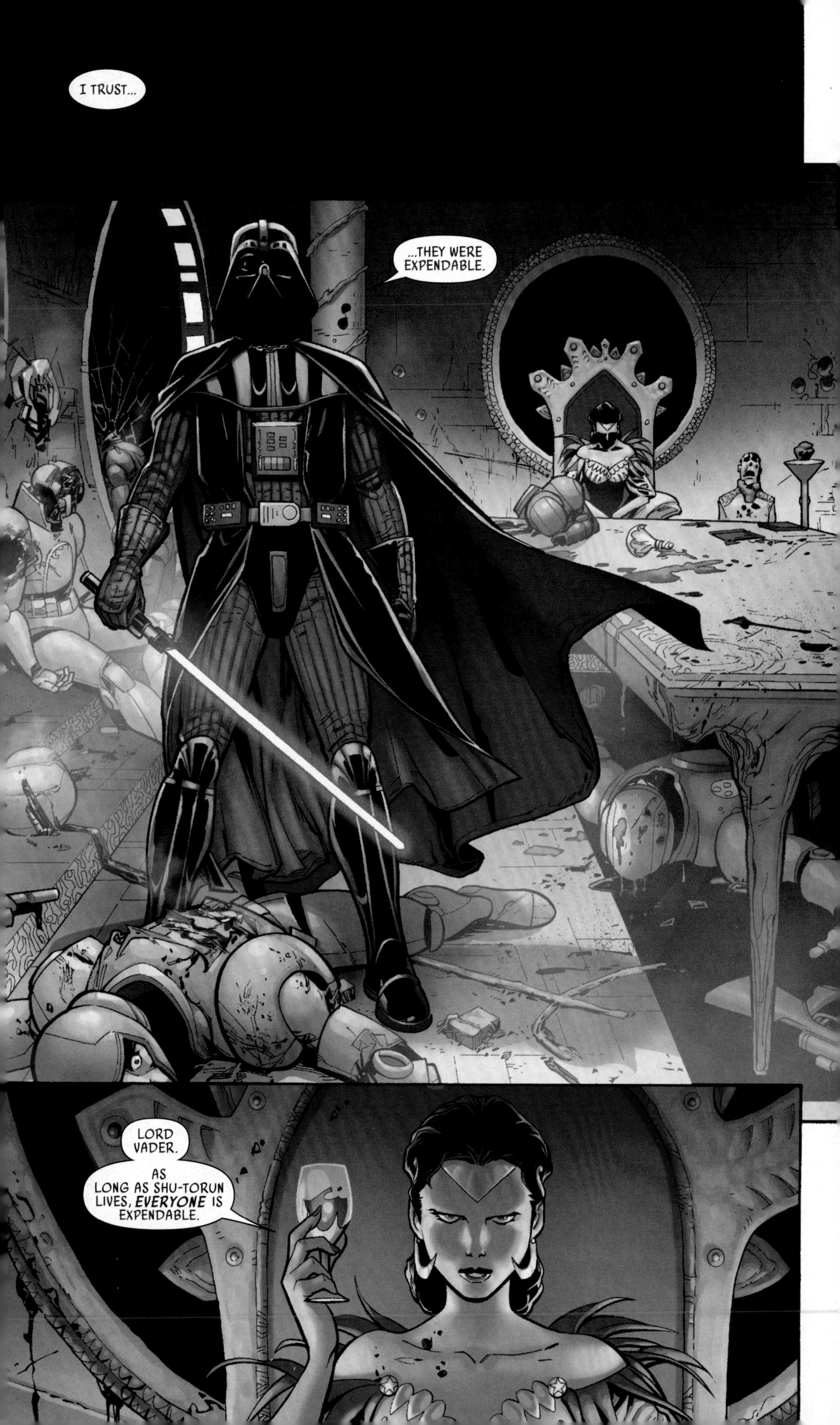
I TRUST...
...THEY WERE EXPENDABLE.
LORD VADER.
AS LONG AS SHU-TORUN LIVES, *EVERYONE* IS EXPENDABLE.

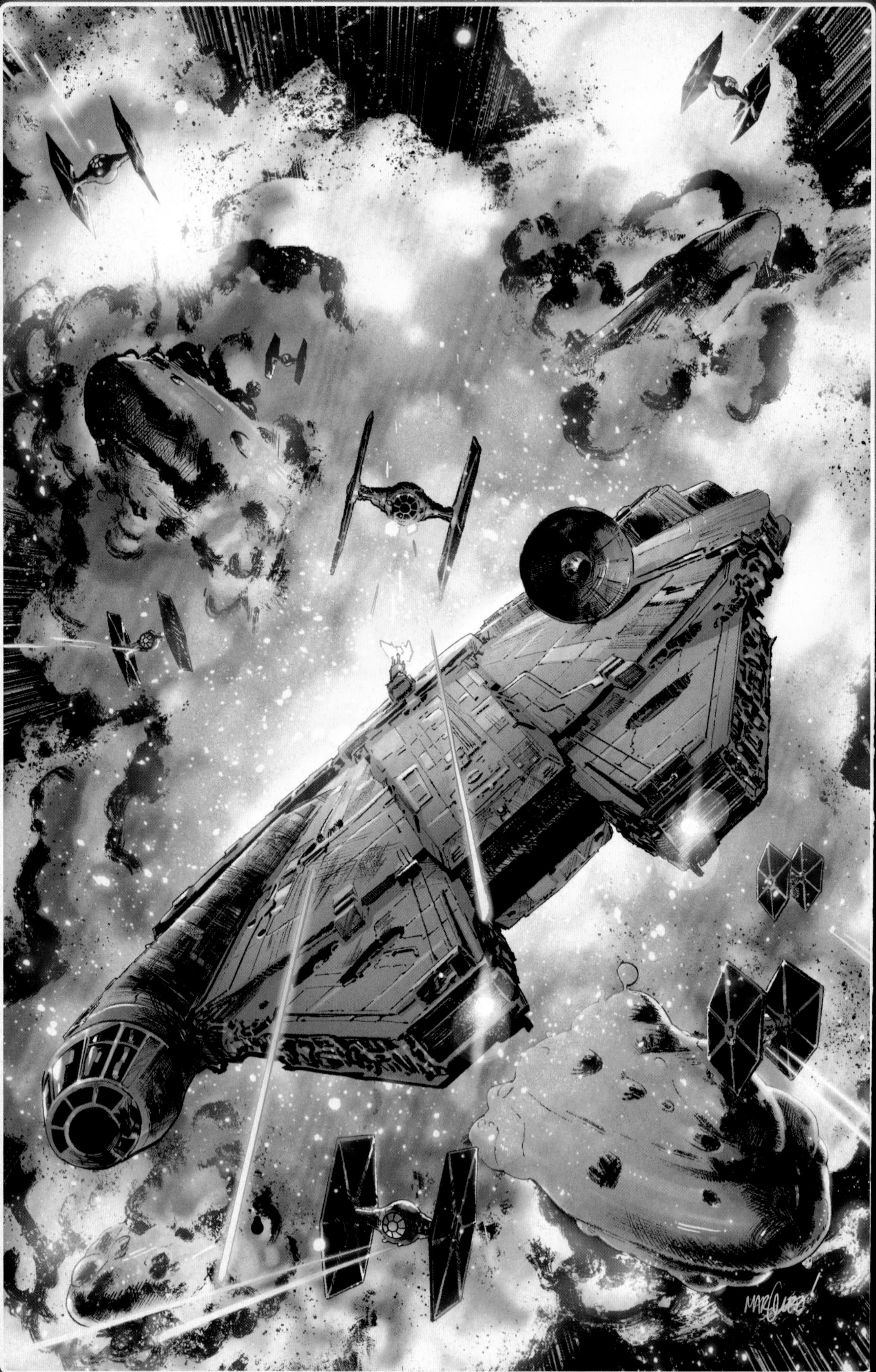

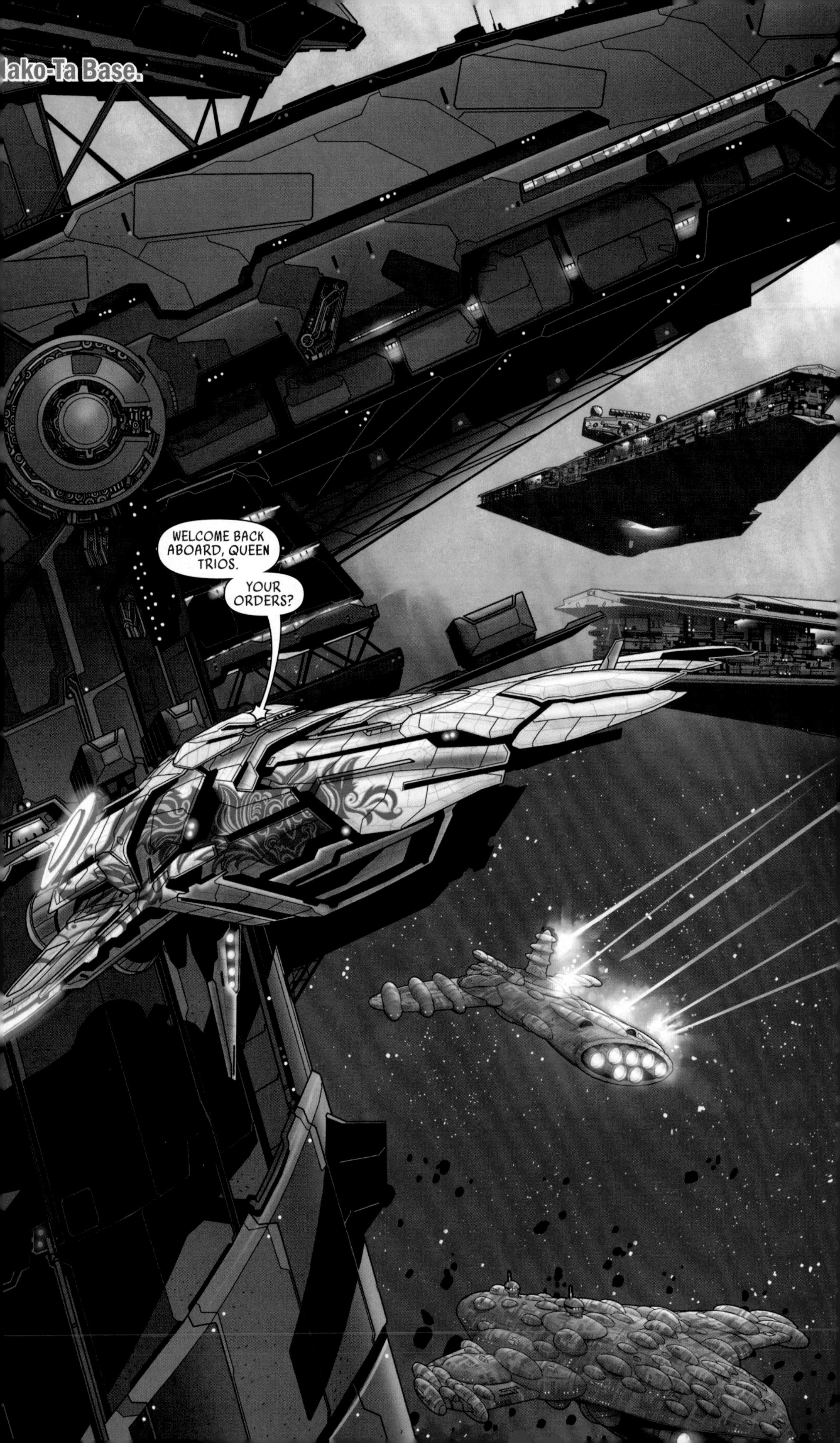
lako-Ta Base.
WELCOME BACK ABOARD, QUEEN TRIOS.
YOUR ORDERS?

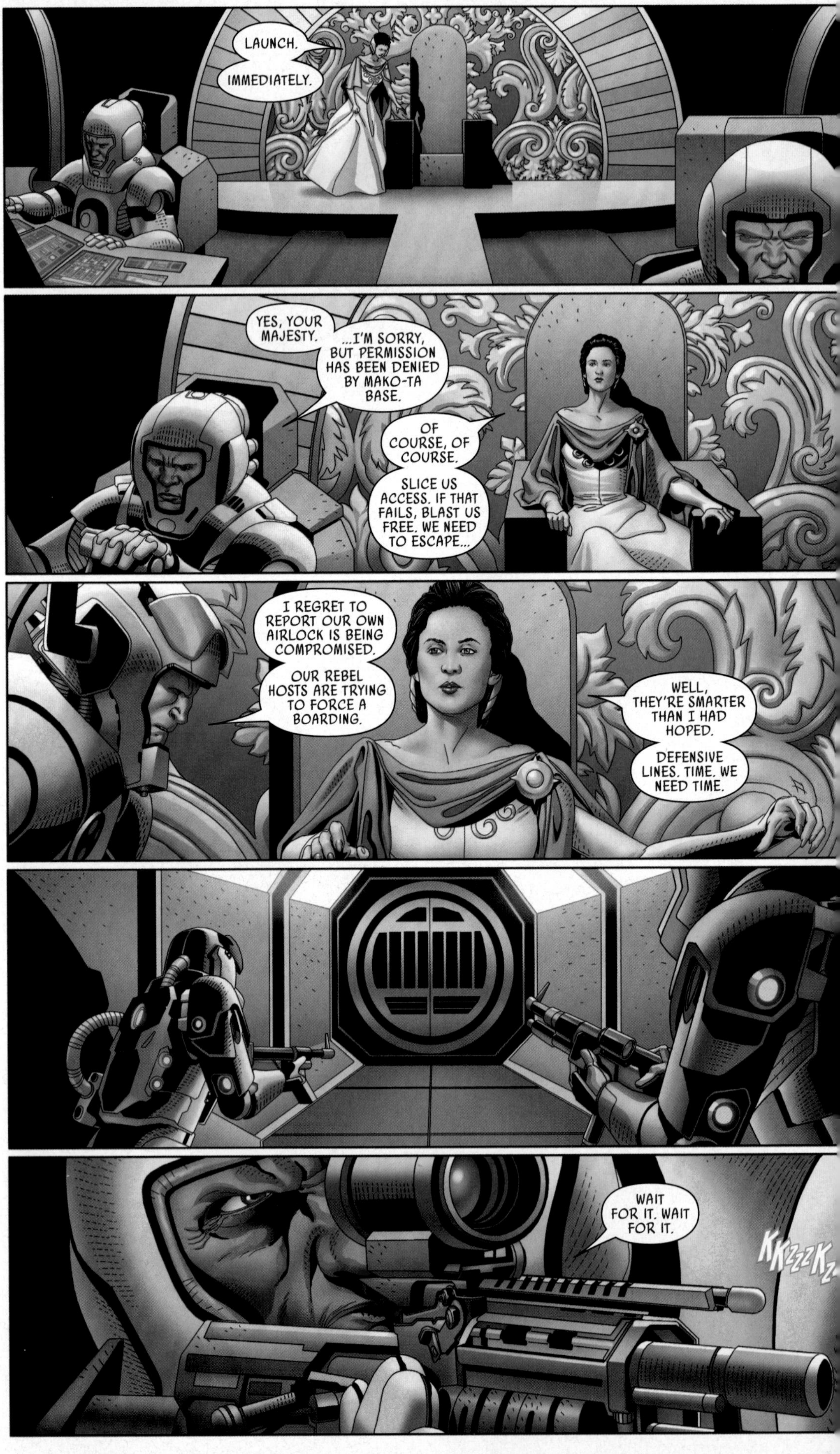
LAUNCH.
IMMEDIATELY.
YES, YOUR MAJESTY.
...I'M SORRY, BUT PERMISSION HAS BEEN DENIED BY MAKO-TA BASE.
OF COURSE, OF COURSE.
SLICE US ACCESS. IF THAT FAILS, BLAST US FREE. WE NEED TO ESCAPE...
I REGRET TO REPORT OUR OWN AIRLOCK IS BEING COMPROMISED.
OUR REBEL HOSTS ARE TRYING TO FORCE A BOARDING.
WELL, THEY'RE SMARTER THAN I HAD HOPED.
DEFENSIVE LINES. TIME. WE NEED TIME.
WAIT FOR IT. WAIT FOR IT.
KKZZZKZ

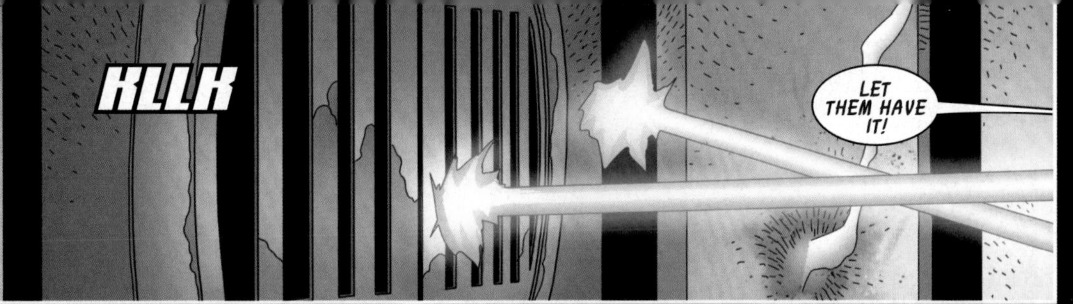
KLLK
LET THEM HAVE IT!

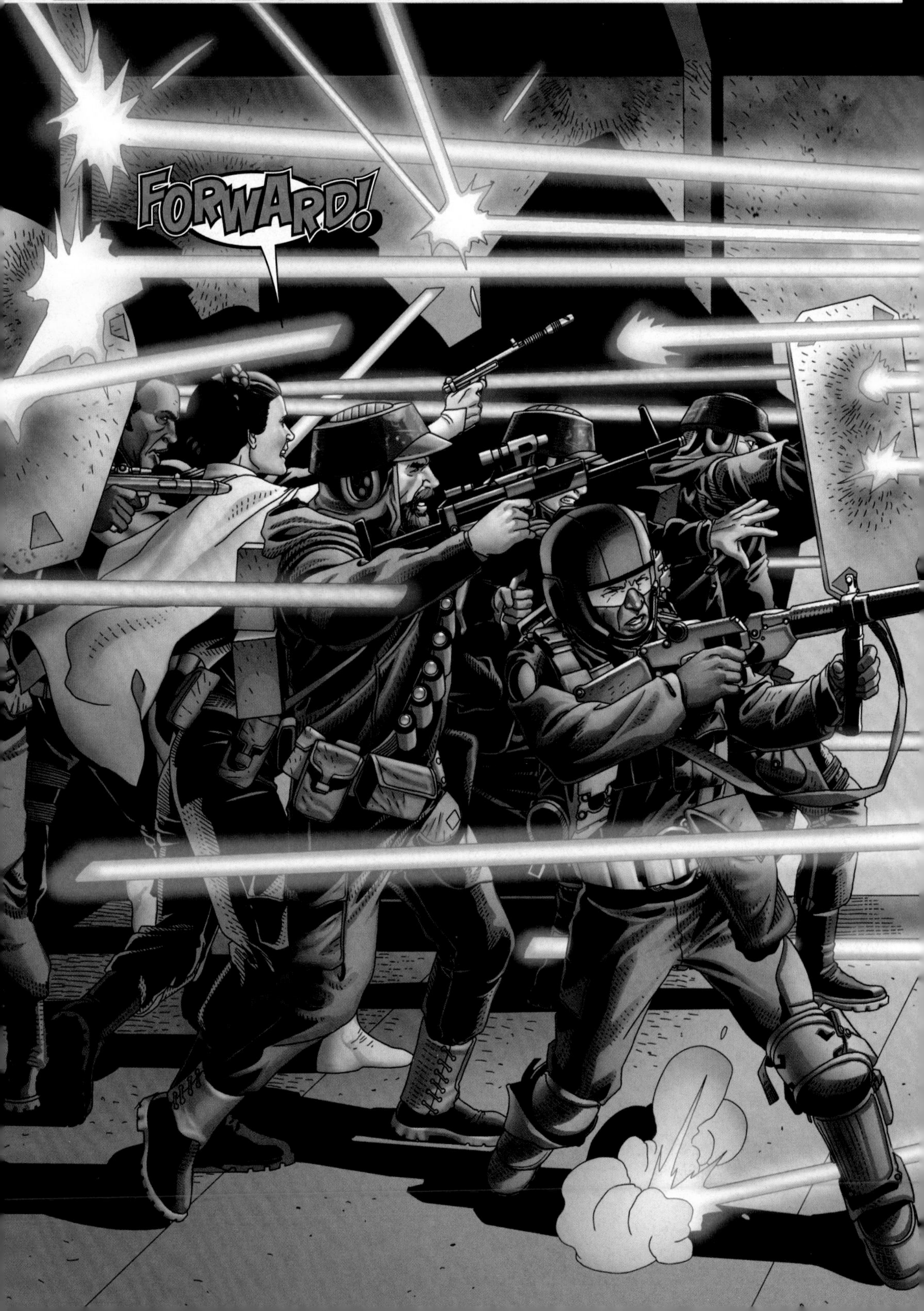
FORWARD!

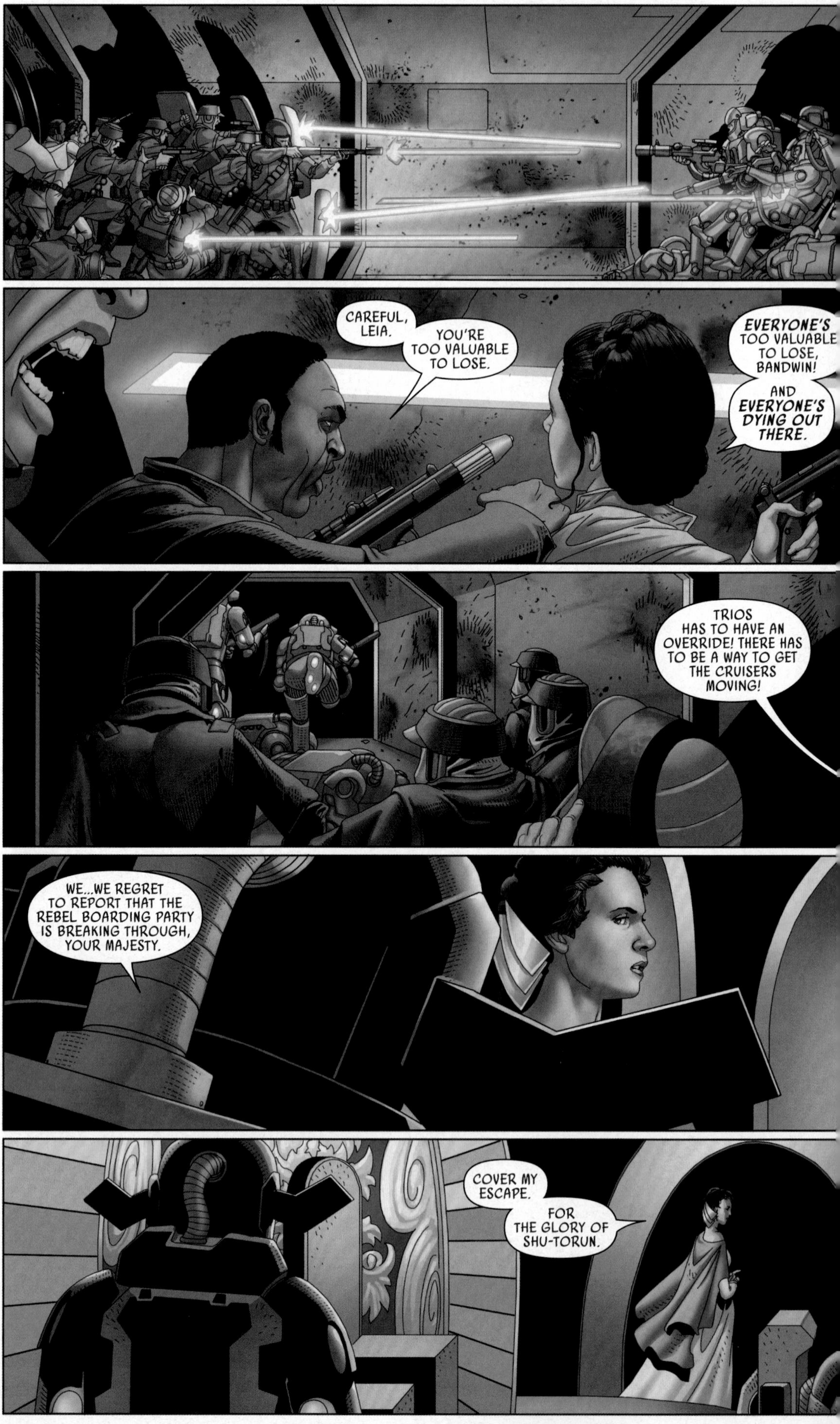
CAREFUL, LEIA.
YOU'RE TOO VALUABLE TO LOSE.
EVERYONE'S TOO VALUABLE TO LOSE, BANDWIN!
AND EVERYONE'S DYING OUT THERE.
TRIOS HAS TO HAVE AN OVERRIDE! THERE HAS TO BE A WAY TO GET THE CRUISERS MOVING!
WE...WE REGRET TO REPORT THAT THE REBEL BOARDING PARTY IS BREAKING THROUGH, YOUR MAJESTY.
COVER MY ESCAPE.
FOR THE GLORY OF SHU-TORUN.

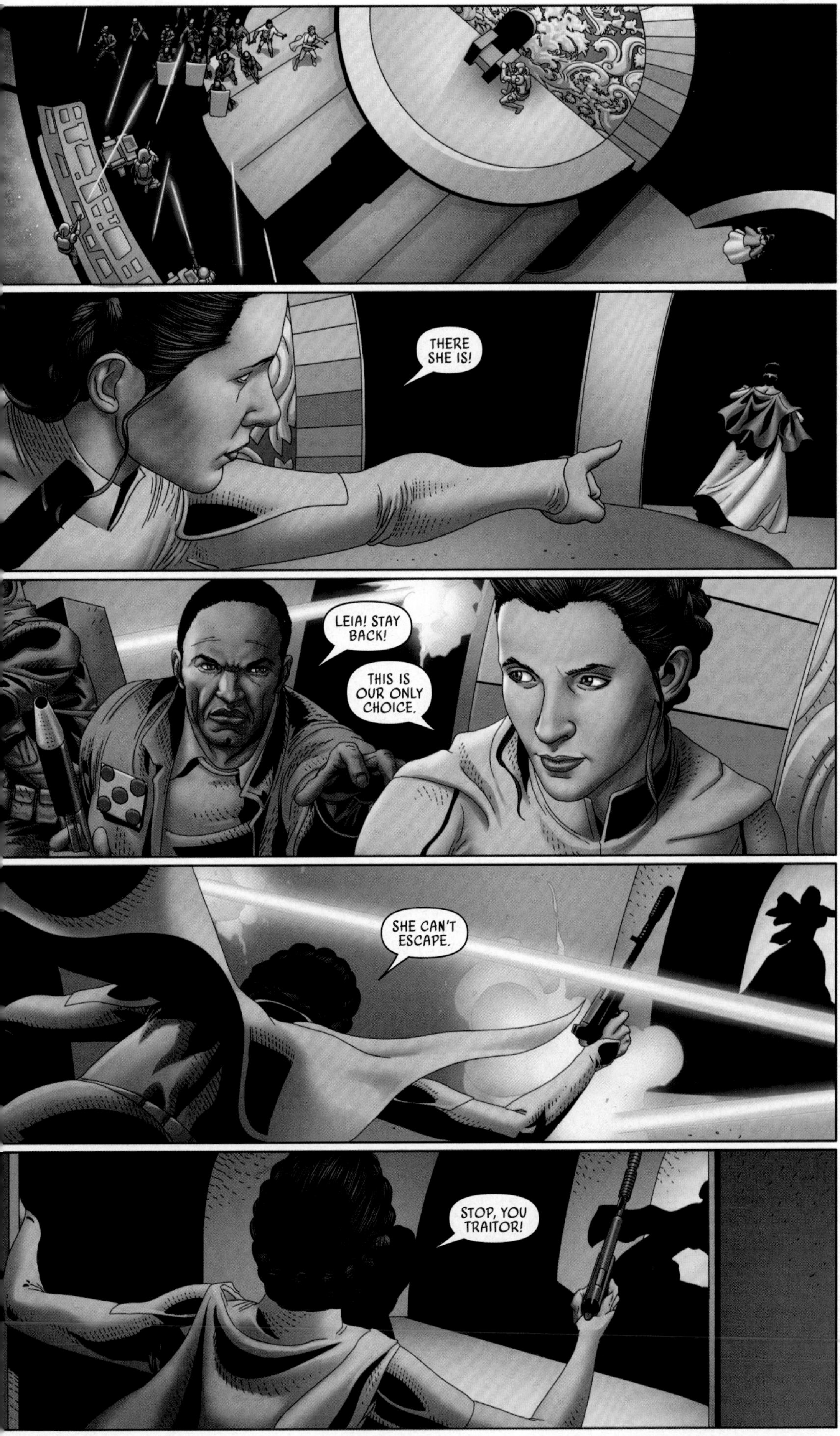
THERE SHE IS!
LEIA! STAY BACK!
THIS IS OUR ONLY CHOICE.
SHE CAN'T ESCAPE.
STOP, YOU TRAITOR!

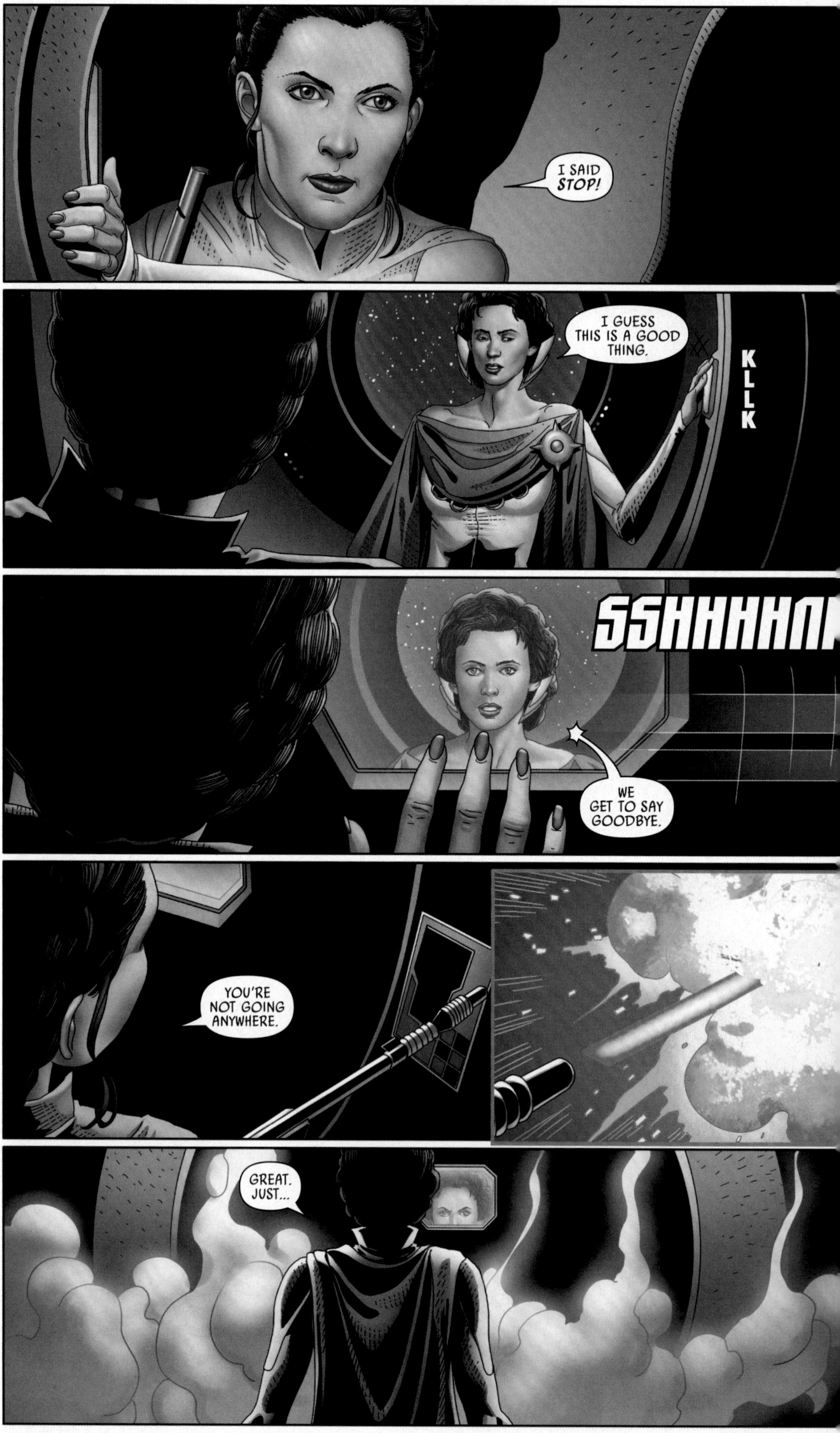
I SAID STOP!
I GUESS THIS IS A GOOD THING.
KLLK
WE GET TO SAY GOODBYE.
YOU'RE NOT GOING ANYWHERE.
GREAT. JUST...

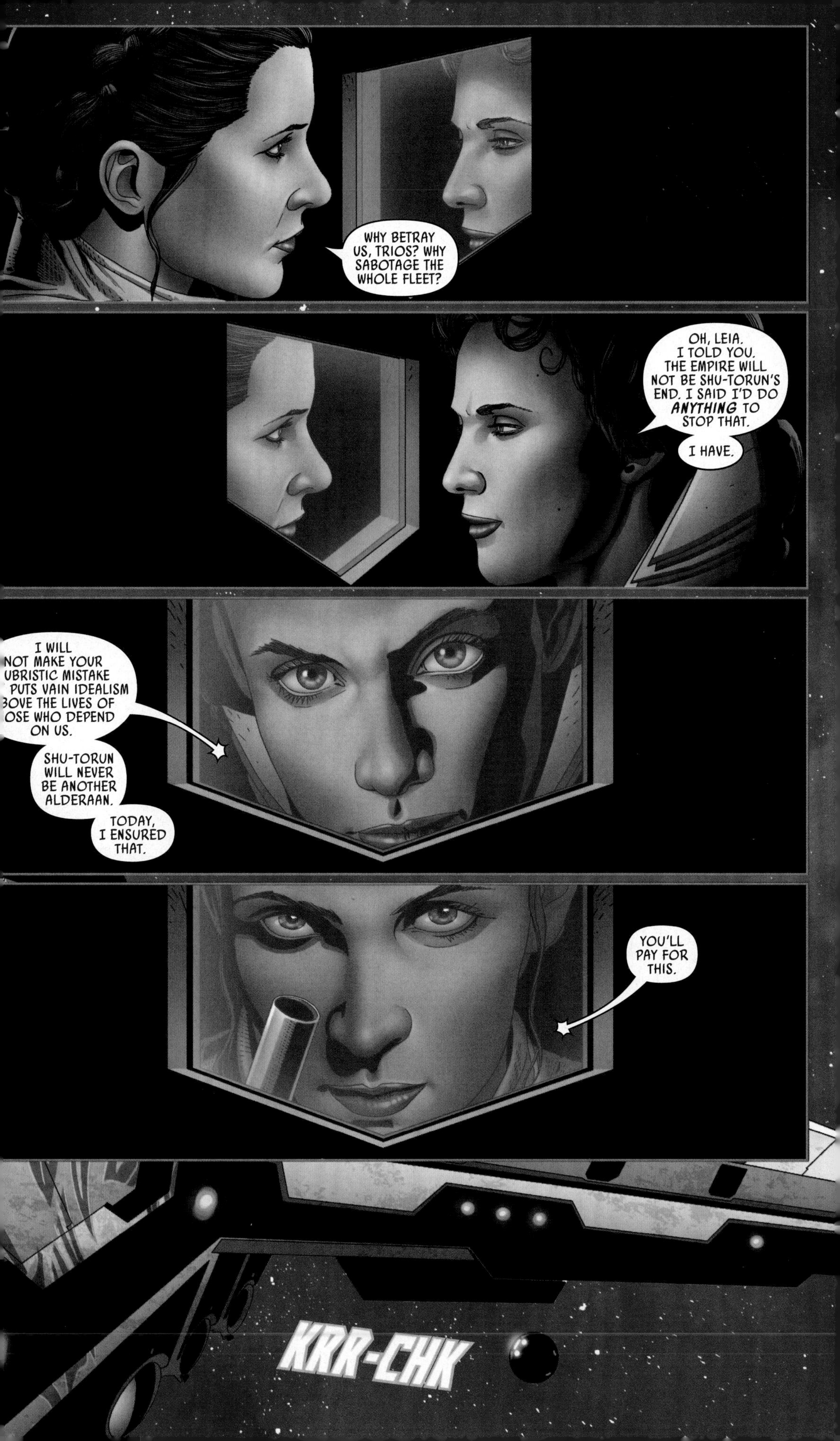
WHY BETRAY US, TRIOS? WHY SABOTAGE THE WHOLE FLEET?
OH, LEIA. I TOLD YOU. THE EMPIRE WILL NOT BE SHU-TORUN'S END. I SAID I'D DO ANYTHING TO STOP THAT.
I HAVE.
I WILL NOT MAKE YOUR UBRISTIC MISTAKE PUTS VAIN IDEALISM BOVE THE LIVES OF OSE WHO DEPEND ON US.
SHU-TORUN WILL NEVER BE ANOTHER ALDERAAN.
TODAY, I ENSURED THAT.
YOU'LL PAY FOR THIS.
KRR-CHK

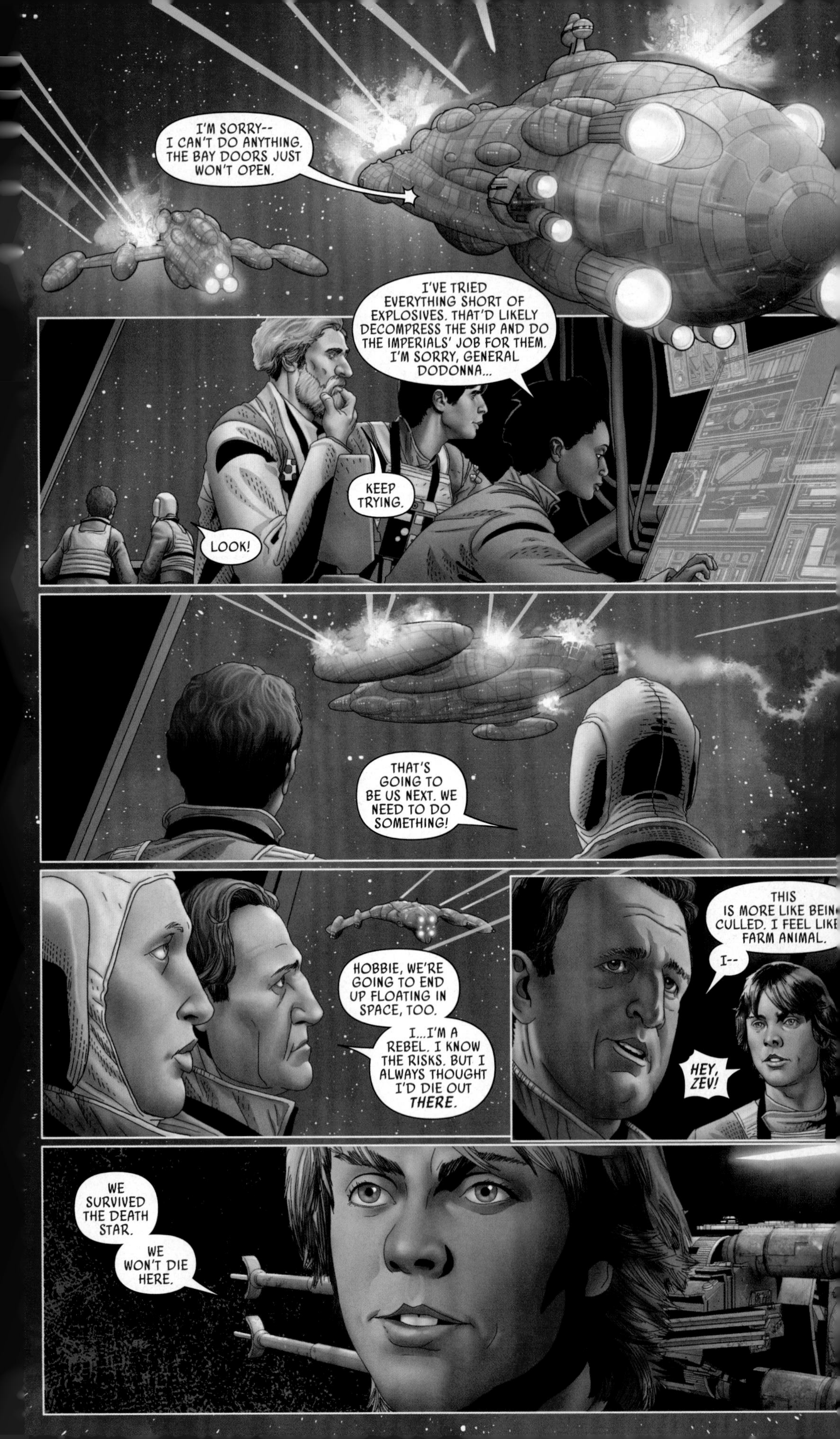
I'M SORRY-- I CAN'T DO ANYTHING. THE BAY DOORS JUST WON'T OPEN.
I'VE TRIED EVERYTHING SHORT OF EXPLOSIVES. THAT'D LIKELY DECOMPRESS THE SHIP AND DO THE IMPERIALS' JOB FOR THEM. I'M SORRY, GENERAL DODONNA...
KEEP TRYING.
LOOK!
THAT'S GOING TO BE US NEXT. WE NEED TO DO SOMETHING!
HOBBIE, WE'RE GOING TO END UP FLOATING IN SPACE, TOO.
I...I'M A REBEL. I KNOW THE RISKS. BUT I ALWAYS THOUGHT I'D DIE OUT *THERE*.
THIS IS MORE LIKE BEIN CULLED. I FEEL LIKE FARM ANIMAL.
I--
HEY, ZEV!
WE SURVIVED THE DEATH STAR.
WE WON'T DIE HERE.

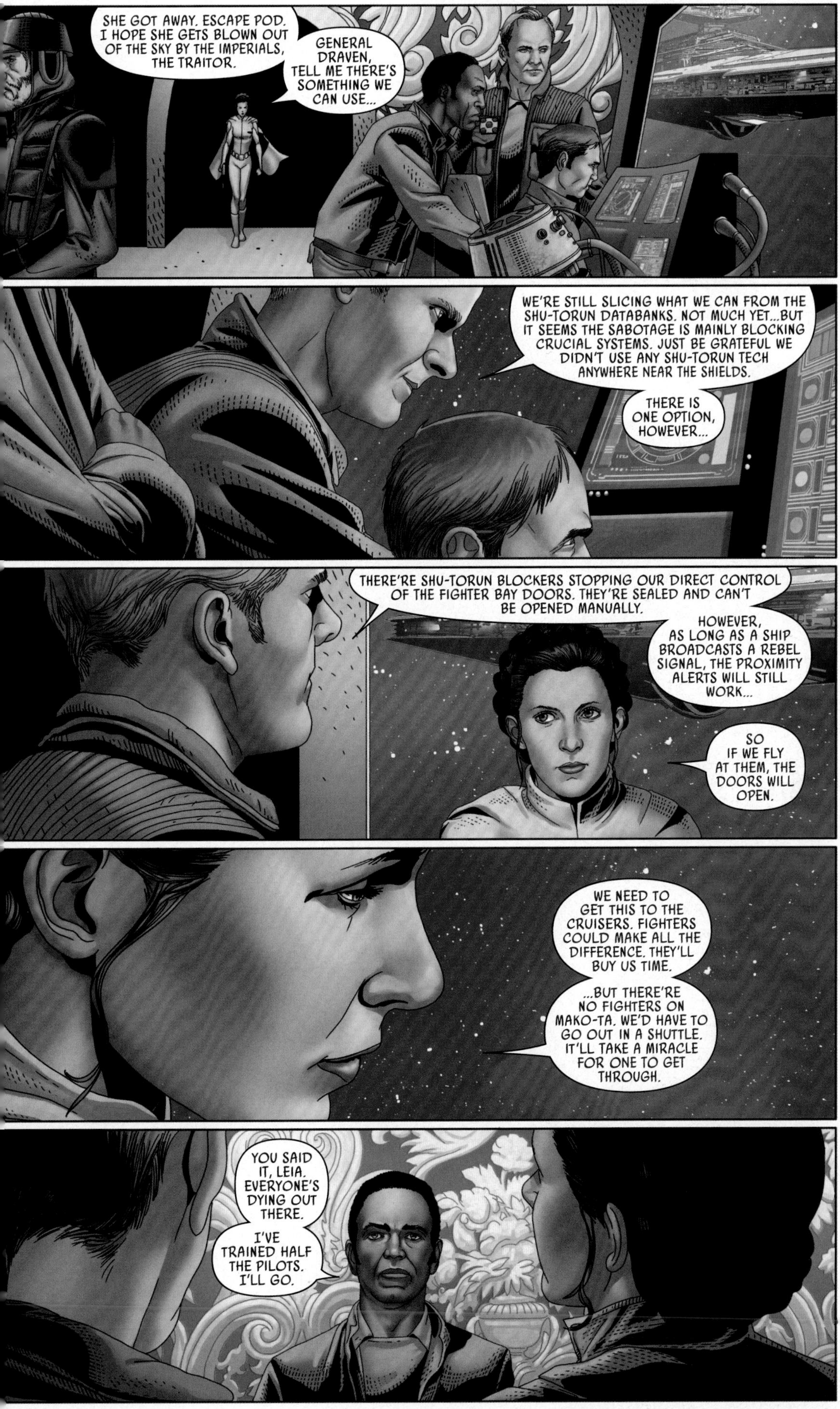
SHE GOT AWAY. ESCAPE POD. I HOPE SHE GETS BLOWN OUT OF THE SKY BY THE IMPERIALS, THE TRAITOR.
GENERAL DRAVEN, TELL ME THERE'S SOMETHING WE CAN USE...
WE'RE STILL SLICING WHAT WE CAN FROM THE SHU-TORUN DATABANKS. NOT MUCH YET...BUT IT SEEMS THE SABOTAGE IS MAINLY BLOCKING CRUCIAL SYSTEMS. JUST BE GRATEFUL WE DIDN'T USE ANY SHU-TORUN TECH ANYWHERE NEAR THE SHIELDS.
THERE IS ONE OPTION, HOWEVER...
THERE'RE SHU-TORUN BLOCKERS STOPPING OUR DIRECT CONTROL OF THE FIGHTER BAY DOORS. THEY'RE SEALED AND CAN'T BE OPENED MANUALLY.
HOWEVER, AS LONG AS A SHIP BROADCASTS A REBEL SIGNAL, THE PROXIMITY ALERTS WILL STILL WORK...
SO IF WE FLY AT THEM, THE DOORS WILL OPEN.
WE NEED TO GET THIS TO THE CRUISERS. FIGHTERS COULD MAKE ALL THE DIFFERENCE. THEY'LL BUY US TIME.
...BUT THERE'RE NO FIGHTERS ON MAKO-TA. WE'D HAVE TO GO OUT IN A SHUTTLE. IT'LL TAKE A MIRACLE FOR ONE TO GET THROUGH.
YOU SAID IT, LEIA. EVERYONE'S DYING OUT THERE.
I'VE TRAINED HALF THE PILOTS. I'LL GO.

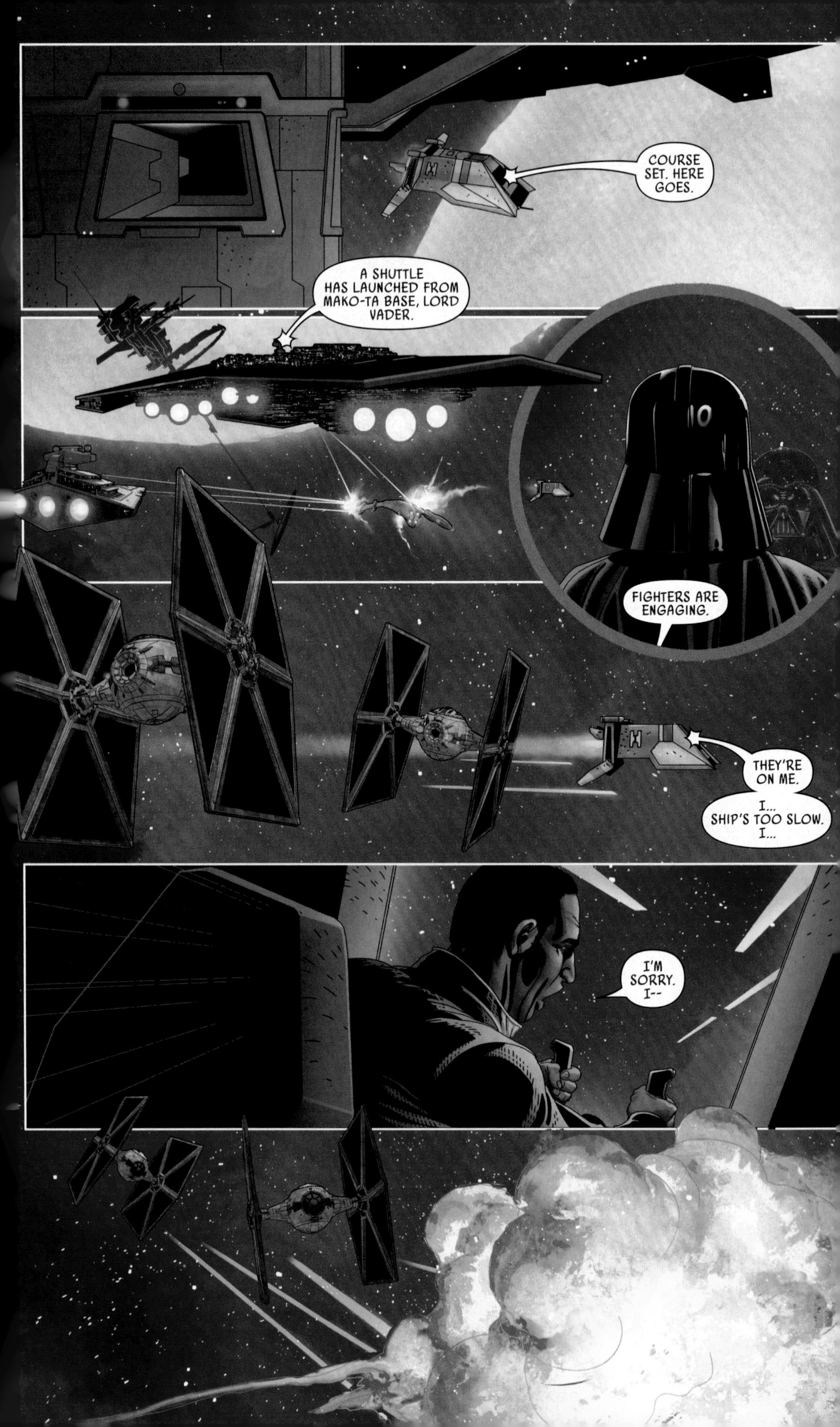
COURSE SET. HERE GOES.
A SHUTTLE HAS LAUNCHED FROM MAKO-TA BASE, LORD VADER.
FIGHTERS ARE ENGAGING.
THEY'RE ON ME.
I... SHIP'S TOO SLOW. I...
I'M SORRY. I--

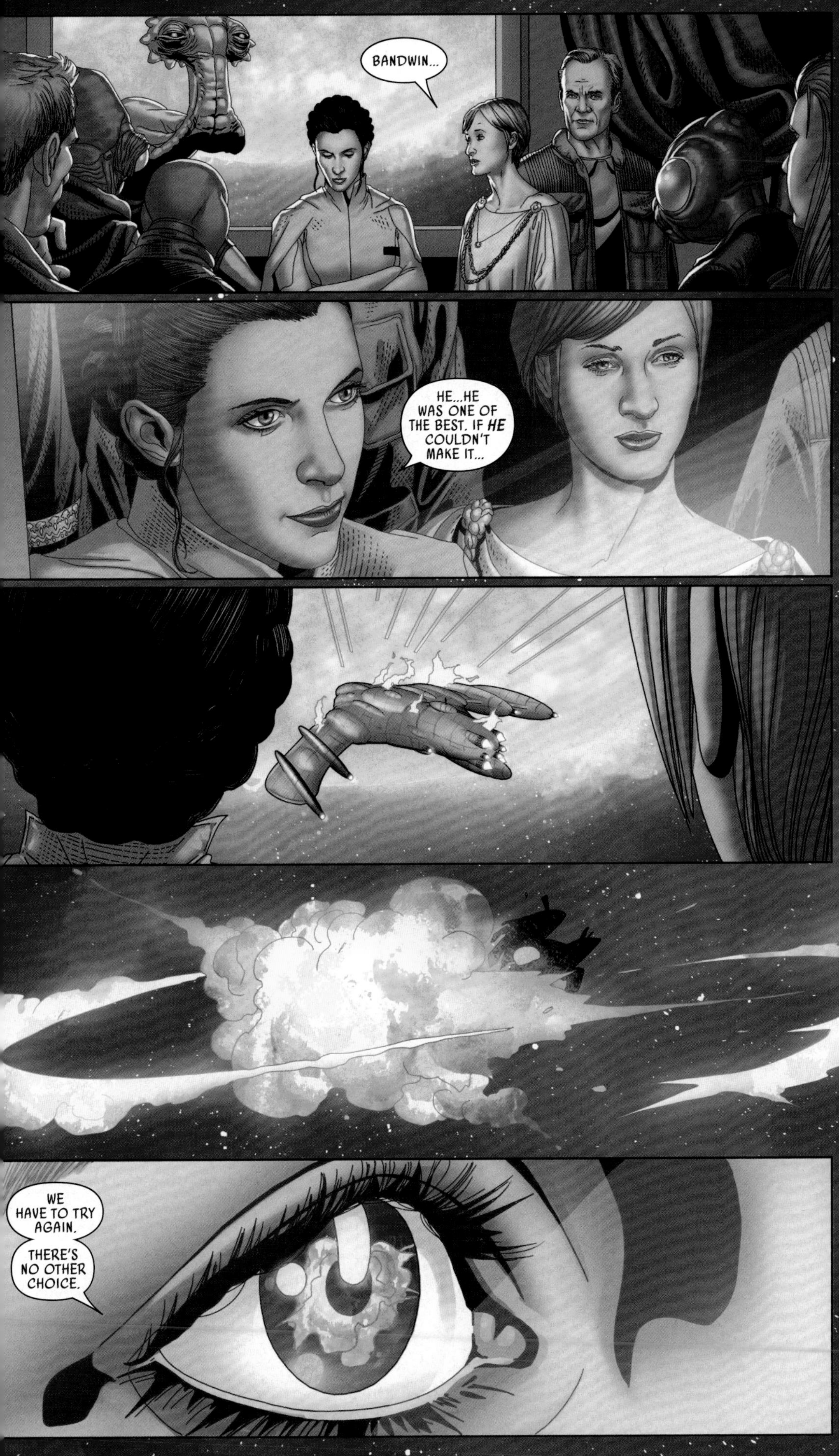
BANDWIN...
HE...HE WAS ONE OF THE BEST. IF ***HE*** COULDN'T MAKE IT...
WE HAVE TO TRY AGAIN.
THERE'S NO OTHER CHOICE.

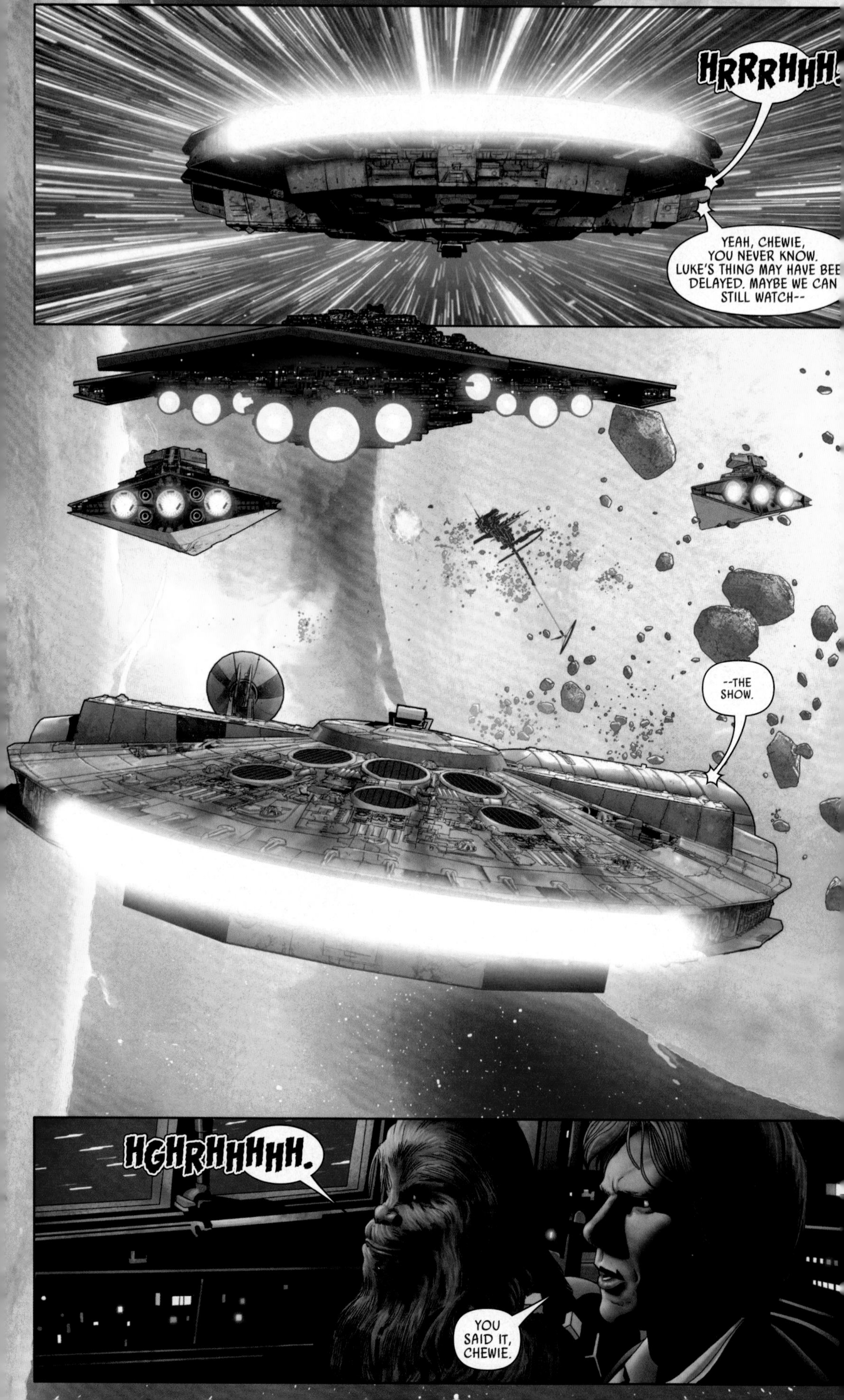
HRRRHHH!
YEAH, CHEWIE, YOU NEVER KNOW. LUKE'S THING MAY HAVE BEE DELAYED. MAYBE WE CAN STILL WATCH--
--THE SHOW.
HGHRHHHHH.
YOU SAID IT, CHEWIE.

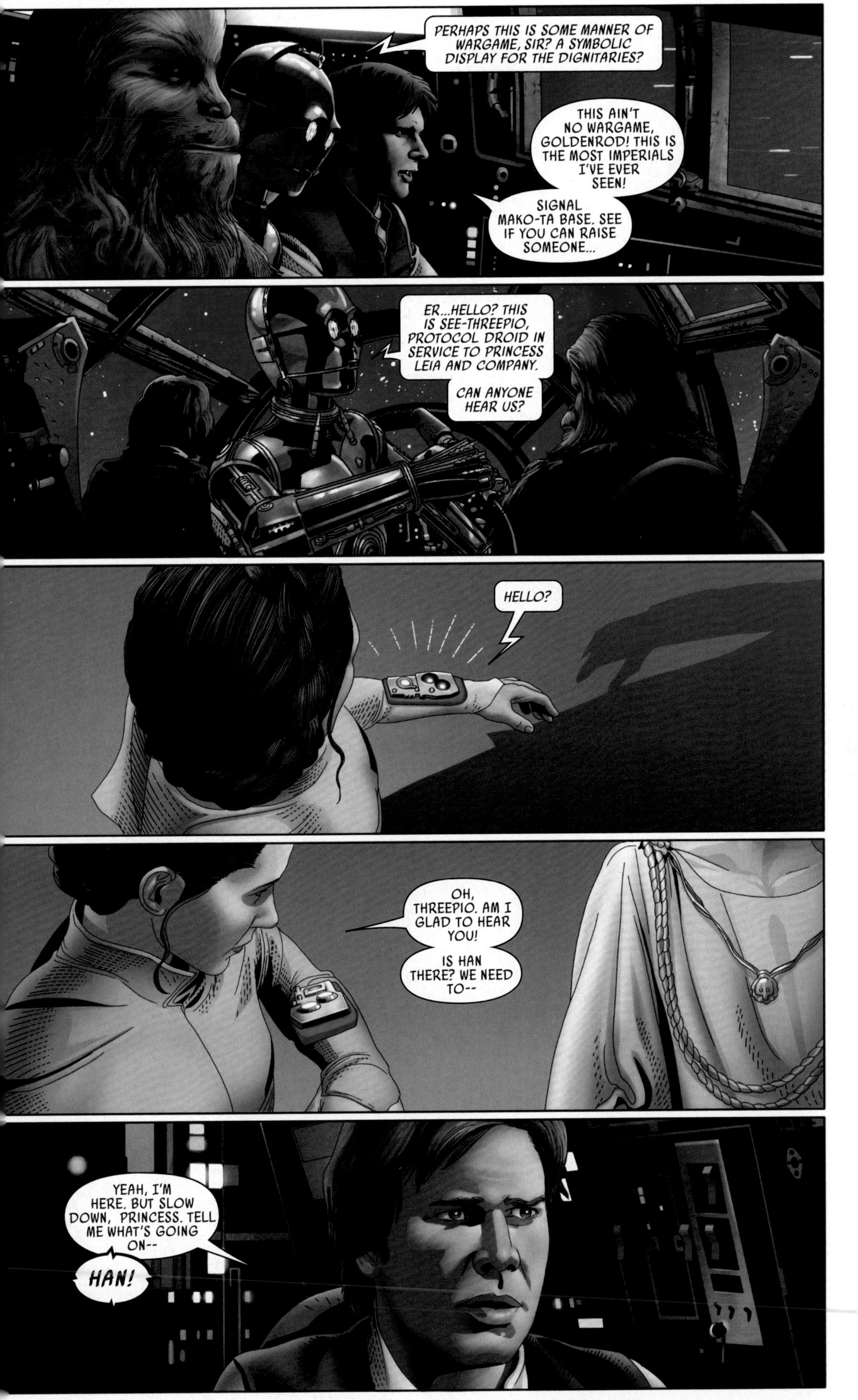
PERHAPS THIS IS SOME MANNER OF WARGAME, SIR? A SYMBOLIC DISPLAY FOR THE DIGNITARIES?
THIS AIN'T NO WARGAME, GOLDENROD! THIS IS THE MOST IMPERIALS I'VE EVER SEEN!
SIGNAL MAKO-TA BASE. SEE IF YOU CAN RAISE SOMEONE...
ER...HELLO? THIS IS SEE-THREEPIO, PROTOCOL DROID IN SERVICE TO PRINCESS LEIA AND COMPANY.
CAN ANYONE HEAR US?
HELLO?
OH, THREEPIO. AM I GLAD TO HEAR YOU!
IS HAN THERE? WE NEED TO--
YEAH, I'M HERE. BUT SLOW DOWN, PRINCESS. TELL ME WHAT'S GOING ON--
HAN!

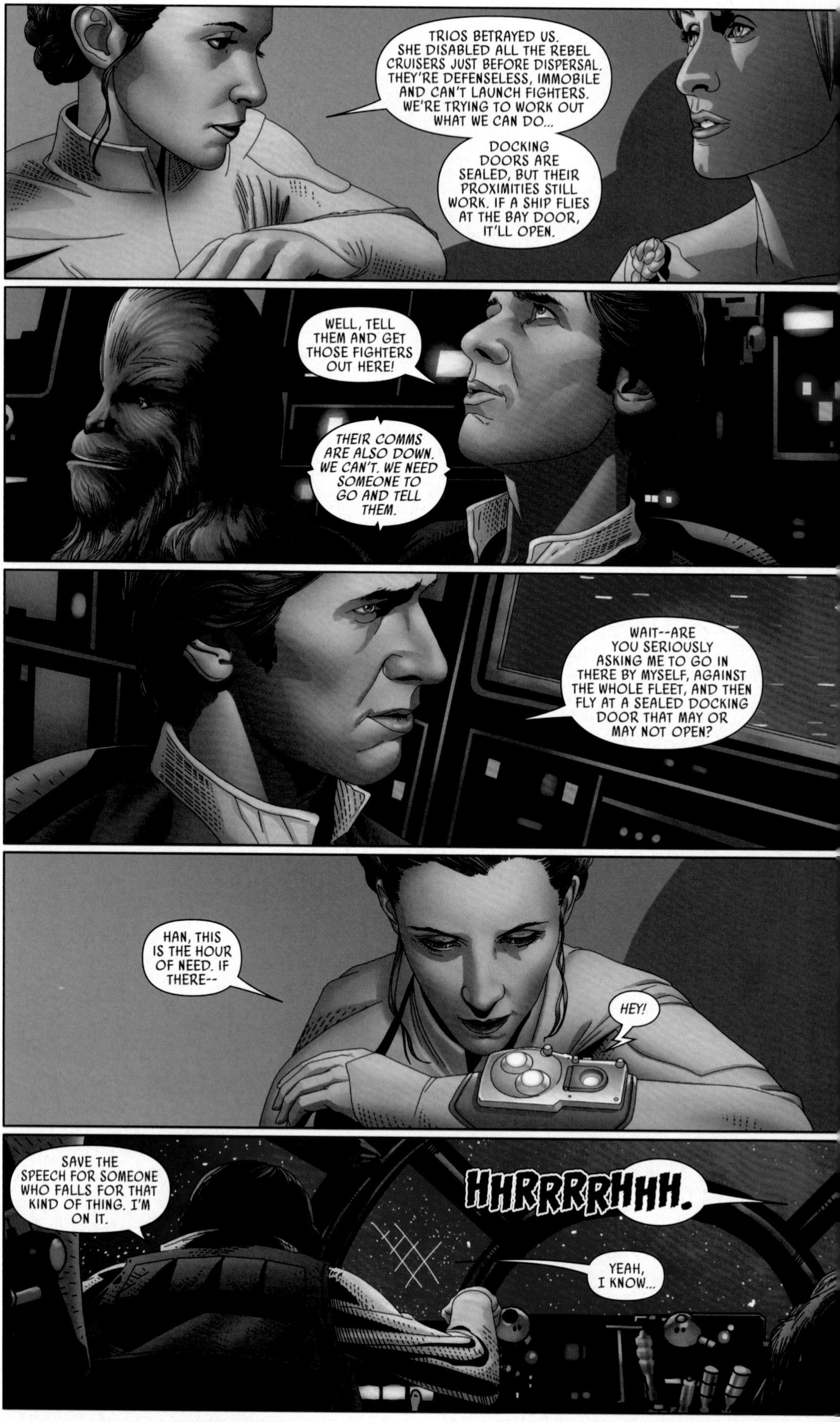
TRIOS BETRAYED US. SHE DISABLED ALL THE REBEL CRUISERS JUST BEFORE DISPERSAL. THEY'RE DEFENSELESS, IMMOBILE AND CAN'T LAUNCH FIGHTERS. WE'RE TRYING TO WORK OUT WHAT WE CAN DO...
DOCKING DOORS ARE SEALED, BUT THEIR PROXIMITIES STILL WORK. IF A SHIP FLIES AT THE BAY DOOR, IT'LL OPEN.
WELL, TELL THEM AND GET THOSE FIGHTERS OUT HERE!
THEIR COMMS ARE ALSO DOWN. WE CAN'T. WE NEED SOMEONE TO GO AND TELL THEM.
WAIT--ARE YOU SERIOUSLY ASKING ME TO GO IN THERE BY MYSELF, AGAINST THE WHOLE FLEET, AND THEN FLY AT A SEALED DOCKING DOOR THAT MAY OR MAY NOT OPEN?
HAN, THIS IS THE HOUR OF NEED. IF THERE--
HEY!
SAVE THE SPEECH FOR SOMEONE WHO FALLS FOR THAT KIND OF THING. I'M ON IT.
HHRRRRHHH.
YEAH, I KNOW...

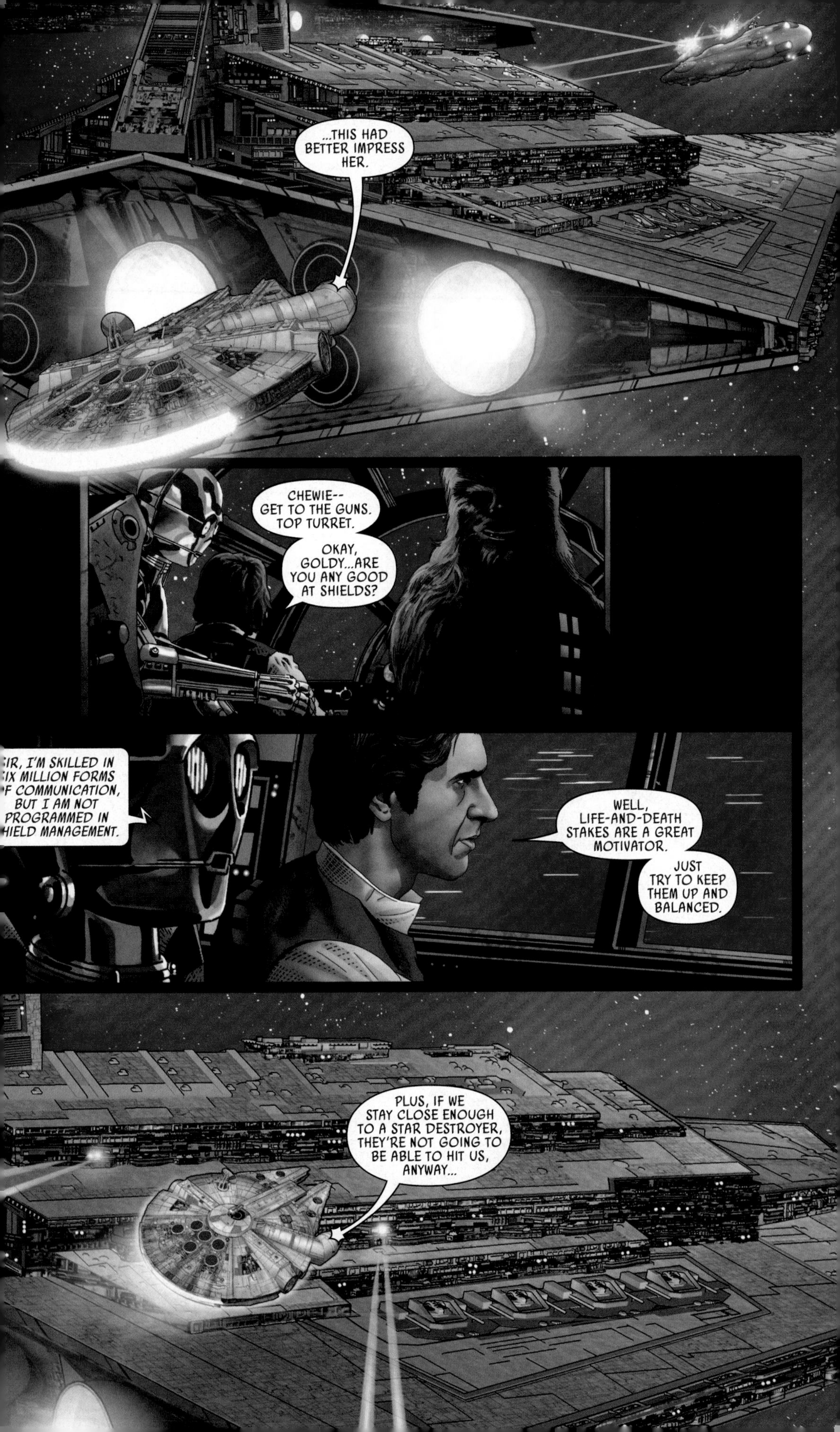
...THIS HAD BETTER IMPRESS HER.
CHEWIE-- GET TO THE GUNS. TOP TURRET.
OKAY, GOLDY...ARE YOU ANY GOOD AT SHIELDS?
IR, I'M SKILLED IN IX MILLION FORMS F COMMUNICATION, BUT I AM NOT PROGRAMMED IN HIELD MANAGEMENT.
WELL, LIFE-AND-DEATH STAKES ARE A GREAT MOTIVATOR.
JUST TRY TO KEEP THEM UP AND BALANCED.
PLUS, IF WE STAY CLOSE ENOUGH TO A STAR DESTROYER, THEY'RE NOT GOING TO BE ABLE TO HIT US, ANYWAY...

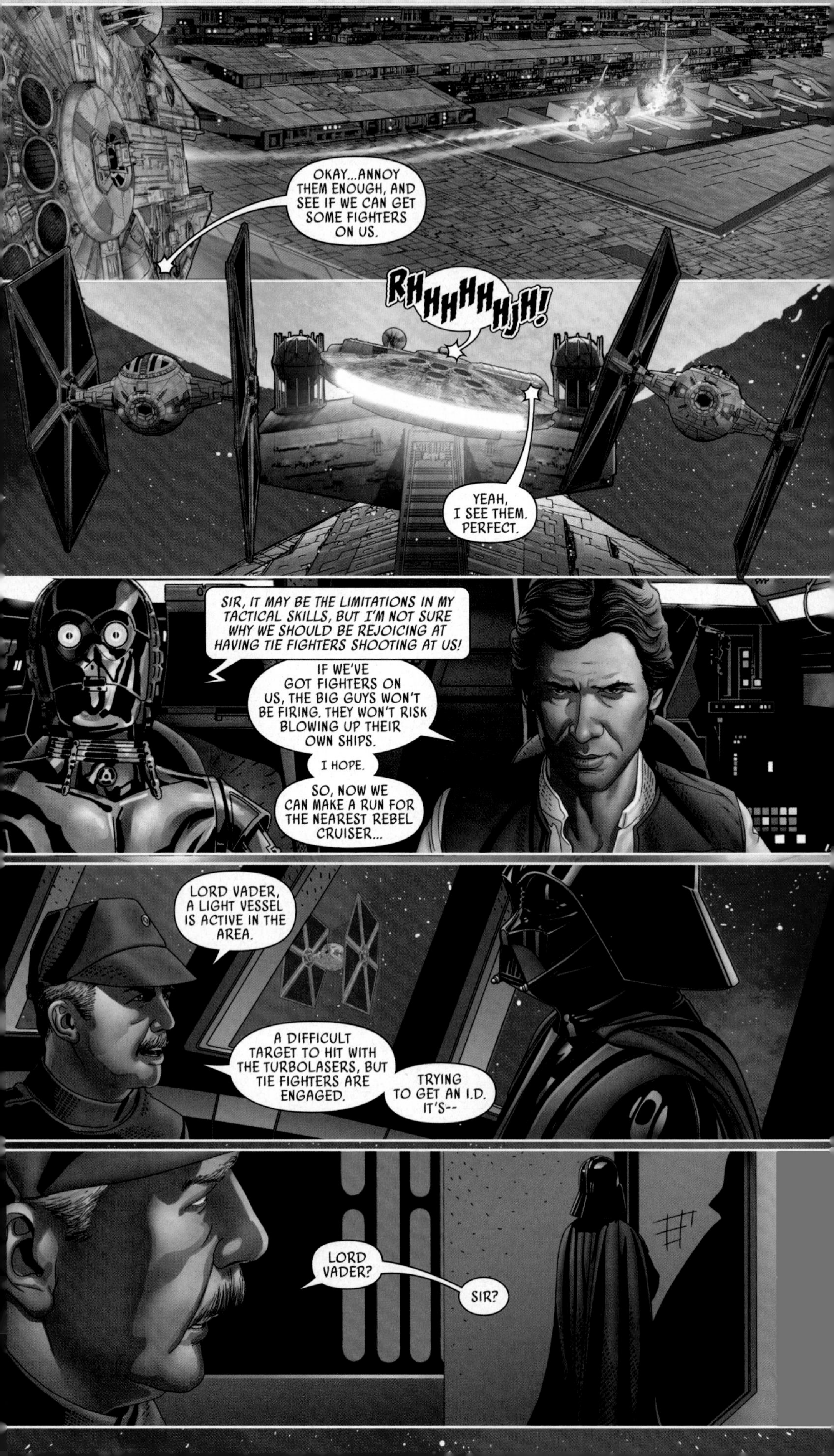
OKAY...ANNOY THEM ENOUGH, AND SEE IF WE CAN GET SOME FIGHTERS ON US.
RHHHHHJH!
YEAH, I SEE THEM. PERFECT.
SIR, IT MAY BE THE LIMITATIONS IN MY TACTICAL SKILLS, BUT I'M NOT SURE WHY WE SHOULD BE REJOICING AT HAVING TIE FIGHTERS SHOOTING AT US!
IF WE'VE GOT FIGHTERS ON US, THE BIG GUYS WON'T BE FIRING. THEY WON'T RISK BLOWING UP THEIR OWN SHIPS.
I HOPE.
SO, NOW WE CAN MAKE A RUN FOR THE NEAREST REBEL CRUISER...
LORD VADER, A LIGHT VESSEL IS ACTIVE IN THE AREA.
A DIFFICULT TARGET TO HIT WITH THE TURBOLASERS, BUT TIE FIGHTERS ARE ENGAGED.
TRYING TO GET AN I.D. IT'S--
LORD VADER?
SIR?

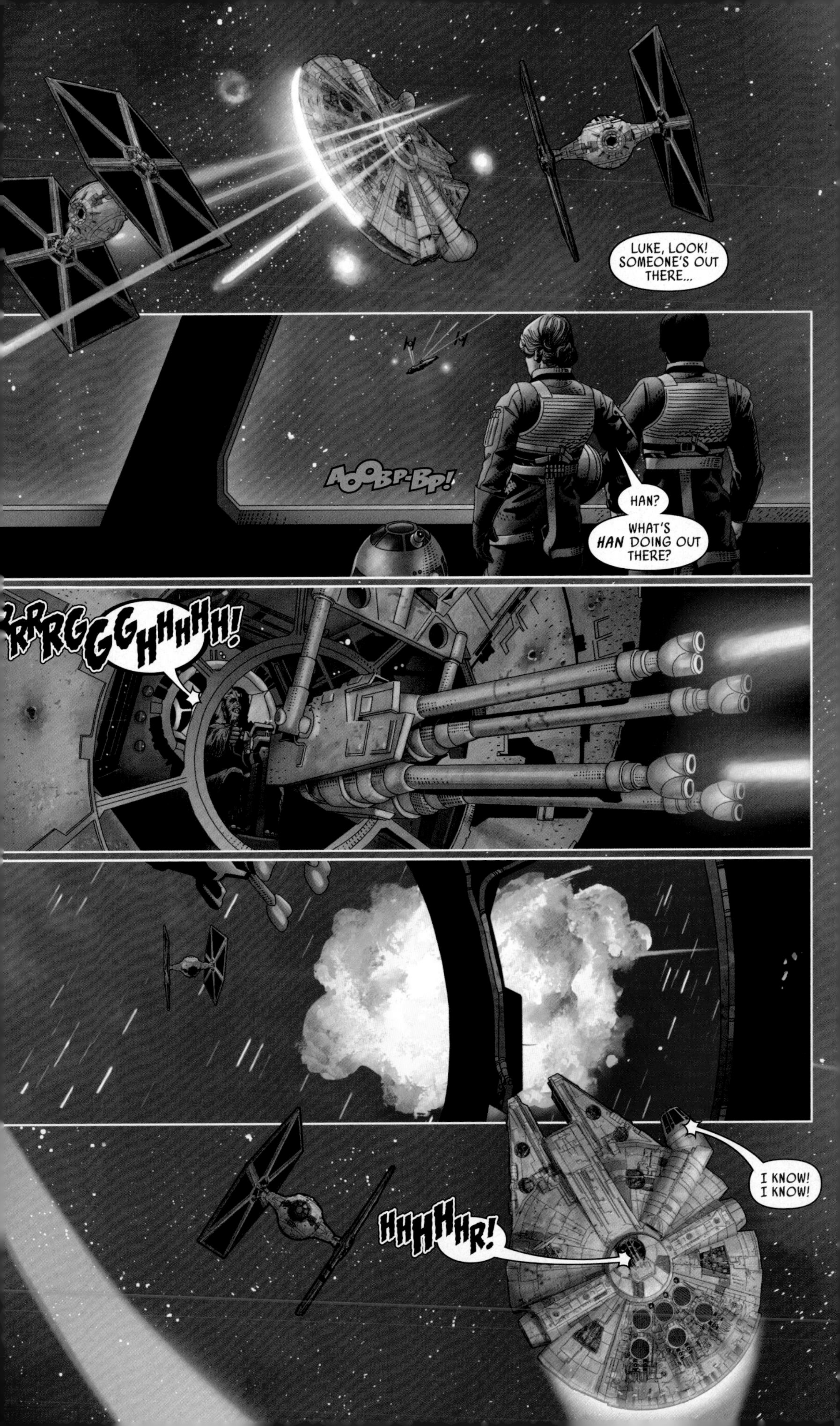
LUKE, LOOK! SOMEONE'S OUT THERE...
AOOBP-BP!
HAN?
WHAT'S HAN DOING OUT THERE?
RRRGGGHHHHH!
HHHHHR!
I KNOW! I KNOW!

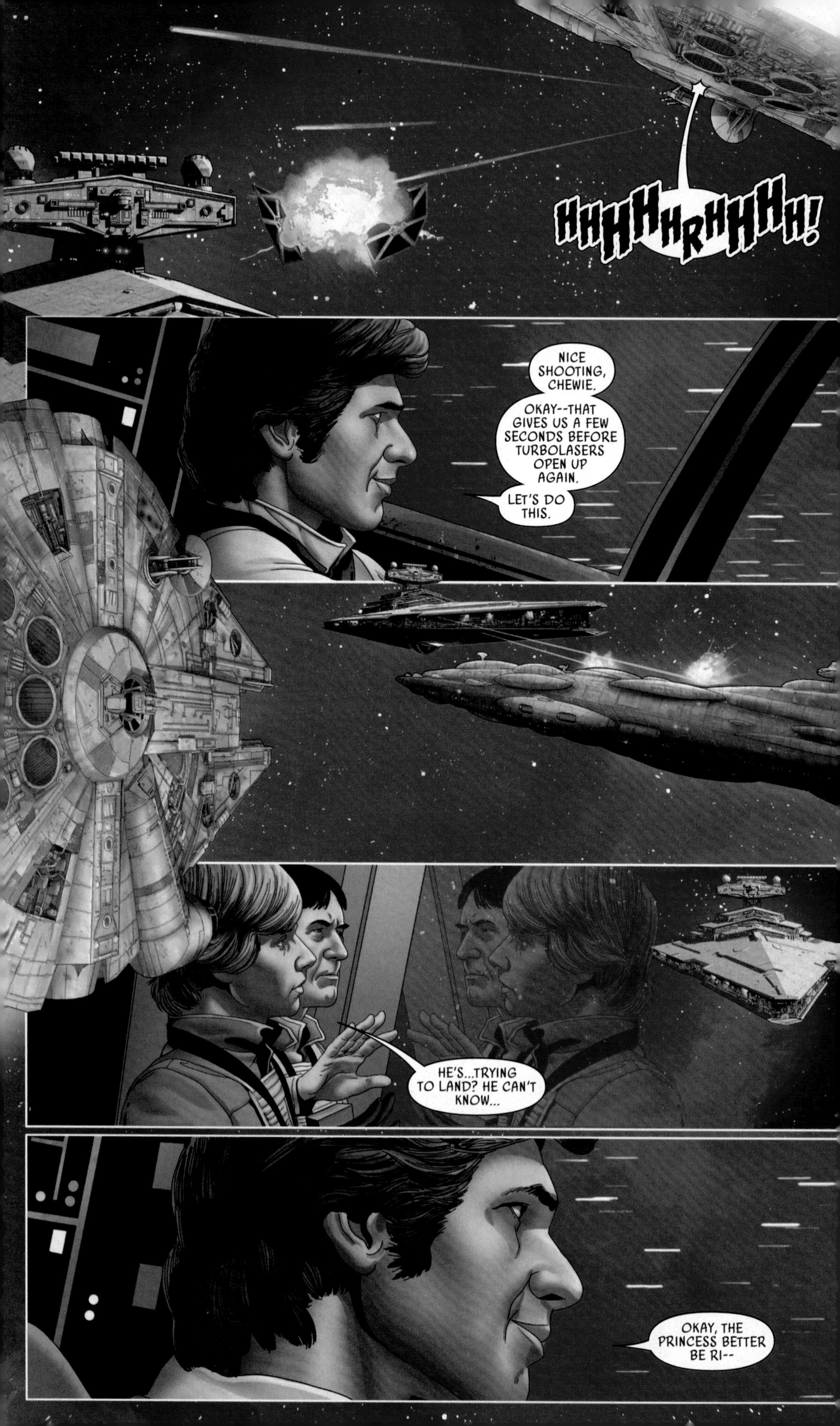
HHHHHRHHHH!
NICE SHOOTING, CHEWIE.
OKAY--THAT GIVES US A FEW SECONDS BEFORE TURBOLASERS OPEN UP AGAIN.
LET'S DO THIS.
HE'S...TRYING TO LAND? HE CAN'T KNOW...
OKAY, THE PRINCESS BETTER BE RI--

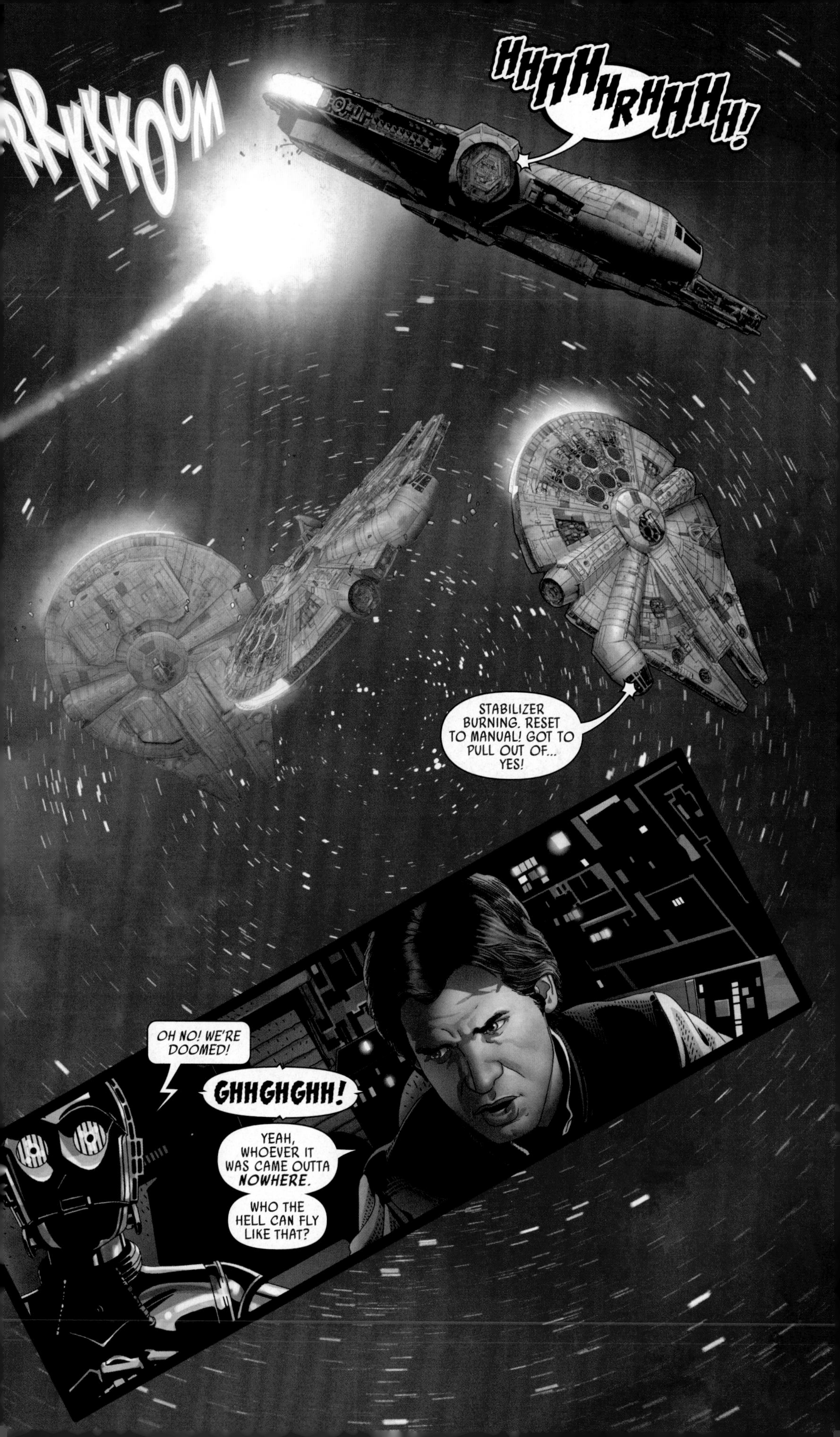
RRKKKOOM
HHHHHRHHHHH!
STABILIZER BURNING. RESET TO MANUAL! GOT TO PULL OUT OF... YES!
OH NO! WE'RE DOOMED!
GHHGHGHH!
YEAH, WHOEVER IT WAS CAME OUTTA *NOWHERE*.
WHO THE HELL CAN FLY LIKE THAT?

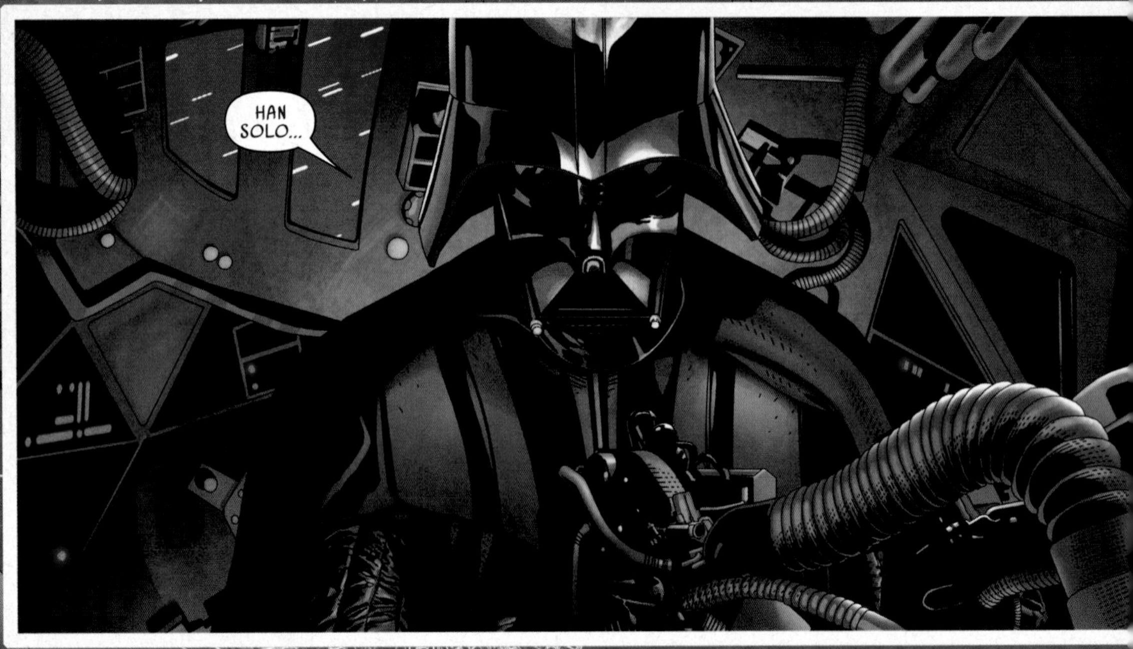
HAN SOLO...

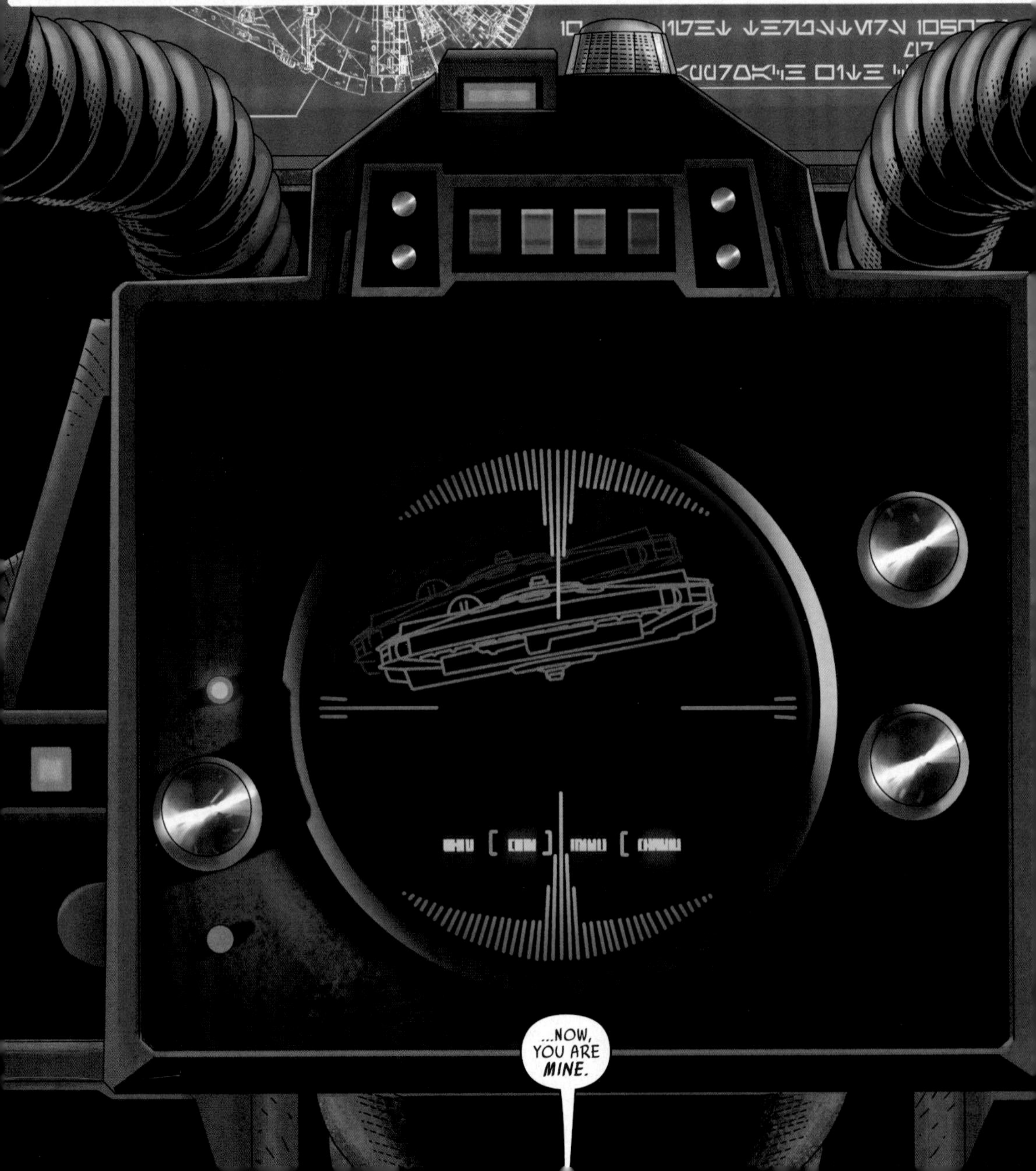
...NOW, YOU ARE MINE.

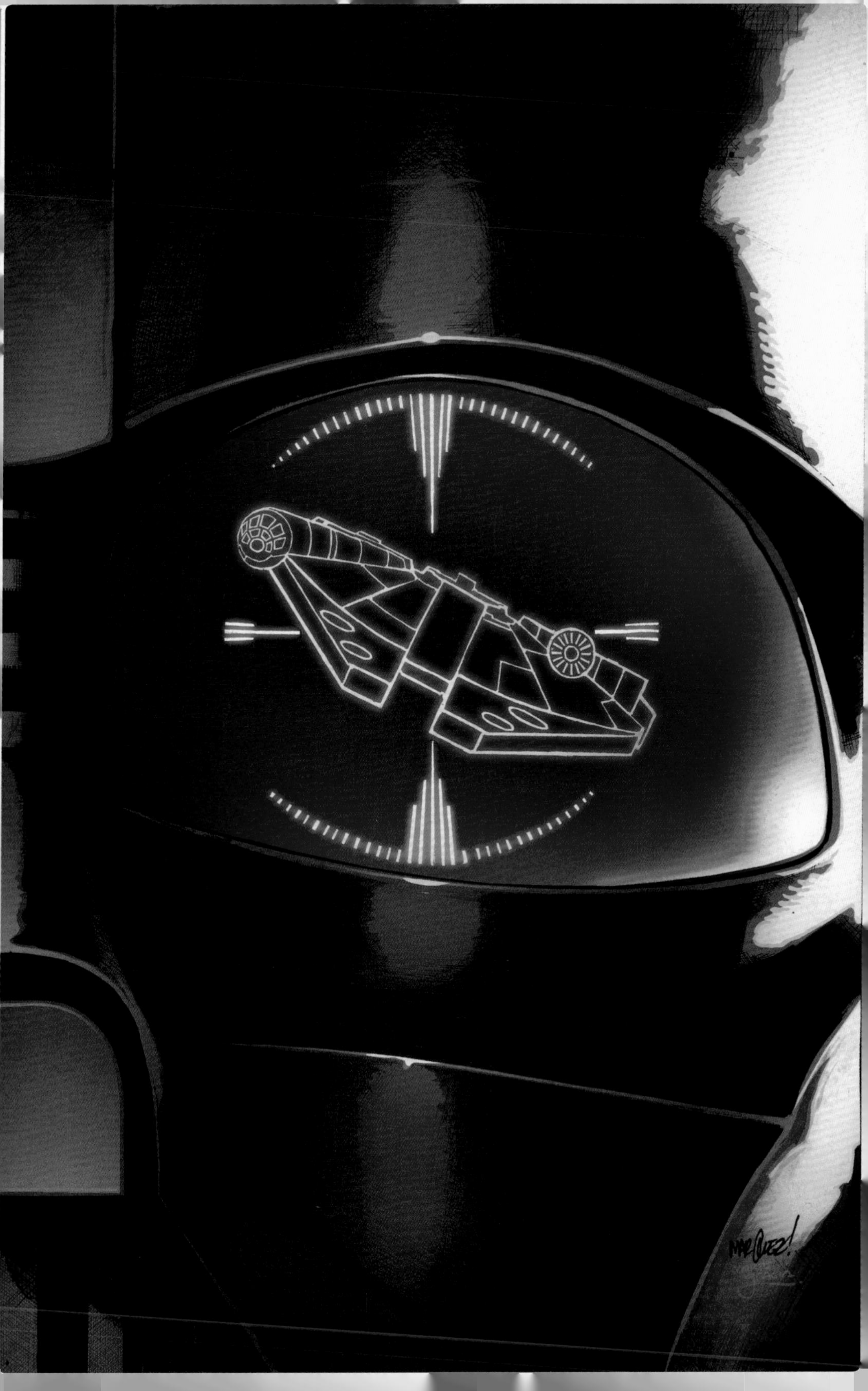

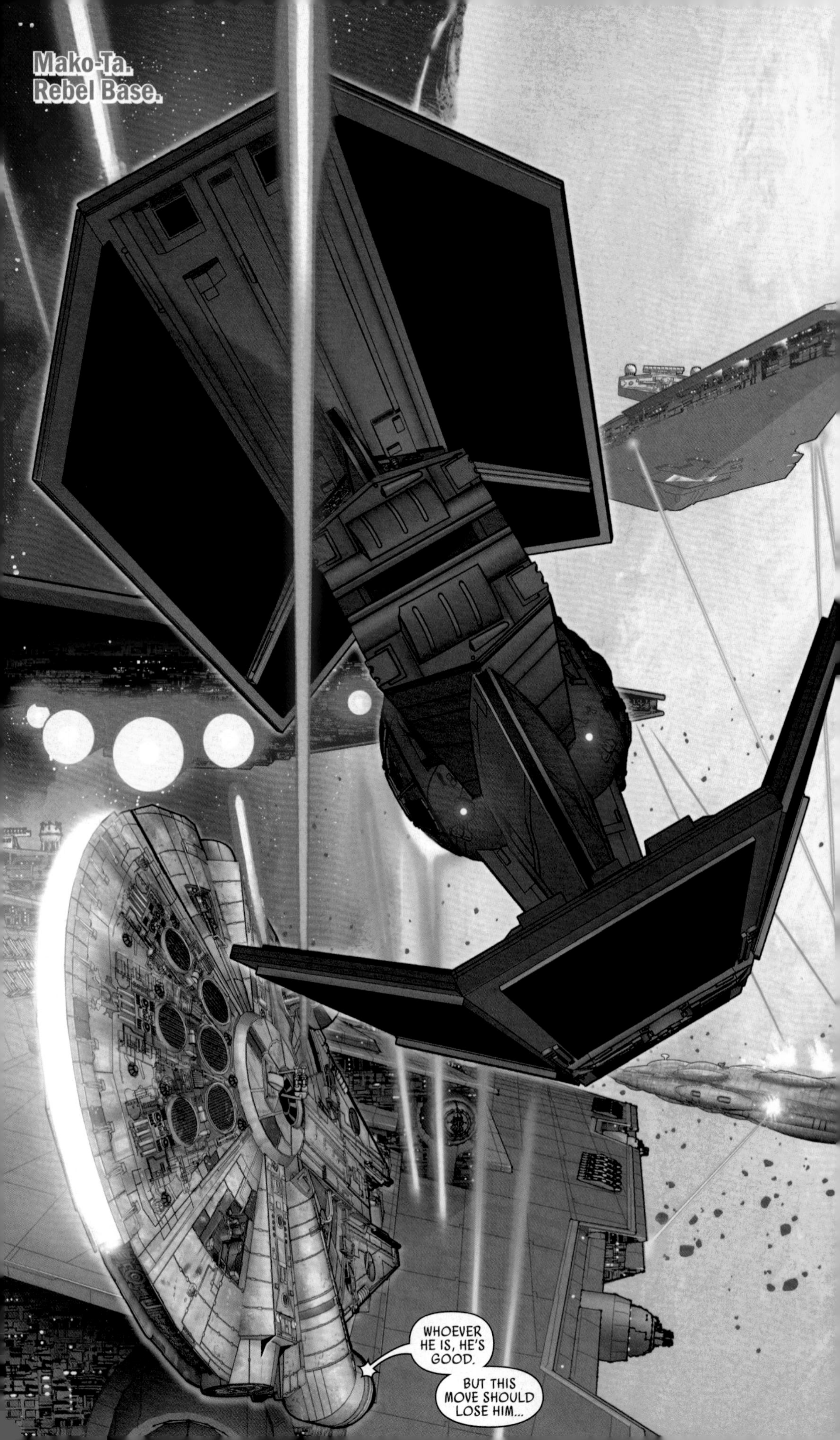
Mako-Ta.
Rebel Base.
WHOEVER HE IS, HE'S GOOD.
BUT THIS MOVE SHOULD LOSE HIM...

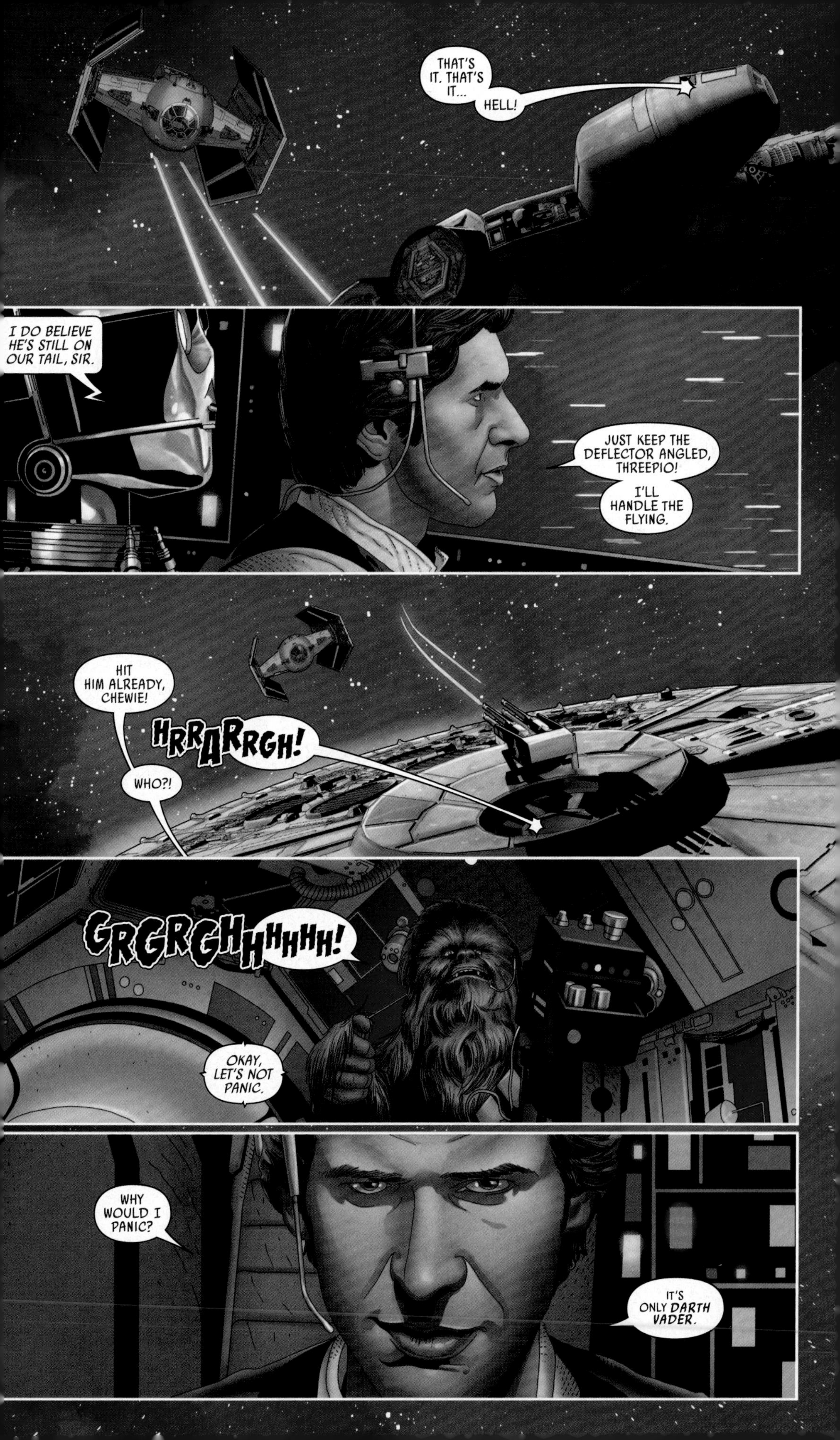

THAT'S IT. THAT'S IT...
HELL!
I DO BELIEVE HE'S STILL ON OUR TAIL, SIR.
JUST KEEP THE DEFLECTOR ANGLED, THREEPIO!
I'LL HANDLE THE FLYING.
HIT HIM ALREADY, CHEWIE!
HRRARRGH!
WHO?!
GRGRGHHHHHH!
OKAY, LET'S NOT PANIC.
WHY WOULD I PANIC?
IT'S ONLY DARTH VADER.

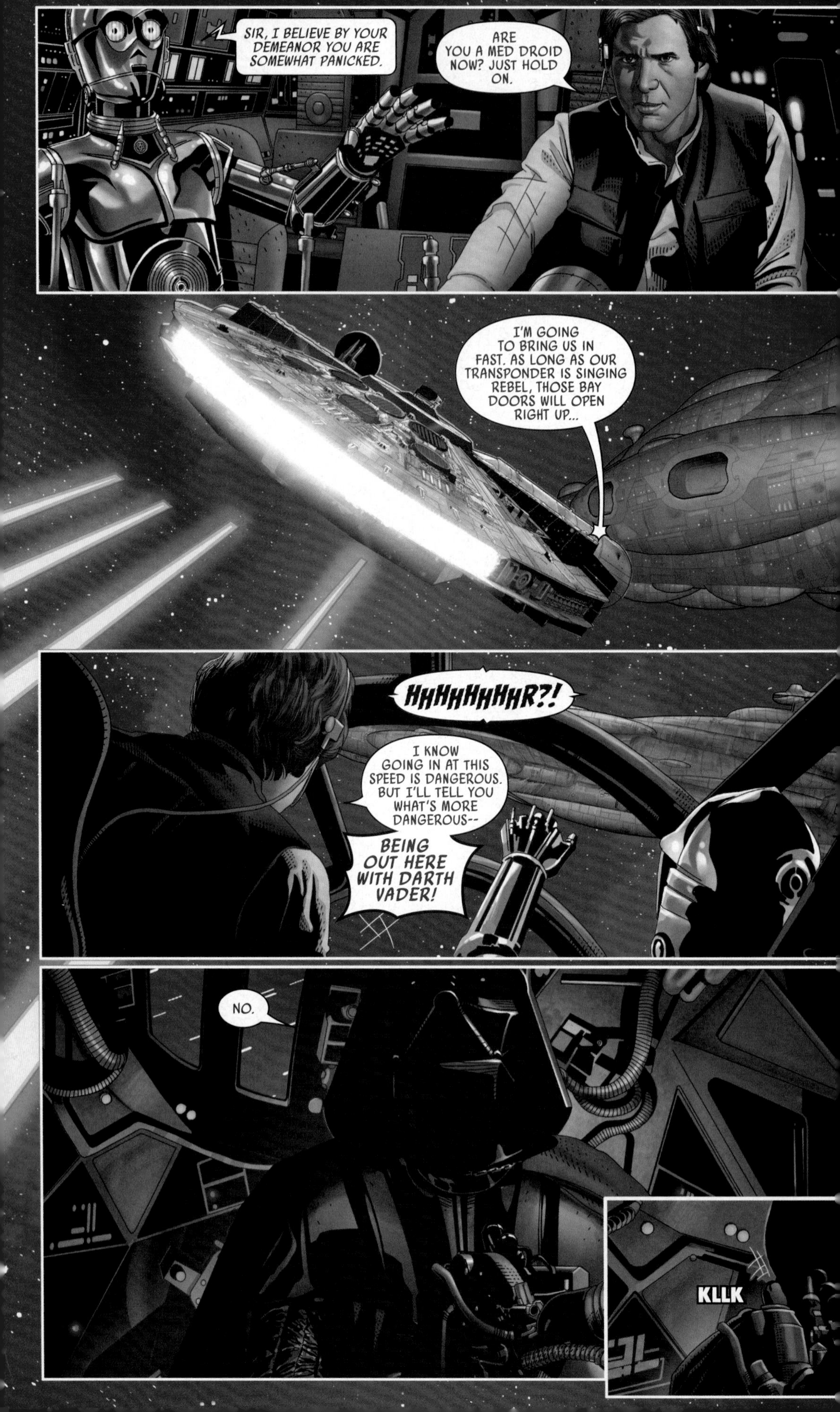
SIR, I BELIEVE BY YOUR DEMEANOR YOU ARE SOMEWHAT PANICKED.
ARE YOU A MED DROID NOW? JUST HOLD ON.
I'M GOING TO BRING US IN FAST. AS LONG AS OUR TRANSPONDER IS SINGING REBEL, THOSE BAY DOORS WILL OPEN RIGHT UP...
HHHHHHHHR?!
I KNOW GOING IN AT THIS SPEED IS DANGEROUS. BUT I'LL TELL YOU WHAT'S MORE DANGEROUS--
BEING OUT HERE WITH DARTH VADER!
NO.
KLLK

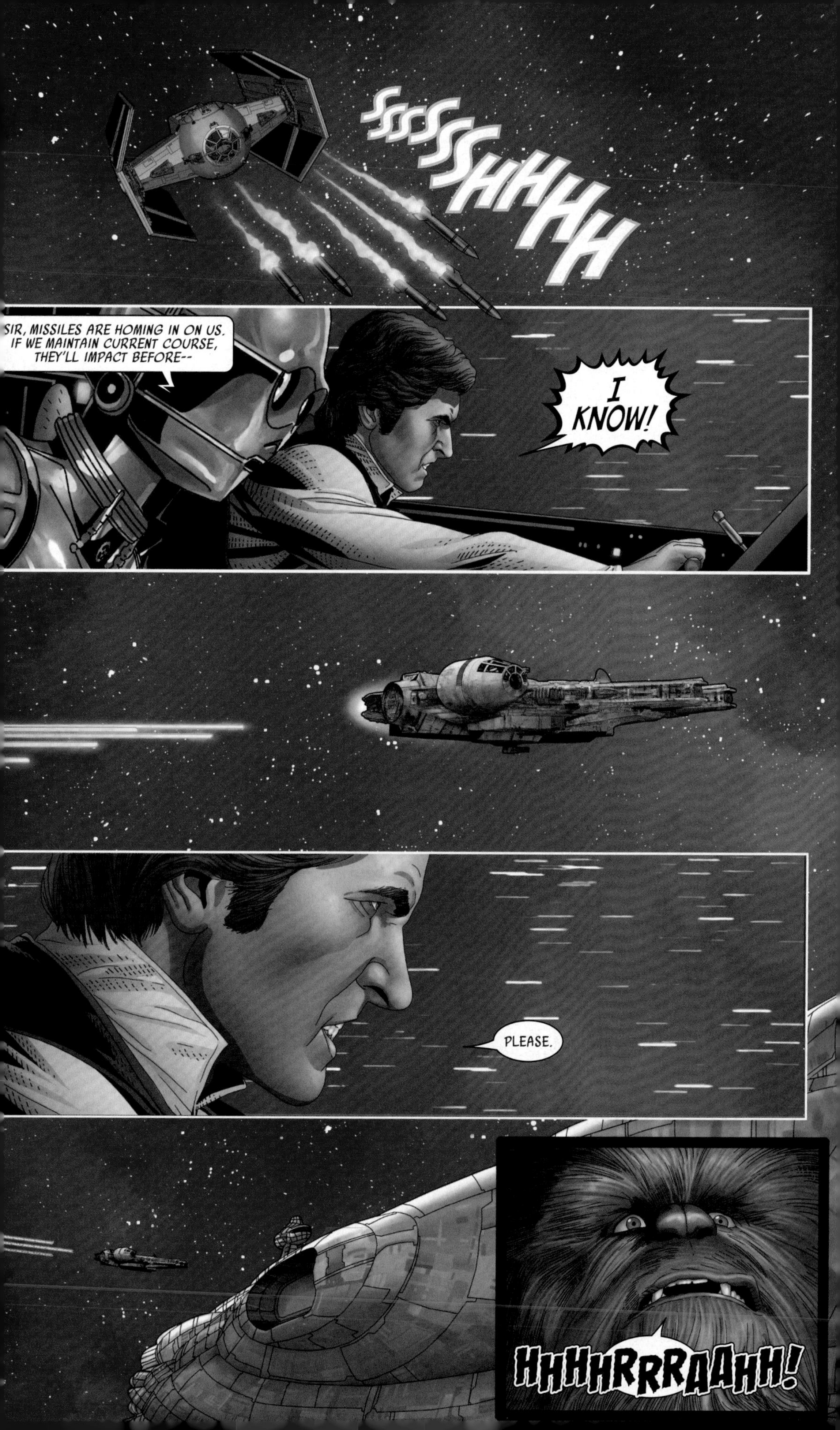
SSSSSHHHHHH
SIR, MISSILES ARE HOMING IN ON US. IF WE MAINTAIN CURRENT COURSE, THEY'LL IMPACT BEFORE--
I KNOW!
PLEASE.
HHHHRRRAAHH!

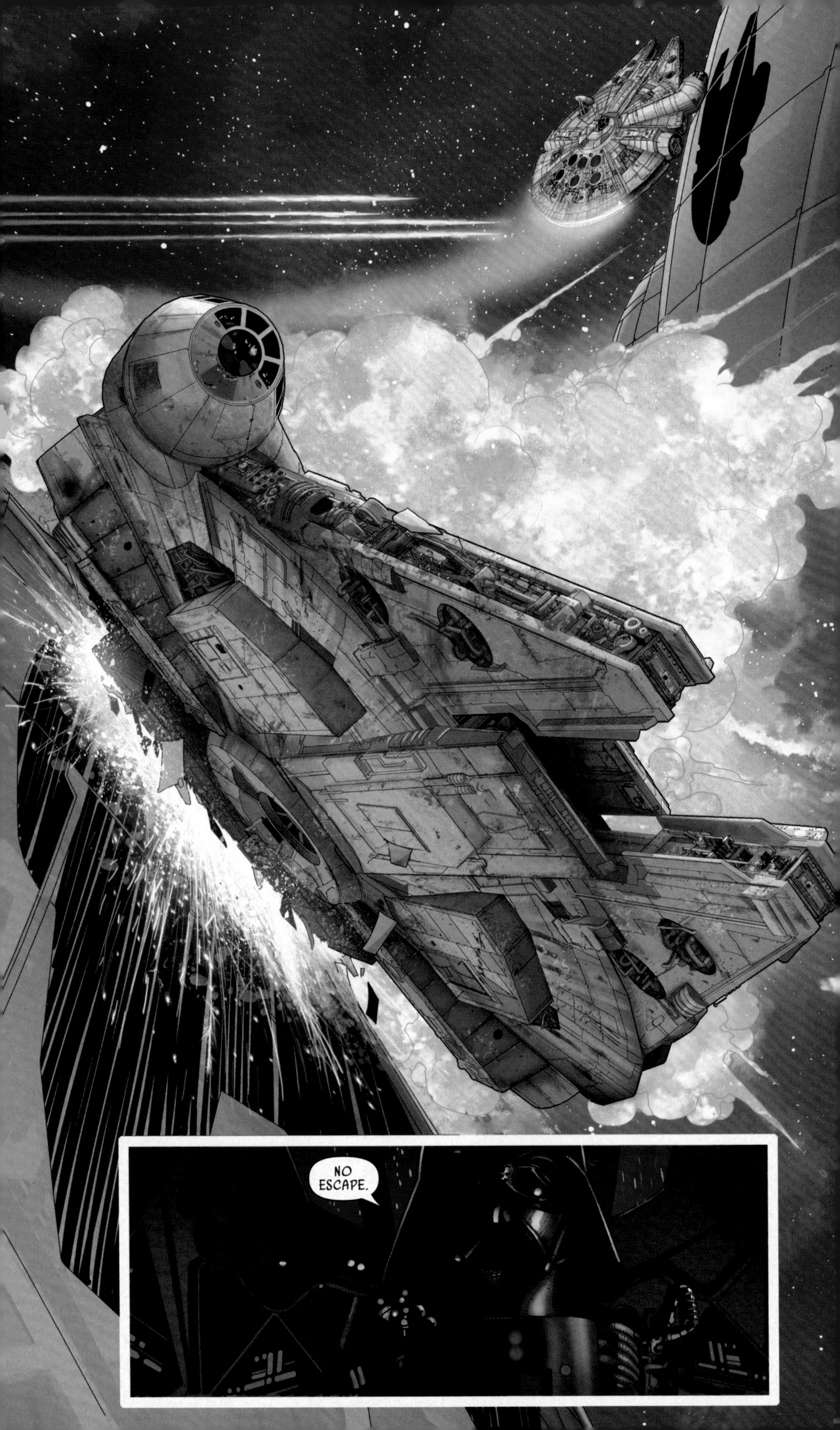
NO ESCAPE.

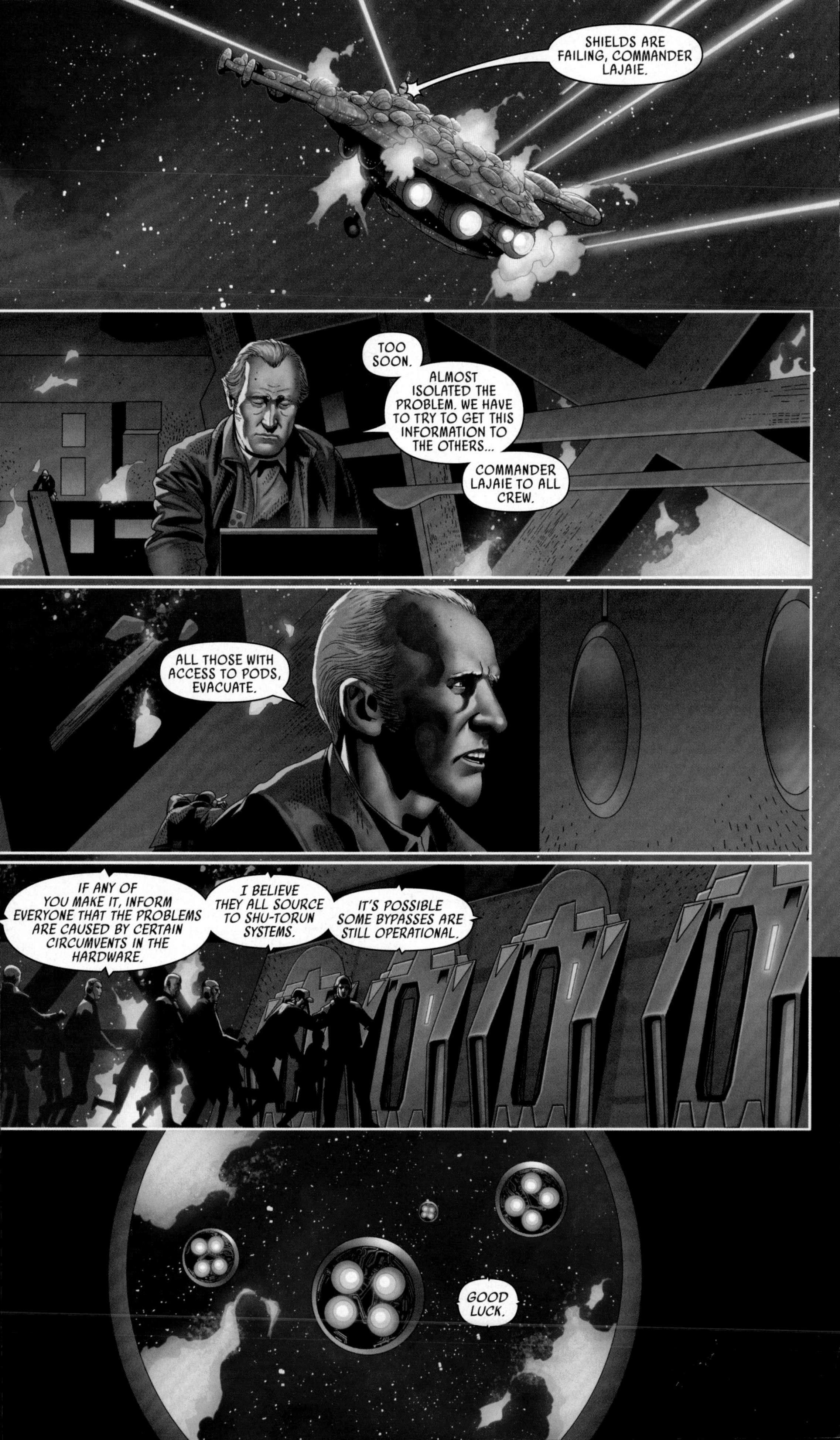
SHIELDS ARE FAILING, COMMANDER LAJAIE.
TOO SOON.
ALMOST ISOLATED THE PROBLEM. WE HAVE TO TRY TO GET THIS INFORMATION TO THE OTHERS...
COMMANDER LAJAIE TO ALL CREW.
ALL THOSE WITH ACCESS TO PODS, EVACUATE.
IF ANY OF YOU MAKE IT, INFORM EVERYONE THAT THE PROBLEMS ARE CAUSED BY CERTAIN CIRCUMVENTS IN THE HARDWARE.
I BELIEVE THEY ALL SOURCE TO SHU-TORUN SYSTEMS.
IT'S POSSIBLE SOME BYPASSES ARE STILL OPERATIONAL.
GOOD LUCK.

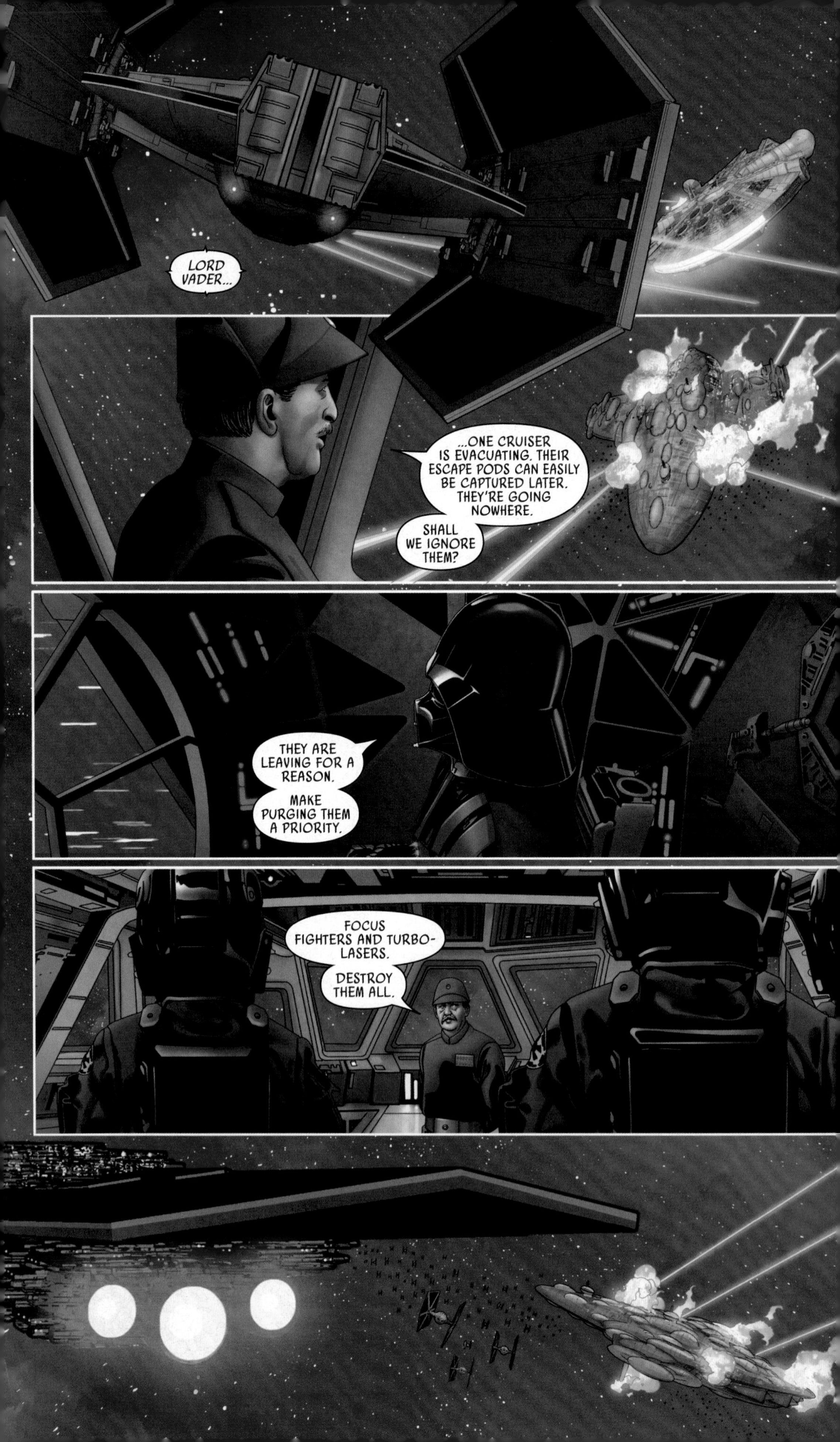
LORD VADER...
...ONE CRUISER IS EVACUATING. THEIR ESCAPE PODS CAN EASILY BE CAPTURED LATER. THEY'RE GOING NOWHERE.
SHALL WE IGNORE THEM?
THEY ARE LEAVING FOR A REASON.
MAKE PURGING THEM A PRIORITY.
FOCUS FIGHTERS AND TURBO-LASERS.
DESTROY THEM ALL.

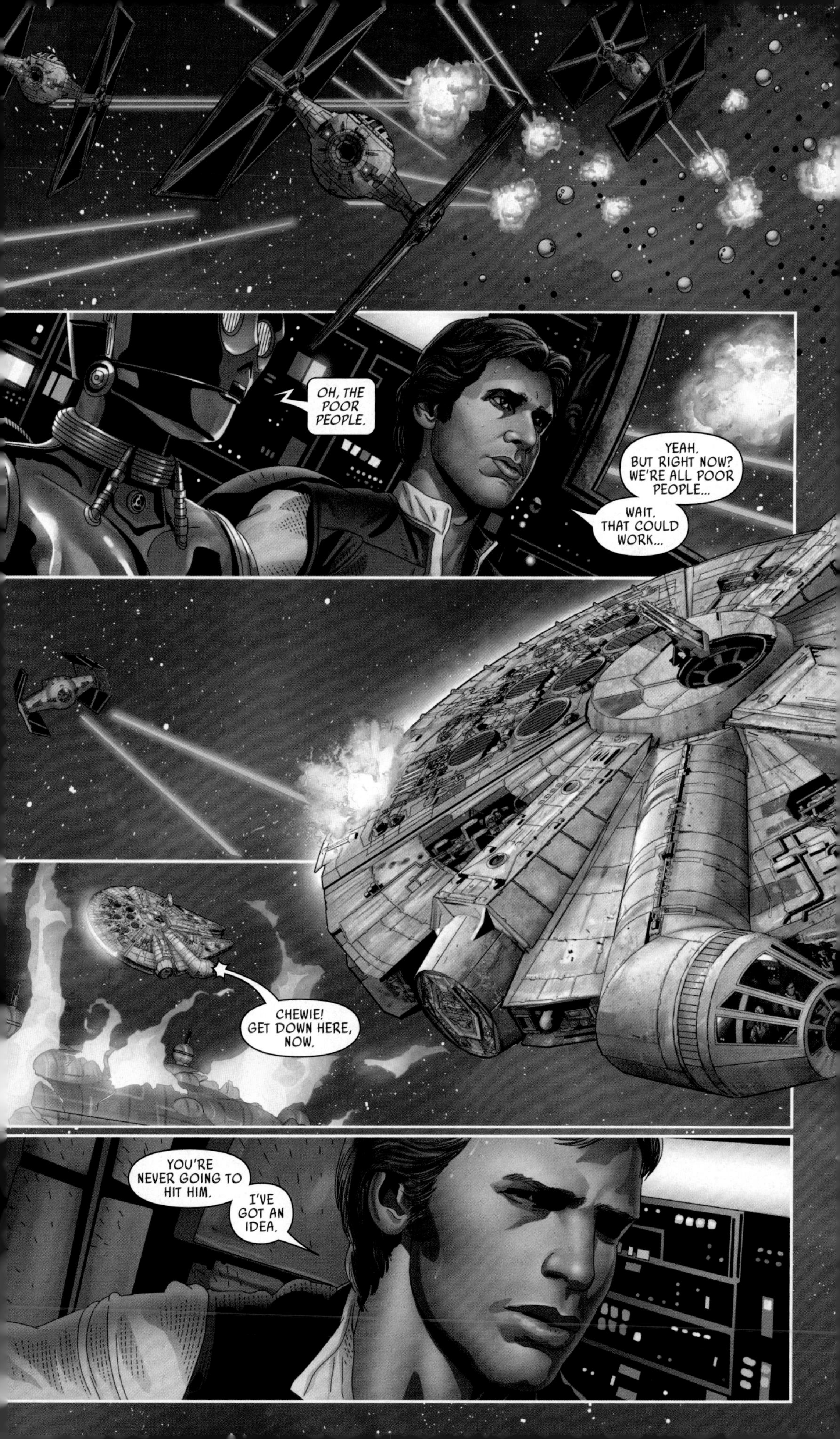
OH, THE POOR PEOPLE.
YEAH. BUT RIGHT NOW? WE'RE ALL POOR PEOPLE...
WAIT. THAT COULD WORK...
CHEWIE! GET DOWN HERE, NOW.
YOU'RE NEVER GOING TO HIT HIM.
I'VE GOT AN IDEA.

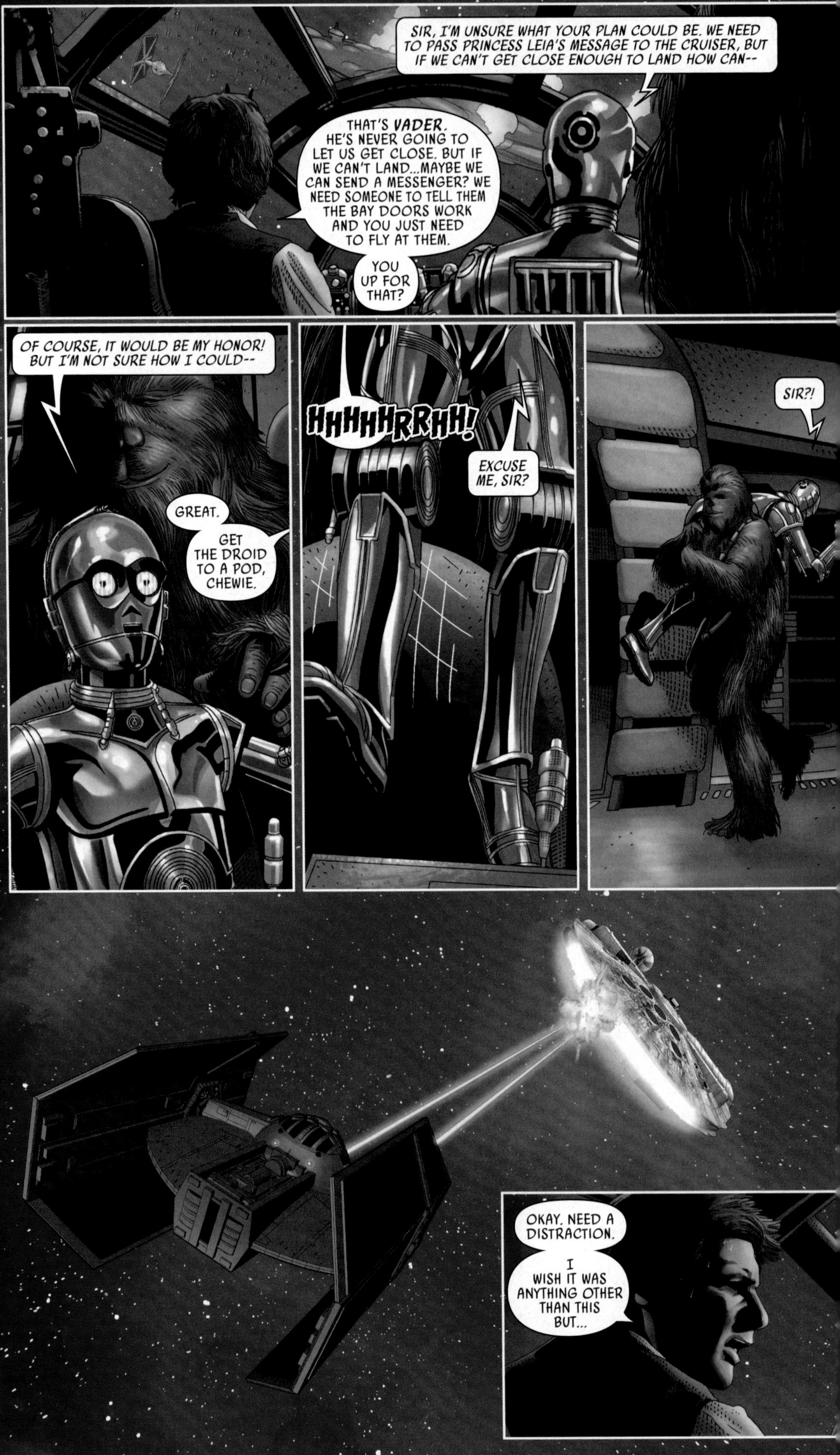

SIR, I'M UNSURE WHAT YOUR PLAN COULD BE. WE NEED TO PASS PRINCESS LEIA'S MESSAGE TO THE CRUISER, BUT IF WE CAN'T GET CLOSE ENOUGH TO LAND HOW CAN--
THAT'S VADER. HE'S NEVER GOING TO LET US GET CLOSE. BUT IF WE CAN'T LAND...MAYBE WE CAN SEND A MESSENGER? WE NEED SOMEONE TO TELL THEM THE BAY DOORS WORK AND YOU JUST NEED TO FLY AT THEM.
YOU UP FOR THAT?
OF COURSE, IT WOULD BE MY HONOR! BUT I'M NOT SURE HOW I COULD--
GREAT.
GET THE DROID TO A POD, CHEWIE.
HHHHHRRHH!
EXCUSE ME, SIR?
SIR?!
OKAY. NEED A DISTRACTION.
I WISH IT WAS ANYTHING OTHER THAN THIS BUT...

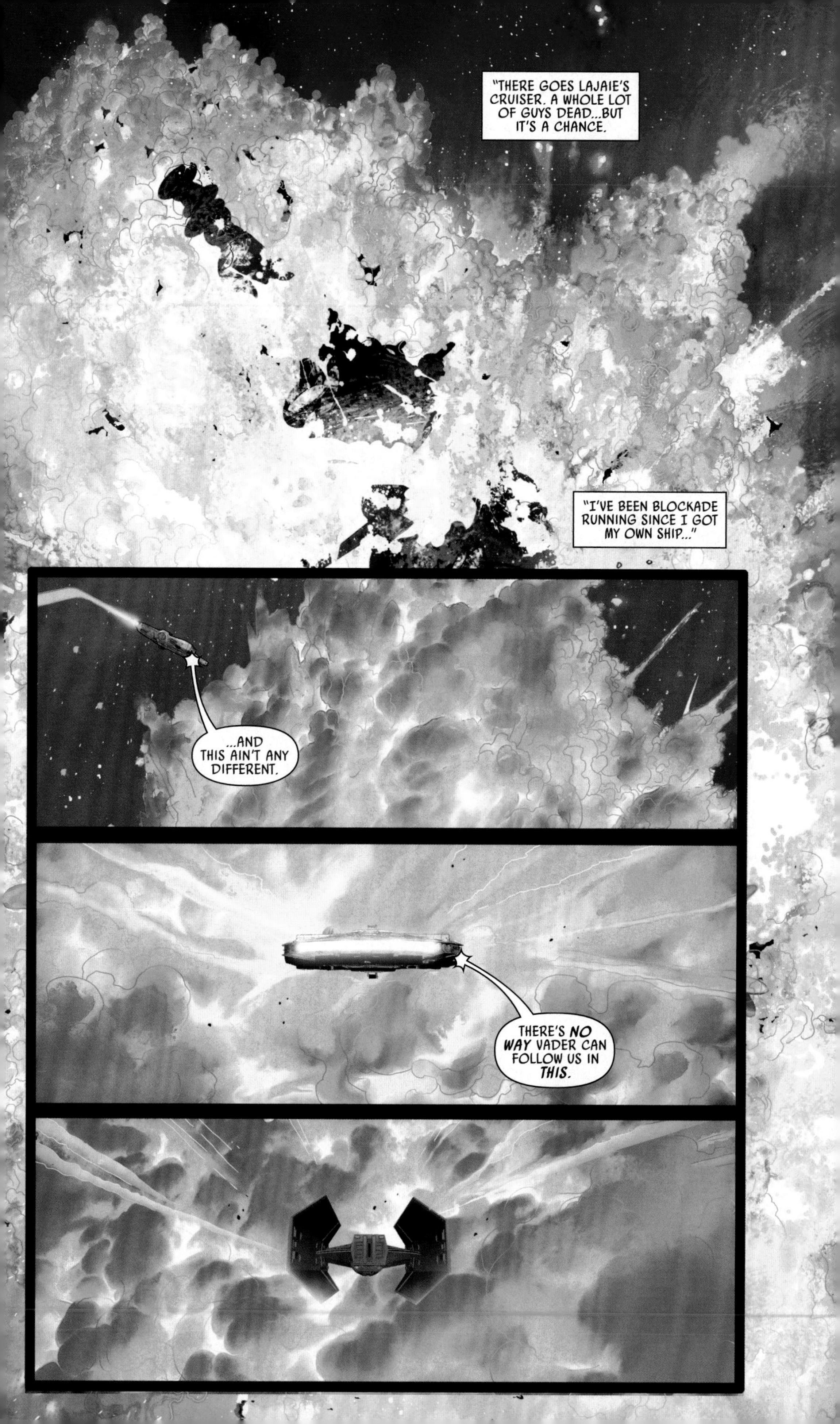
"THERE GOES LAJAIE'S CRUISER. A WHOLE LOT OF GUYS DEAD...BUT IT'S A CHANCE.
"I'VE BEEN BLOCKADE RUNNING SINCE I GOT MY OWN SHIP..."
...AND THIS AIN'T ANY DIFFERENT.
THERE'S **NO WAY** VADER CAN FOLLOW US IN ***THIS.***

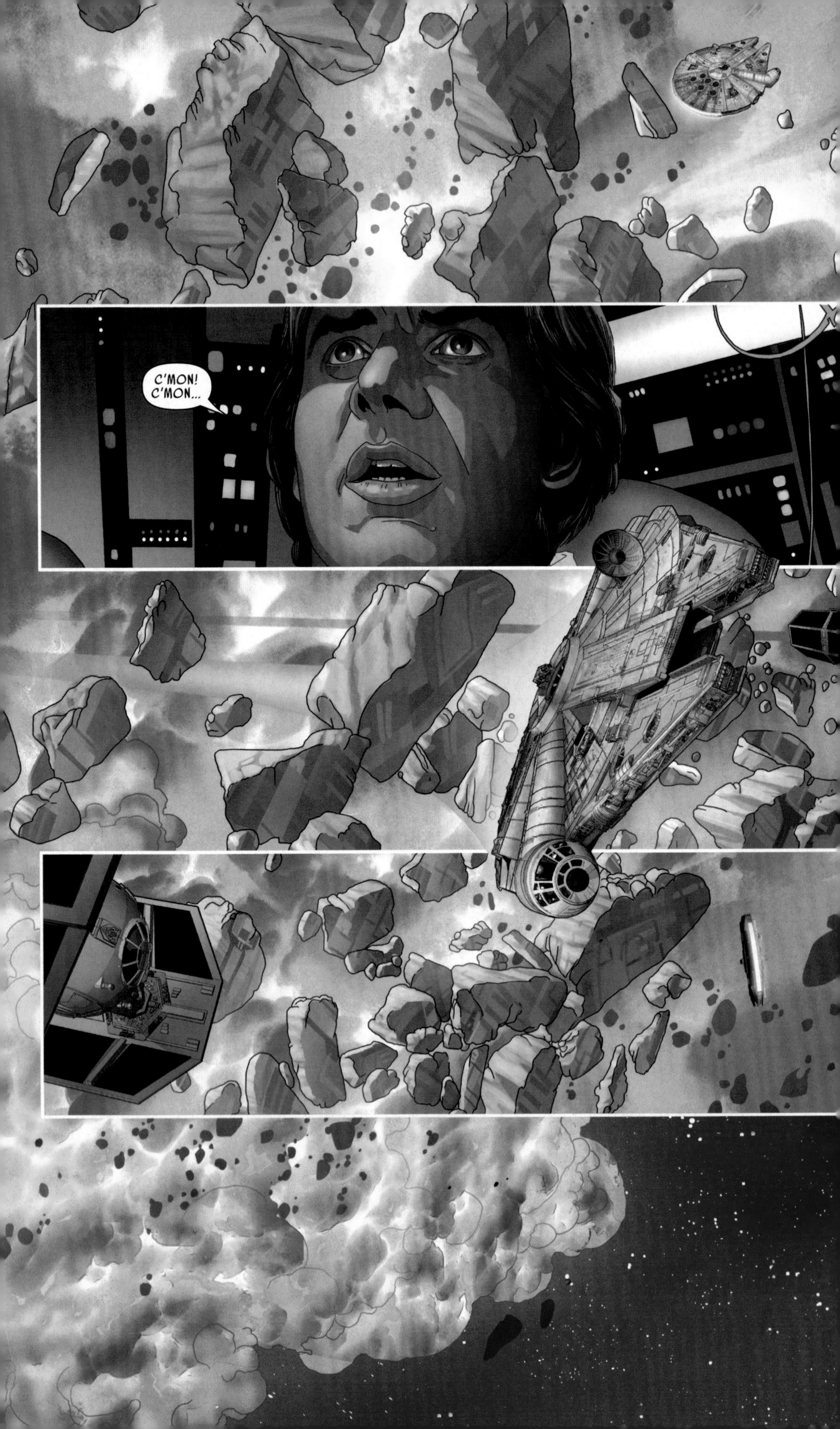
C'MON! C'MON...

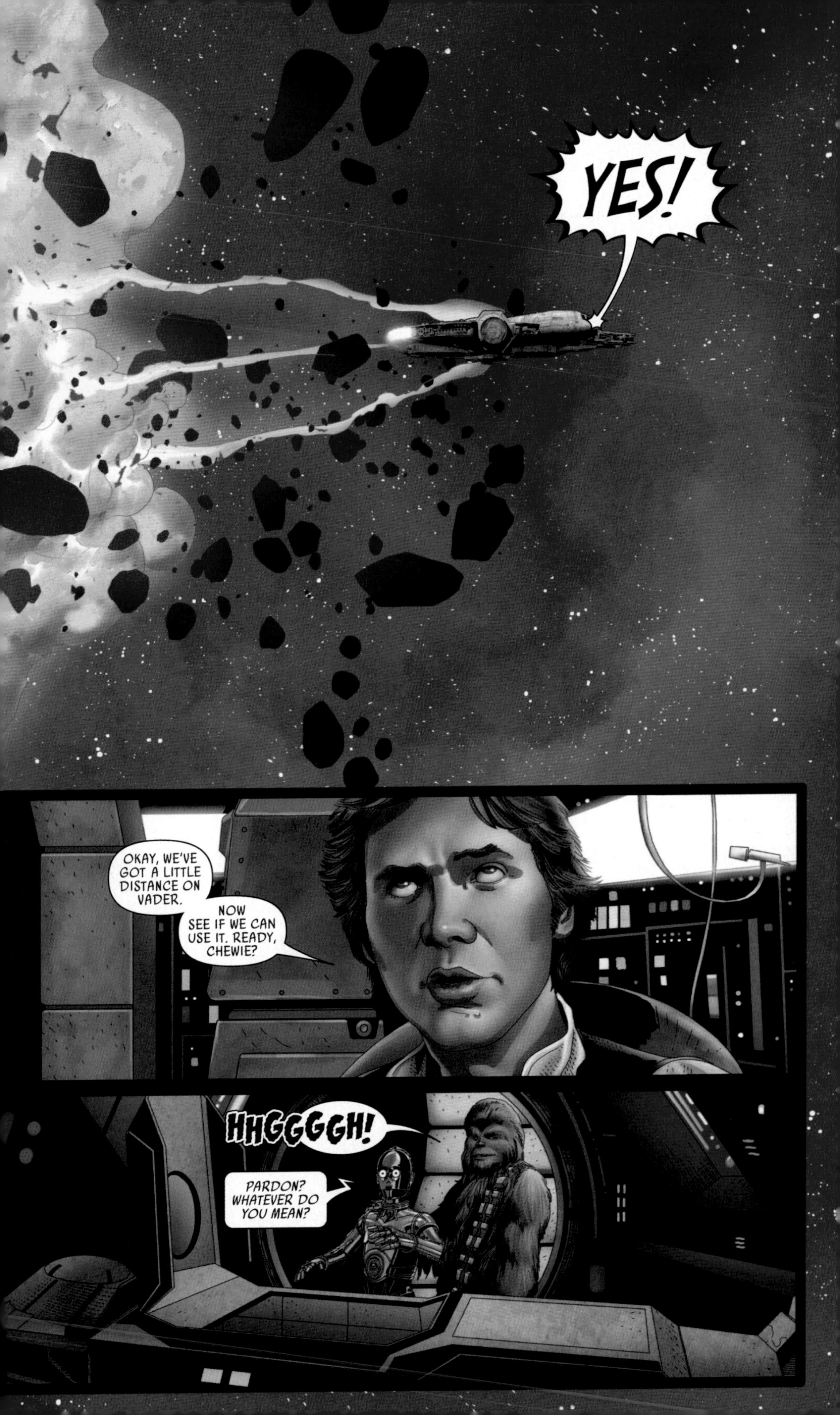
YES!
OKAY, WE'VE GOT A LITTLE DISTANCE ON VADER.
NOW SEE IF WE CAN USE IT. READY, CHEWIE?
HHGGGGH!
PARDON? WHATEVER DO YOU MEAN?

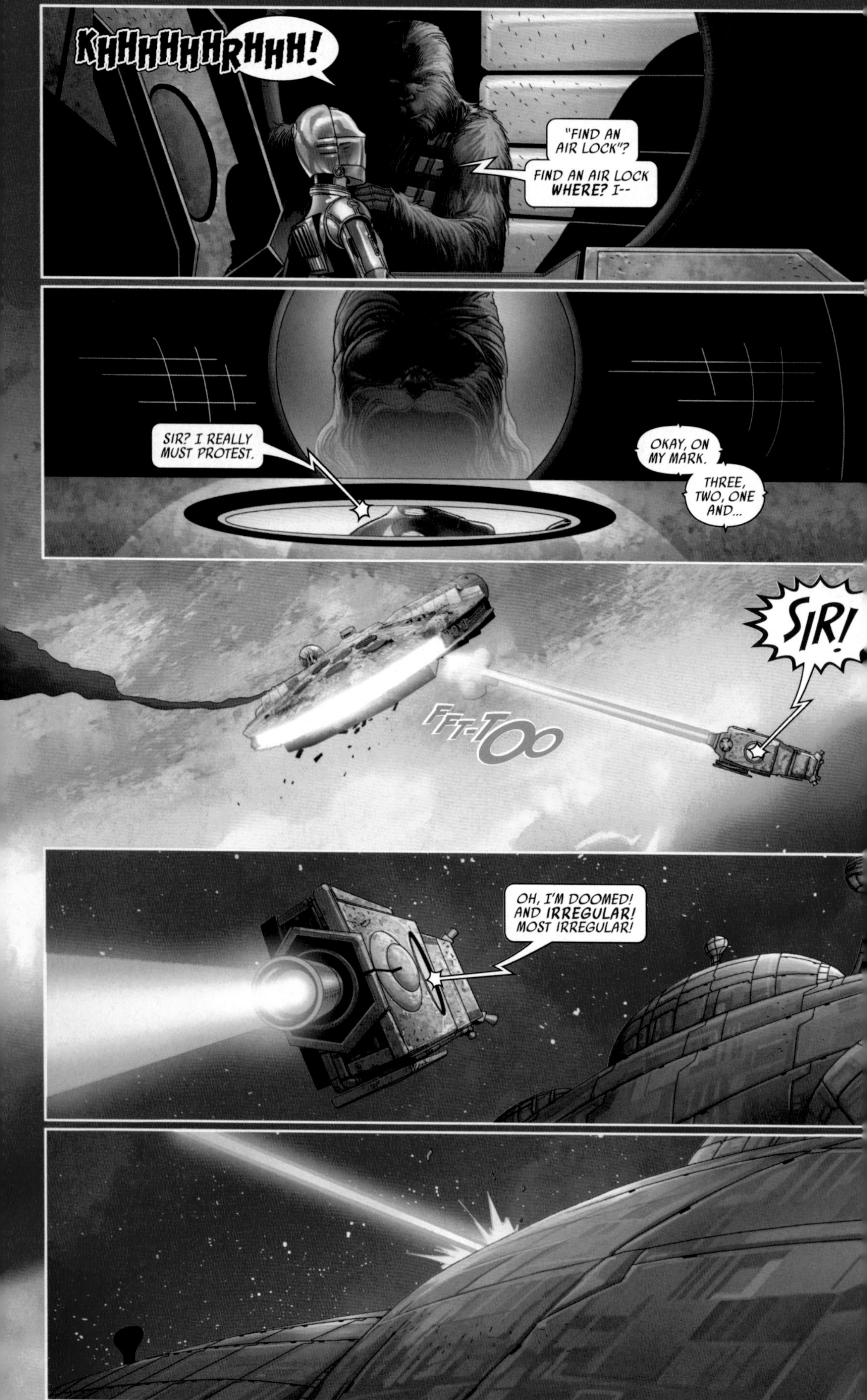
KHHHHHHRHHH!
"FIND AN AIR LOCK"?
FIND AN AIR LOCK WHERE? I--
SIR? I REALLY MUST PROTEST.
OKAY, ON MY MARK.
THREE, TWO, ONE AND...
SIR!
FFT-TOO
OH, I'M DOOMED! AND IRREGULAR! MOST IRREGULAR!

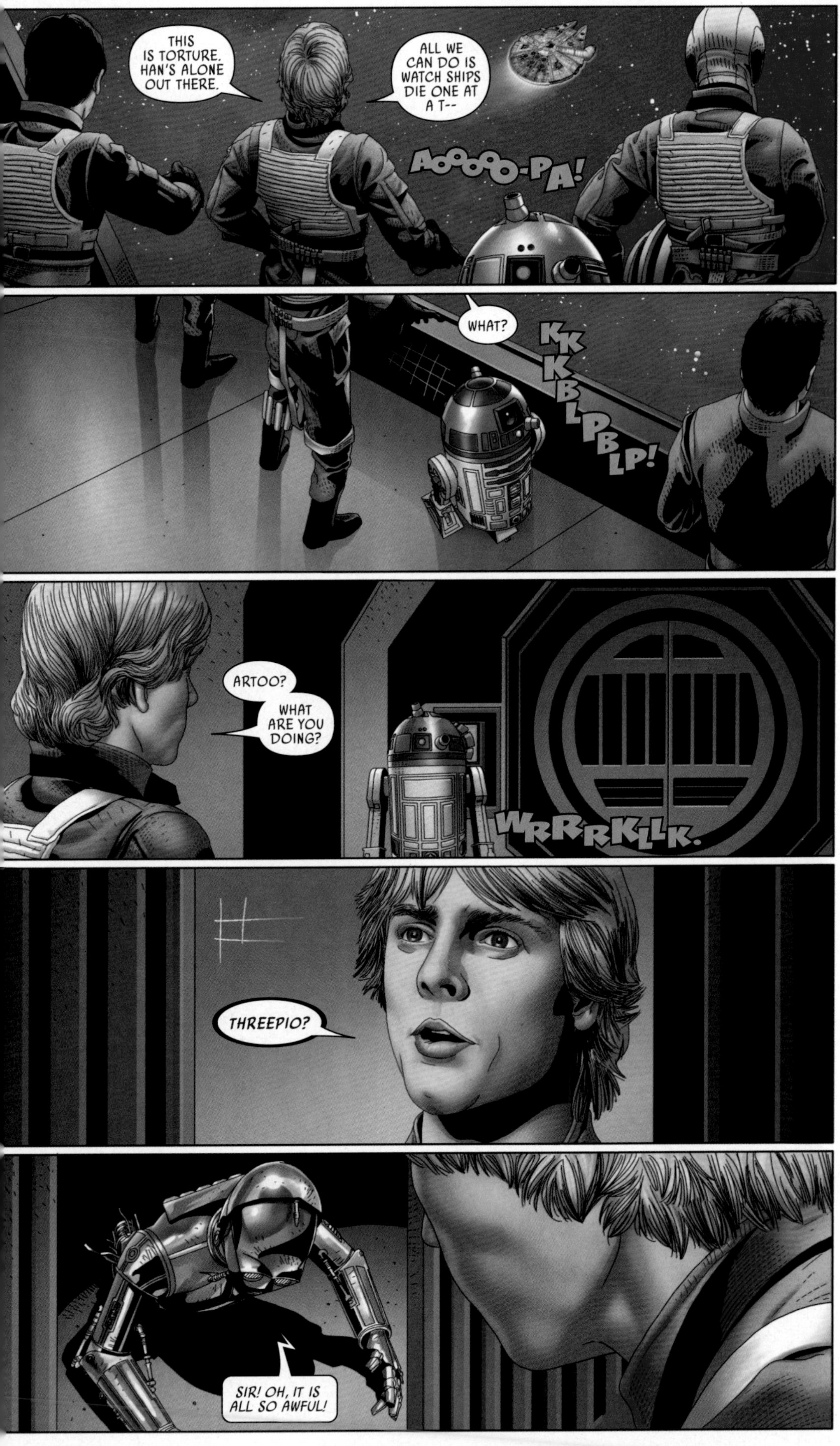
THIS IS TORTURE. HAN'S ALONE OUT THERE.
ALL WE CAN DO IS WATCH SHIPS DIE ONE AT A T--
AOOOOO-PA!
WHAT?
KKKBLPBLP!
ARTOO? WHAT ARE YOU DOING?
WRRRRKLLK.
THREEPIO?
SIR! OH, IT IS ALL SO AWFUL!

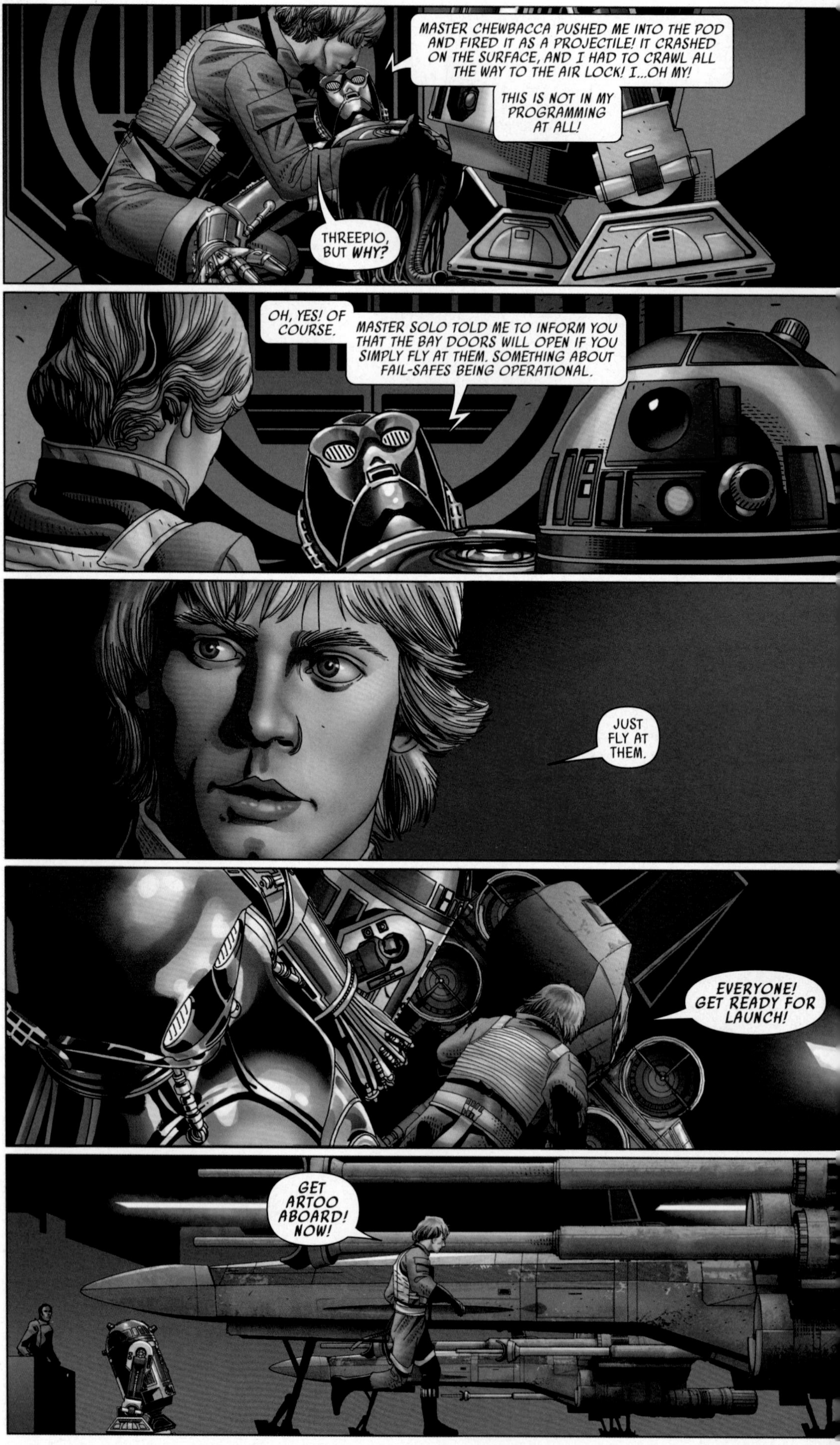
MASTER CHEWBACCA PUSHED ME INTO THE POD AND FIRED IT AS A PROJECTILE! IT CRASHED ON THE SURFACE, AND I HAD TO CRAWL ALL THE WAY TO THE AIR LOCK! I...OH MY!
THIS IS NOT IN MY PROGRAMMING AT ALL!
THREEPIO, BUT WHY?
OH, YES! OF COURSE.
MASTER SOLO TOLD ME TO INFORM YOU THAT THE BAY DOORS WILL OPEN IF YOU SIMPLY FLY AT THEM. SOMETHING ABOUT FAIL-SAFES BEING OPERATIONAL.
JUST FLY AT THEM.
EVERYONE! GET READY FOR LAUNCH!
GET ARTOO ABOARD! NOW!

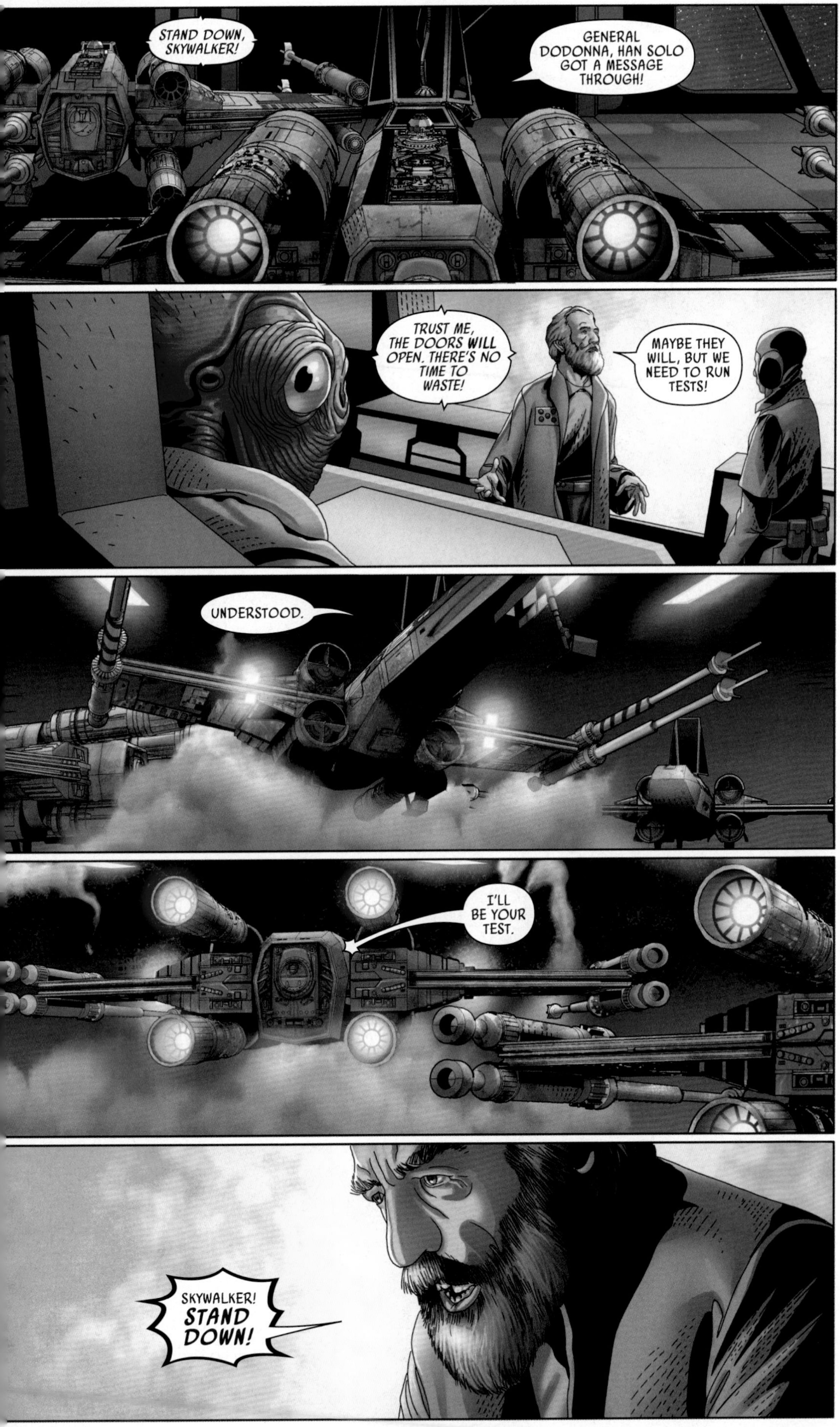
STAND DOWN, SKYWALKER!
GENERAL DODONNA, HAN SOLO GOT A MESSAGE THROUGH!
TRUST ME, THE DOORS WILL OPEN. THERE'S NO TIME TO WASTE!
MAYBE THEY WILL, BUT WE NEED TO RUN TESTS!
UNDERSTOOD.
I'LL BE YOUR TEST.
SKYWALKER! STAND DOWN!

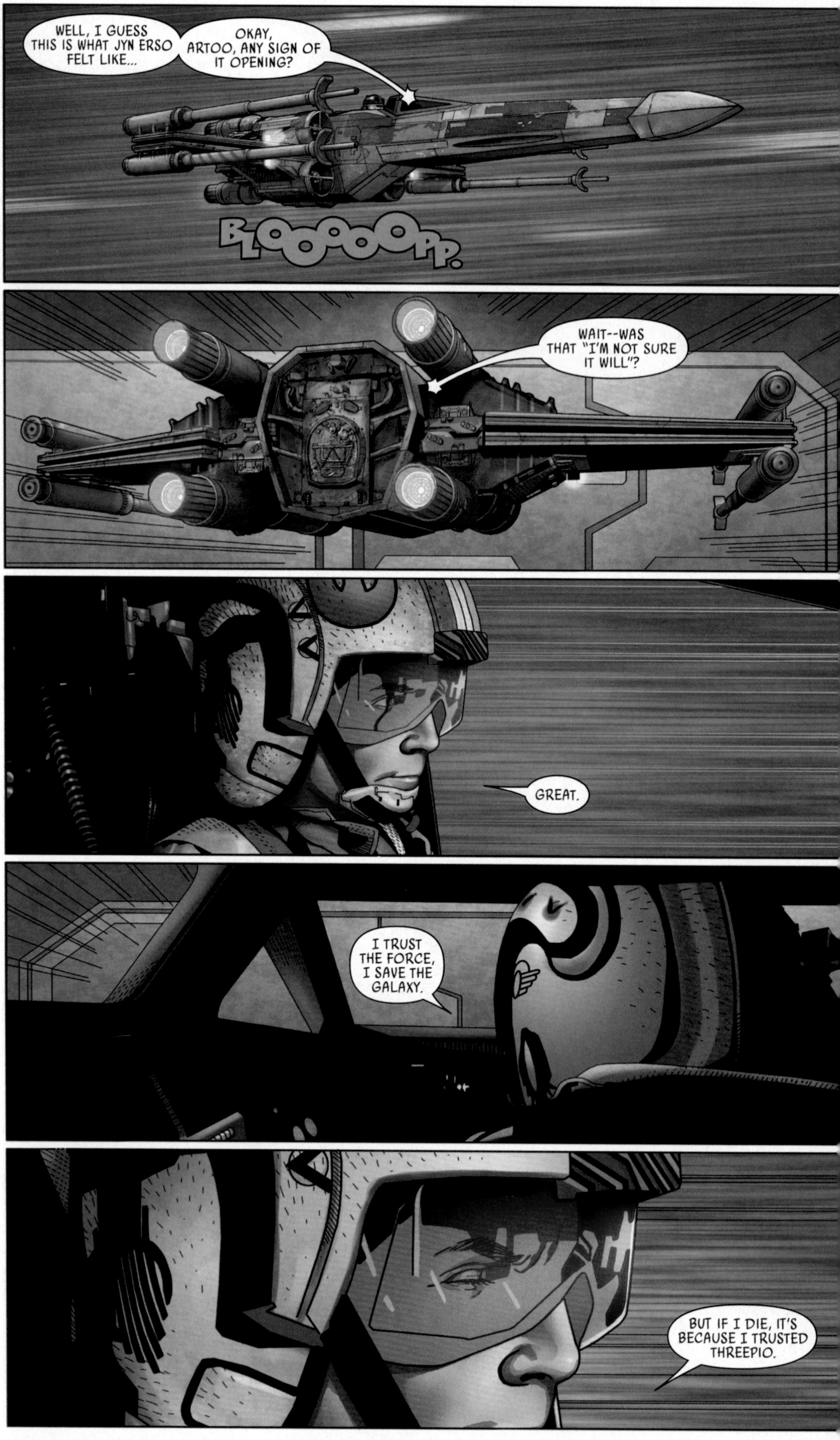
WELL, I GUESS THIS IS WHAT JYN ERSO FELT LIKE...
OKAY, ARTOO, ANY SIGN OF IT OPENING?
BLOOOOOOPP.
WAIT--WAS THAT "I'M NOT SURE IT WILL"?
GREAT.
I TRUST THE FORCE, I SAVE THE GALAXY.
BUT IF I DIE, IT'S BECAUSE I TRUSTED THREEPIO.

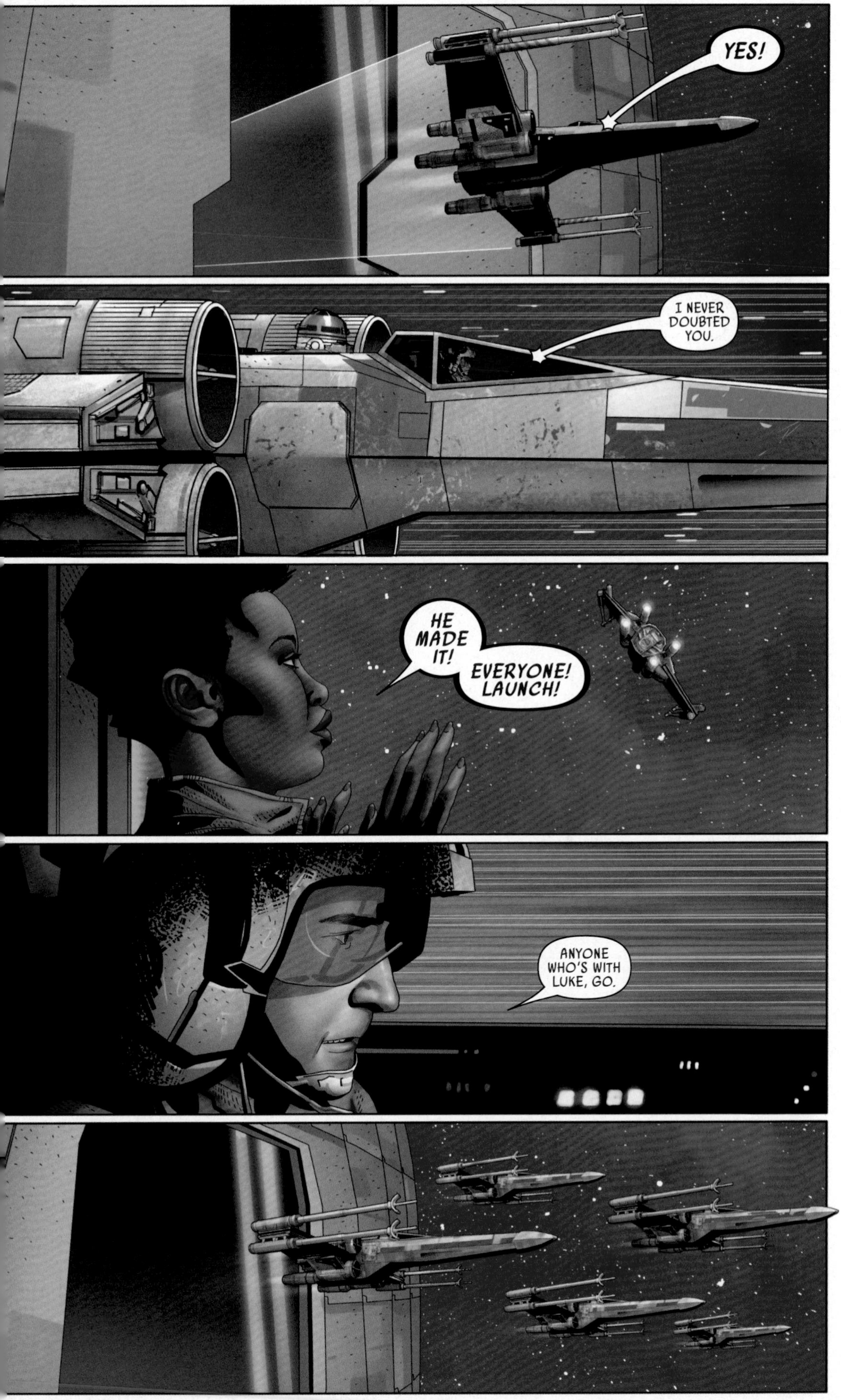
YES!
I NEVER DOUBTED YOU.
HE MADE IT!
EVERYONE! LAUNCH!
ANYONE WHO'S WITH LUKE, GO.

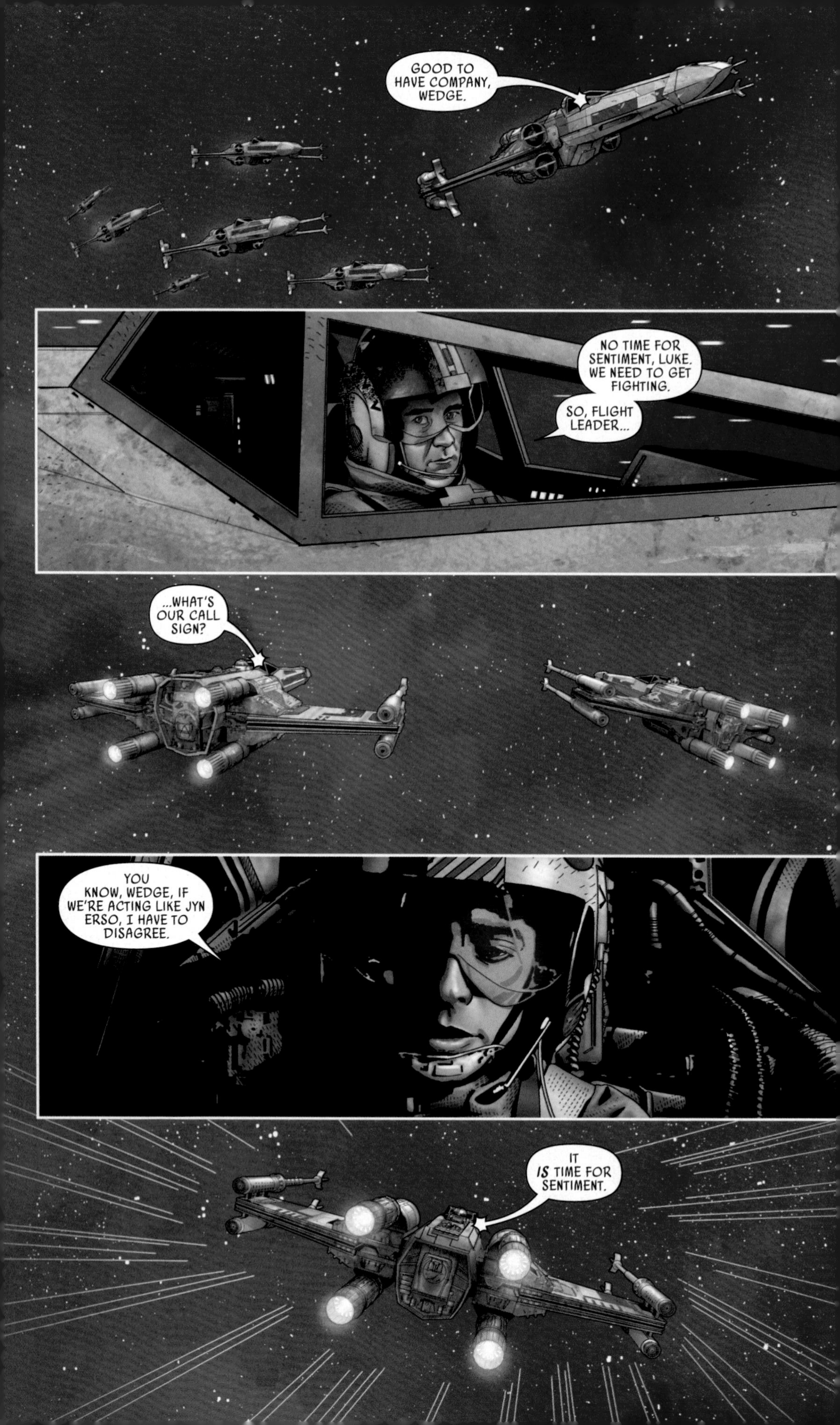
GOOD TO HAVE COMPANY, WEDGE.
NO TIME FOR SENTIMENT, LUKE. WE NEED TO GET FIGHTING.
SO, FLIGHT LEADER...
...WHAT'S OUR CALL SIGN?
YOU KNOW, WEDGE, IF WE'RE ACTING LIKE JYN ERSO, I HAVE TO DISAGREE.
IT *IS* TIME FOR SENTIMENT.

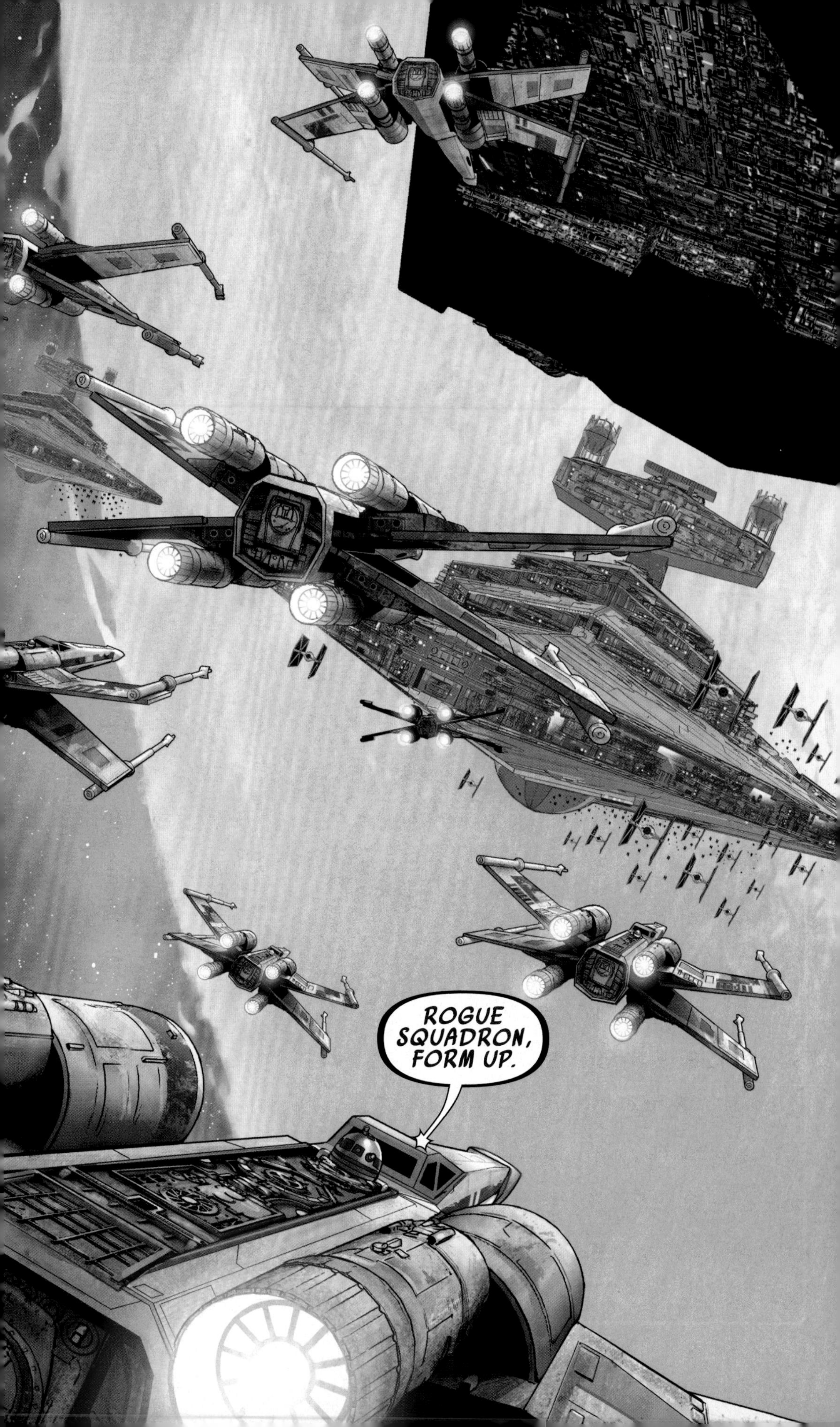
ROGUE SQUADRON, FORM UP.

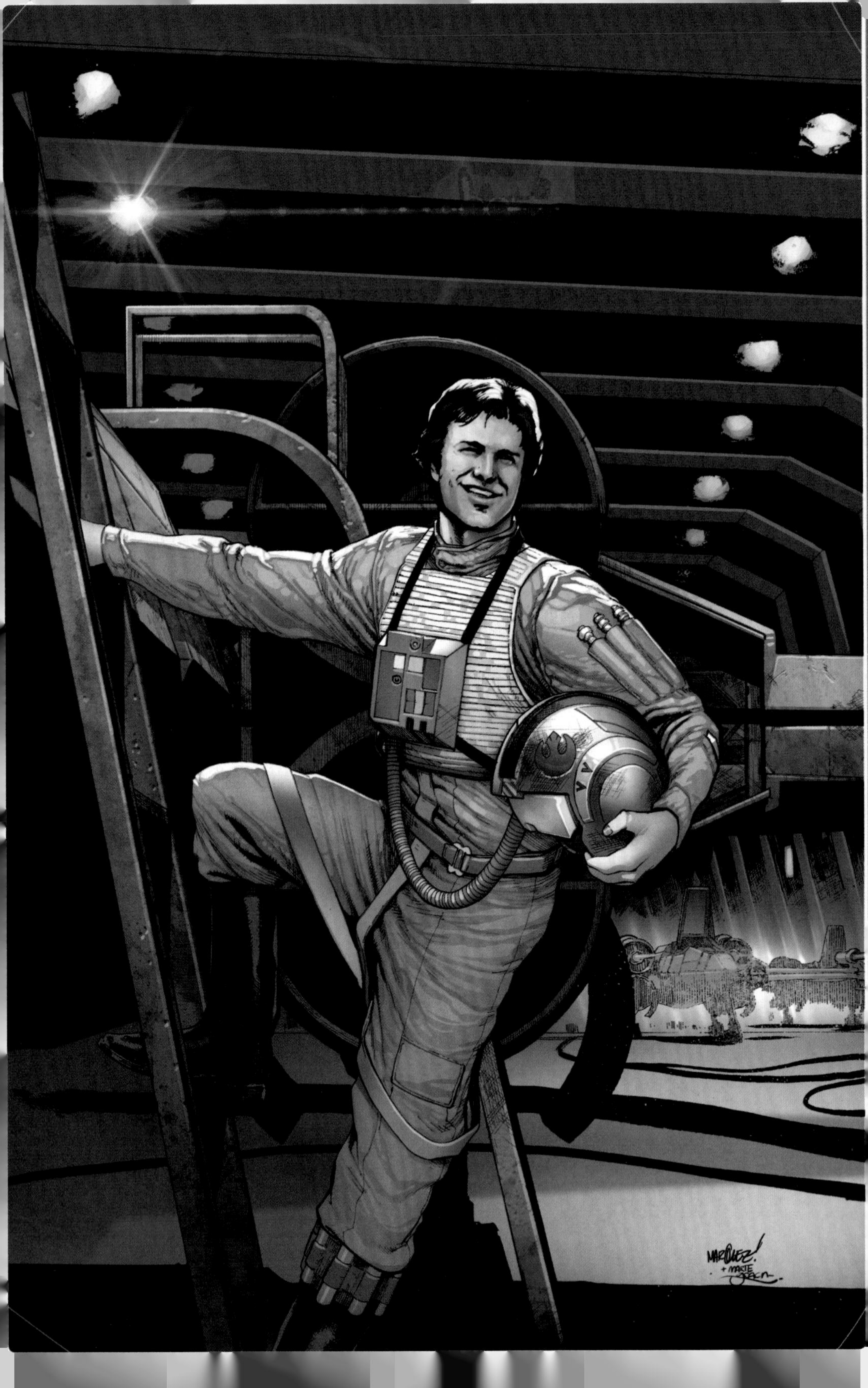
MARQUEZ!
+ MARTE

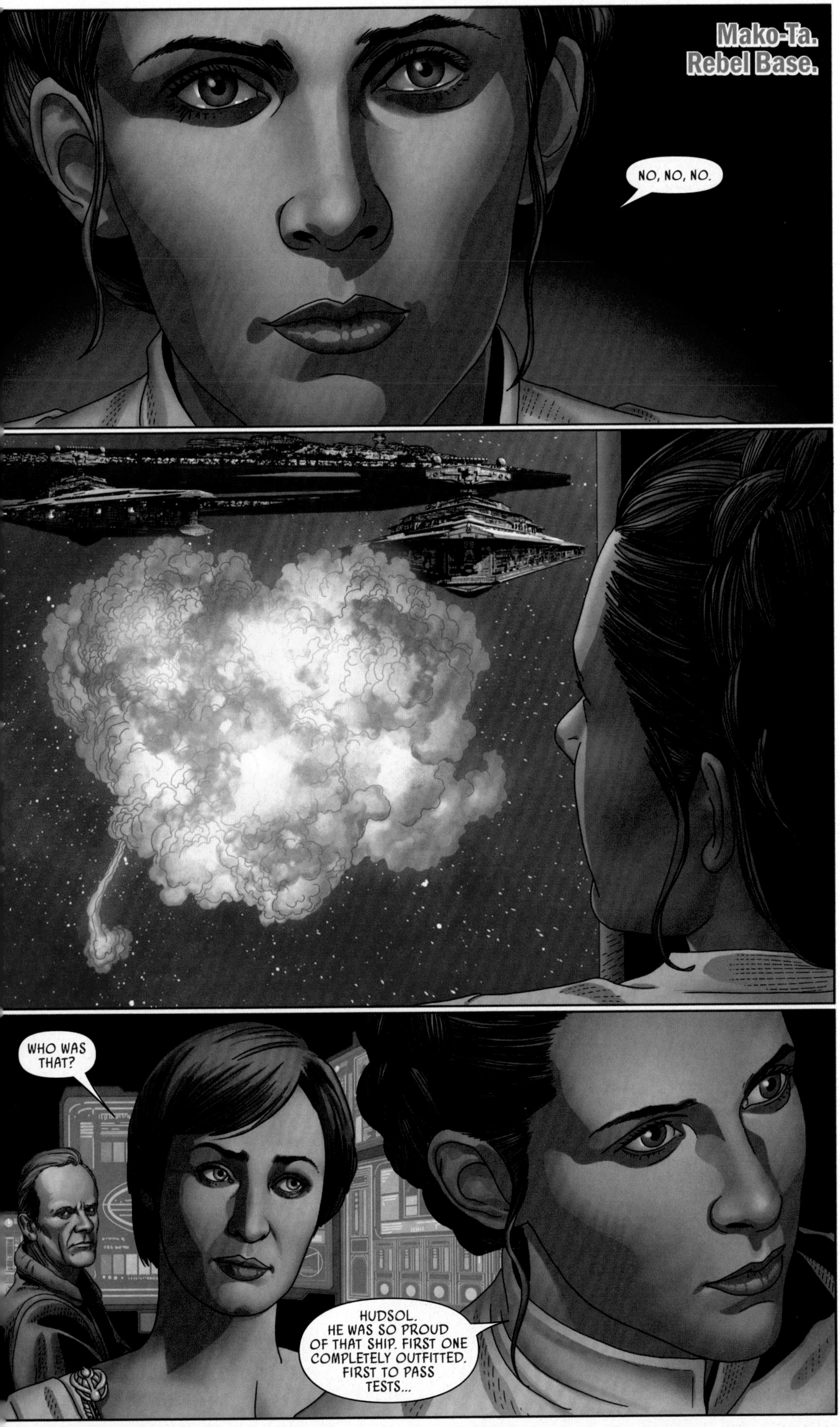
Mako-Ta.
Rebel Base.
NO, NO, NO.
WHO WAS THAT?
HUDSOL. HE WAS SO PROUD OF THAT SHIP. FIRST ONE COMPLETELY OUTFITTED. FIRST TO PASS TESTS...

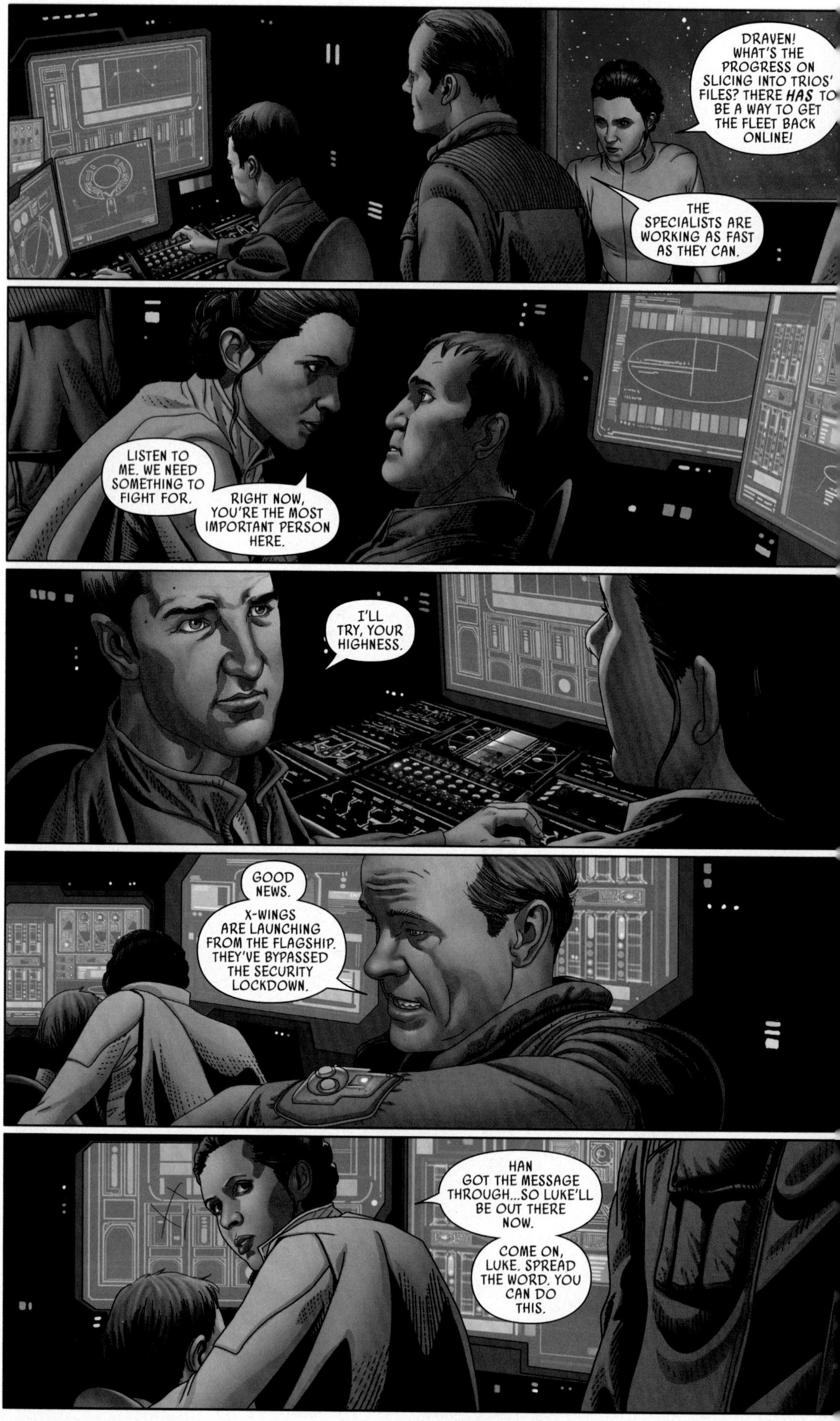
DRAVEN! WHAT'S THE PROGRESS ON SLICING INTO TRIOS' FILES? THERE HAS TO BE A WAY TO GET THE FLEET BACK ONLINE!
THE SPECIALISTS ARE WORKING AS FAST AS THEY CAN.
LISTEN TO ME. WE NEED SOMETHING TO FIGHT FOR.
RIGHT NOW, YOU'RE THE MOST IMPORTANT PERSON HERE.
I'LL TRY, YOUR HIGHNESS.
GOOD NEWS.
X-WINGS ARE LAUNCHING FROM THE FLAGSHIP. THEY'VE BYPASSED THE SECURITY LOCKDOWN.
HAN GOT THE MESSAGE THROUGH...SO LUKE'LL BE OUT THERE NOW.
COME ON, LUKE. SPREAD THE WORD. YOU CAN DO THIS.

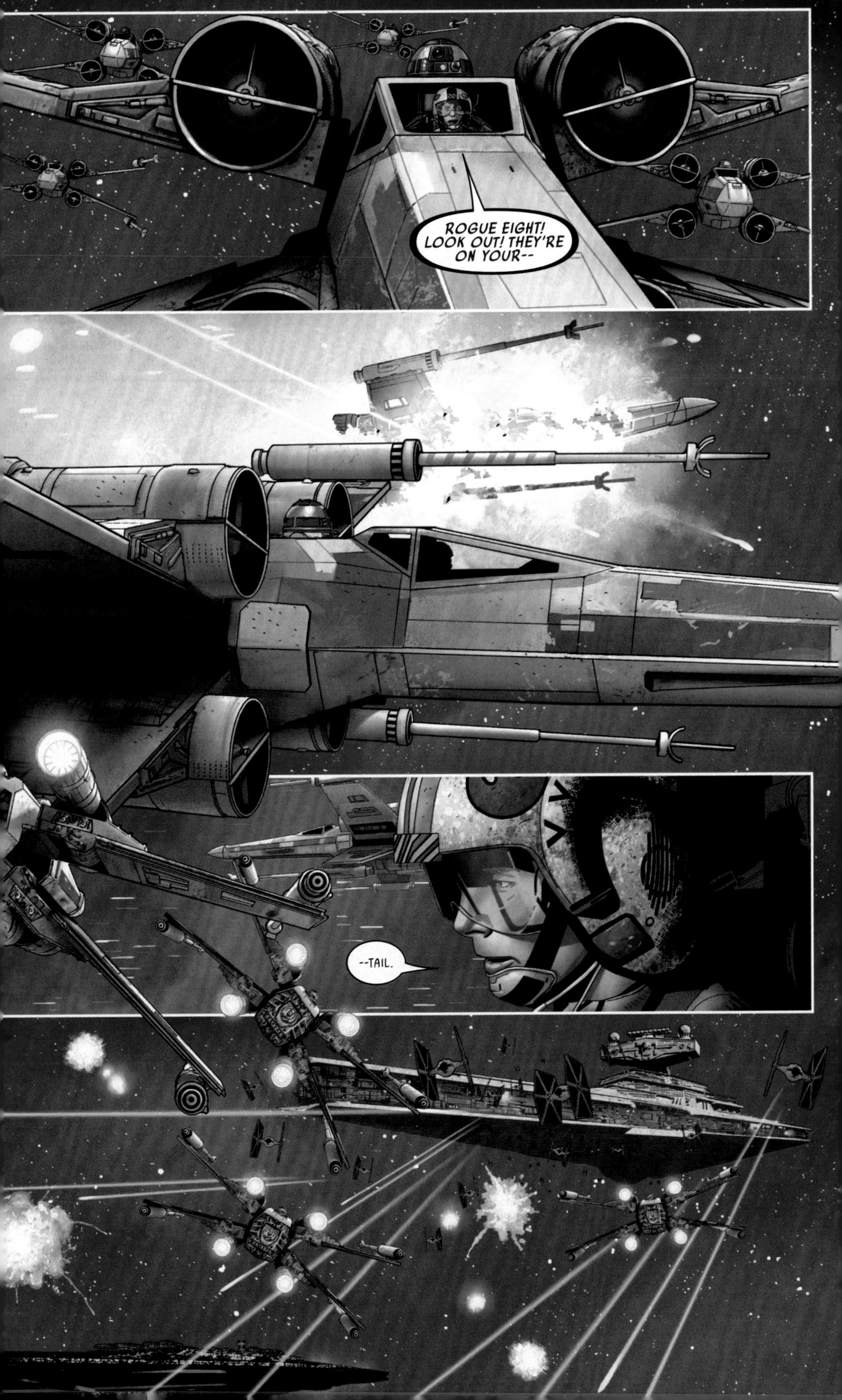
ROGUE EIGHT! LOOK OUT! THEY'RE ON YOUR--
--TAIL.

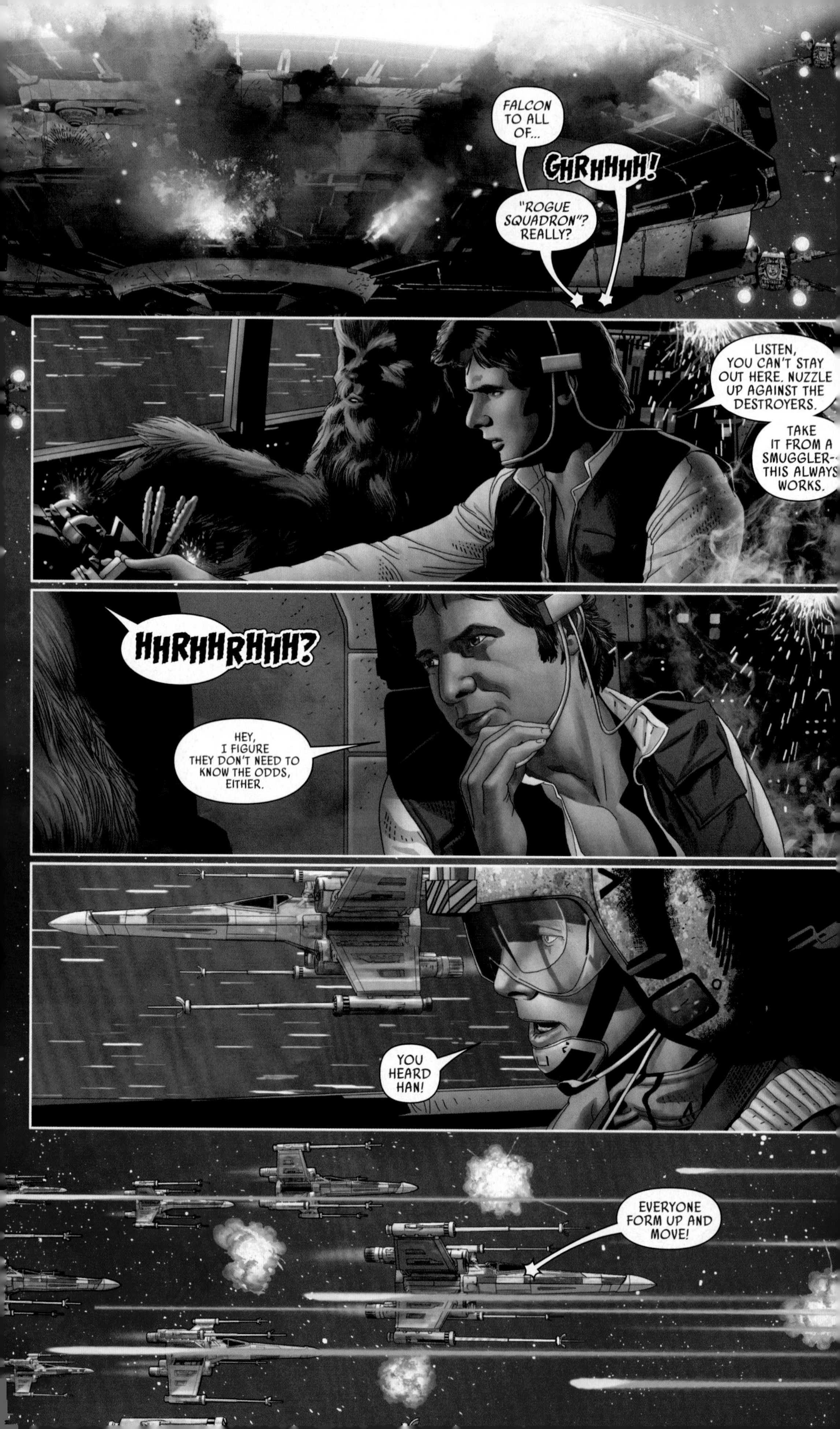
FALCON TO ALL OF...
GHRHHHH!
"ROGUE SQUADRON"? REALLY?
LISTEN, YOU CAN'T STAY OUT HERE. NUZZLE UP AGAINST THE DESTROYERS.
TAKE IT FROM A SMUGGLER-- THIS ALWAYS WORKS.
HHRHHRHHH?
HEY, I FIGURE THEY DON'T NEED TO KNOW THE ODDS, EITHER.
YOU HEARD HAN!
EVERYONE FORM UP AND MOVE!

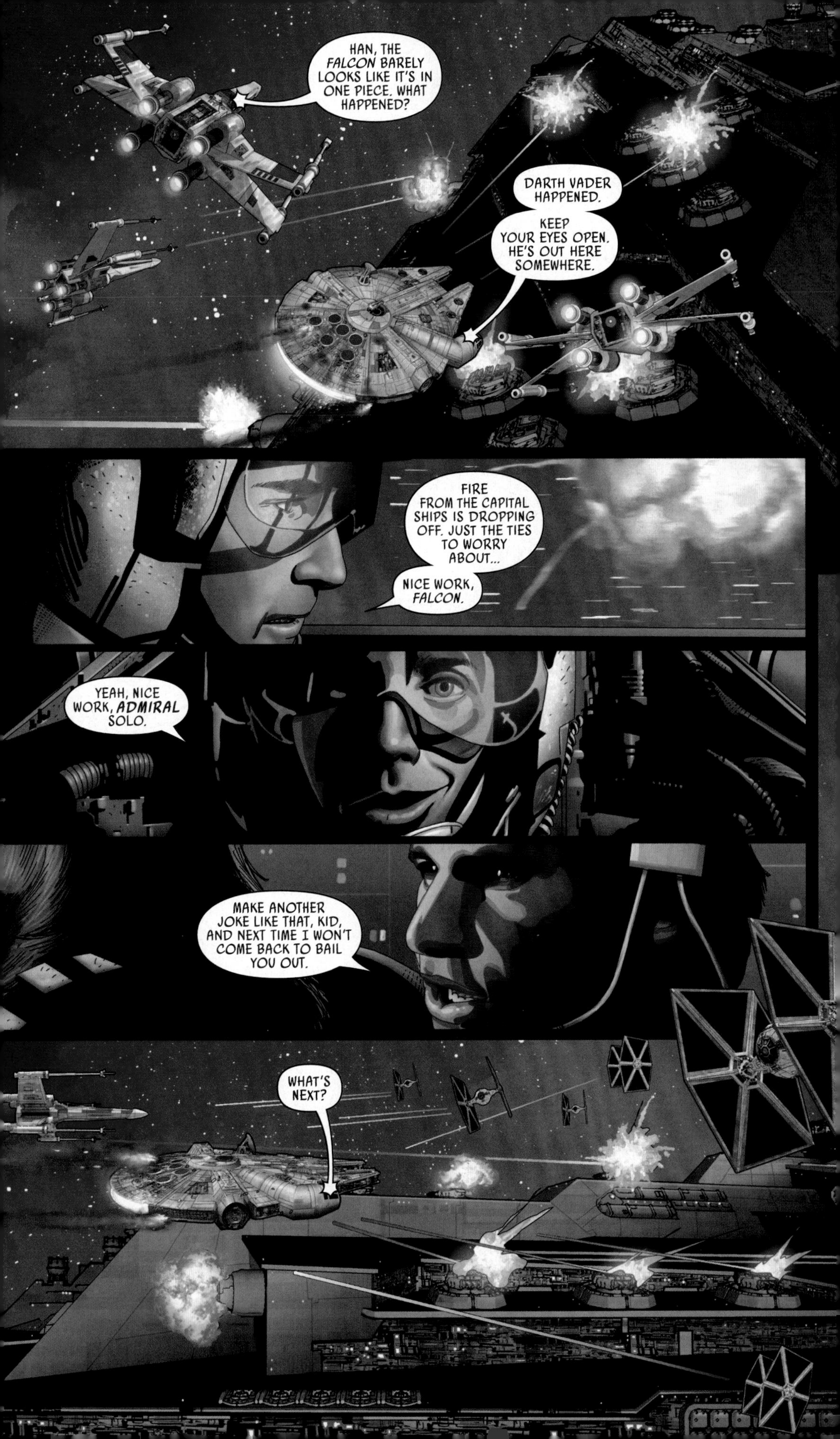

HAN, THE FALCON BARELY LOOKS LIKE IT'S IN ONE PIECE. WHAT HAPPENED?
DARTH VADER HAPPENED.
KEEP YOUR EYES OPEN. HE'S OUT HERE SOMEWHERE.
FIRE FROM THE CAPITAL SHIPS IS DROPPING OFF. JUST THE TIES TO WORRY ABOUT...
NICE WORK, FALCON.
YEAH, NICE WORK, ADMIRAL SOLO.
MAKE ANOTHER JOKE LIKE THAT, KID, AND NEXT TIME I WON'T COME BACK TO BAIL YOU OUT.
WHAT'S NEXT?

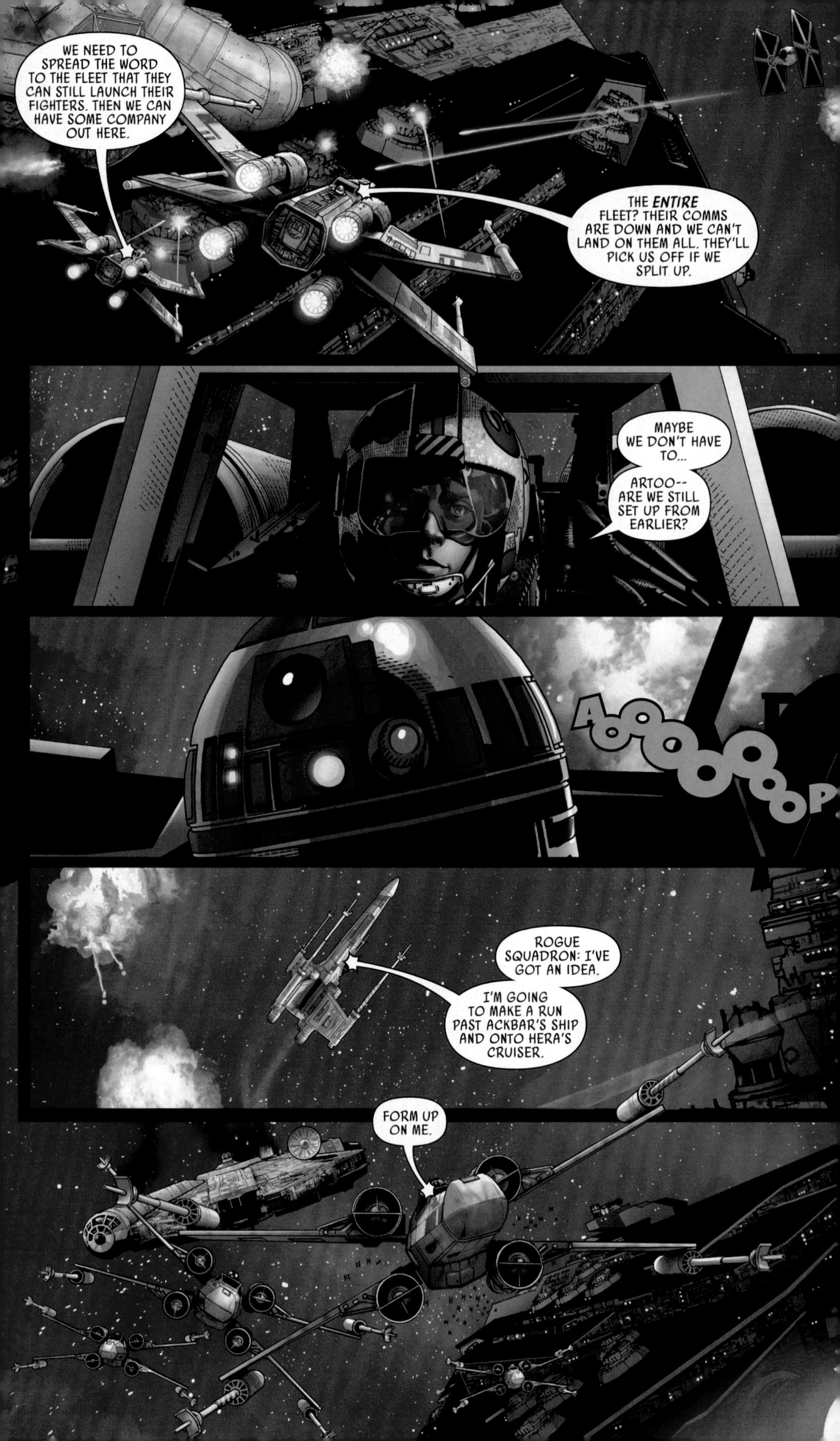
WE NEED TO SPREAD THE WORD TO THE FLEET THAT THEY CAN STILL LAUNCH THEIR FIGHTERS. THEN WE CAN HAVE SOME COMPANY OUT HERE.
THE *ENTIRE* FLEET? THEIR COMMS ARE DOWN AND WE CAN'T LAND ON THEM ALL. THEY'LL PICK US OFF IF WE SPLIT UP.
MAYBE WE DON'T HAVE TO...
ARTOO-- ARE WE STILL SET UP FROM EARLIER?
AOOOOOOOOP
ROGUE SQUADRON: I'VE GOT AN IDEA.
I'M GOING TO MAKE A RUN PAST ACKBAR'S SHIP AND ONTO HERA'S CRUISER.
FORM UP ON ME.

Ackbar's cruiser.

MON CALA DIDN'T SACRIFICE EVERYTHING IT HAS FOR IT TO END HERE.

IF JAN HAS DEPLOYED HIS FIGHTERS, IT MEANS WE CAN, TOO. WE'RE MISSING SOMETHING OBVIOUS. THERE HAS TO BE A WAY.

WE MUST FIND IT.

ARTOO-- HIT IT.

HMM. A DISPLAY TRAIL. ATTENTION GRABBING, DANGEROUS.

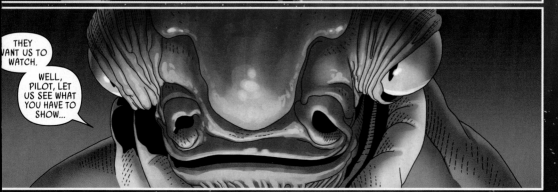

THEY WANT US TO WATCH.

WELL, PILOT, LET US SEE WHAT YOU HAVE TO SHOW...

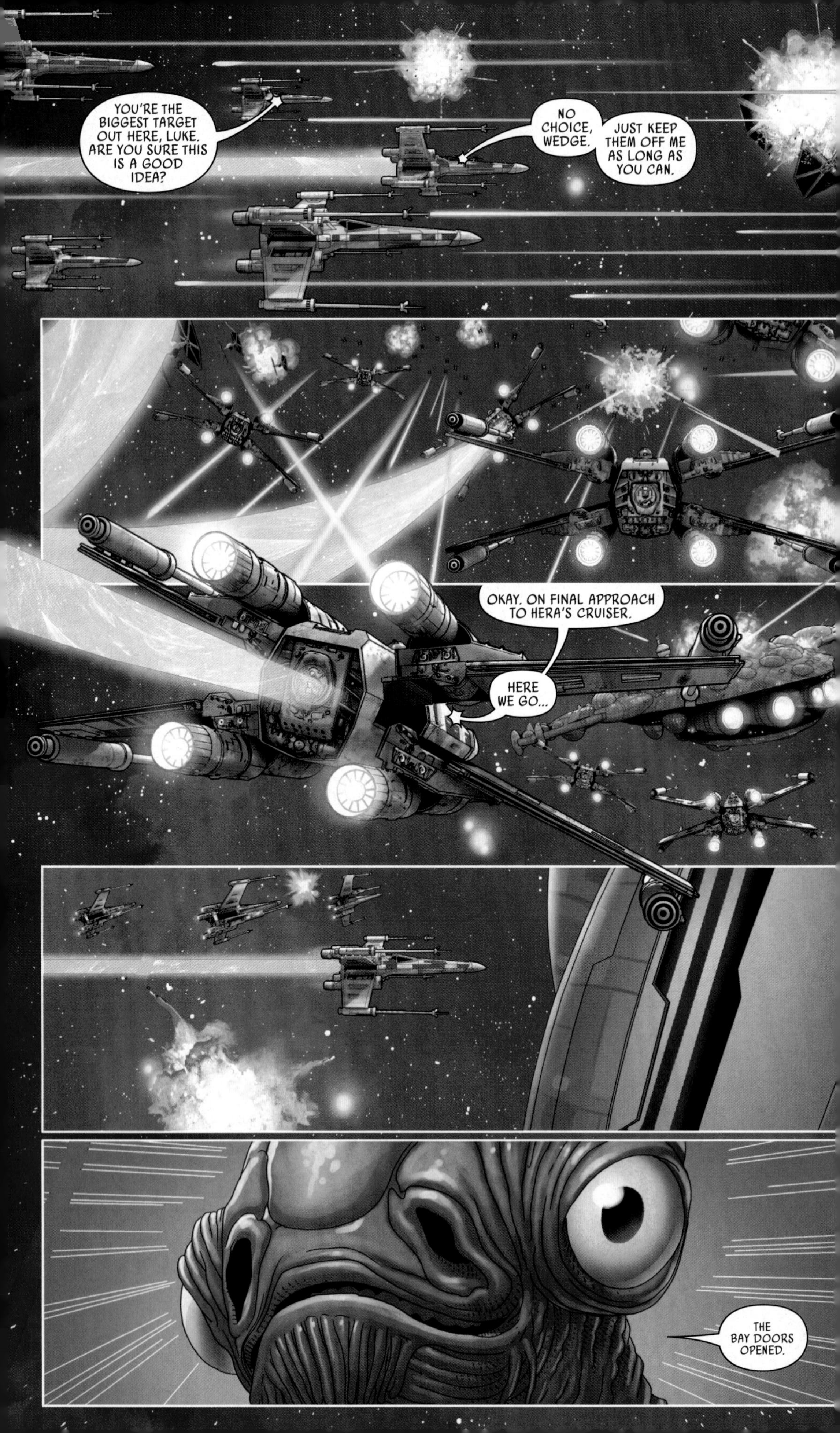
YOU'RE THE BIGGEST TARGET OUT HERE, LUKE. ARE YOU SURE THIS IS A GOOD IDEA?
NO CHOICE, WEDGE.
JUST KEEP THEM OFF ME AS LONG AS YOU CAN.
OKAY. ON FINAL APPROACH TO HERA'S CRUISER.
HERE WE GO...
THE BAY DOORS OPENED.

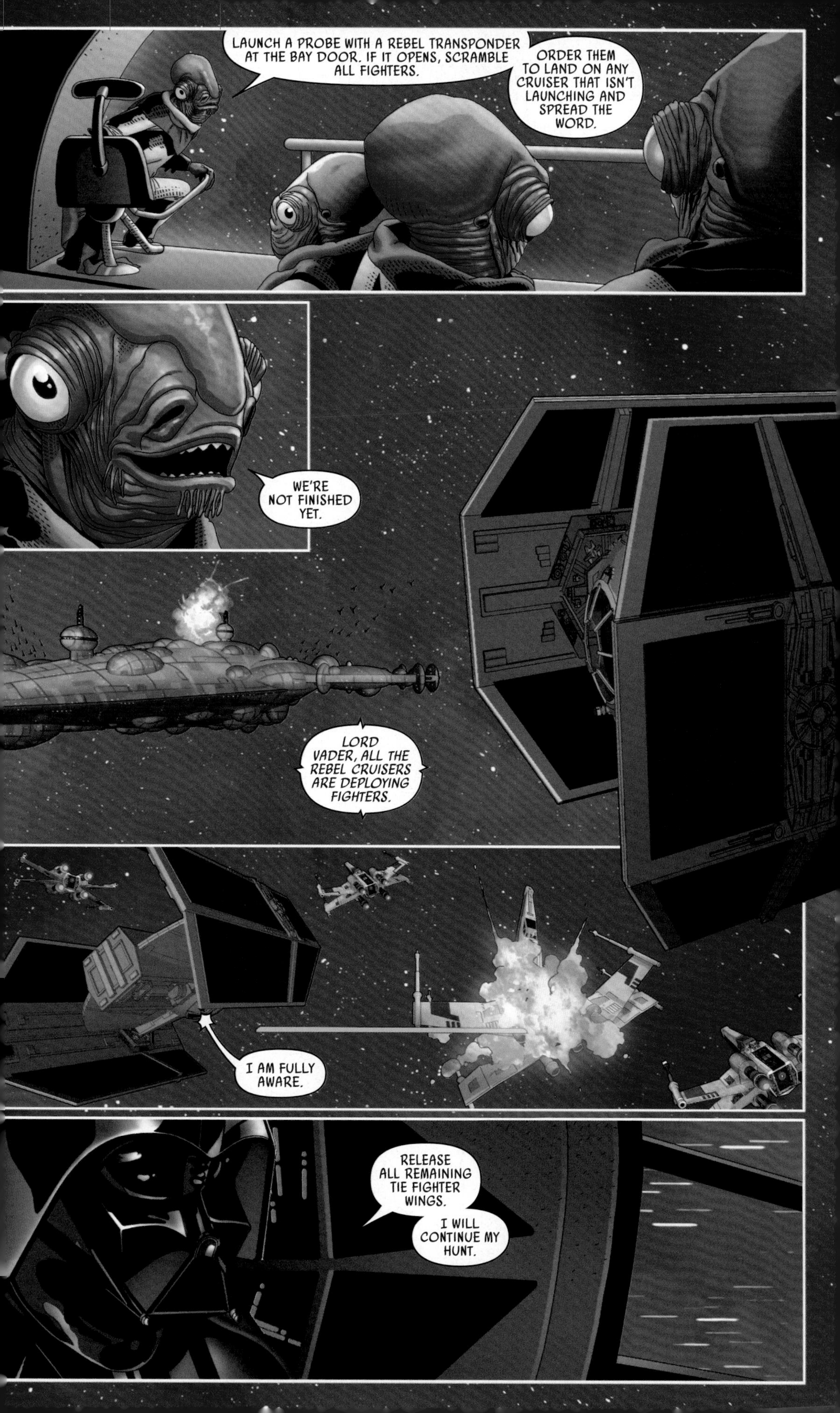
LAUNCH A PROBE WITH A REBEL TRANSPONDER AT THE BAY DOOR. IF IT OPENS, SCRAMBLE ALL FIGHTERS.
ORDER THEM TO LAND ON ANY CRUISER THAT ISN'T LAUNCHING AND SPREAD THE WORD.
WE'RE NOT FINISHED YET.
LORD VADER, ALL THE REBEL CRUISERS ARE DEPLOYING FIGHTERS.
I AM FULLY AWARE.
RELEASE ALL REMAINING TIE FIGHTER WINGS.
I WILL CONTINUE MY HUNT.

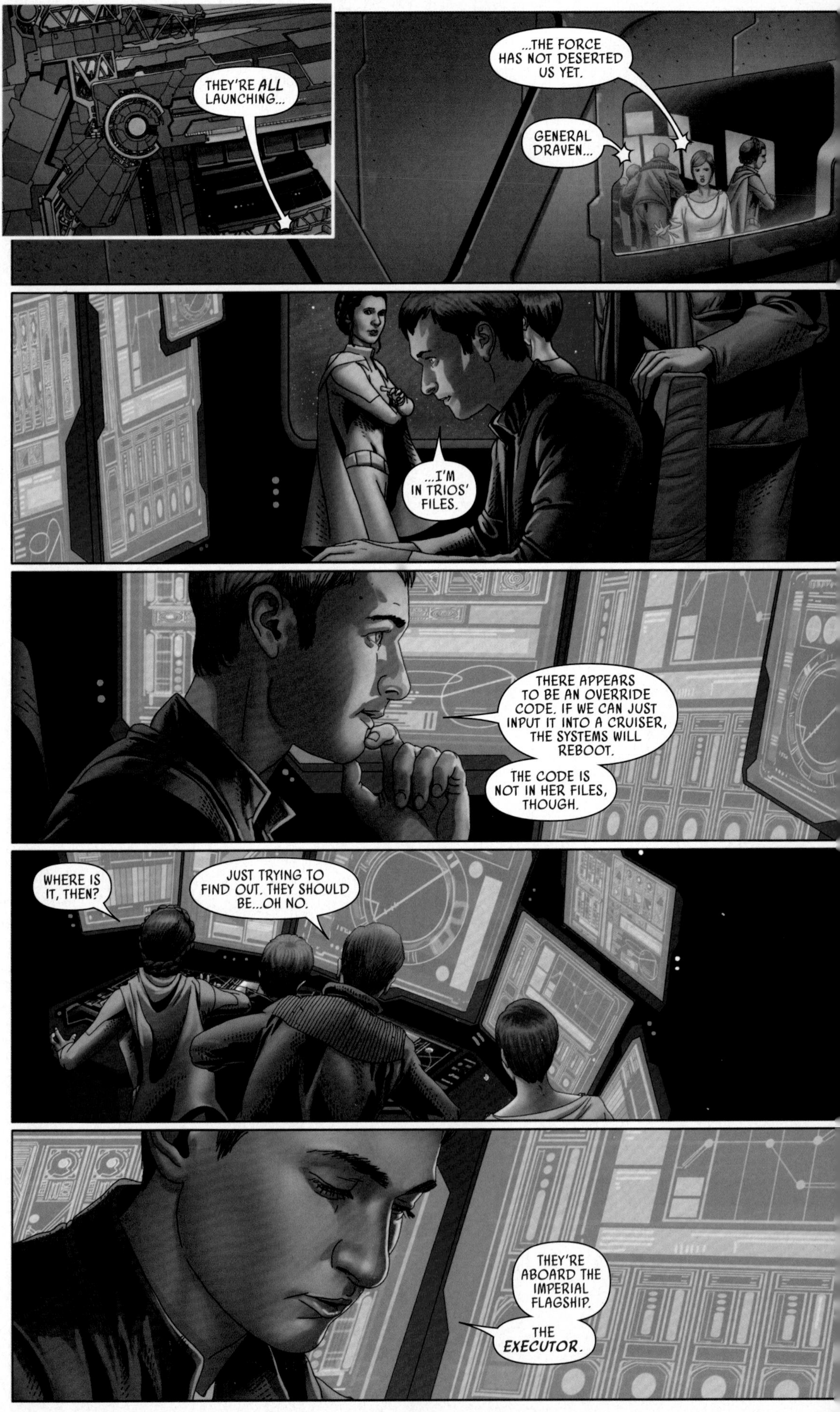
THEY'RE *ALL* LAUNCHING...
...THE FORCE HAS NOT DESERTED US YET.
GENERAL DRAVEN...
...I'M IN TRIOS' FILES.
THERE APPEARS TO BE AN OVERRIDE CODE. IF WE CAN JUST INPUT IT INTO A CRUISER, THE SYSTEMS WILL REBOOT.
THE CODE IS NOT IN HER FILES, THOUGH.
WHERE IS IT, THEN?
JUST TRYING TO FIND OUT. THEY SHOULD BE...OH NO.
THEY'RE ABOARD THE IMPERIAL FLAGSHIP.
THE *EXECUTOR*.

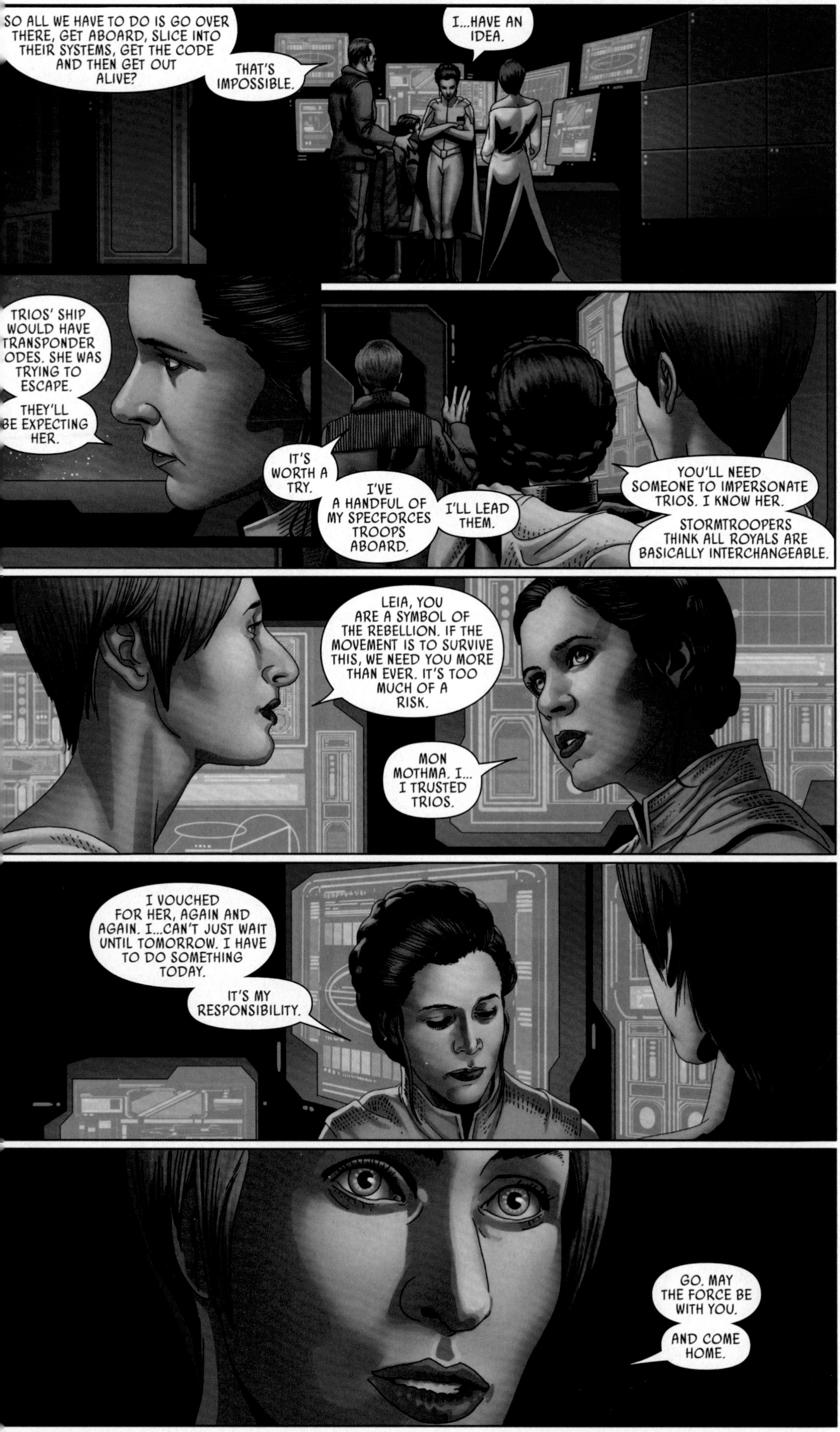
SO ALL WE HAVE TO DO IS GO OVER THERE, GET ABOARD, SLICE INTO THEIR SYSTEMS, GET THE CODE AND THEN GET OUT ALIVE?
THAT'S IMPOSSIBLE.
I...HAVE AN IDEA.
TRIOS' SHIP WOULD HAVE TRANSPONDER ODES. SHE WAS TRYING TO ESCAPE.
THEY'LL BE EXPECTING HER.
IT'S WORTH A TRY.
I'VE A HANDFUL OF MY SPECFORCES TROOPS ABOARD.
I'LL LEAD THEM.
YOU'LL NEED SOMEONE TO IMPERSONATE TRIOS. I KNOW HER.
STORMTROOPERS THINK ALL ROYALS ARE BASICALLY INTERCHANGEABLE.
LEIA, YOU ARE A SYMBOL OF THE REBELLION. IF THE MOVEMENT IS TO SURVIVE THIS, WE NEED YOU MORE THAN EVER. IT'S TOO MUCH OF A RISK.
MON MOTHMA. I... I TRUSTED TRIOS.
I VOUCHED FOR HER, AGAIN AND AGAIN. I...CAN'T JUST WAIT UNTIL TOMORROW. I HAVE TO DO SOMETHING TODAY.
IT'S MY RESPONSIBILITY.
GO. MAY THE FORCE BE WITH YOU.
AND COME HOME.

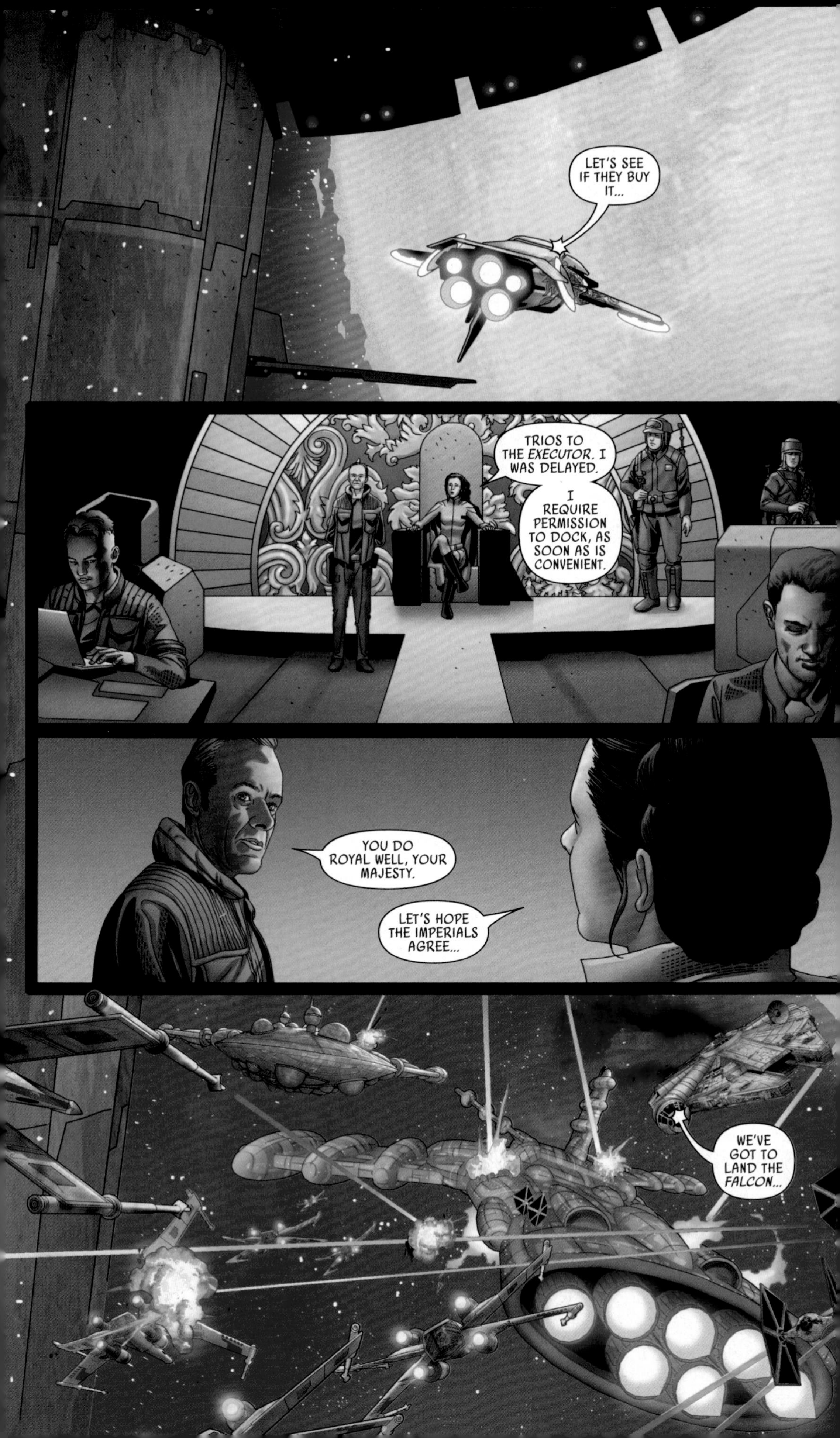
LET'S SEE IF THEY BUY IT...
TRIOS TO THE *EXECUTOR*. I WAS DELAYED.
I REQUIRE PERMISSION TO DOCK, AS SOON AS IS CONVENIENT.
YOU DO ROYAL WELL, YOUR MAJESTY.
LET'S HOPE THE IMPERIALS AGREE...
WE'VE GOT TO LAND THE *FALCON*...

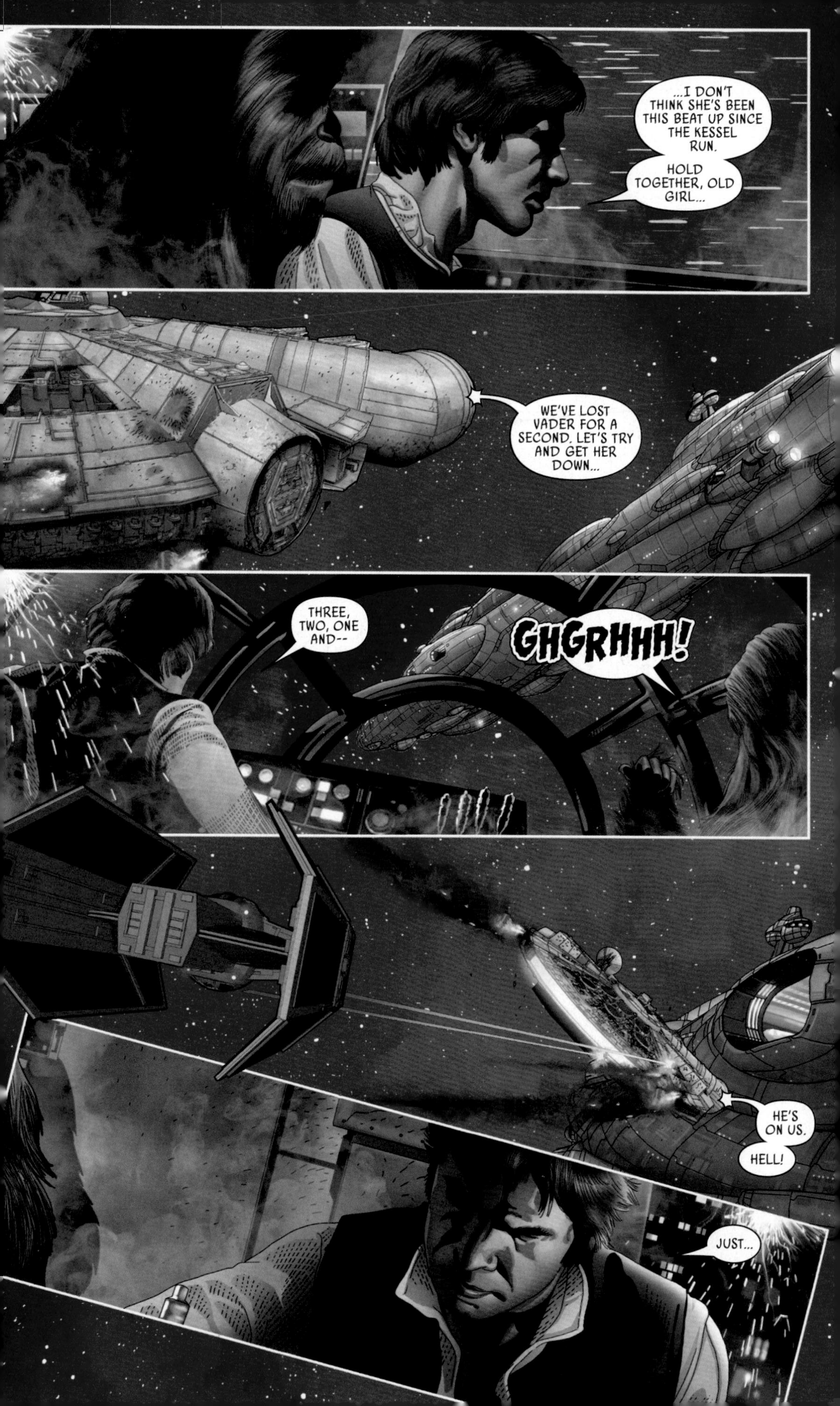
...I DON'T THINK SHE'S BEEN THIS BEAT UP SINCE THE KESSEL RUN.
HOLD TOGETHER, OLD GIRL...
WE'VE LOST VADER FOR A SECOND. LET'S TRY AND GET HER DOWN...
THREE, TWO, ONE AND--
GHGRHHH!
HE'S ON US.
HELL!
JUST...

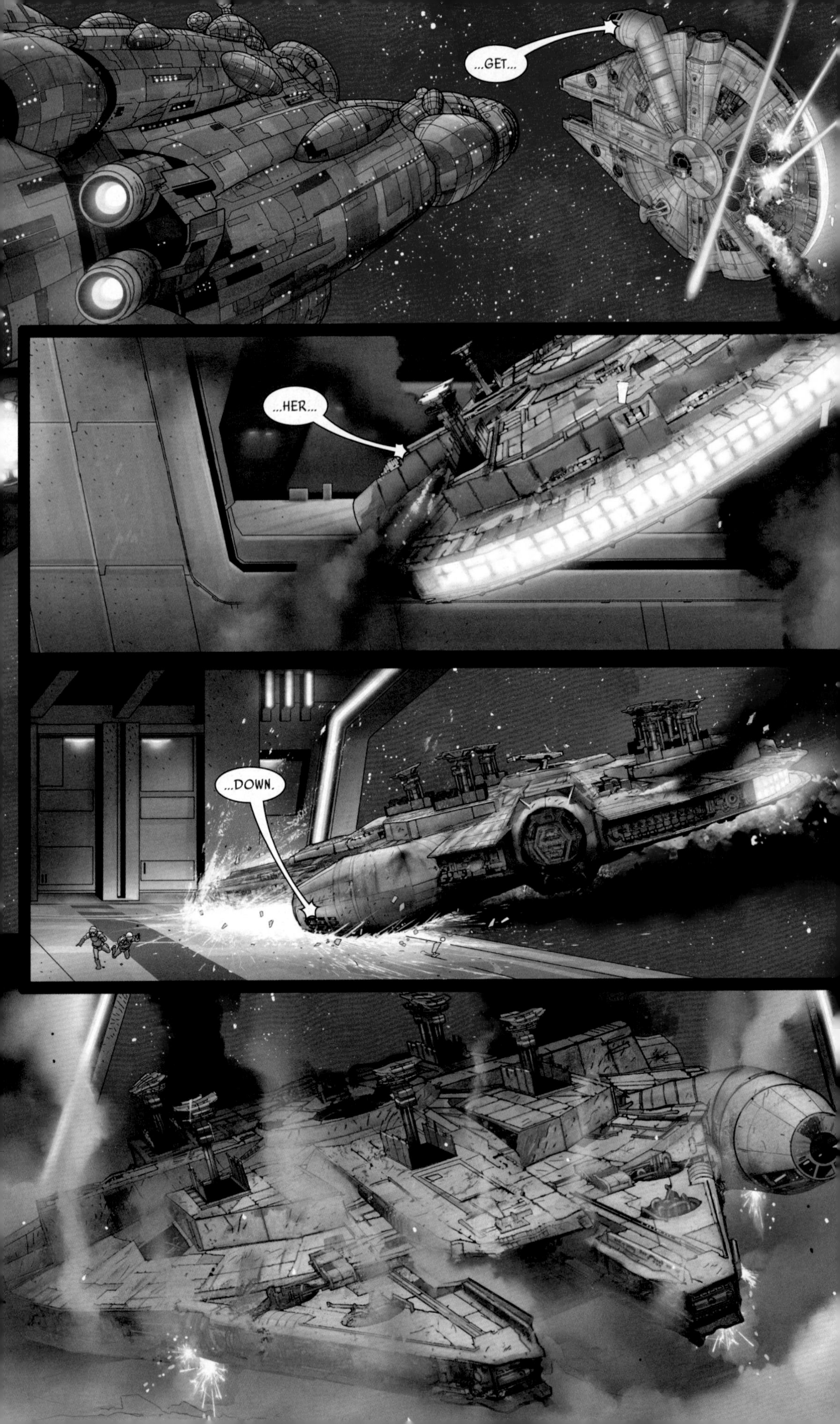
...GET...
...HER...
...DOWN.

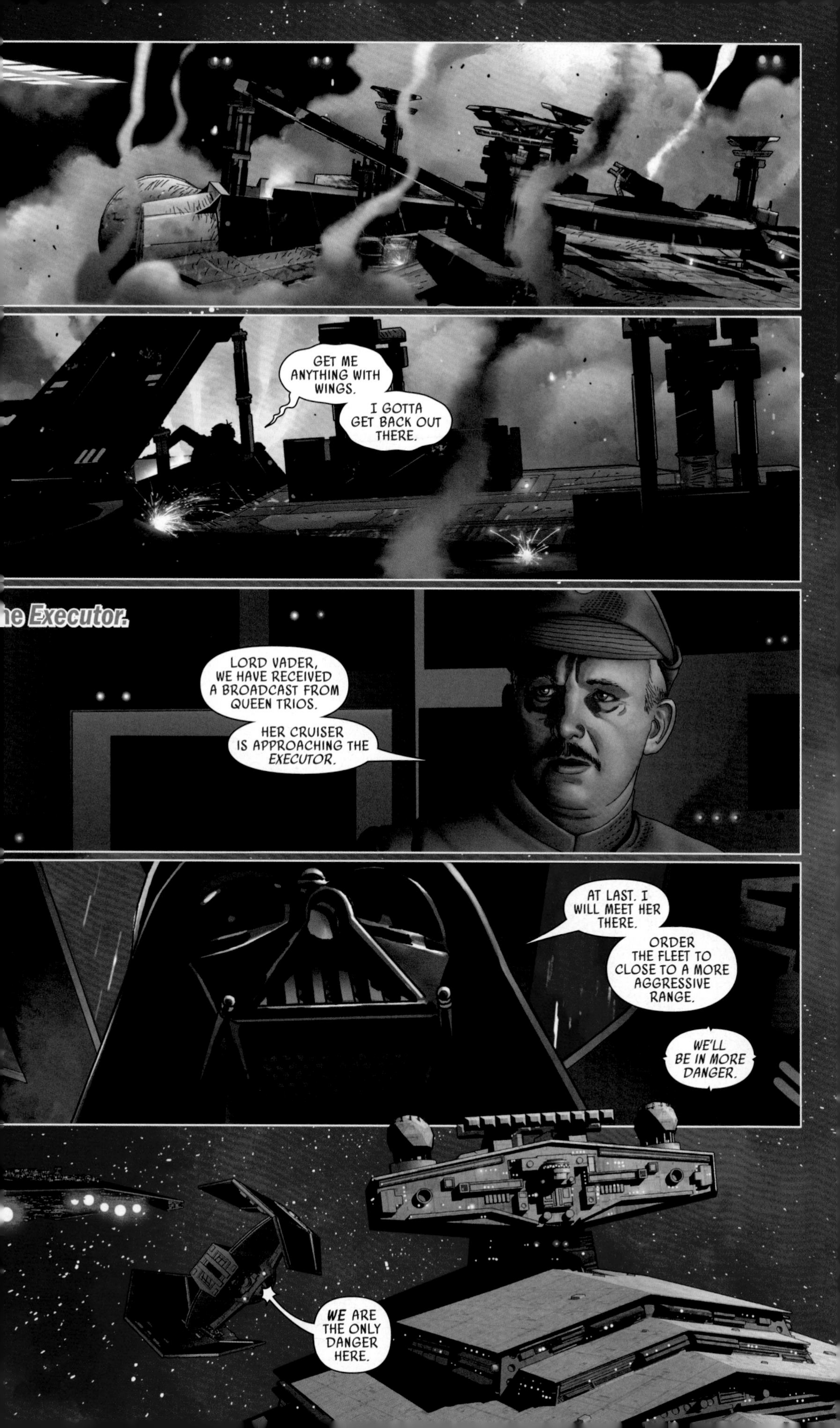
GET ME ANYTHING WITH WINGS.
I GOTTA GET BACK OUT THERE.
he Executor.
LORD VADER, WE HAVE RECEIVED A BROADCAST FROM QUEEN TRIOS.
HER CRUISER IS APPROACHING THE EXECUTOR.
AT LAST. I WILL MEET HER THERE.
ORDER THE FLEET TO CLOSE TO A MORE AGGRESSIVE RANGE.
WE'LL BE IN MORE DANGER.
WE ARE THE ONLY DANGER HERE.

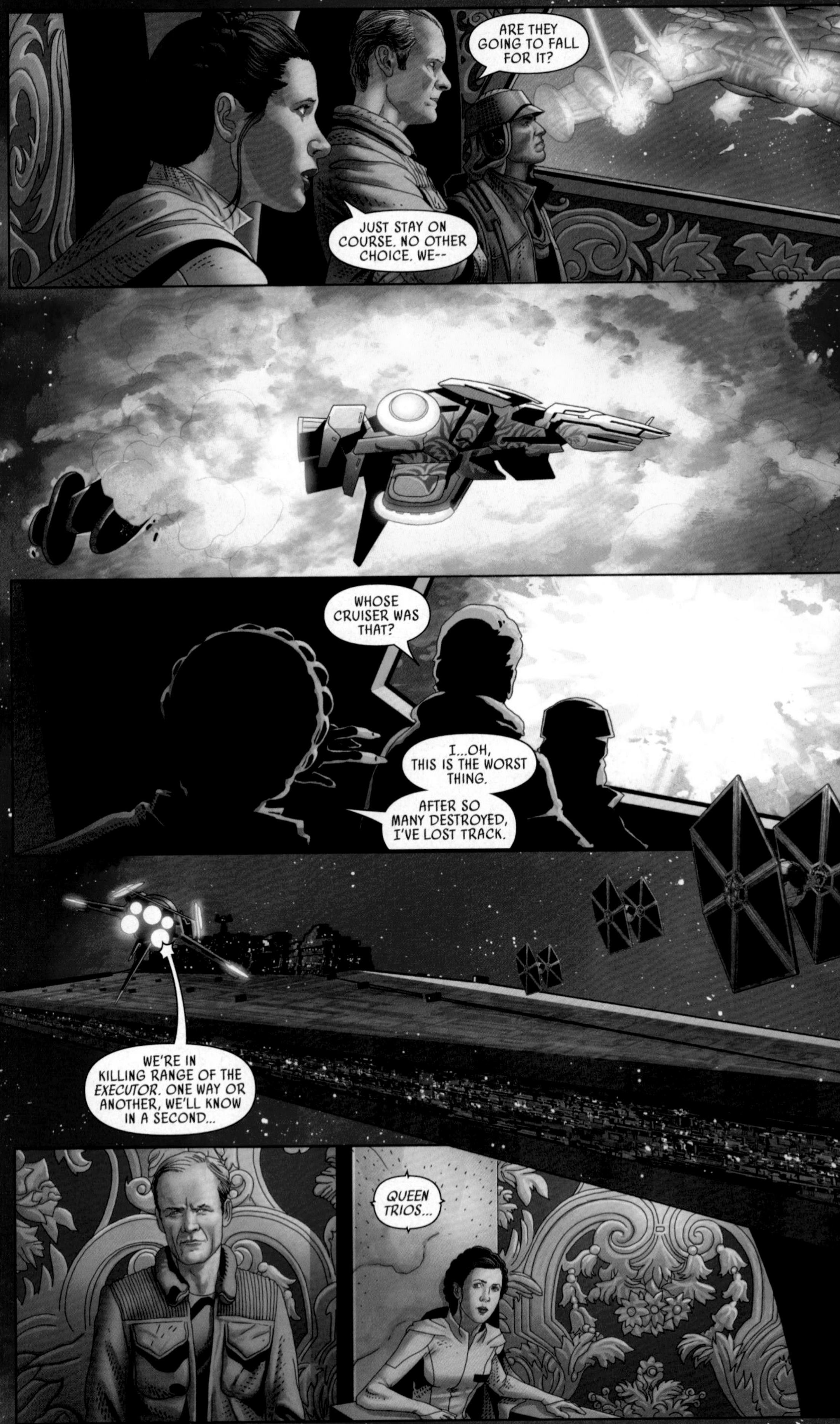
ARE THEY GOING TO FALL FOR IT?
JUST STAY ON COURSE. NO OTHER CHOICE. WE--
WHOSE CRUISER WAS THAT?
I...OH, THIS IS THE WORST THING.
AFTER SO MANY DESTROYED, I'VE LOST TRACK.
WE'RE IN KILLING RANGE OF THE *EXECUTOR*. ONE WAY OR ANOTHER, WE'LL KNOW IN A SECOND...
QUEEN TRIOS...

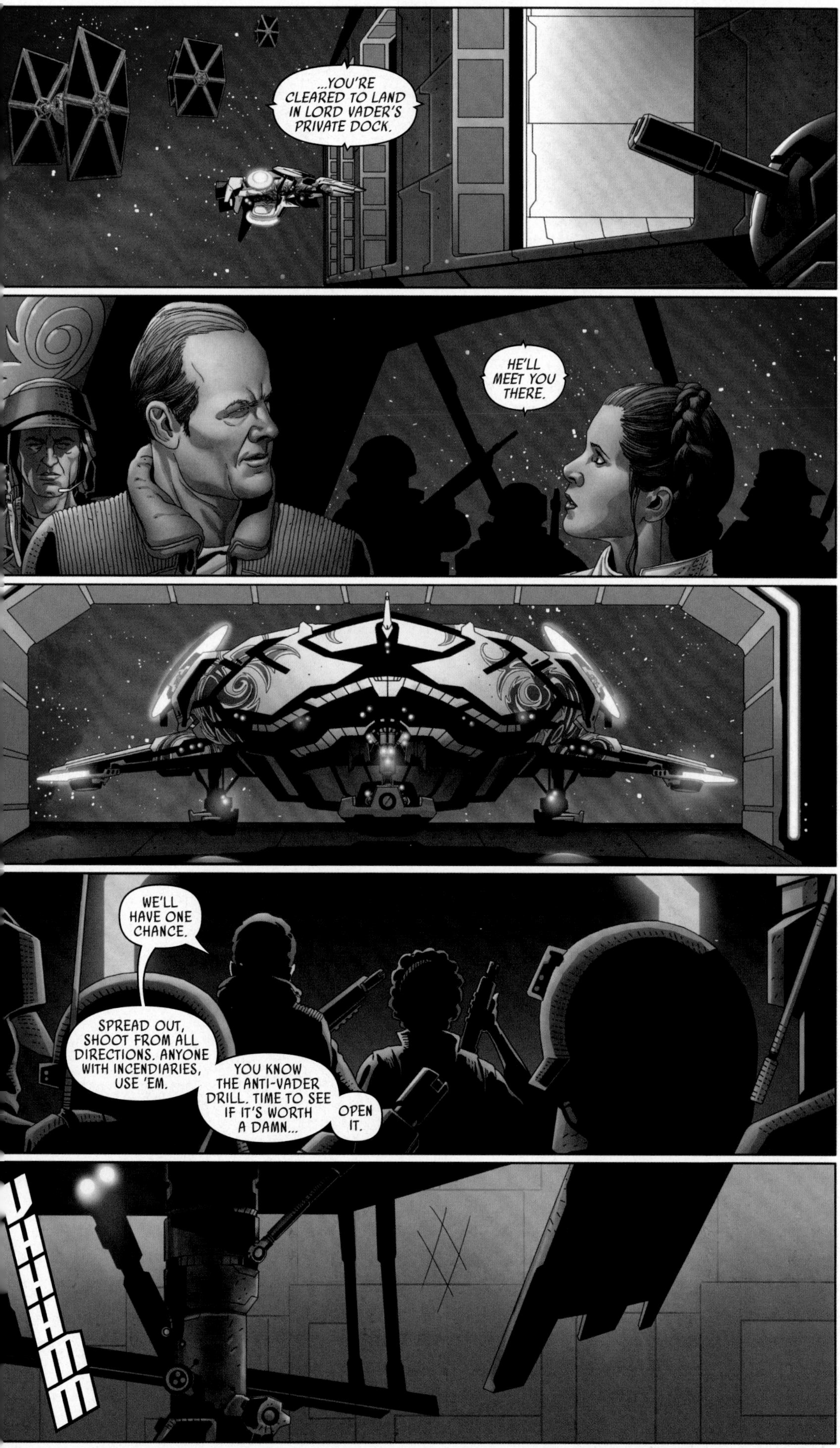

...YOU'RE CLEARED TO LAND IN LORD VADER'S PRIVATE DOCK.
HE'LL MEET YOU THERE.
WE'LL HAVE ONE CHANCE.
SPREAD OUT, SHOOT FROM ALL DIRECTIONS. ANYONE WITH INCENDIARIES, USE 'EM.
YOU KNOW THE ANTI-VADER DRILL. TIME TO SEE IF IT'S WORTH A DAMN...
OPEN IT.
VHHHMM

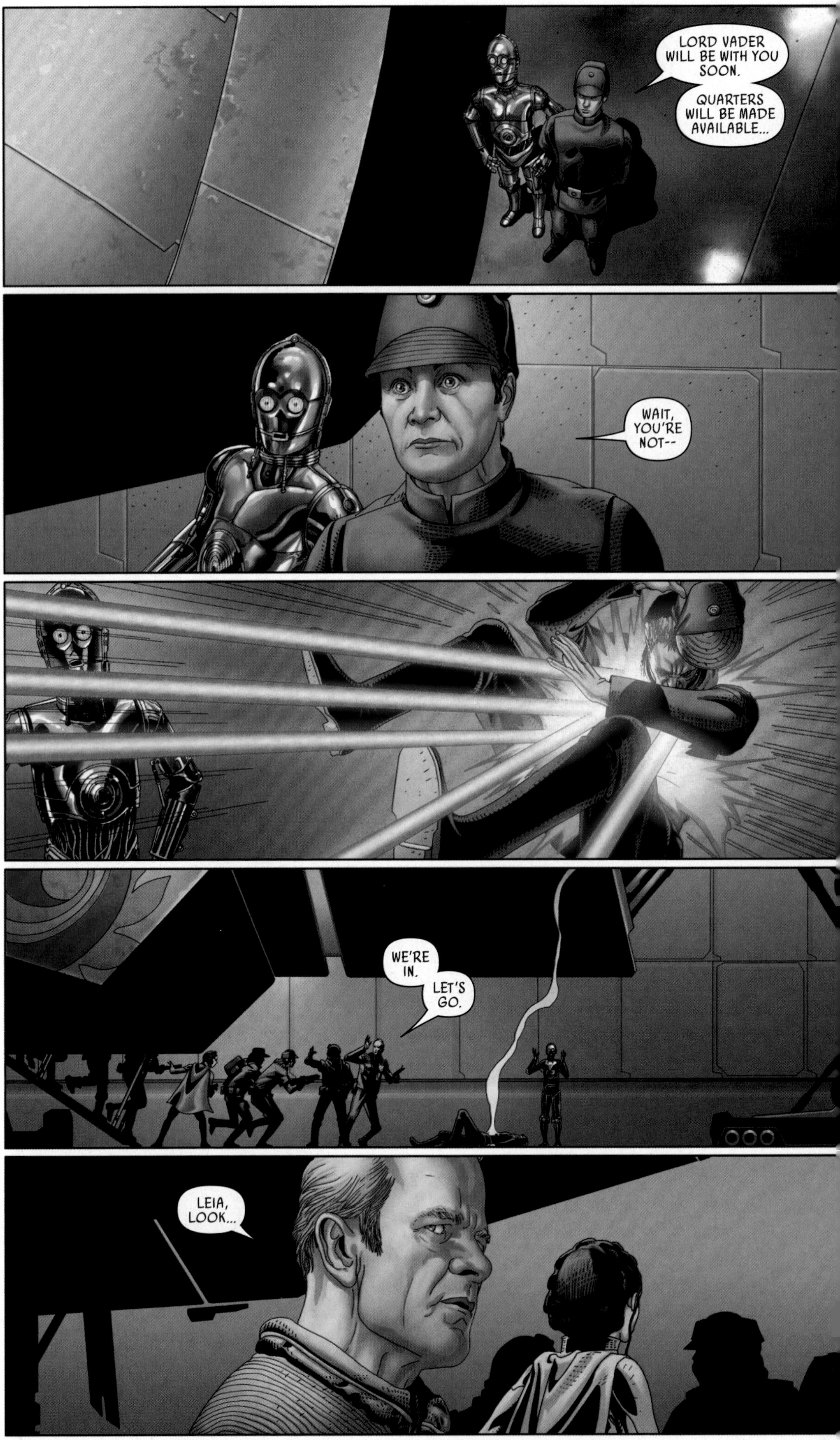
LORD VADER WILL BE WITH YOU SOON.
QUARTERS WILL BE MADE AVAILABLE...
WAIT, YOU'RE NOT--
WE'RE IN.
LET'S GO.
LEIA, LOOK...

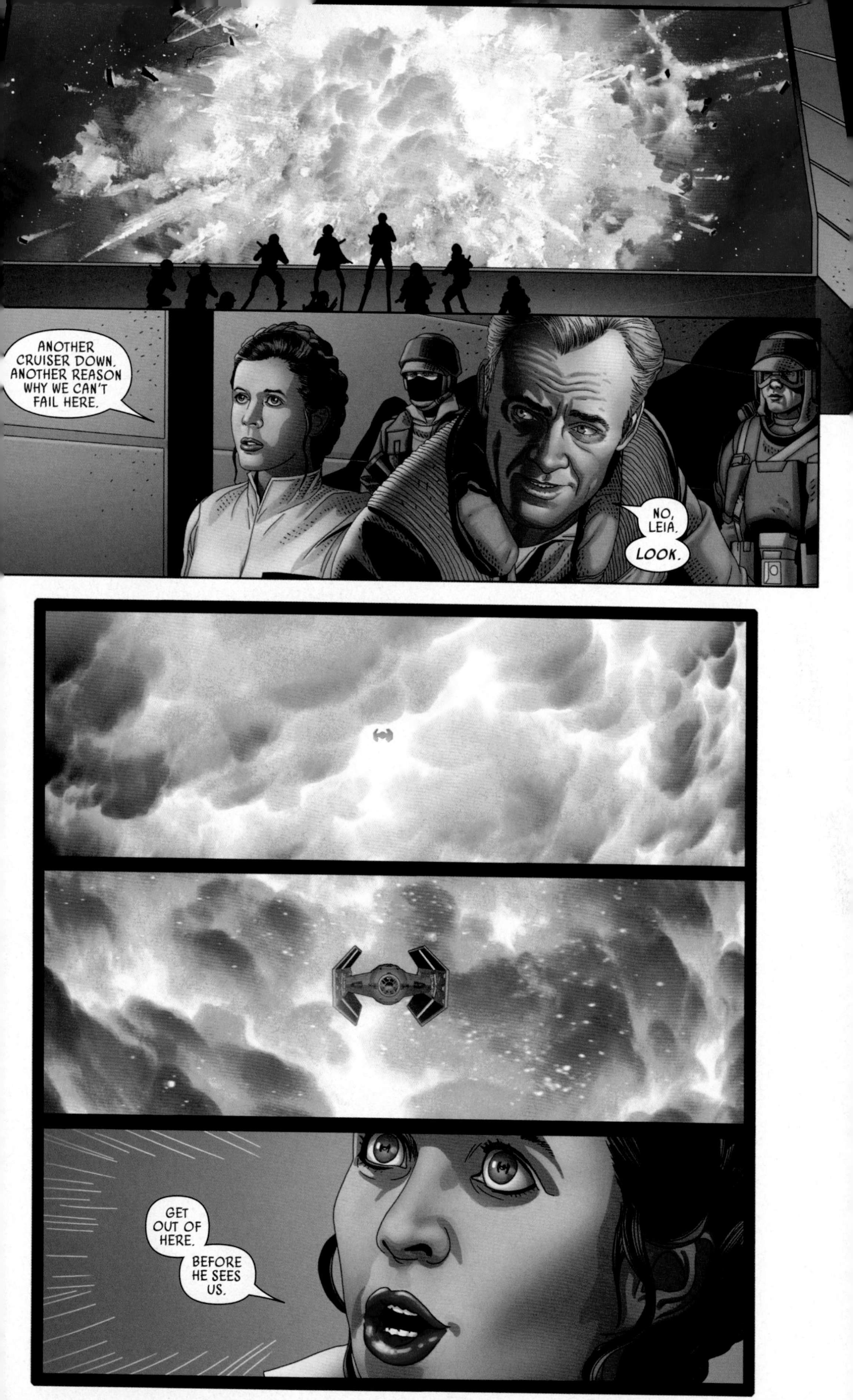
ANOTHER CRUISER DOWN. ANOTHER REASON WHY WE CAN'T FAIL HERE.
NO, LEIA.
LOOK.
GET OUT OF HERE.
BEFORE HE SEES US.

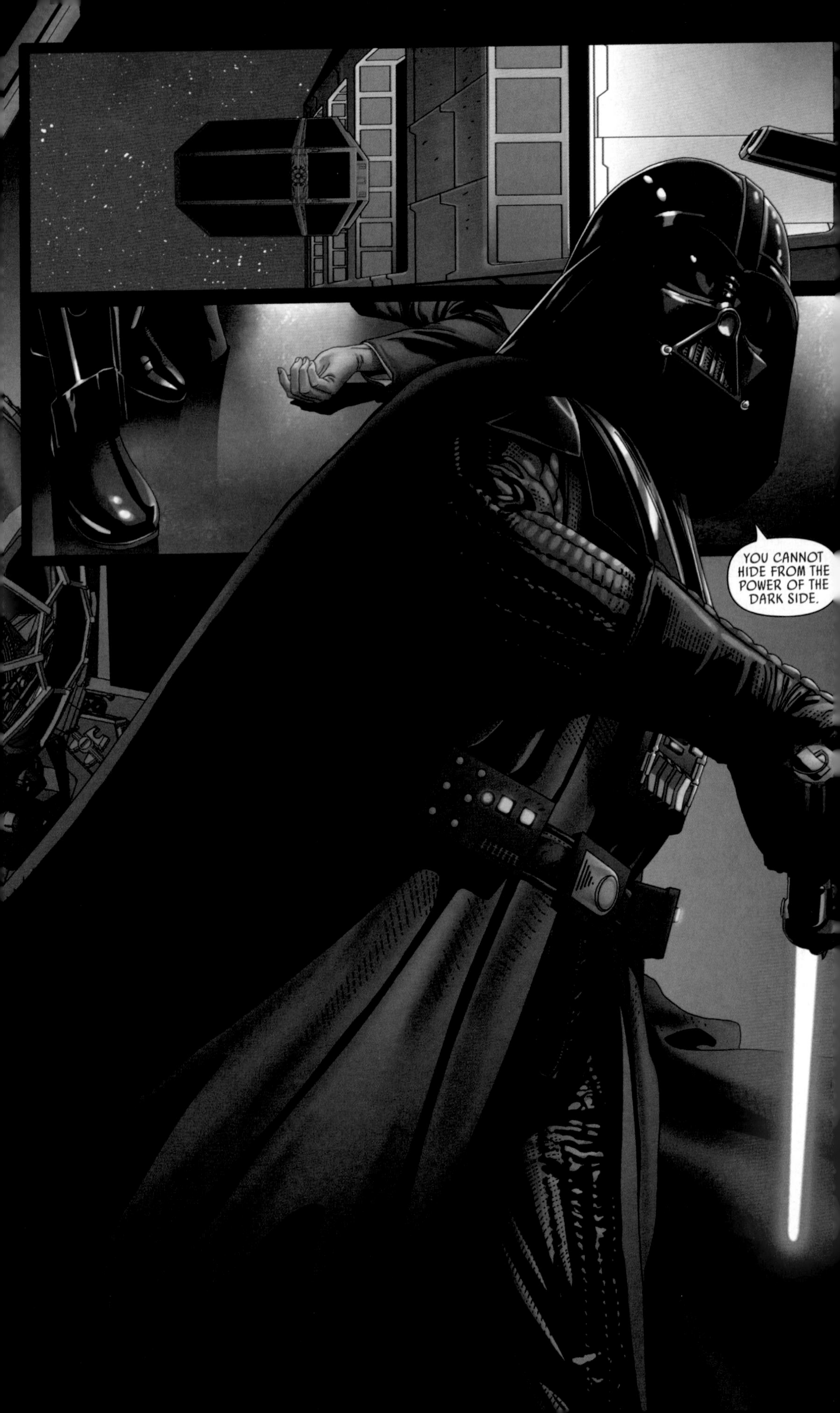
YOU CANNOT HIDE FROM THE POWER OF THE DARK SIDE.

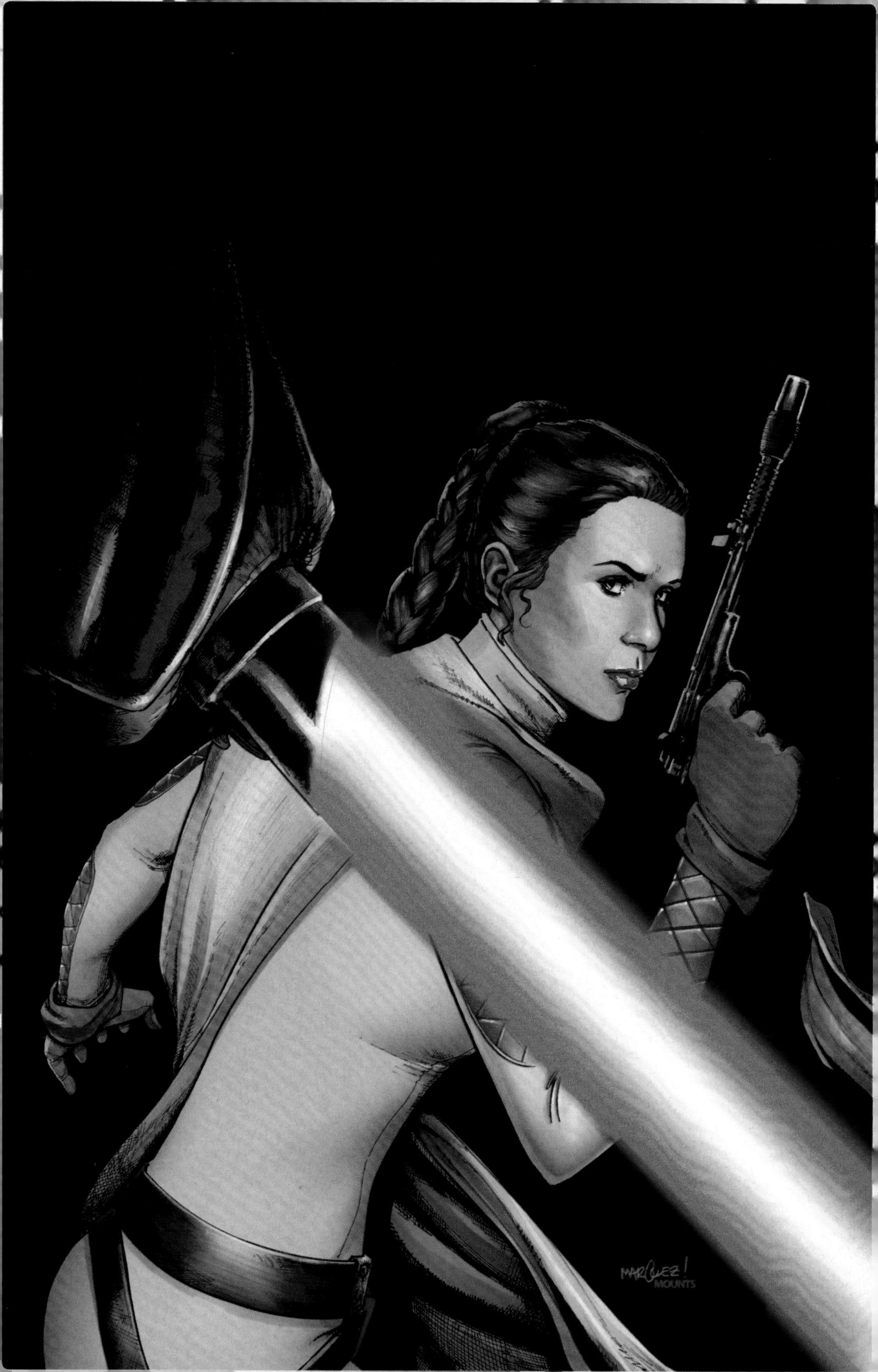
MARQUEZ!
MOUNTS

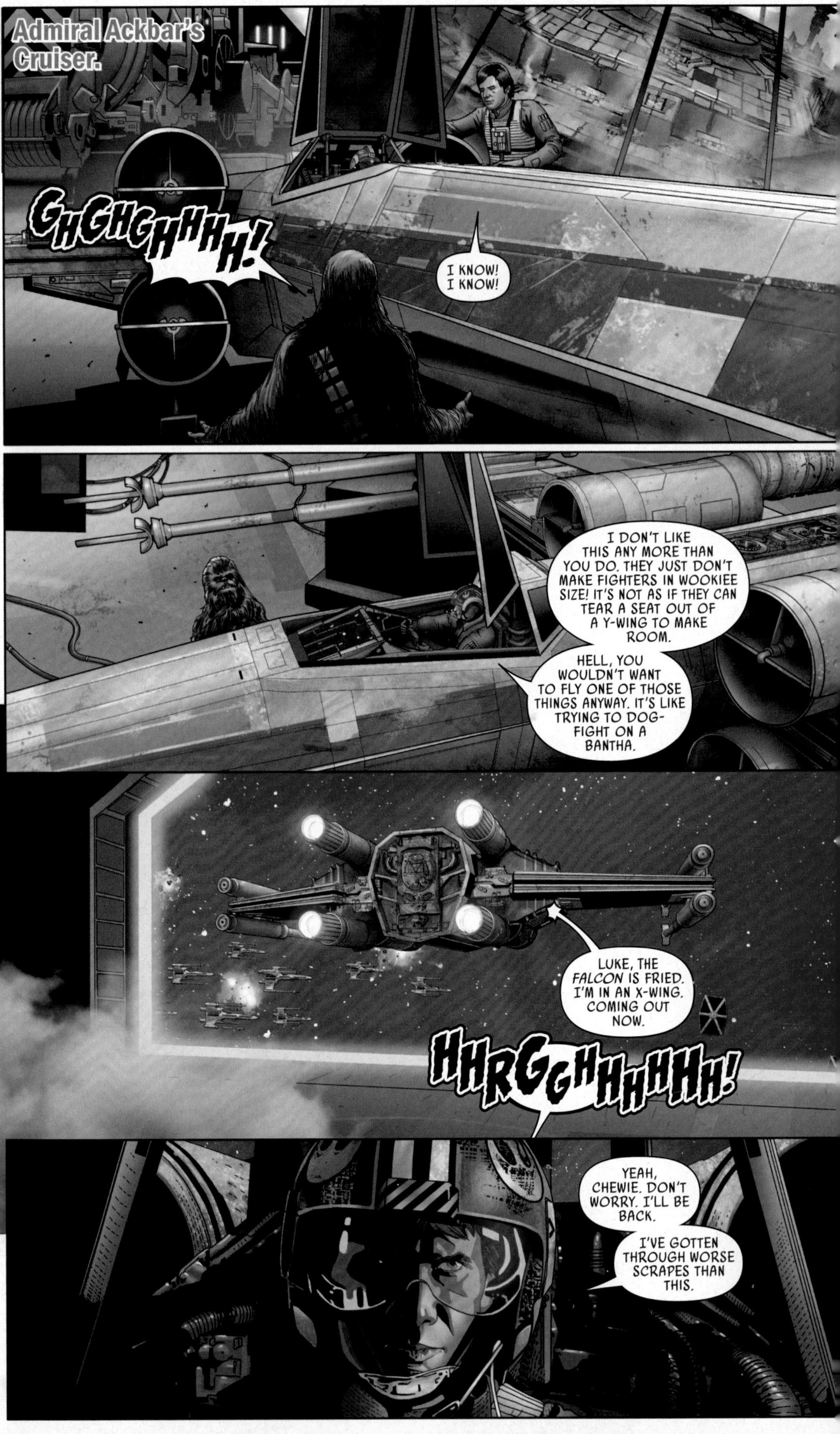
Admiral Ackbar's Cruiser.
GHGHGHHHH!
I KNOW! I KNOW!
I DON'T LIKE THIS ANY MORE THAN YOU DO. THEY JUST DON'T MAKE FIGHTERS IN WOOKIEE SIZE! IT'S NOT AS IF THEY CAN TEAR A SEAT OUT OF A Y-WING TO MAKE ROOM.
HELL, YOU WOULDN'T WANT TO FLY ONE OF THOSE THINGS ANYWAY. IT'S LIKE TRYING TO DOG-FIGHT ON A BANTHA.
LUKE, THE *FALCON* IS FRIED. I'M IN AN X-WING. COMING OUT NOW.
HHRGGHHHHHH!
YEAH, CHEWIE. DON'T WORRY. I'LL BE BACK.
I'VE GOTTEN THROUGH WORSE SCRAPES THAN THIS.

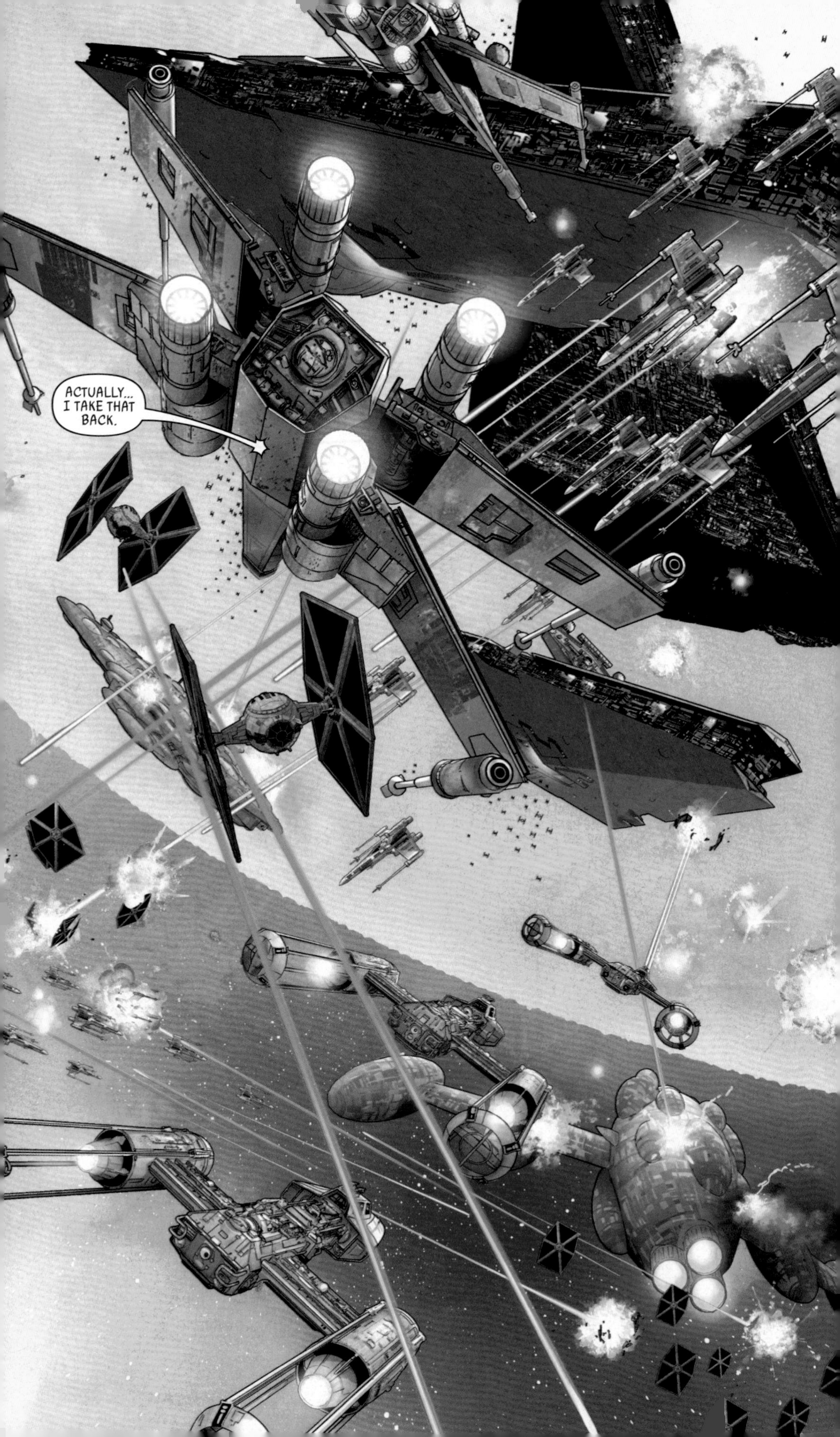
ACTUALLY... I TAKE THAT BACK.

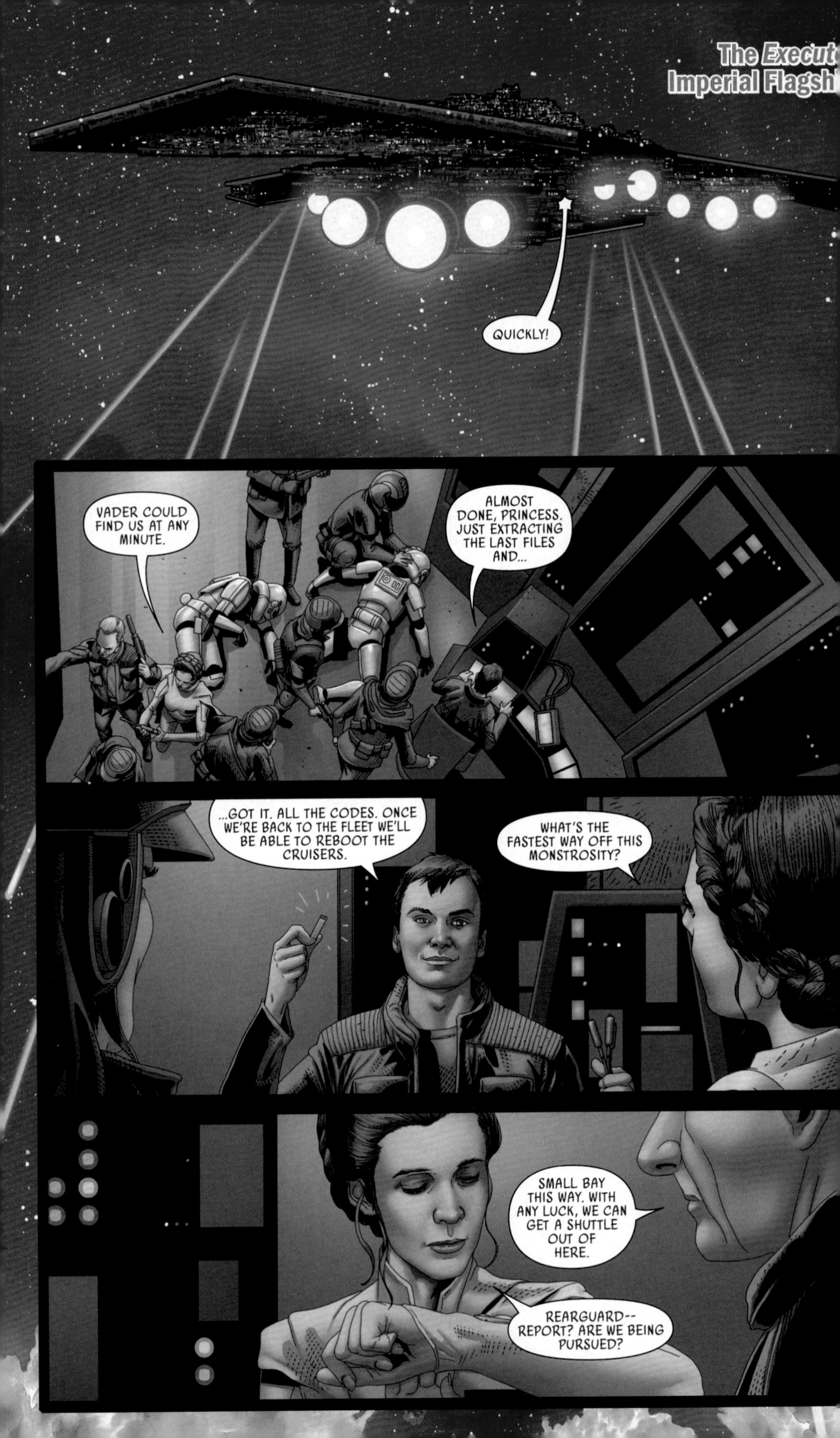
The Execut
Imperial Flagsh
QUICKLY!
VADER COULD FIND US AT ANY MINUTE.
ALMOST DONE, PRINCESS. JUST EXTRACTING THE LAST FILES AND...
...GOT IT. ALL THE CODES. ONCE WE'RE BACK TO THE FLEET WE'LL BE ABLE TO REBOOT THE CRUISERS.
WHAT'S THE FASTEST WAY OFF THIS MONSTROSITY?
SMALL BAY THIS WAY. WITH ANY LUCK, WE CAN GET A SHUTTLE OUT OF HERE.
REARGUARD-- REPORT? ARE WE BEING PURSUED?

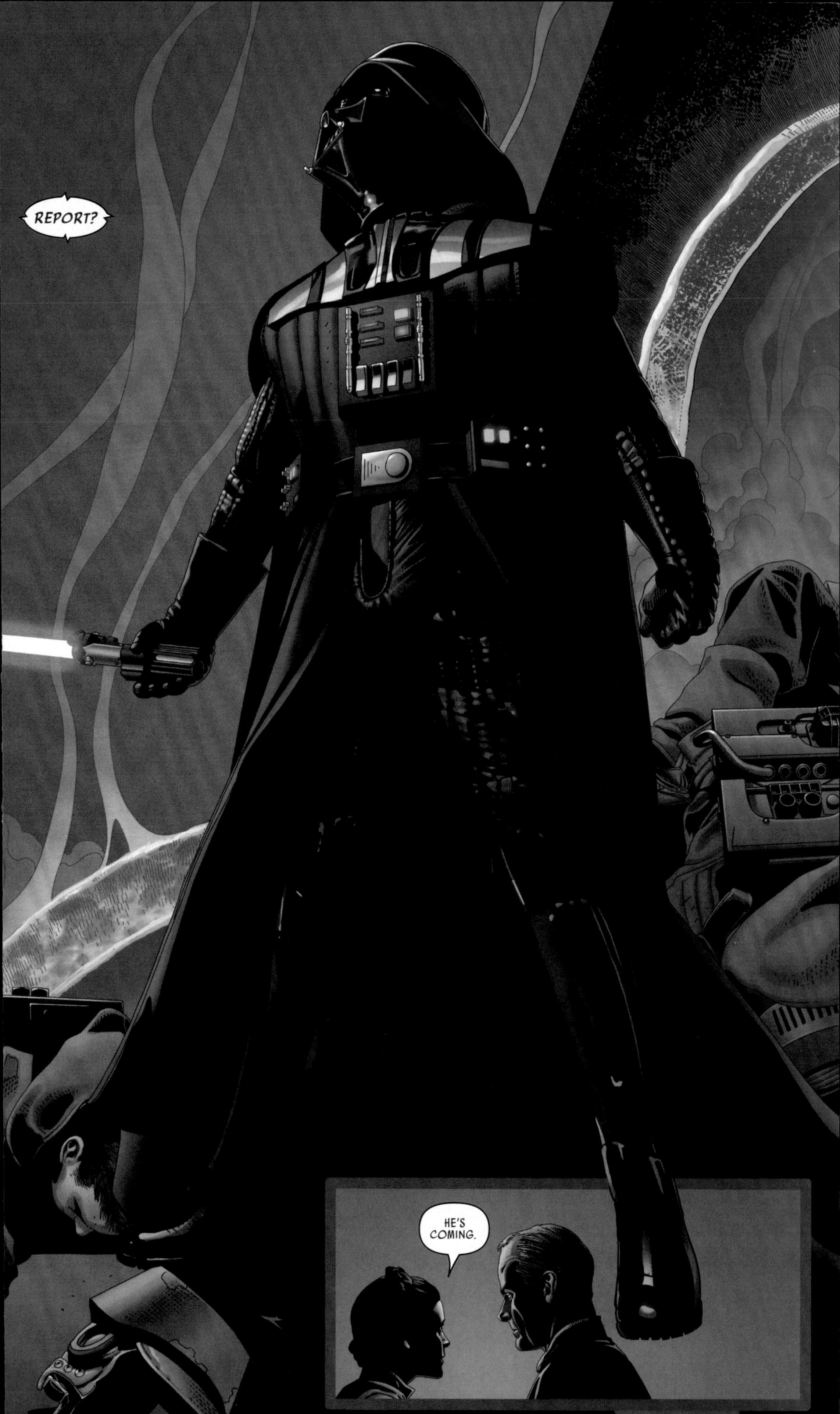
REPORT?
HE'S COMING.

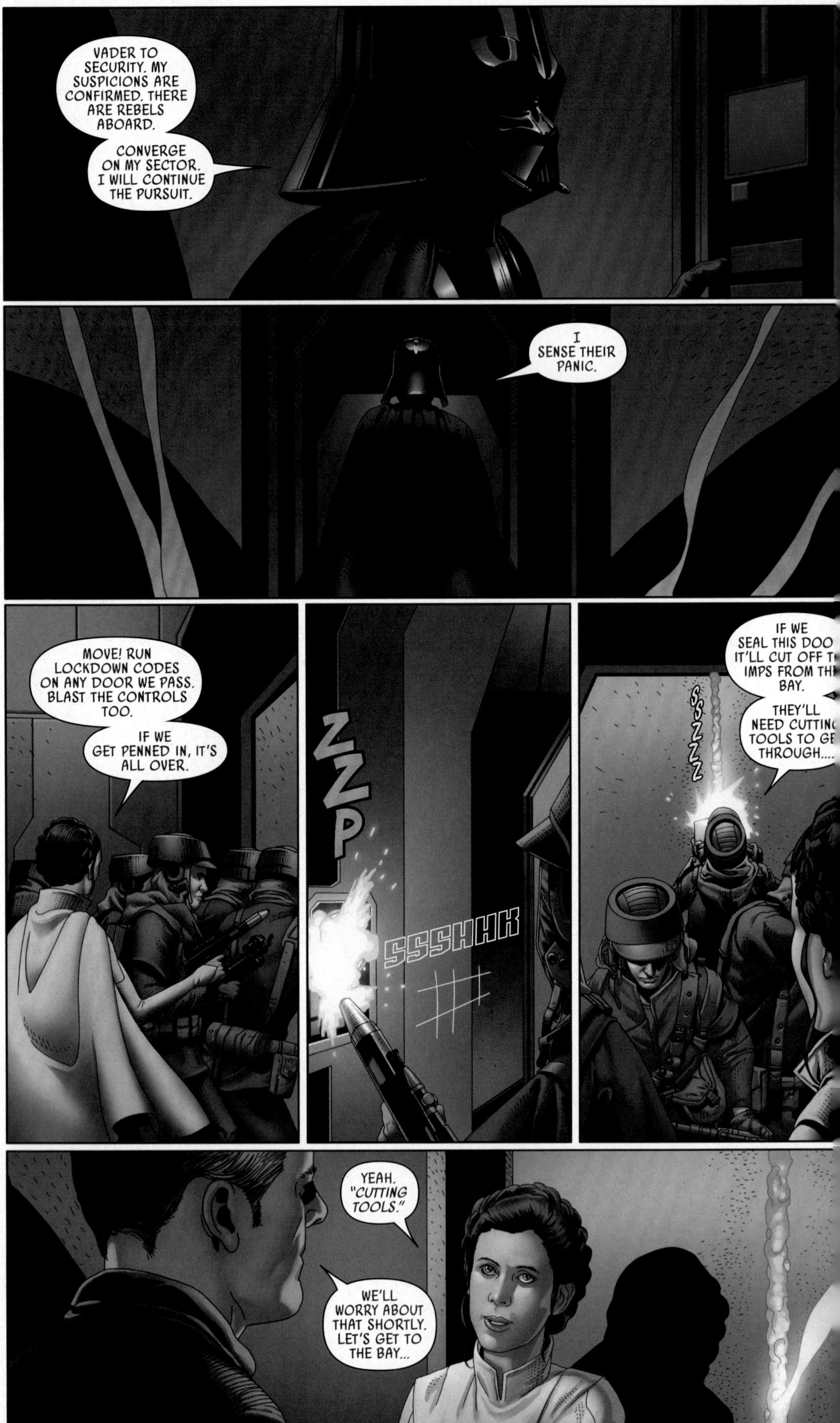
VADER TO SECURITY. MY SUSPICIONS ARE CONFIRMED. THERE ARE REBELS ABOARD.
CONVERGE ON MY SECTOR. I WILL CONTINUE THE PURSUIT.
I SENSE THEIR PANIC.
MOVE! RUN LOCKDOWN CODES ON ANY DOOR WE PASS. BLAST THE CONTROLS TOO.
IF WE GET PENNED IN, IT'S ALL OVER.
ZZP
SSSHHK
SSZZZ
IF WE SEAL THIS DOO
IT'LL CUT OFF T
IMPS FROM TH
BAY.
THEY'LL NEED CUTTIN
TOOLS TO GE
THROUGH....
YEAH. "CUTTING TOOLS."
WE'LL WORRY ABOUT THAT SHORTLY. LET'S GET TO THE BAY...

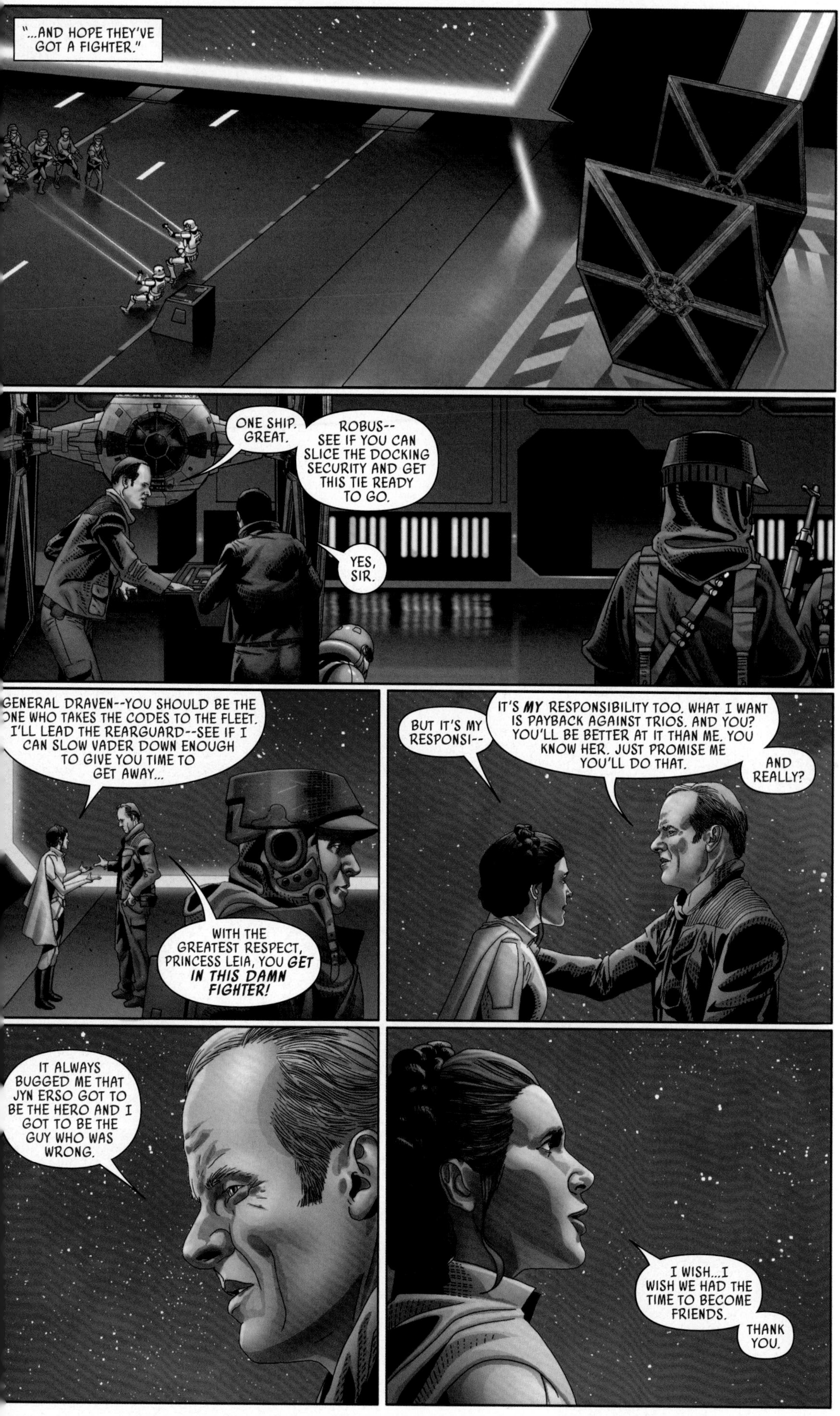

"...AND HOPE THEY'VE GOT A FIGHTER."
ONE SHIP. GREAT.
ROBUS-- SEE IF YOU CAN SLICE THE DOCKING SECURITY AND GET THIS TIE READY TO GO.
YES, SIR.
GENERAL DRAVEN--YOU SHOULD BE THE ONE WHO TAKES THE CODES TO THE FLEET. I'LL LEAD THE REARGUARD--SEE IF I CAN SLOW VADER DOWN ENOUGH TO GIVE YOU TIME TO GET AWAY...
WITH THE GREATEST RESPECT, PRINCESS LEIA, YOU GET IN THIS DAMN FIGHTER!
BUT IT'S MY RESPONSI--
IT'S MY RESPONSIBILITY TOO. WHAT I WANT IS PAYBACK AGAINST TRIOS. AND YOU? YOU'LL BE BETTER AT IT THAN ME. YOU KNOW HER. JUST PROMISE ME YOU'LL DO THAT.
AND REALLY?
IT ALWAYS BUGGED ME THAT JYN ERSO GOT TO BE THE HERO AND I GOT TO BE THE GUY WHO WAS WRONG.
I WISH...I WISH WE HAD THE TIME TO BECOME FRIENDS.
THANK YOU.

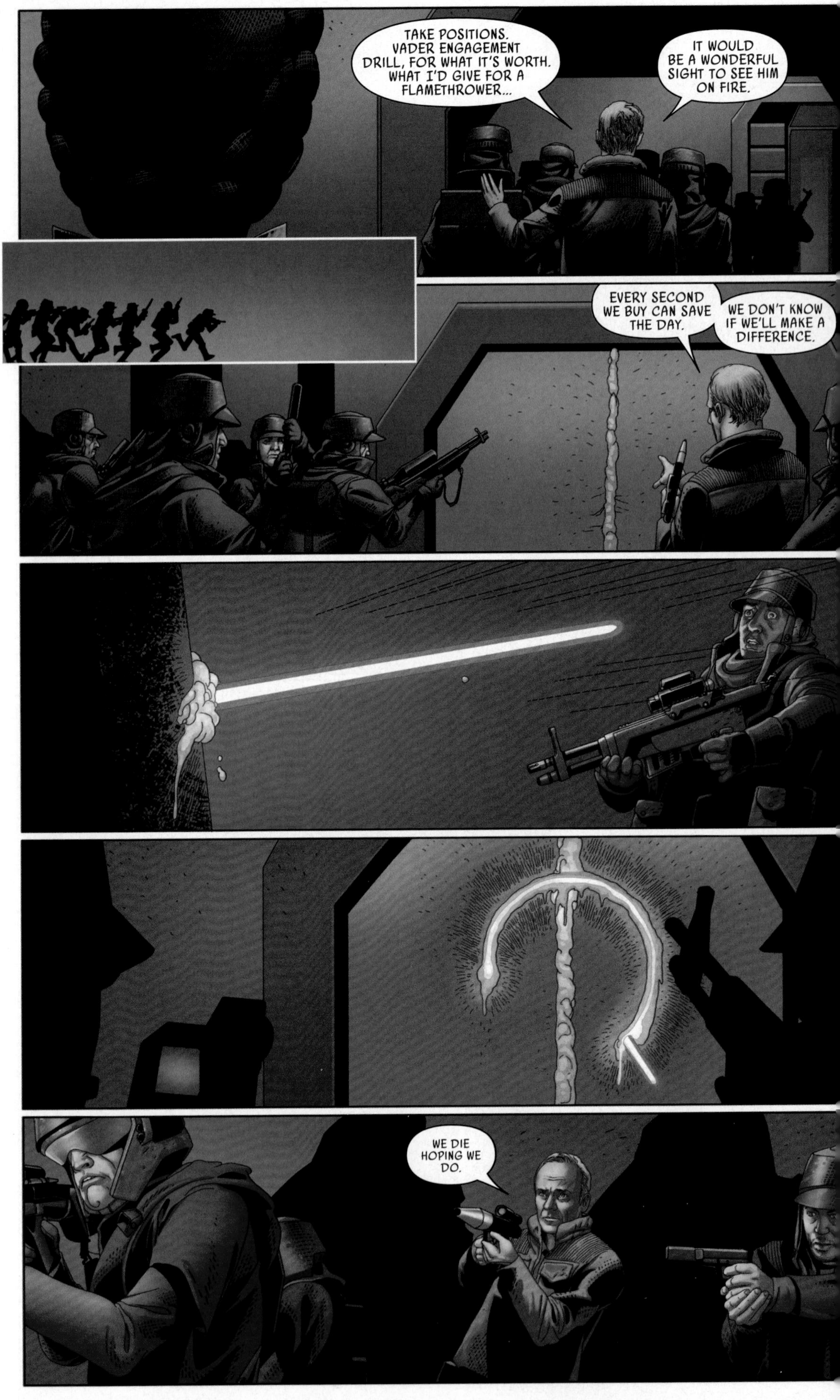
TAKE POSITIONS. VADER ENGAGEMENT DRILL, FOR WHAT IT'S WORTH. WHAT I'D GIVE FOR A FLAMETHROWER...
IT WOULD BE A WONDERFUL SIGHT TO SEE HIM ON FIRE.
EVERY SECOND WE BUY CAN SAVE THE DAY.
WE DON'T KNOW IF WE'LL MAKE A DIFFERENCE.
WE DIE HOPING WE DO.

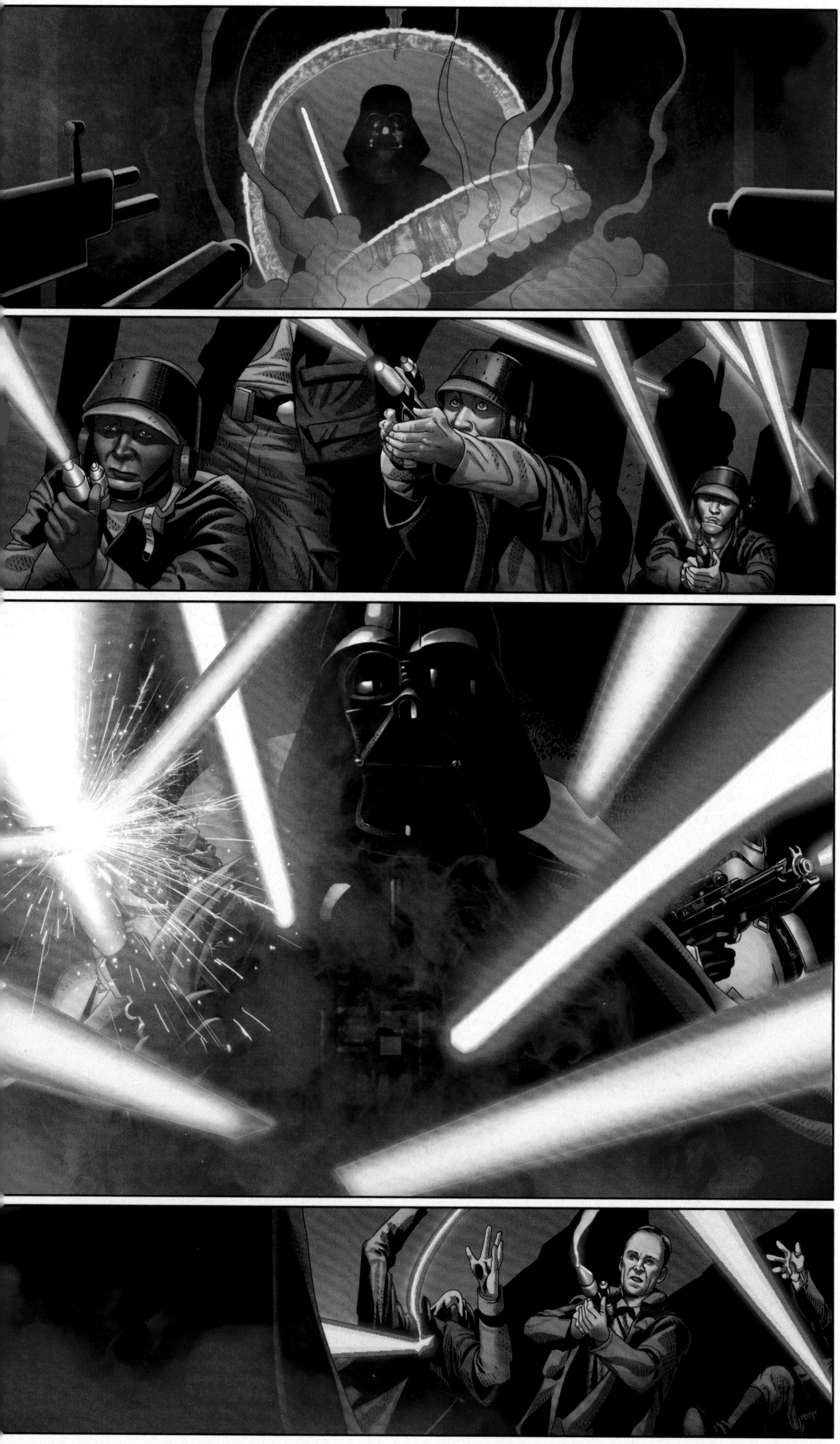

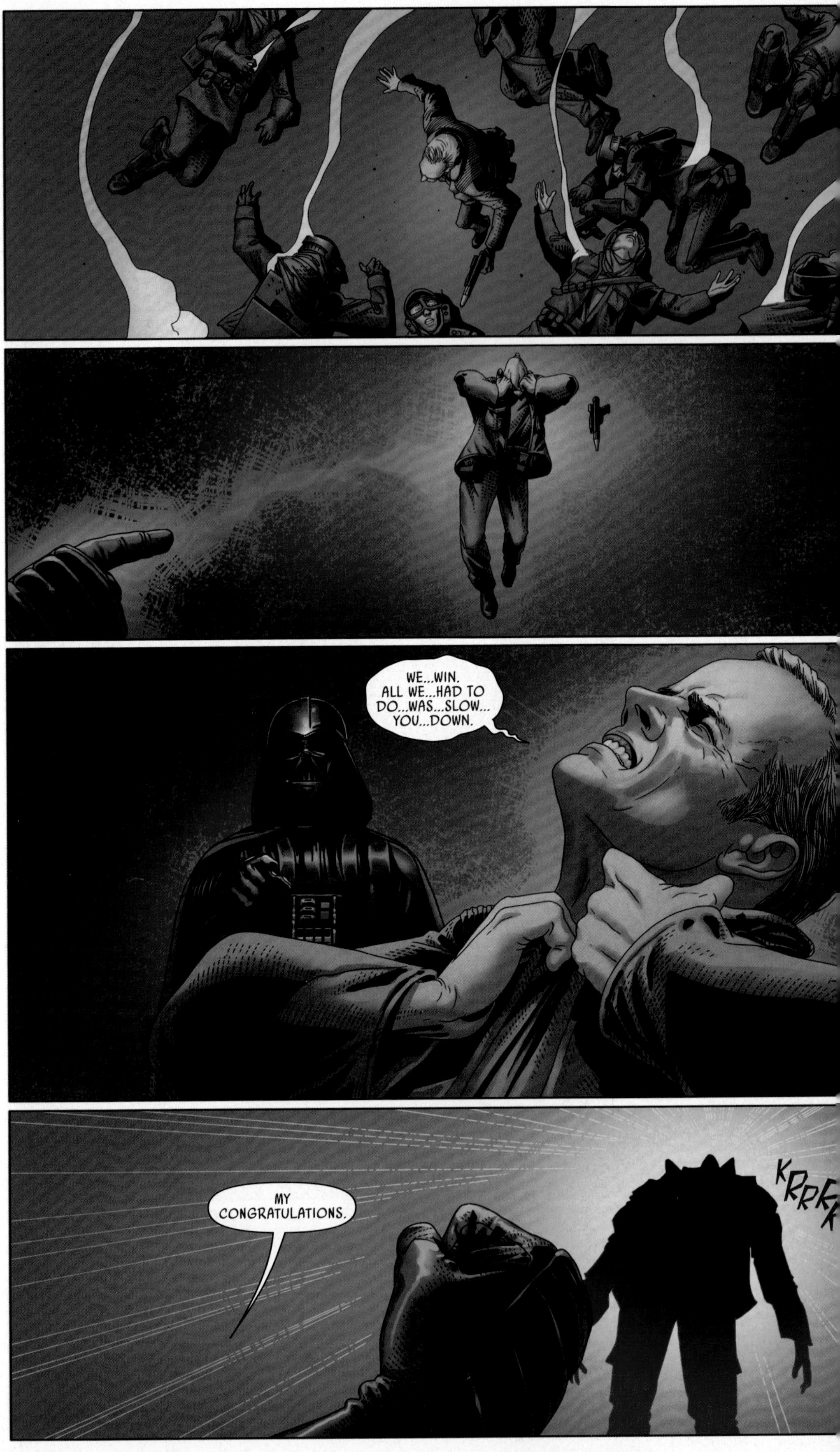
WE...WIN.
ALL WE...HAD TO
DO...WAS...SLOW...
YOU...DOWN.
MY
CONGRATULATIONS.
KRRKK

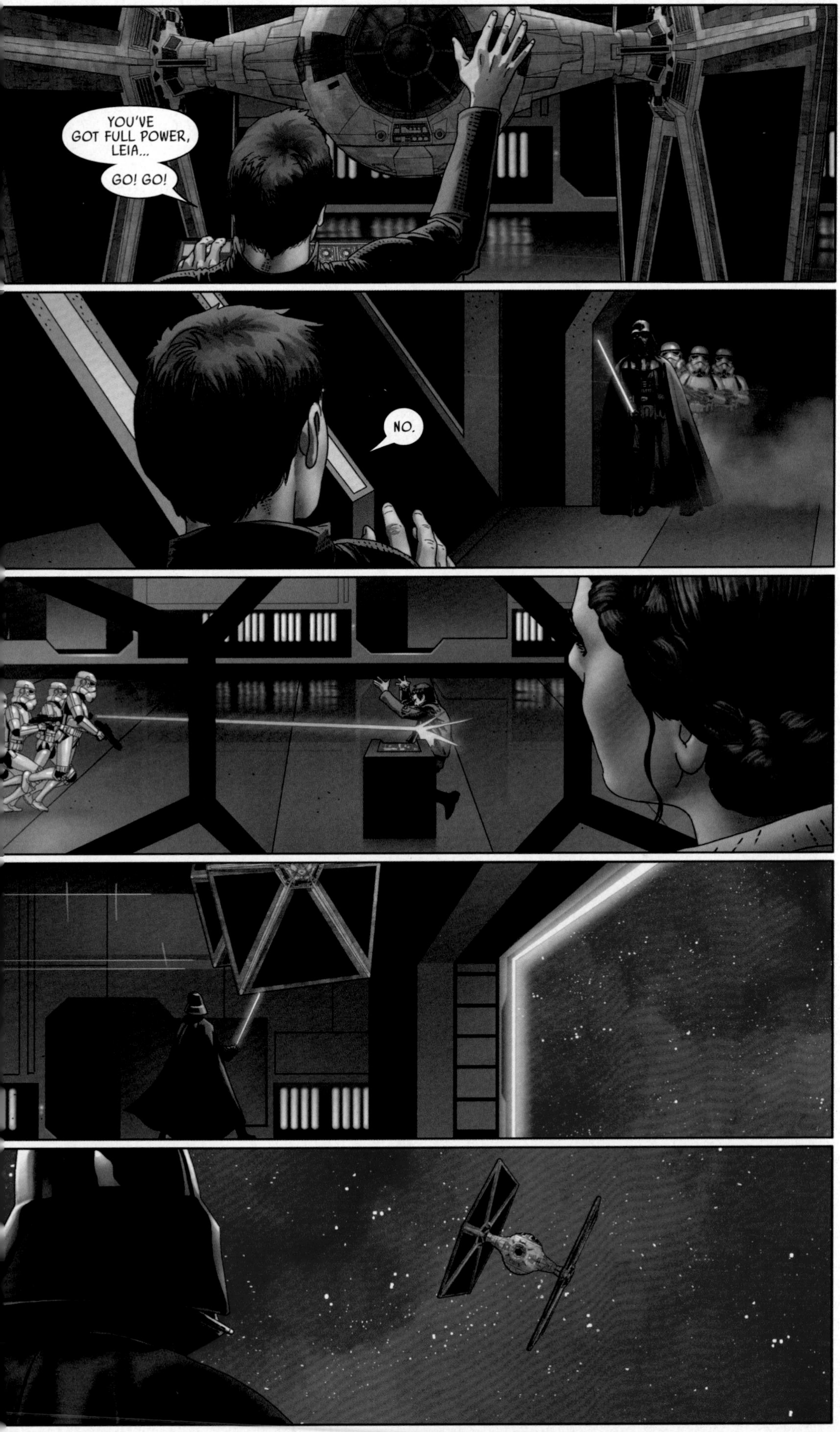
YOU'VE GOT FULL POWER, LEIA...
GO! GO!
NO.

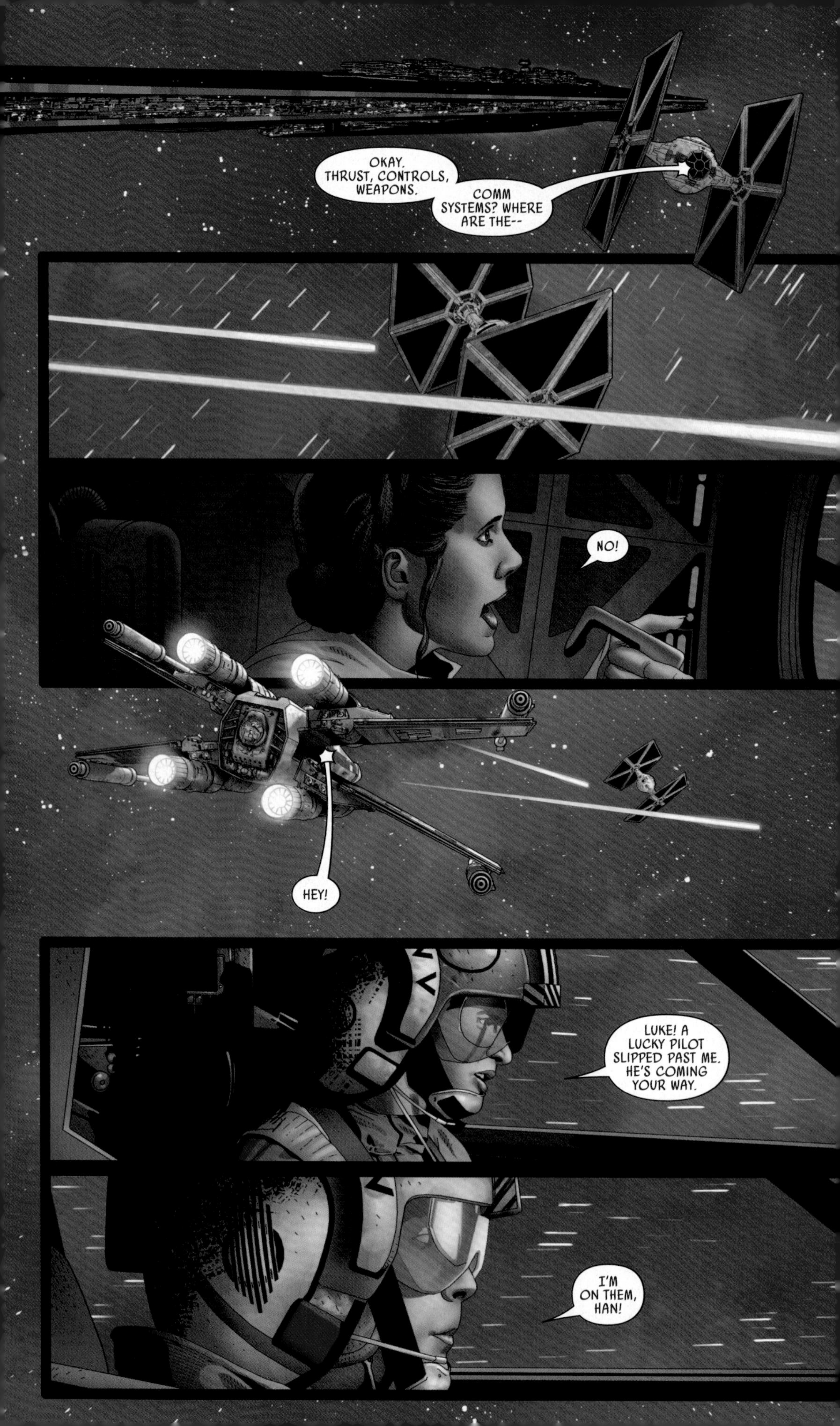
OKAY. THRUST, CONTROLS, WEAPONS.
COMM SYSTEMS? WHERE ARE THE--
NO!
HEY!
LUKE! A LUCKY PILOT SLIPPED PAST ME. HE'S COMING YOUR WAY.
I'M ON THEM, HAN!

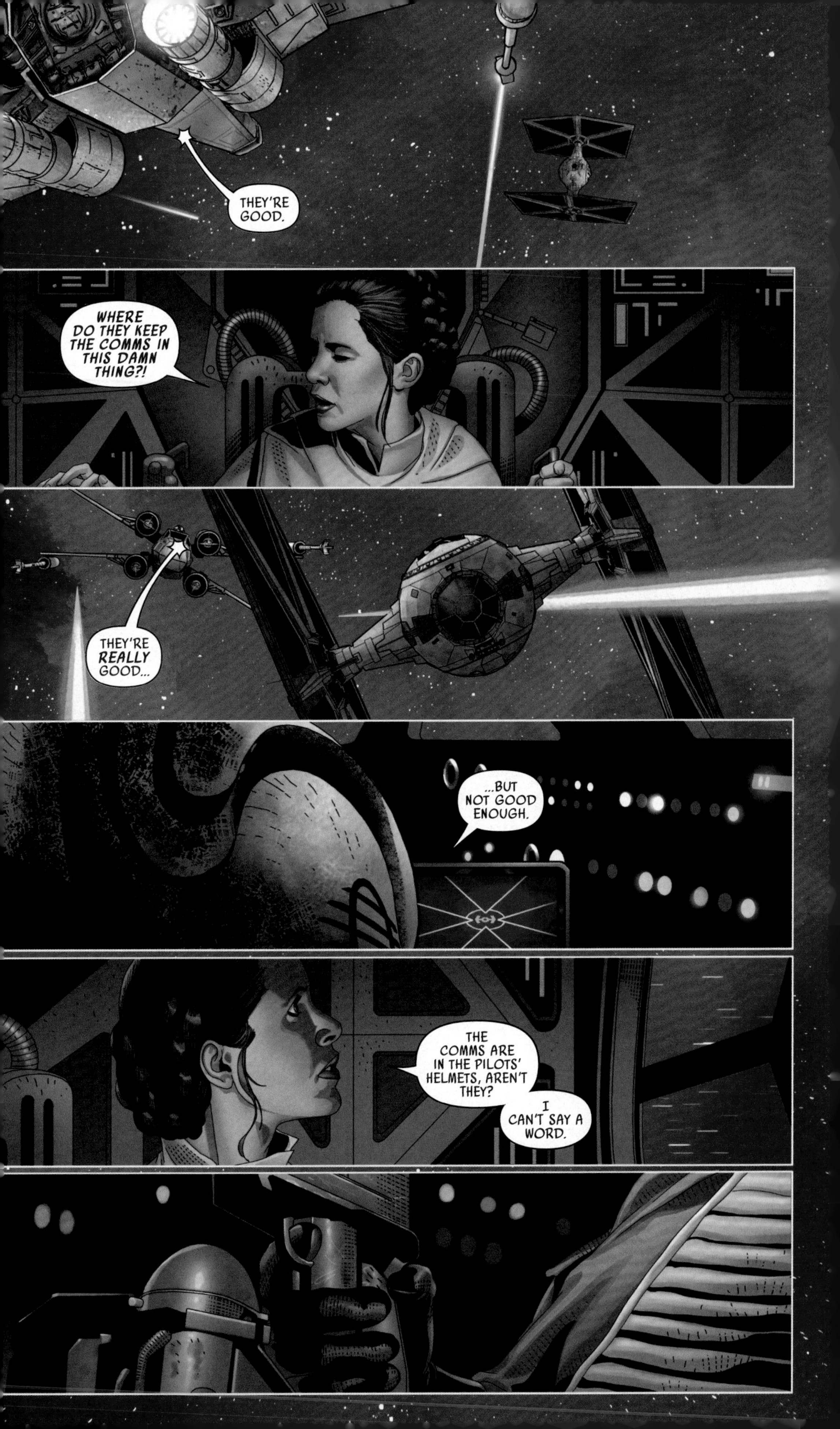
THEY'RE GOOD.
WHERE DO THEY KEEP THE COMMS IN THIS DAMN THING?!
THEY'RE REALLY GOOD...
...BUT NOT GOOD ENOUGH.
THE COMMS ARE IN THE PILOTS' HELMETS, AREN'T THEY?
I CAN'T SAY A WORD.

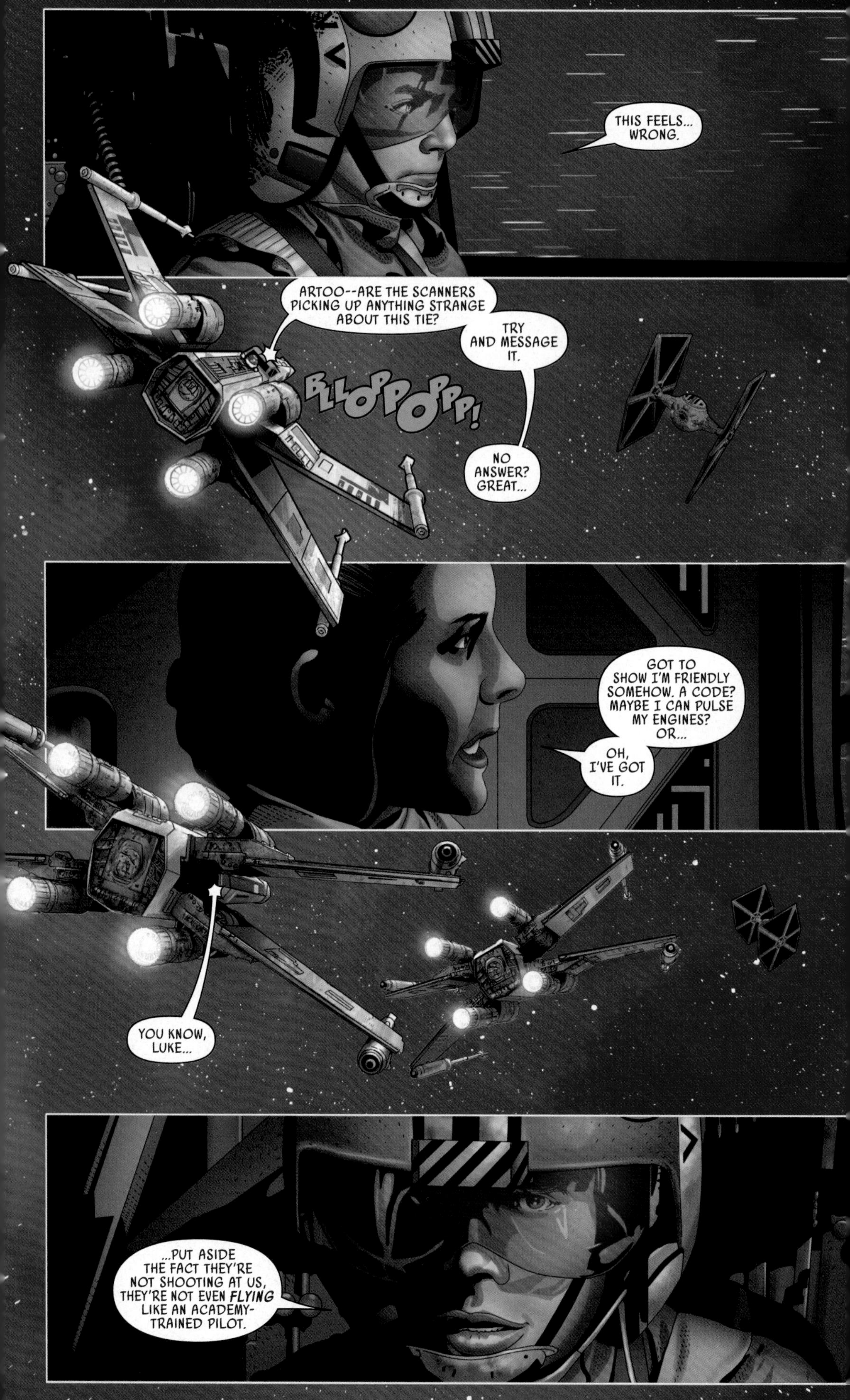

THIS FEELS... WRONG.
ARTOO--ARE THE SCANNERS PICKING UP ANYTHING STRANGE ABOUT THIS TIE?
TRY AND MESSAGE IT.
BLLOOPOPPP!
NO ANSWER? GREAT...
GOT TO SHOW I'M FRIENDLY SOMEHOW. A CODE? MAYBE I CAN PULSE MY ENGINES? OR...
OH, I'VE GOT IT.
YOU KNOW, LUKE...
...PUT ASIDE THE FACT THEY'RE NOT SHOOTING AT US, THEY'RE NOT EVEN *FLYING* LIKE AN ACADEMY-TRAINED PILOT.

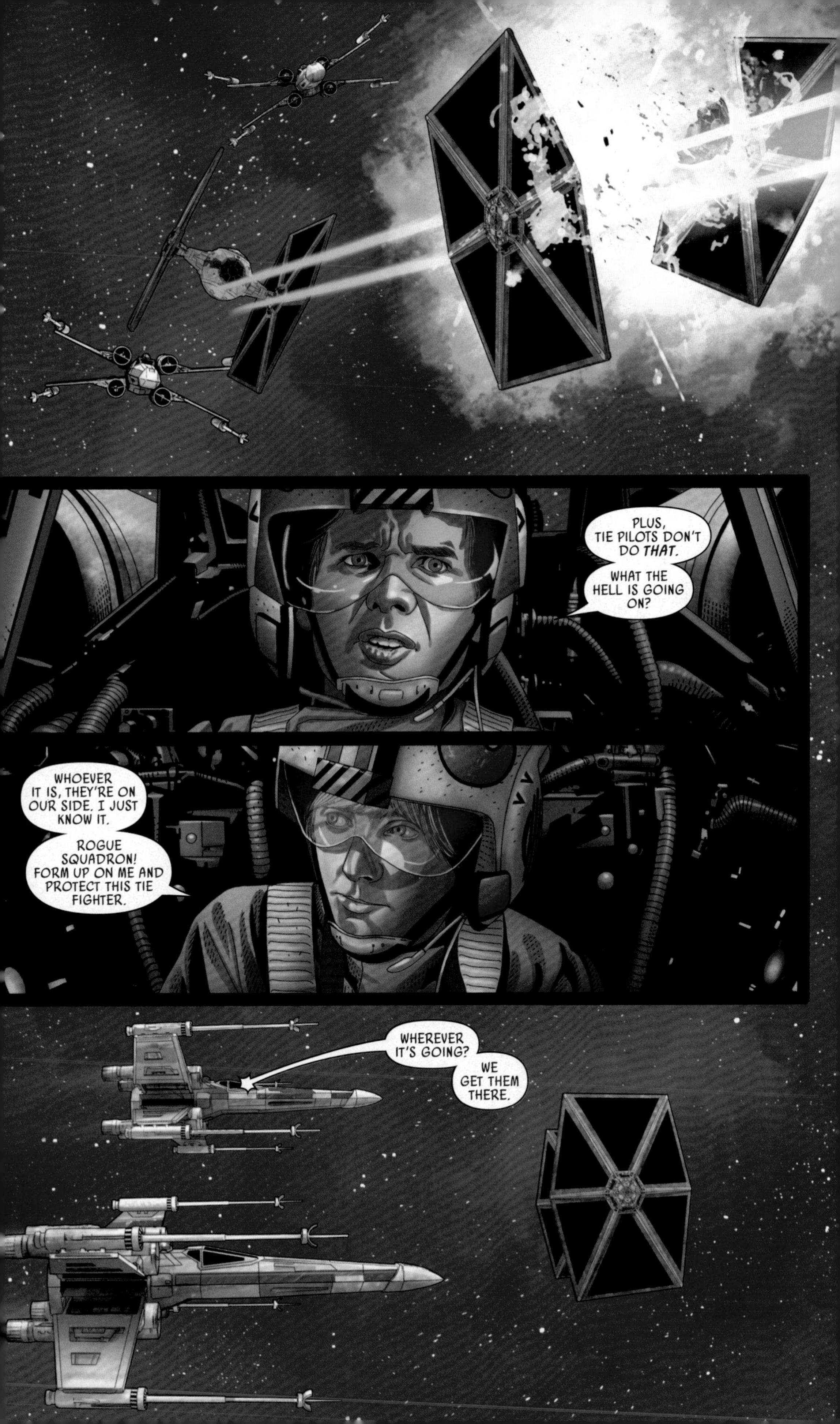
PLUS, TIE PILOTS DON'T DO *THAT.*
WHAT THE HELL IS GOING ON?
WHOEVER IT IS, THEY'RE ON OUR SIDE. I JUST KNOW IT.
ROGUE SQUADRON! FORM UP ON ME AND PROTECT THIS TIE FIGHTER.
WHEREVER IT'S GOING?
WE GET THEM THERE.

OH, THAT TICKLES!

MASTER...

OH, I CAN'T BELIEVE I HAVE BEEN SO RUDE.

I AM SEE-THREEPIO, HUMAN-CYBORG RELATIONS. HOW SHOULD I ADDRESS YOU?

MEORTI.

I AM SO GRATEFUL, MASTER MEORTI. MY DIODES WERE TERRIBLY EXPOSED. THIS IS ALMOST COMFORTABLE.

BUT SHOULDN'T YOU HAVE SOMETHING ELSE TO DO?

RIGHT NOW? MAKING YOU COMFORTABLE IS ALL I CAN DO.

BEING USEFUL WHERE WE CAN. SOMETIM IT'S ALL WE CAN DO.

THAT SEEMS A LOVELY SENTIMENT, MASTER MEORTI. AND--

WHAT'S HAPPENING OUT THERE? THE BATTLE SEEMS TO BE HEADING OUR WAY.

SOMEONE'S COMING IN TO LAND.

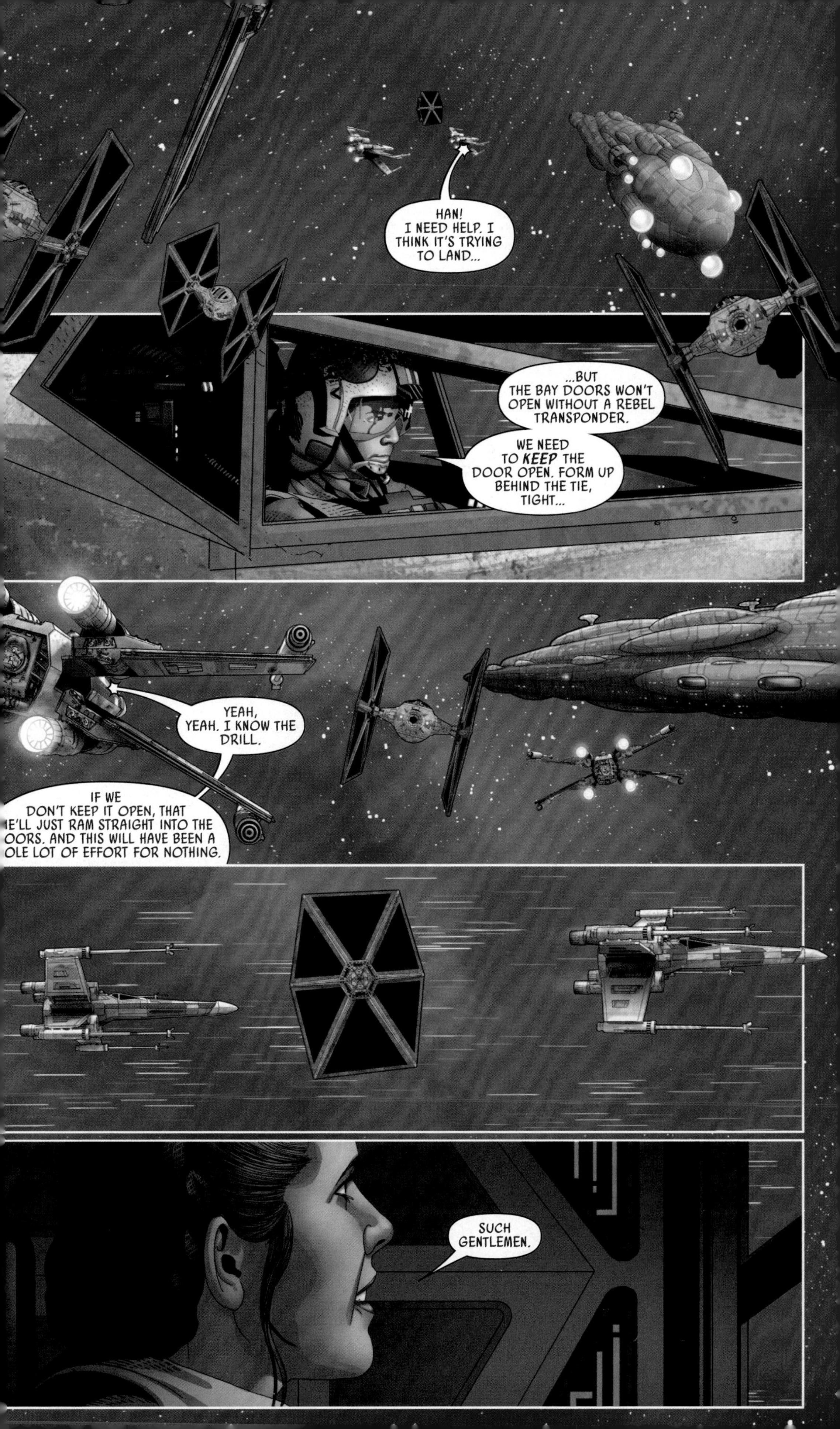
HAN! I NEED HELP. I THINK IT'S TRYING TO LAND...
...BUT THE BAY DOORS WON'T OPEN WITHOUT A REBEL TRANSPONDER.
WE NEED TO **KEEP** THE DOOR OPEN. FORM UP BEHIND THE TIE, TIGHT...
YEAH, YEAH. I KNOW THE DRILL.
IF WE DON'T KEEP IT OPEN, THAT E'LL JUST RAM STRAIGHT INTO THE OORS. AND THIS WILL HAVE BEEN A OLE LOT OF EFFORT FOR NOTHING.
SUCH GENTLEMEN.

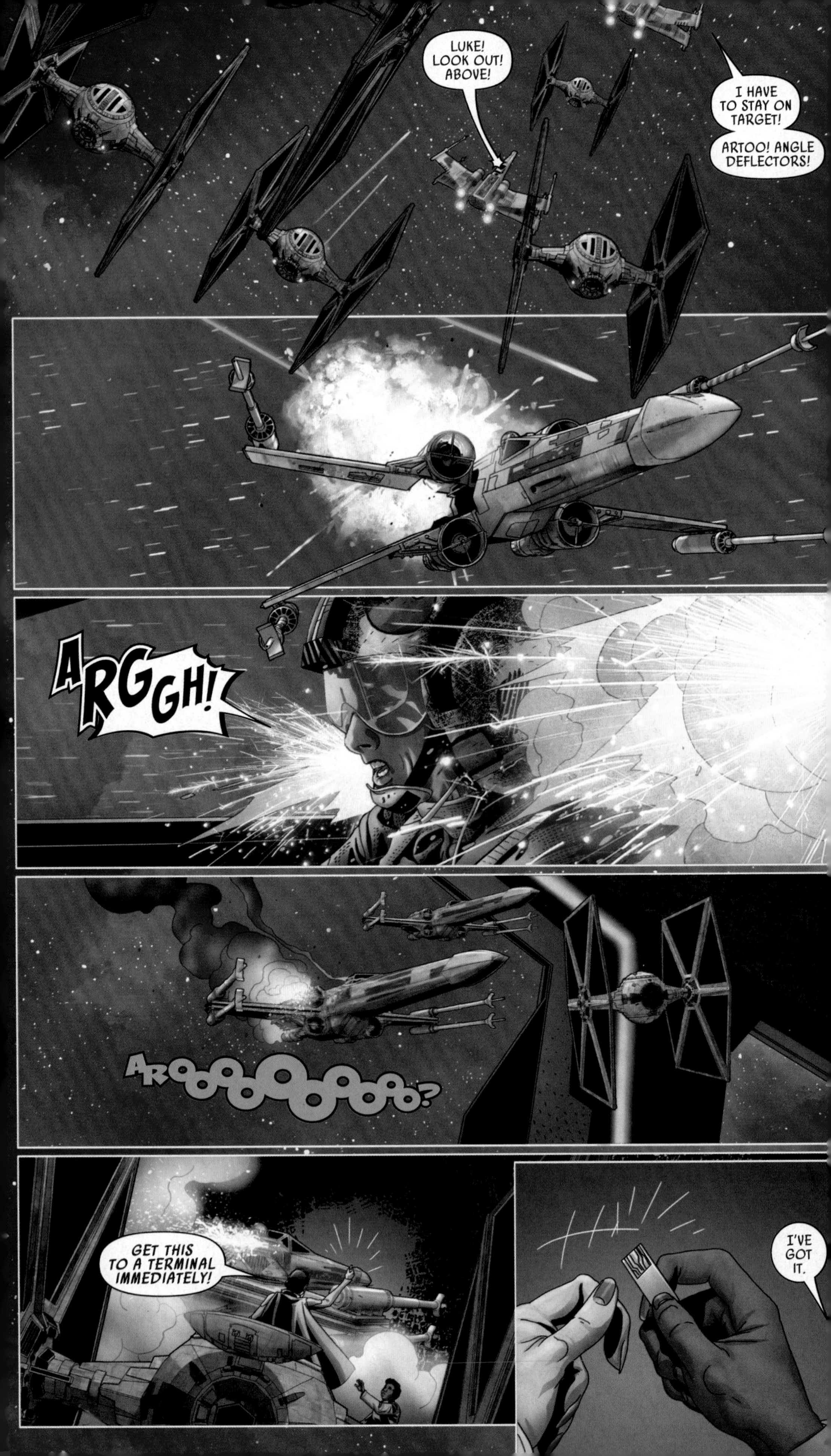
LUKE! LOOK OUT! ABOVE!
I HAVE TO STAY ON TARGET!
ARTOO! ANGLE DEFLECTORS!
ARGGH!
AROOOOOOOOOOO?
GET THIS TO A TERMINAL IMMEDIATELY!
I'VE GOT IT.

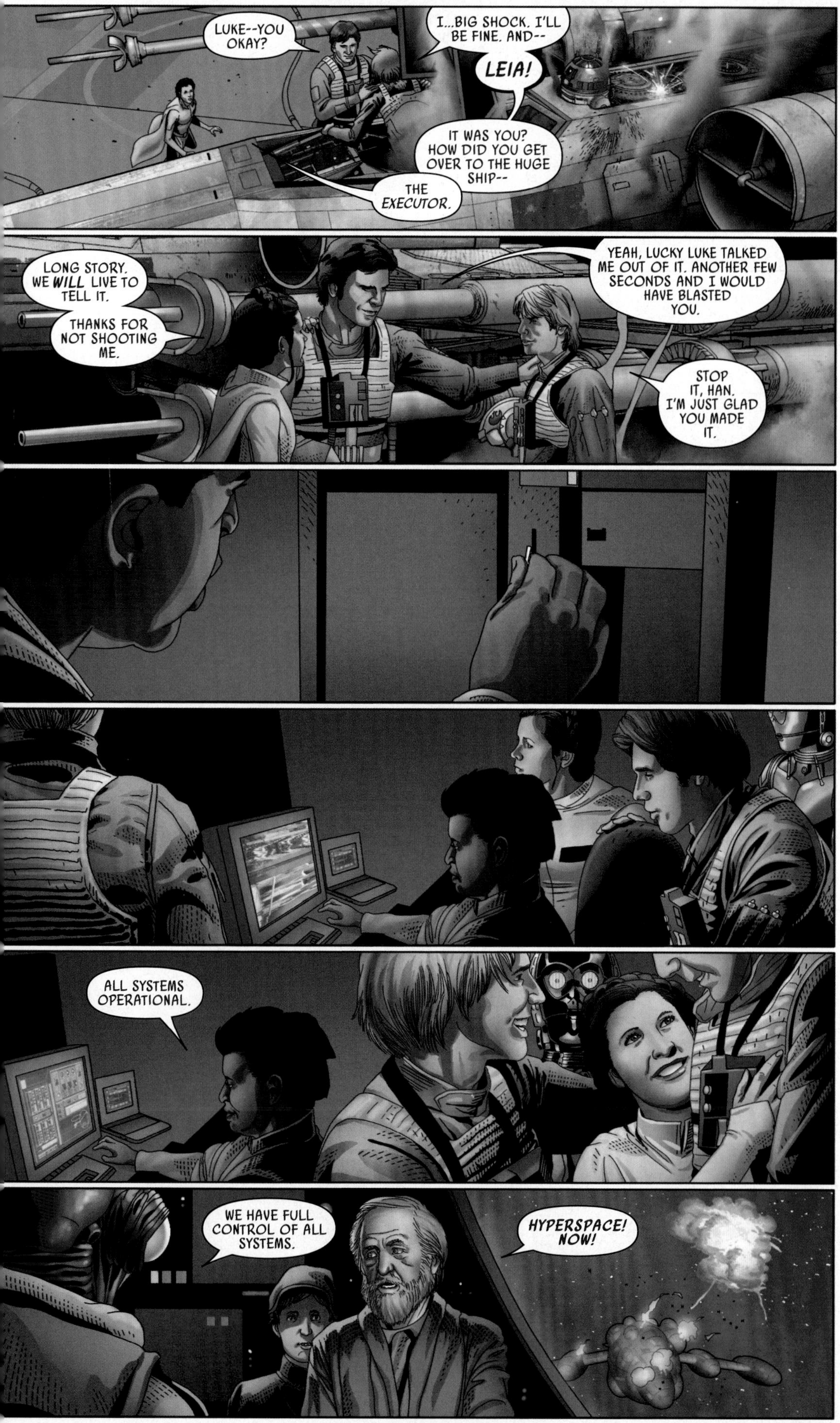
LUKE--YOU OKAY?
I...BIG SHOCK. I'LL BE FINE. AND--
LEIA!
IT WAS YOU? HOW DID YOU GET OVER TO THE HUGE SHIP--
THE EXECUTOR.
LONG STORY. WE WILL LIVE TO TELL IT.
THANKS FOR NOT SHOOTING ME.
YEAH, LUCKY LUKE TALKED ME OUT OF IT. ANOTHER FEW SECONDS AND I WOULD HAVE BLASTED YOU.
STOP IT, HAN. I'M JUST GLAD YOU MADE IT.
ALL SYSTEMS OPERATIONAL.
WE HAVE FULL CONTROL OF ALL SYSTEMS.
HYPERSPACE! NOW!

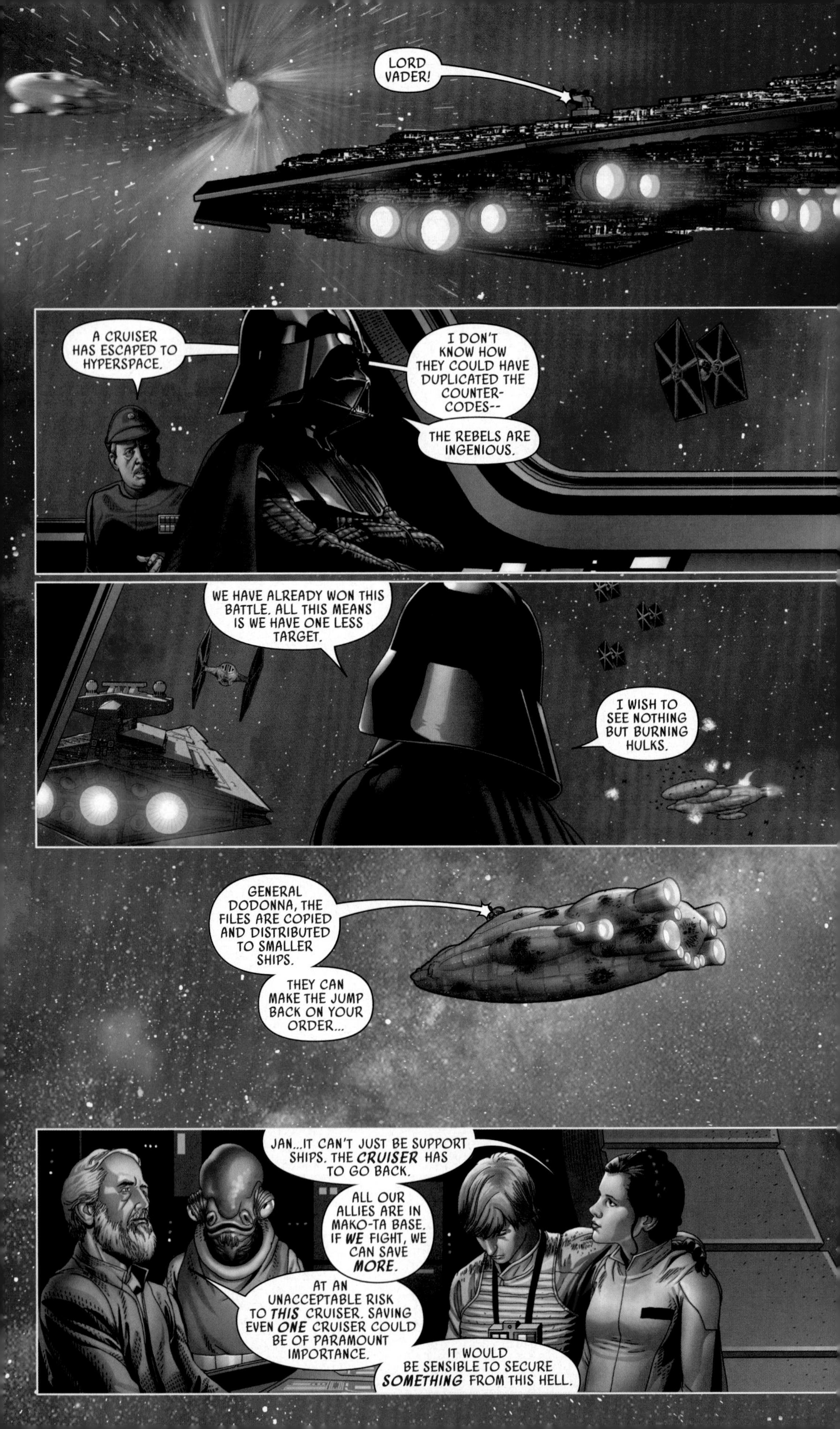
LORD VADER!
A CRUISER HAS ESCAPED TO HYPERSPACE.
I DON'T KNOW HOW THEY COULD HAVE DUPLICATED THE COUNTER-CODES--
THE REBELS ARE INGENIOUS.
WE HAVE ALREADY WON THIS BATTLE. ALL THIS MEANS IS WE HAVE ONE LESS TARGET.
I WISH TO SEE NOTHING BUT BURNING HULKS.
GENERAL DODONNA, THE FILES ARE COPIED AND DISTRIBUTED TO SMALLER SHIPS.
THEY CAN MAKE THE JUMP BACK ON YOUR ORDER...
JAN...IT CAN'T JUST BE SUPPORT SHIPS. THE CRUISER HAS TO GO BACK.
ALL OUR ALLIES ARE IN MAKO-TA BASE. IF WE FIGHT, WE CAN SAVE MORE.
AT AN UNACCEPTABLE RISK TO THIS CRUISER. SAVING EVEN ONE CRUISER COULD BE OF PARAMOUNT IMPORTANCE.
IT WOULD BE SENSIBLE TO SECURE SOMETHING FROM THIS HELL.

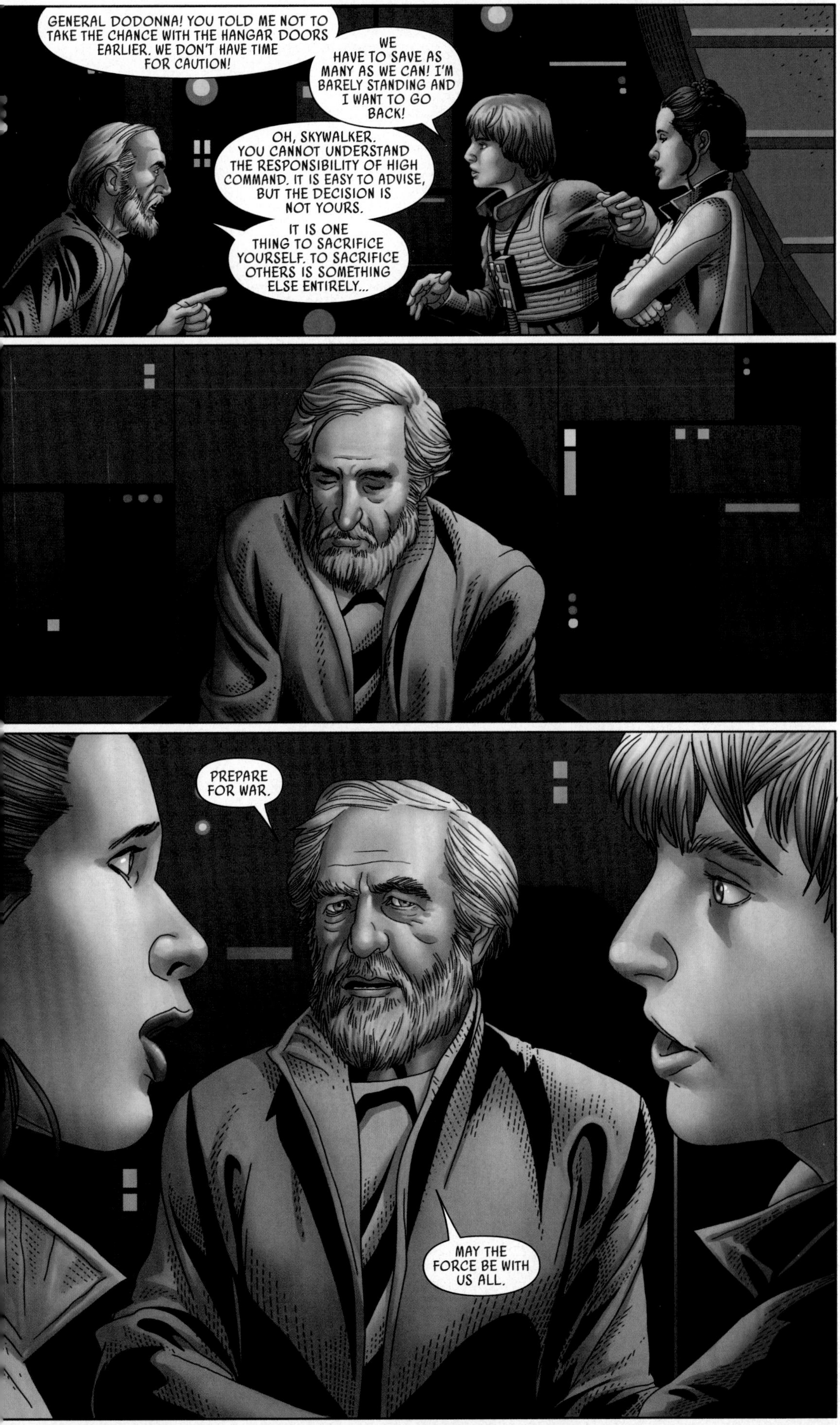
GENERAL DODONNA! YOU TOLD ME NOT TO TAKE THE CHANCE WITH THE HANGAR DOORS EARLIER. WE DON'T HAVE TIME FOR CAUTION!
WE HAVE TO SAVE AS MANY AS WE CAN! I'M BARELY STANDING AND I WANT TO GO BACK!
OH, SKYWALKER. YOU CANNOT UNDERSTAND THE RESPONSIBILITY OF HIGH COMMAND. IT IS EASY TO ADVISE, BUT THE DECISION IS NOT YOURS.
IT IS ONE THING TO SACRIFICE YOURSELF. TO SACRIFICE OTHERS IS SOMETHING ELSE ENTIRELY...
PREPARE FOR WAR.
MAY THE FORCE BE WITH US ALL.

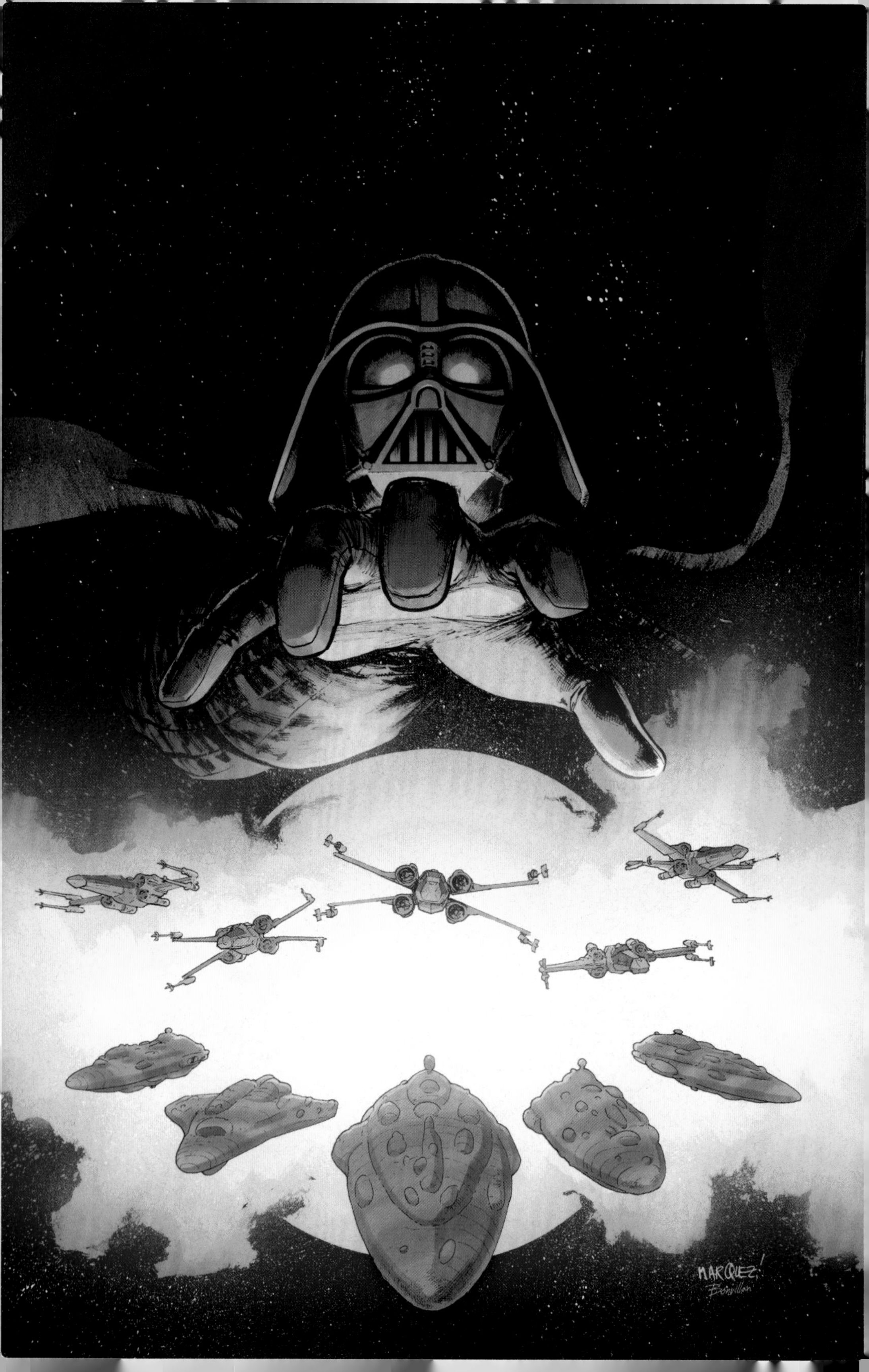
MARQUEZ!

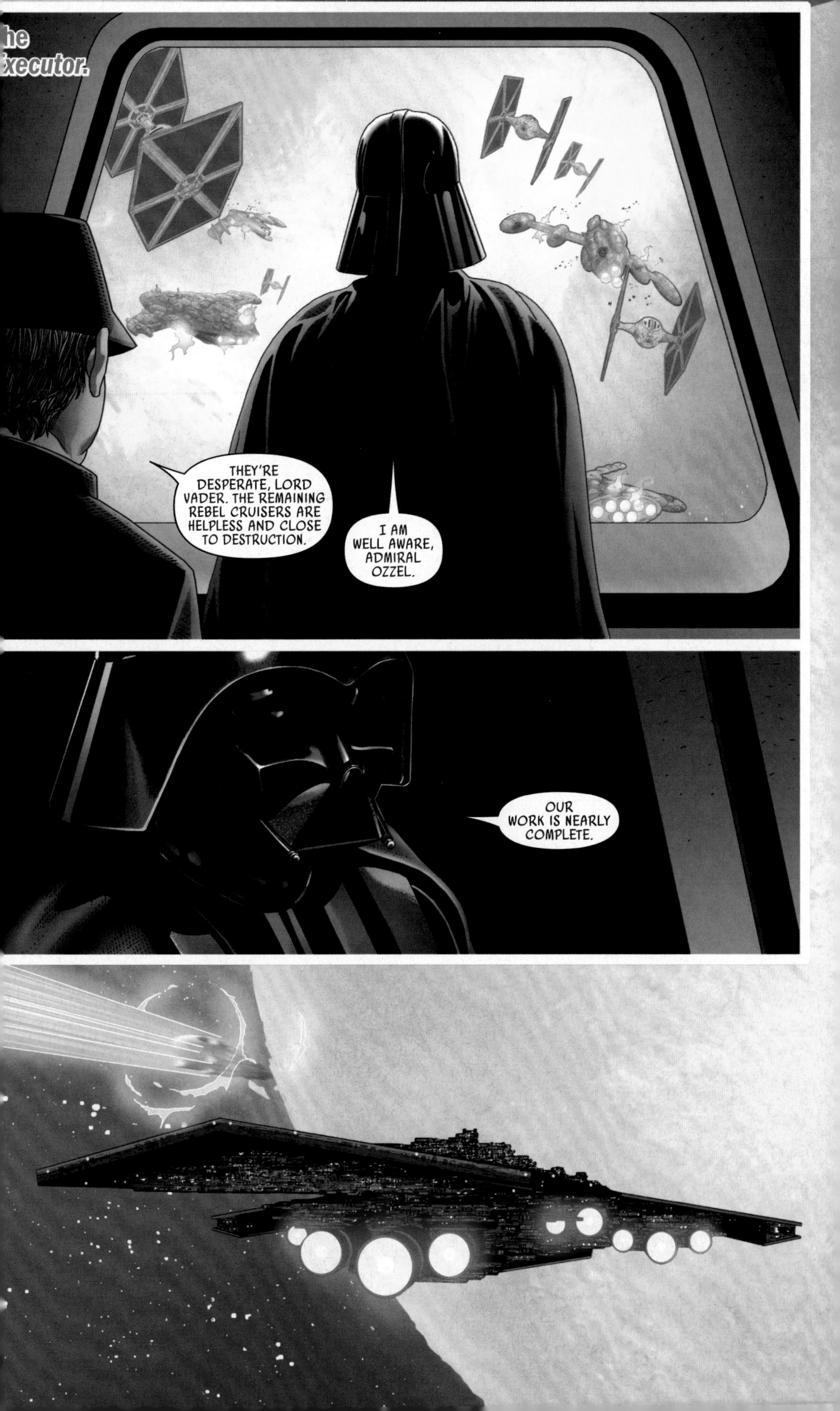

...he ...xecutor.
THEY'RE DESPERATE, LORD VADER. THE REMAINING REBEL CRUISERS ARE HELPLESS AND CLOSE TO DESTRUCTION.
I AM WELL AWARE, ADMIRAL OZZEL.
OUR WORK IS NEARLY COMPLETE.

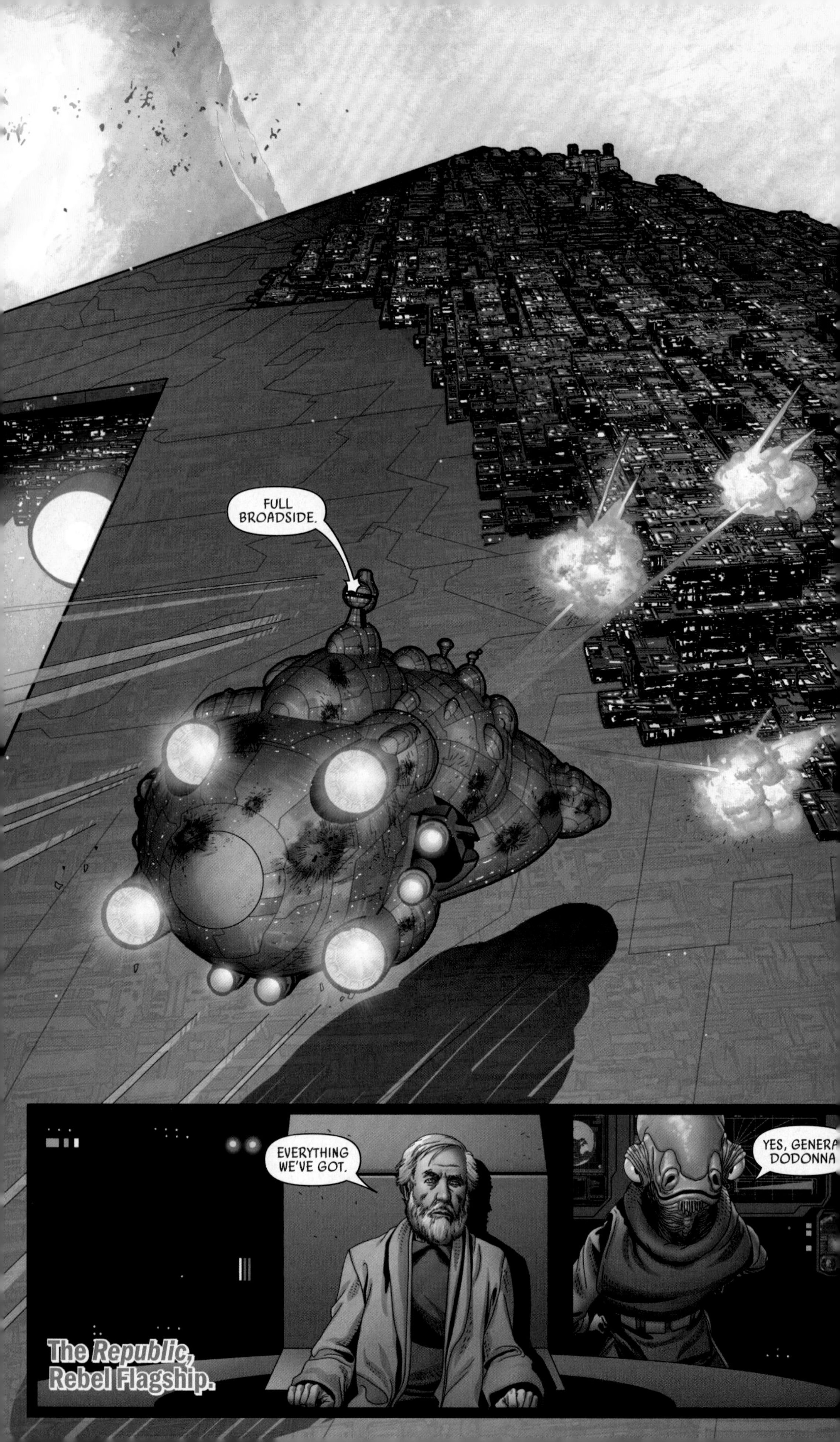
FULL BROADSIDE.
The Republic, Rebel Flagship.
EVERYTHING WE'VE GOT.
YES, GENERA DODONNA

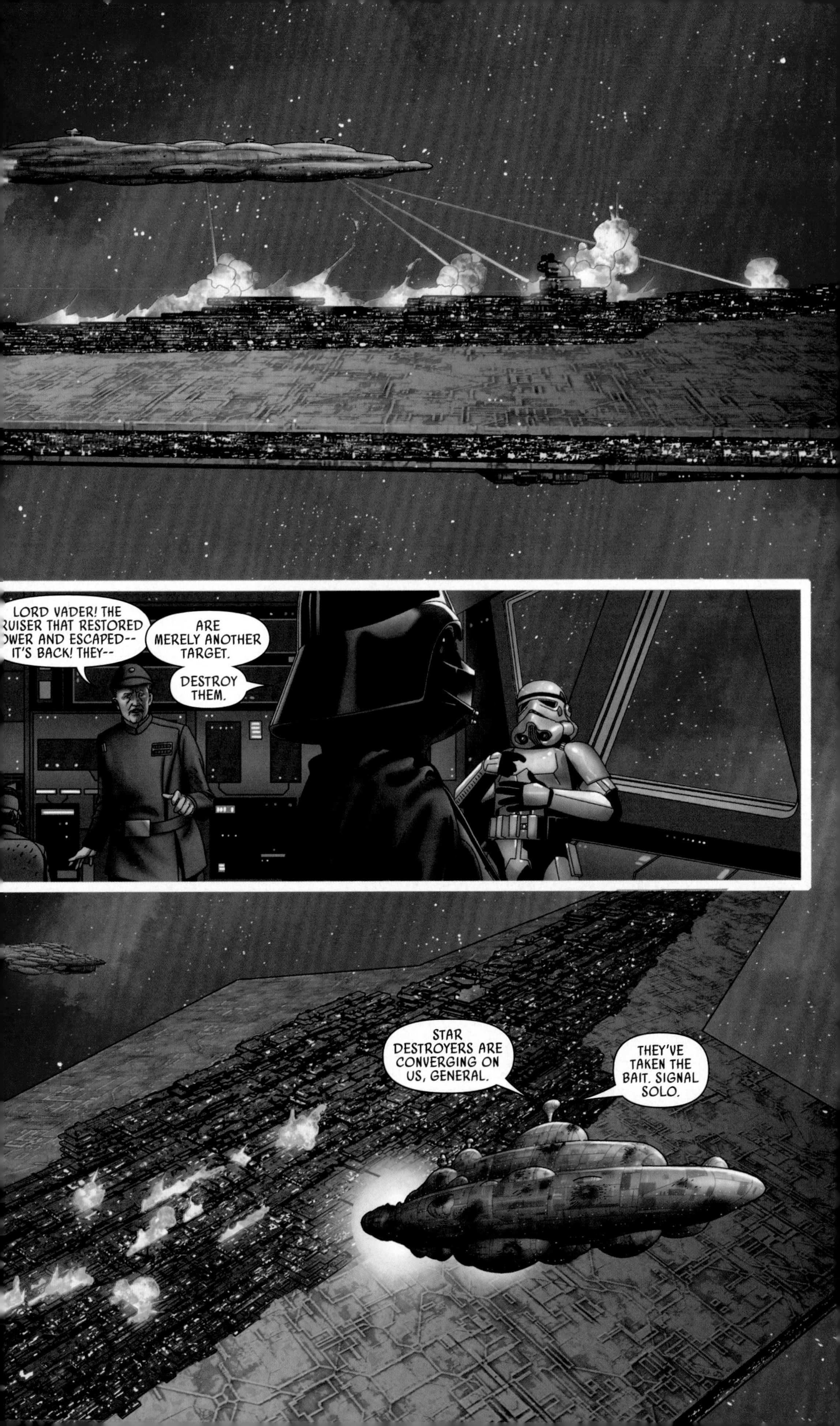
LORD VADER! THE RUISER THAT RESTORED OWER AND ESCAPED-- IT'S BACK! THEY--
ARE MERELY ANOTHER TARGET.
DESTROY THEM.
STAR DESTROYERS ARE CONVERGING ON US, GENERAL.
THEY'VE TAKEN THE BAIT. SIGNAL SOLO.

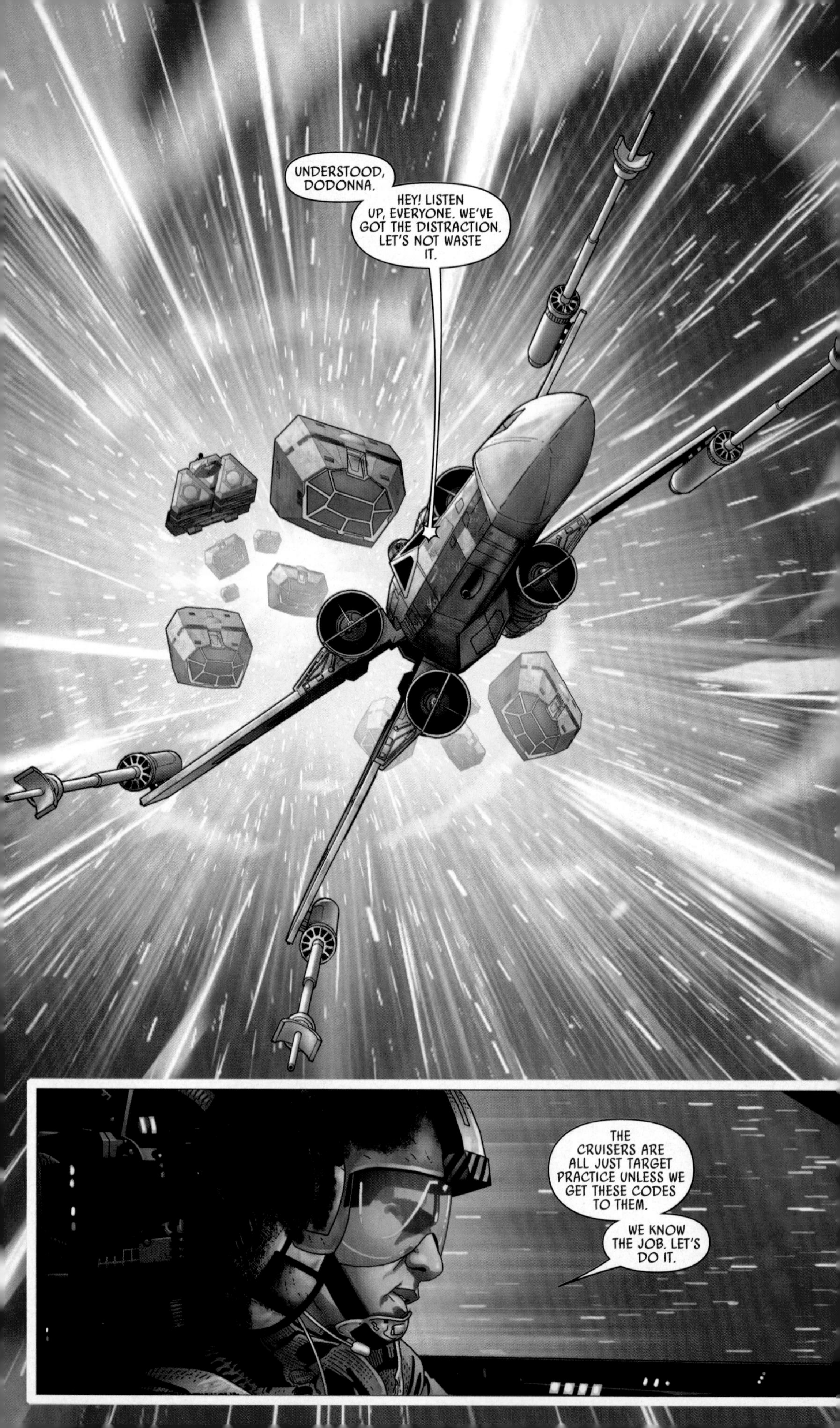
UNDERSTOOD, DODONNA.
HEY! LISTEN UP, EVERYONE. WE'VE GOT THE DISTRACTION. LET'S NOT WASTE IT.
THE CRUISERS ARE ALL JUST TARGET PRACTICE UNLESS WE GET THESE CODES TO THEM.
WE KNOW THE JOB. LET'S DO IT.

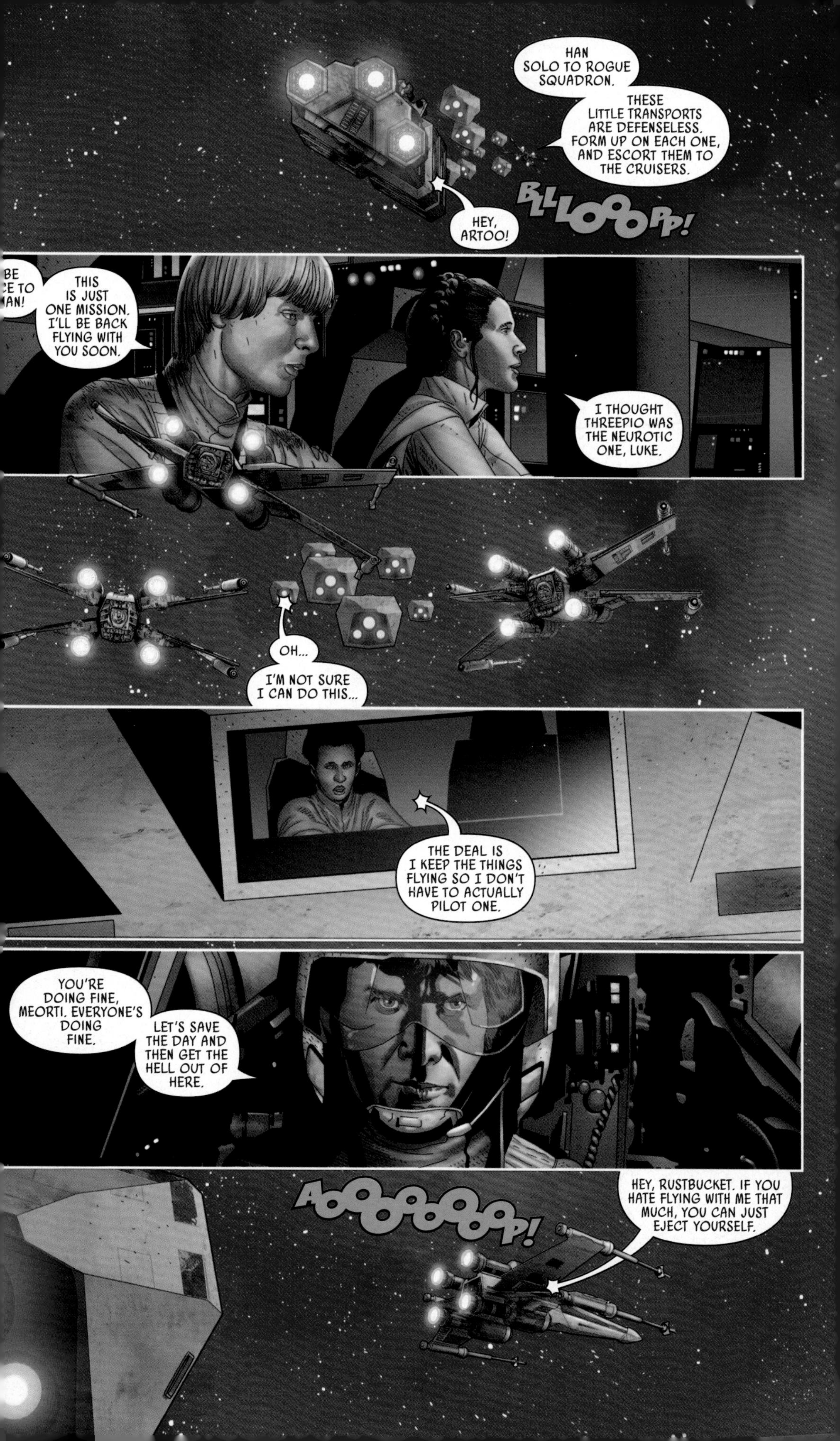
HAN SOLO TO ROGUE SQUADRON.
THESE LITTLE TRANSPORTS ARE DEFENSELESS. FORM UP ON EACH ONE, AND ESCORT THEM TO THE CRUISERS.
HEY, ARTOO!
BLLLOOOPP!
BE
CE TO
MAN!
THIS IS JUST ONE MISSION. I'LL BE BACK FLYING WITH YOU SOON.
I THOUGHT THREEPIO WAS THE NEUROTIC ONE, LUKE.
OH...
I'M NOT SURE I CAN DO THIS...
THE DEAL IS I KEEP THE THINGS FLYING SO I DON'T HAVE TO ACTUALLY PILOT ONE.
YOU'RE DOING FINE, MEORTI. EVERYONE'S DOING FINE.
LET'S SAVE THE DAY AND THEN GET THE HELL OUT OF HERE.
AOOOOOOOOP!
HEY, RUSTBUCKET. IF YOU HATE FLYING WITH ME THAT MUCH, YOU CAN JUST EJECT YOURSELF.

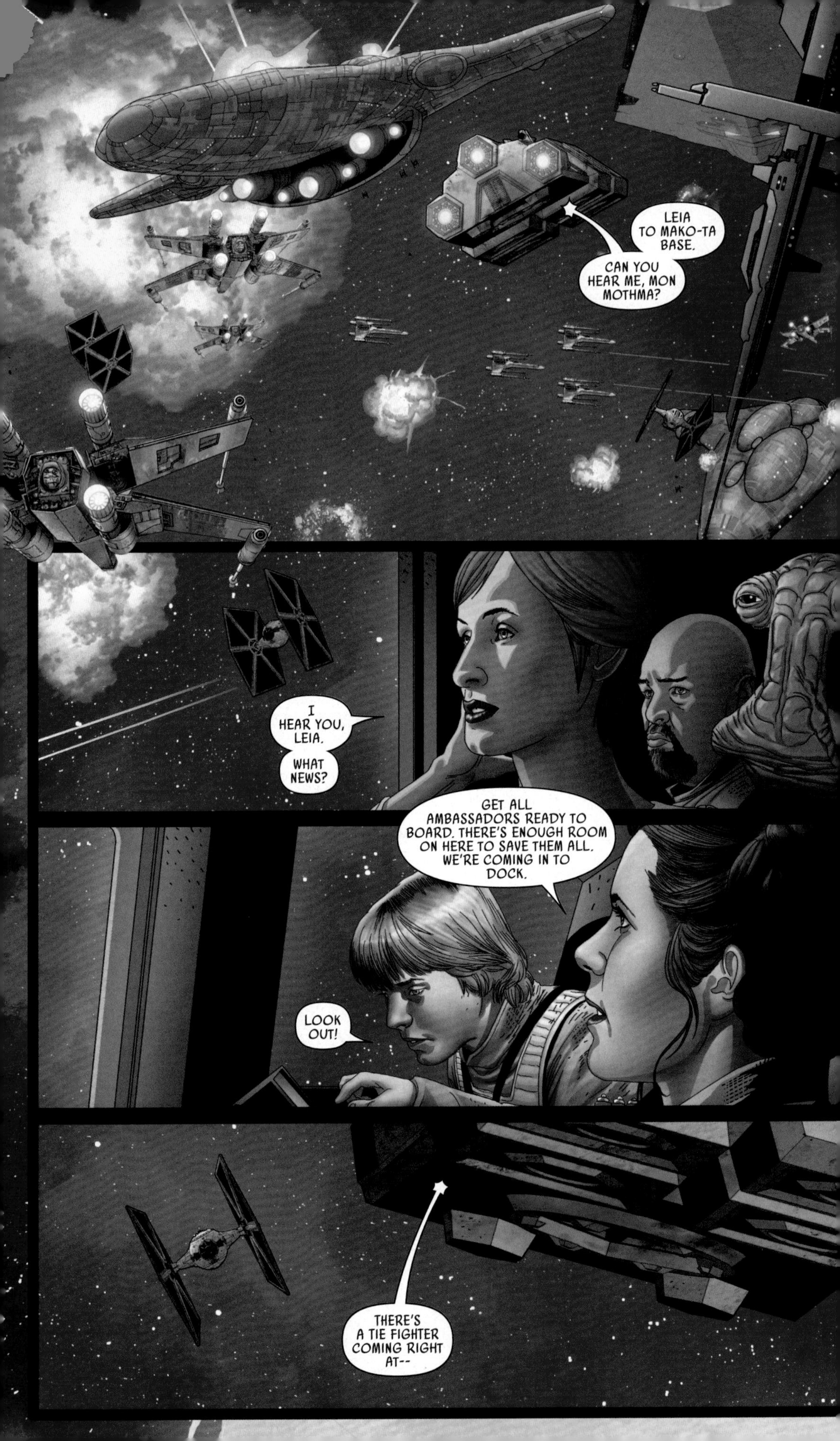
LEIA TO MAKO-TA BASE.
CAN YOU HEAR ME, MON MOTHMA?
I HEAR YOU, LEIA.
WHAT NEWS?
GET ALL AMBASSADORS READY TO BOARD. THERE'S ENOUGH ROOM ON HERE TO SAVE THEM ALL. WE'RE COMING IN TO DOCK.
LOOK OUT!
THERE'S A TIE FIGHTER COMING RIGHT AT--

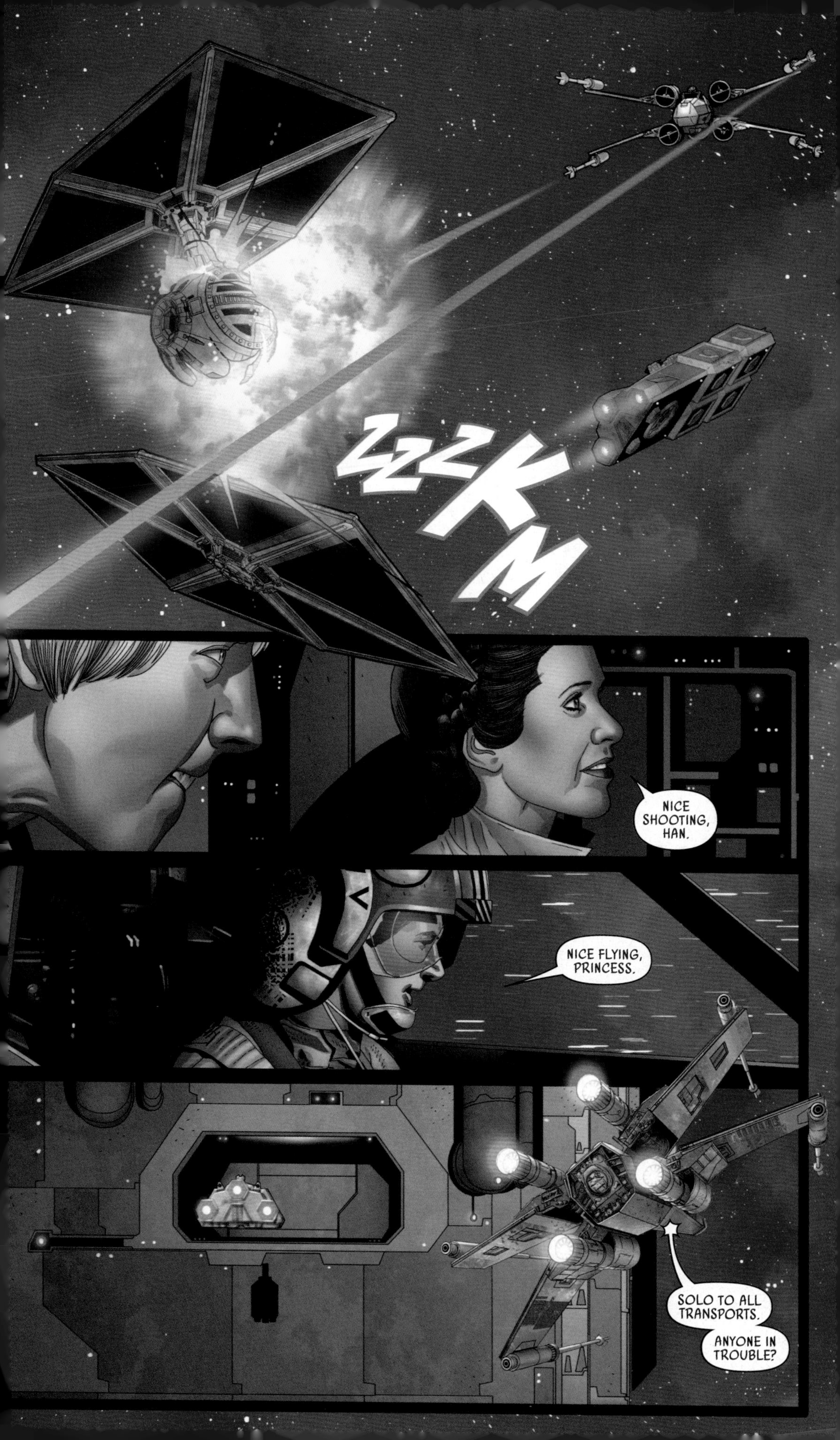
ZZZKM
NICE SHOOTING, HAN.
NICE FLYING, PRINCESS.
SOLO TO ALL TRANSPORTS.
ANYONE IN TROUBLE?

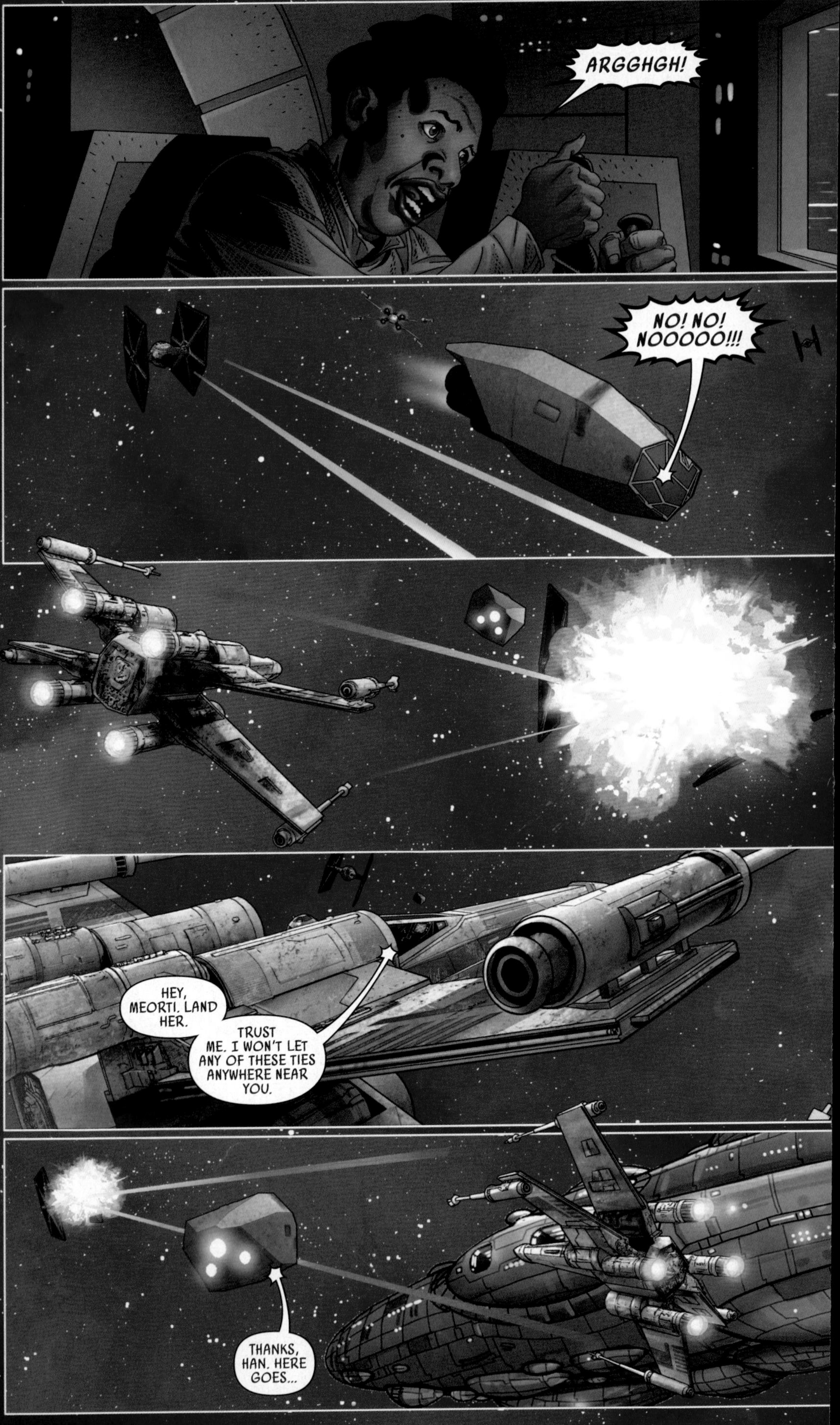

ARGGHGH!
NO! NO! NOOOOO!!!
HEY, MEORTI. LAND HER.
TRUST ME. I WON'T LET ANY OF THESE TIES ANYWHERE NEAR YOU.
THANKS, HAN. HERE GOES...

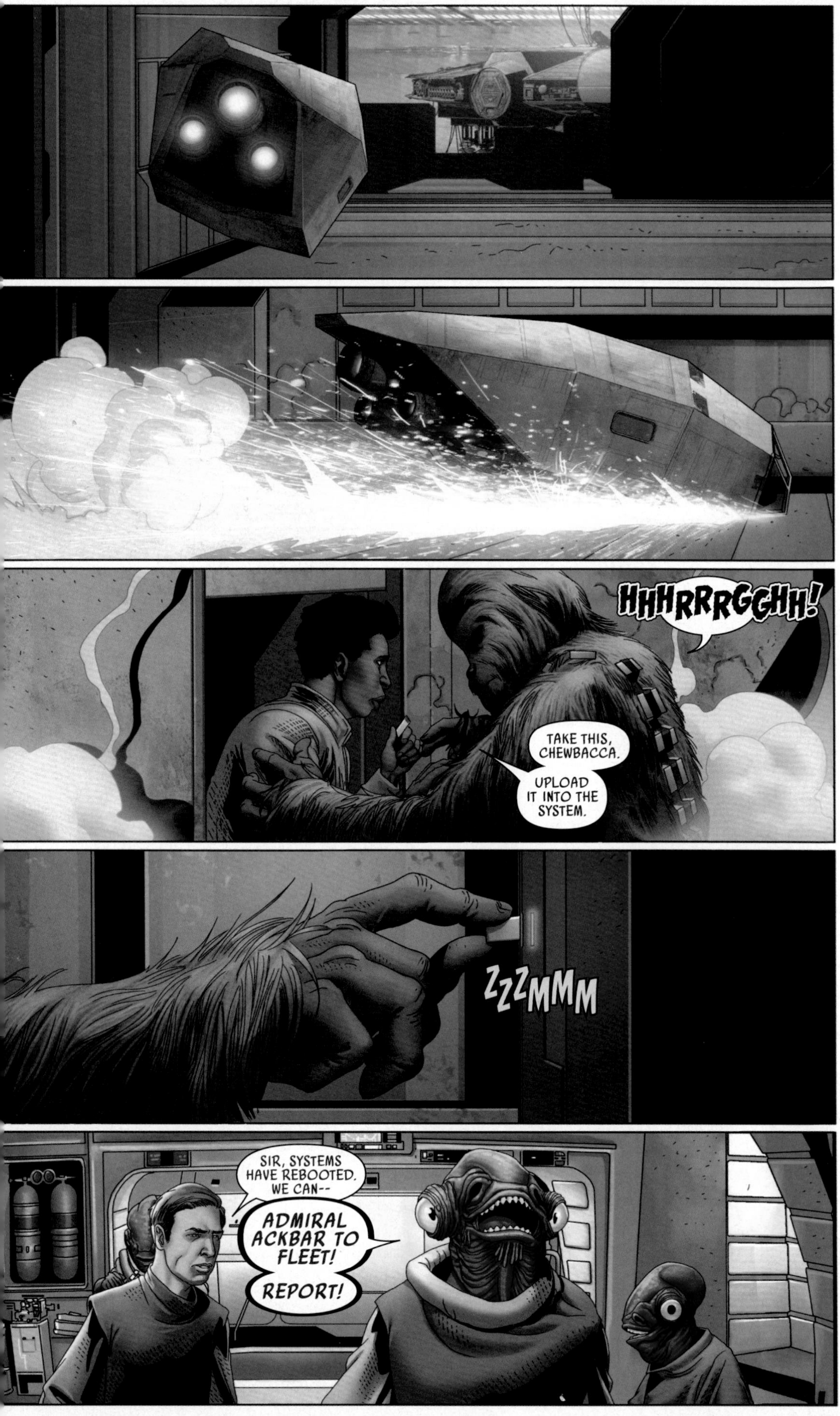
HHHRRRGGHH!
TAKE THIS, CHEWBACCA.
UPLOAD IT INTO THE SYSTEM.
ZZZMMM
SIR, SYSTEMS HAVE REBOOTED. WE CAN--
ADMIRAL ACKBAR TO FLEET!
REPORT!

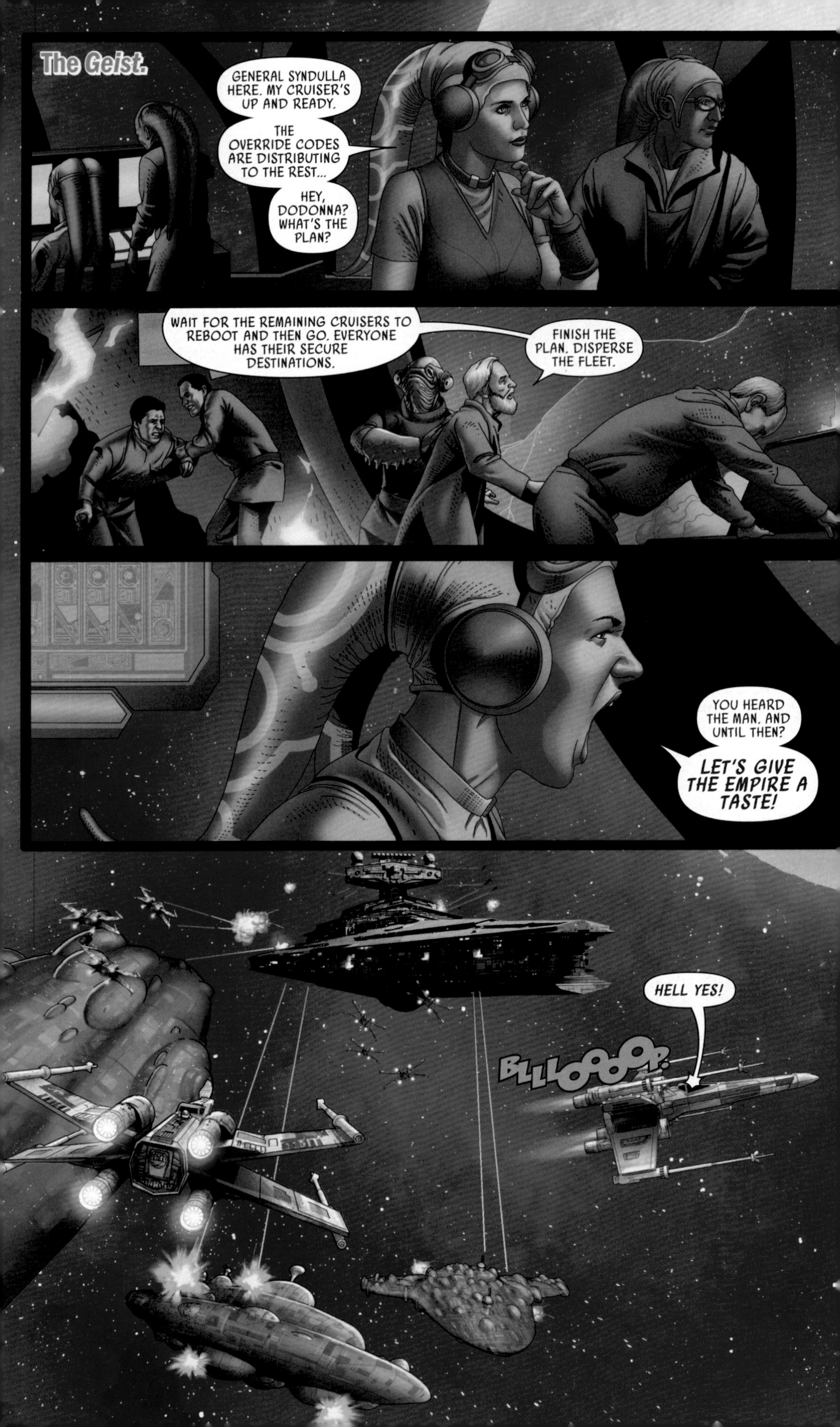

The Geist.
GENERAL SYNDULLA HERE. MY CRUISER'S UP AND READY.
THE OVERRIDE CODES ARE DISTRIBUTING TO THE REST...
HEY, DODONNA? WHAT'S THE PLAN?
WAIT FOR THE REMAINING CRUISERS TO REBOOT AND THEN GO. EVERYONE HAS THEIR SECURE DESTINATIONS.
FINISH THE PLAN. DISPERSE THE FLEET.
YOU HEARD THE MAN. AND UNTIL THEN?
LET'S GIVE THE EMPIRE A TASTE!
HELL YES!
BLLLOOOOP.

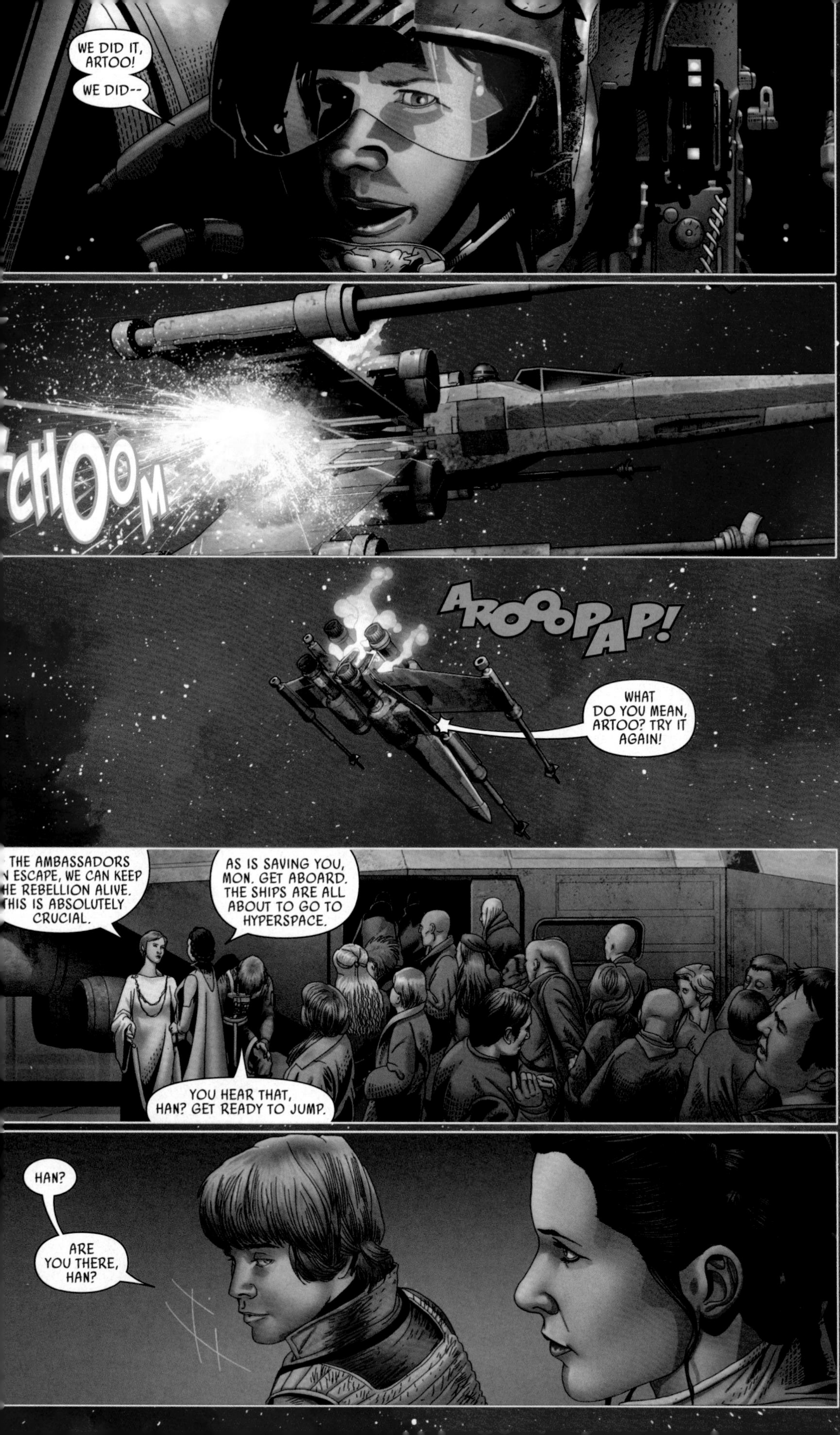
WE DID IT, ARTOO!
WE DID--
CHOOM
AROOOPAP!
WHAT DO YOU MEAN, ARTOO? TRY IT AGAIN!
THE AMBASSADORS N ESCAPE, WE CAN KEEP HE REBELLION ALIVE. THIS IS ABSOLUTELY CRUCIAL.
AS IS SAVING YOU, MON. GET ABOARD. THE SHIPS ARE ALL ABOUT TO GO TO HYPERSPACE.
YOU HEAR THAT, HAN? GET READY TO JUMP.
HAN?
ARE YOU THERE, HAN?

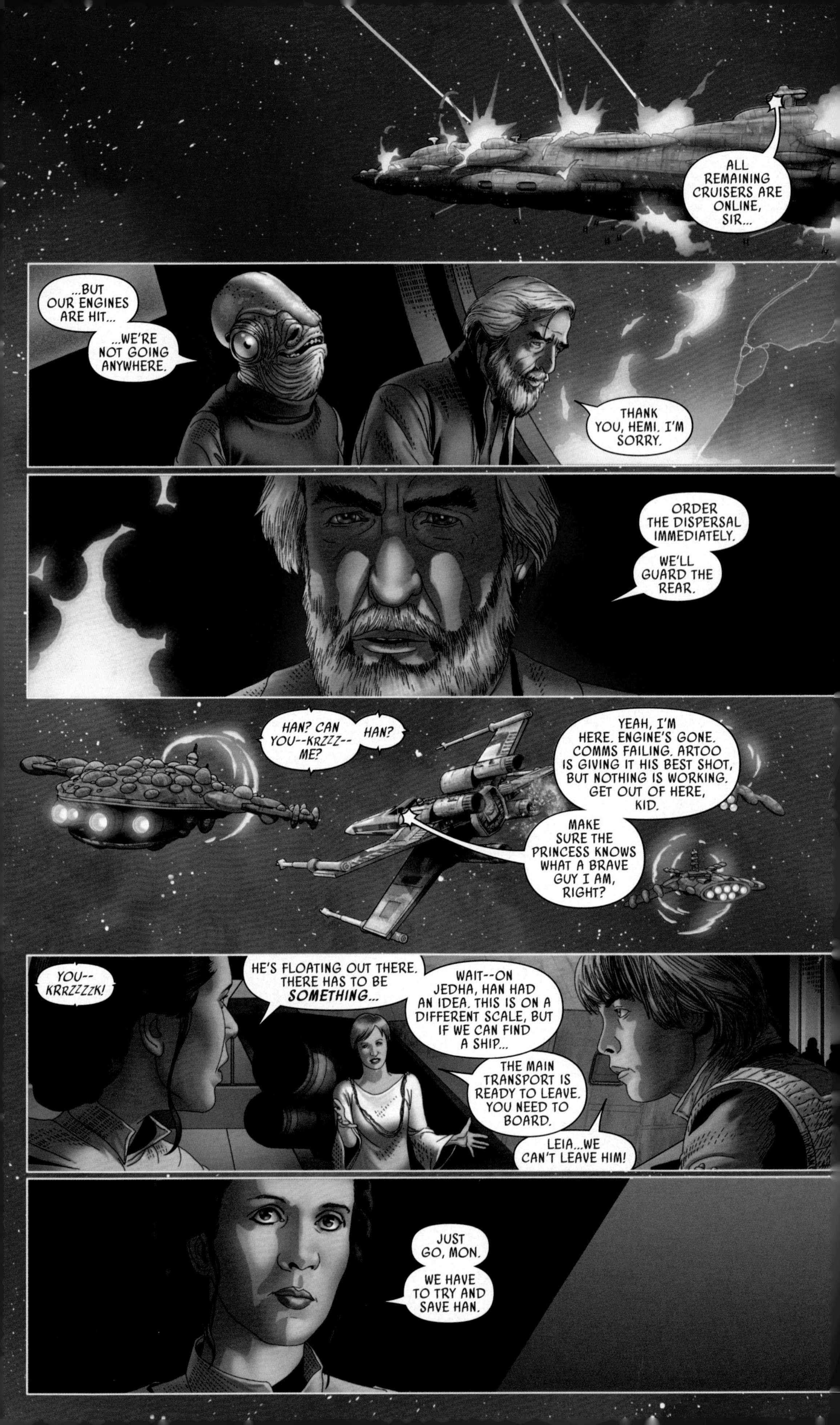
ALL REMAINING CRUISERS ARE ONLINE, SIR...
...BUT OUR ENGINES ARE HIT...
...WE'RE NOT GOING ANYWHERE.
THANK YOU, HEMI. I'M SORRY.
ORDER THE DISPERSAL IMMEDIATELY.
WE'LL GUARD THE REAR.
HAN? CAN YOU--KRZZZ--ME?
HAN?
YEAH, I'M HERE. ENGINE'S GONE. COMMS FAILING. ARTOO IS GIVING IT HIS BEST SHOT, BUT NOTHING IS WORKING. GET OUT OF HERE, KID.
MAKE SURE THE PRINCESS KNOWS WHAT A BRAVE GUY I AM, RIGHT?
YOU--KRRZZZZK!
HE'S FLOATING OUT THERE. THERE HAS TO BE SOMETHING...
WAIT--ON JEDHA, HAN HAD AN IDEA. THIS IS ON A DIFFERENT SCALE, BUT IF WE CAN FIND A SHIP...
THE MAIN TRANSPORT IS READY TO LEAVE. YOU NEED TO BOARD.
LEIA...WE CAN'T LEAVE HIM!
JUST GO, MON.
WE HAVE TO TRY AND SAVE HAN.

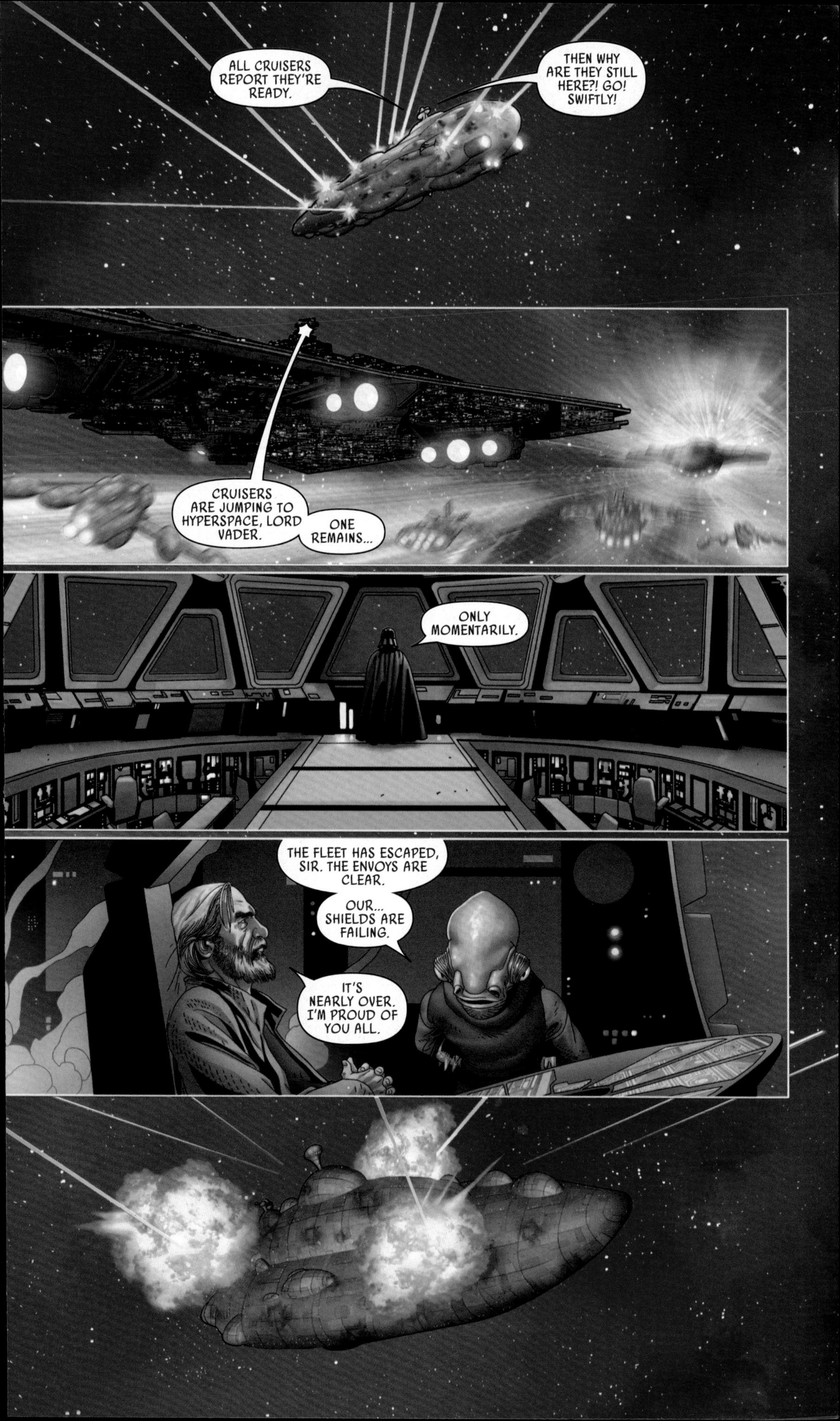
ALL CRUISERS REPORT THEY'RE READY.
THEN WHY ARE THEY STILL HERE?! GO! SWIFTLY!
CRUISERS ARE JUMPING TO HYPERSPACE, LORD VADER.
ONE REMAINS...
ONLY MOMENTARILY.
THE FLEET HAS ESCAPED, SIR. THE ENVOYS ARE CLEAR.
OUR... SHIELDS ARE FAILING.
IT'S NEARLY OVER. I'M PROUD OF YOU ALL.

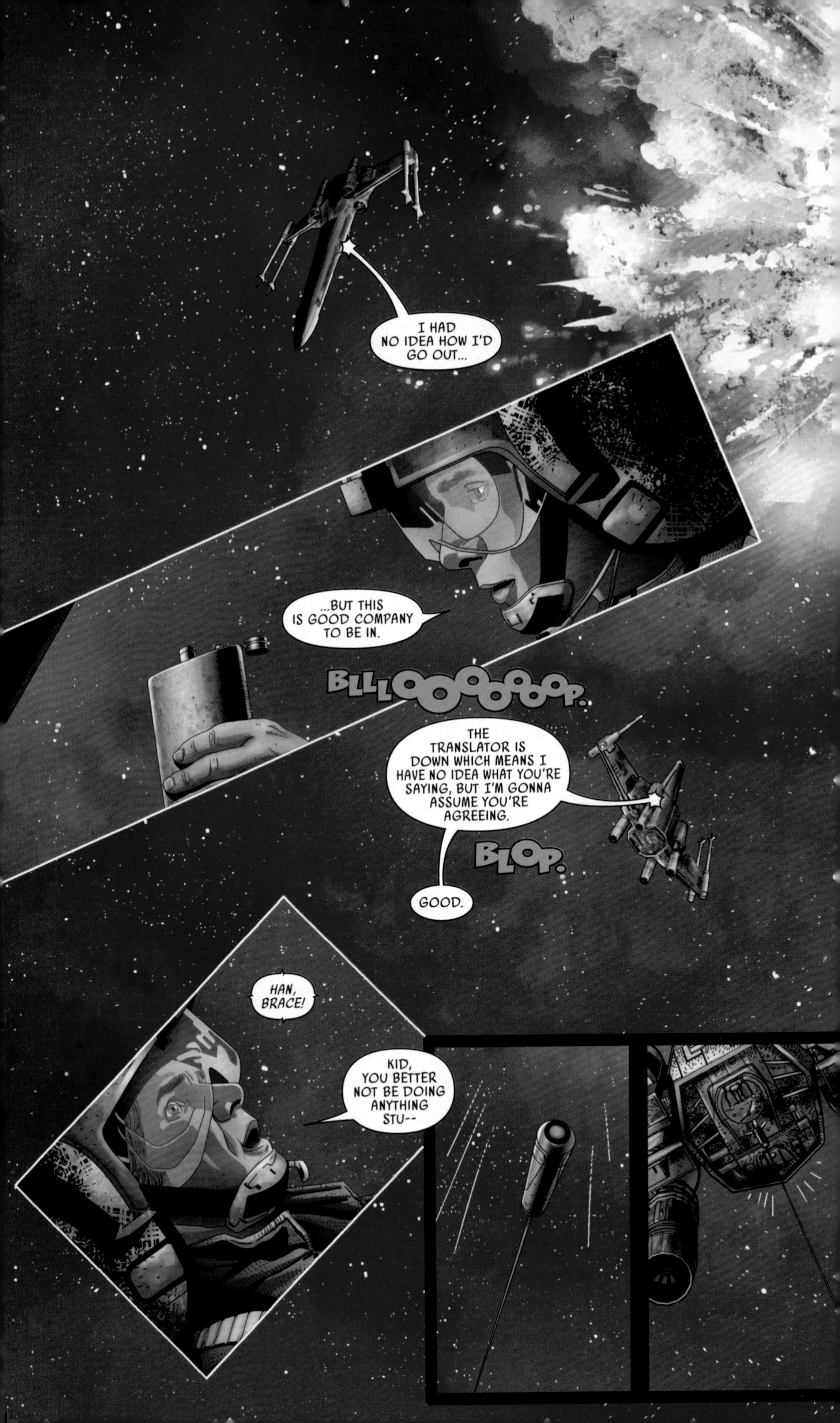
I HAD NO IDEA HOW I'D GO OUT...
...BUT THIS IS GOOD COMPANY TO BE IN.
BLLLOOOOOOOP.
THE TRANSLATOR IS DOWN WHICH MEANS I HAVE NO IDEA WHAT YOU'RE SAYING, BUT I'M GONNA ASSUME YOU'RE AGREEING.
BLOP.
GOOD.
HAN, BRACE!
KID, YOU BETTER NOT BE DOING ANYTHING STU--

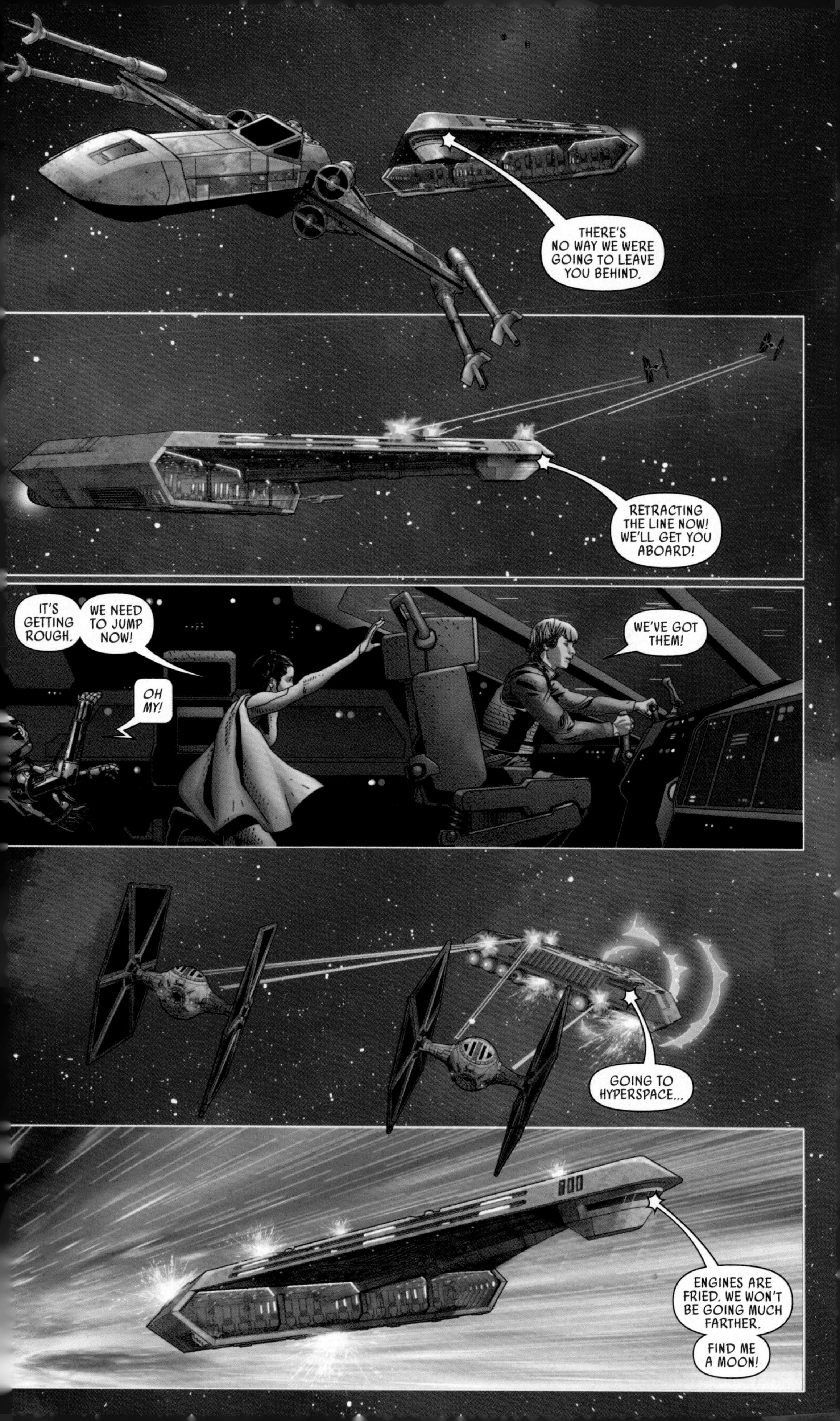
THERE'S NO WAY WE WERE GOING TO LEAVE YOU BEHIND.
RETRACTING THE LINE NOW! WE'LL GET YOU ABOARD!
IT'S GETTING ROUGH.
WE NEED TO JUMP NOW!
OH MY!
WE'VE GOT THEM!
GOING TO HYPERSPACE...
ENGINES ARE FRIED. WE WON'T BE GOING MUCH FARTHER.
FIND ME A MOON!

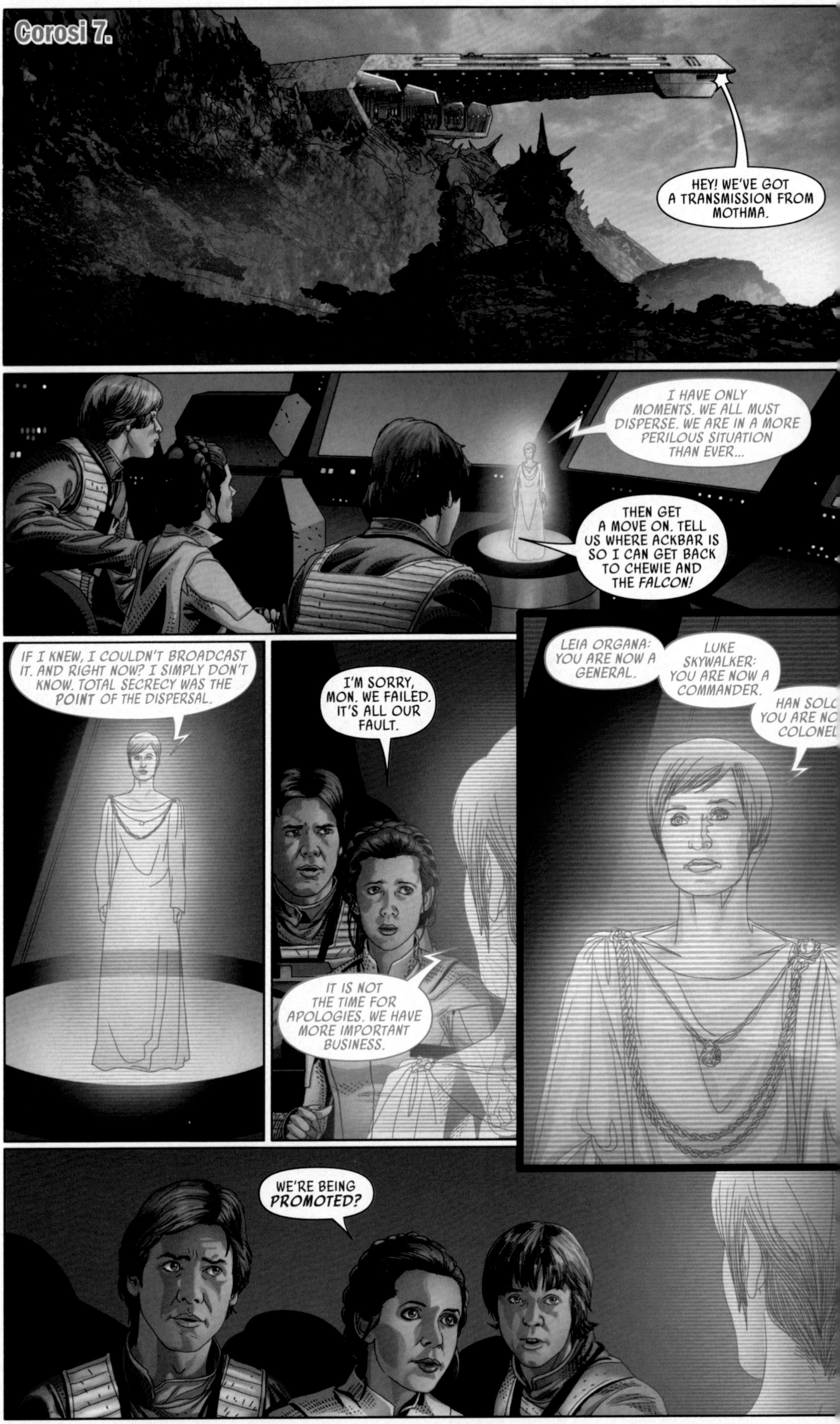
Corosi 7.
HEY! WE'VE GOT A TRANSMISSION FROM MOTHMA.
I HAVE ONLY MOMENTS. WE ALL MUST DISPERSE. WE ARE IN A MORE PERILOUS SITUATION THAN EVER...
THEN GET A MOVE ON. TELL US WHERE ACKBAR IS SO I CAN GET BACK TO CHEWIE AND THE FALCON!
IF I KNEW, I COULDN'T BROADCAST IT. AND RIGHT NOW? I SIMPLY DON'T KNOW. TOTAL SECRECY WAS THE POINT OF THE DISPERSAL.
I'M SORRY, MON. WE FAILED. IT'S ALL OUR FAULT.
IT IS NOT THE TIME FOR APOLOGIES. WE HAVE MORE IMPORTANT BUSINESS.
LEIA ORGANA: YOU ARE NOW A GENERAL.
LUKE SKYWALKER: YOU ARE NOW A COMMANDER.
WE'RE BEING PROMOTED?

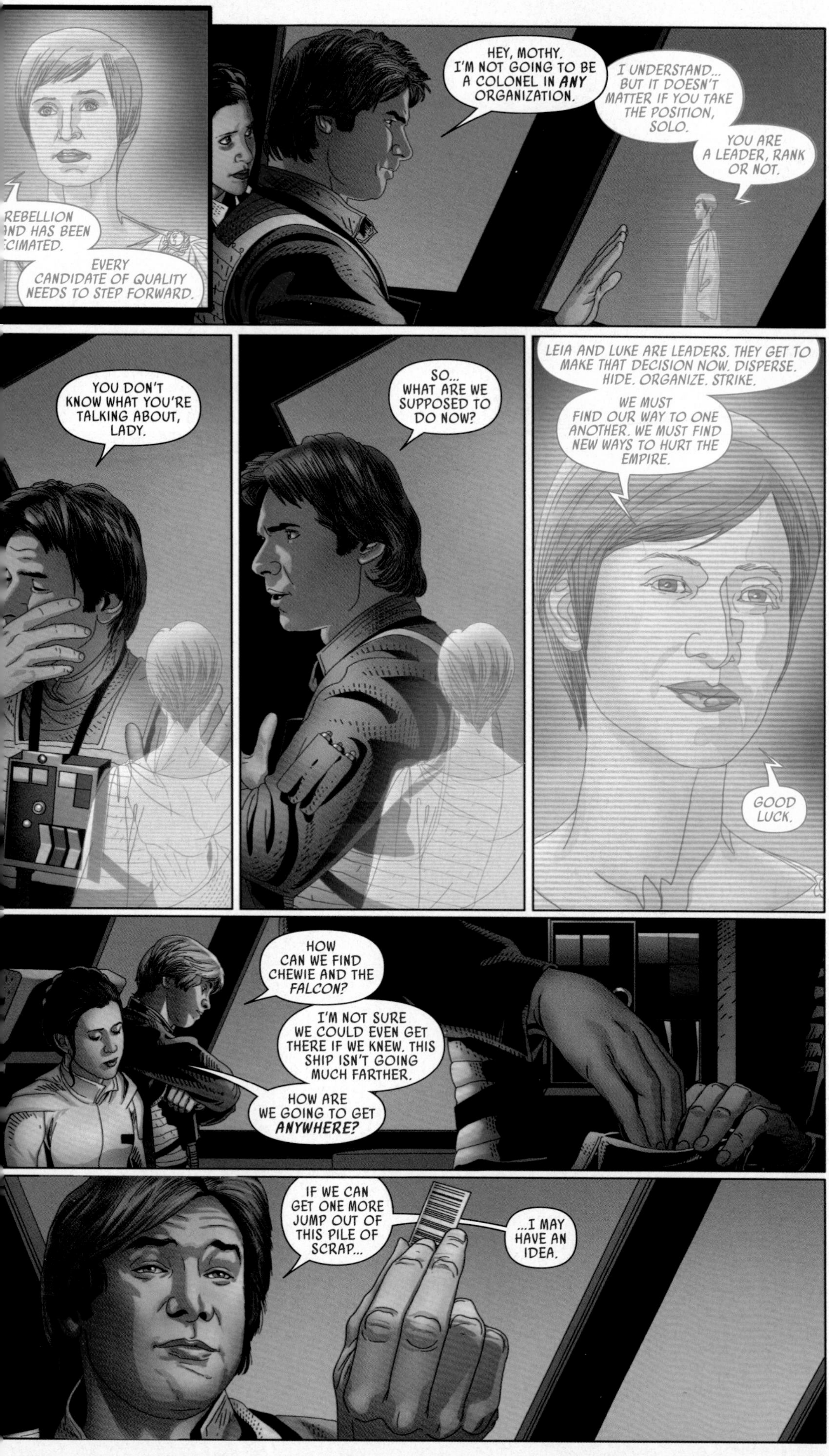

REBELLION
AND HAS BEEN
CIMATED.
EVERY CANDIDATE OF QUALITY NEEDS TO STEP FORWARD.
HEY, MOTHY. I'M NOT GOING TO BE A COLONEL IN ***ANY*** ORGANIZATION.
I UNDERSTAND... BUT IT DOESN'T MATTER IF YOU TAKE THE POSITION, SOLO.
YOU ARE A LEADER, RANK OR NOT.
YOU DON'T KNOW WHAT YOU'RE TALKING ABOUT, LADY.
SO... WHAT ARE WE SUPPOSED TO DO NOW?
LEIA AND LUKE ARE LEADERS. THEY GET TO MAKE THAT DECISION NOW. DISPERSE. HIDE. ORGANIZE. STRIKE.
WE MUST FIND OUR WAY TO ONE ANOTHER. WE MUST FIND NEW WAYS TO HURT THE EMPIRE.
GOOD LUCK.
HOW CAN WE FIND CHEWIE AND THE *FALCON*?
I'M NOT SURE WE COULD EVEN GET THERE IF WE KNEW. THIS SHIP ISN'T GOING MUCH FARTHER.
HOW ARE WE GOING TO GET ***ANYWHERE?***
IF WE CAN GET ONE MORE JUMP OUT OF THIS PILE OF SCRAP...
...I MAY HAVE AN IDEA.

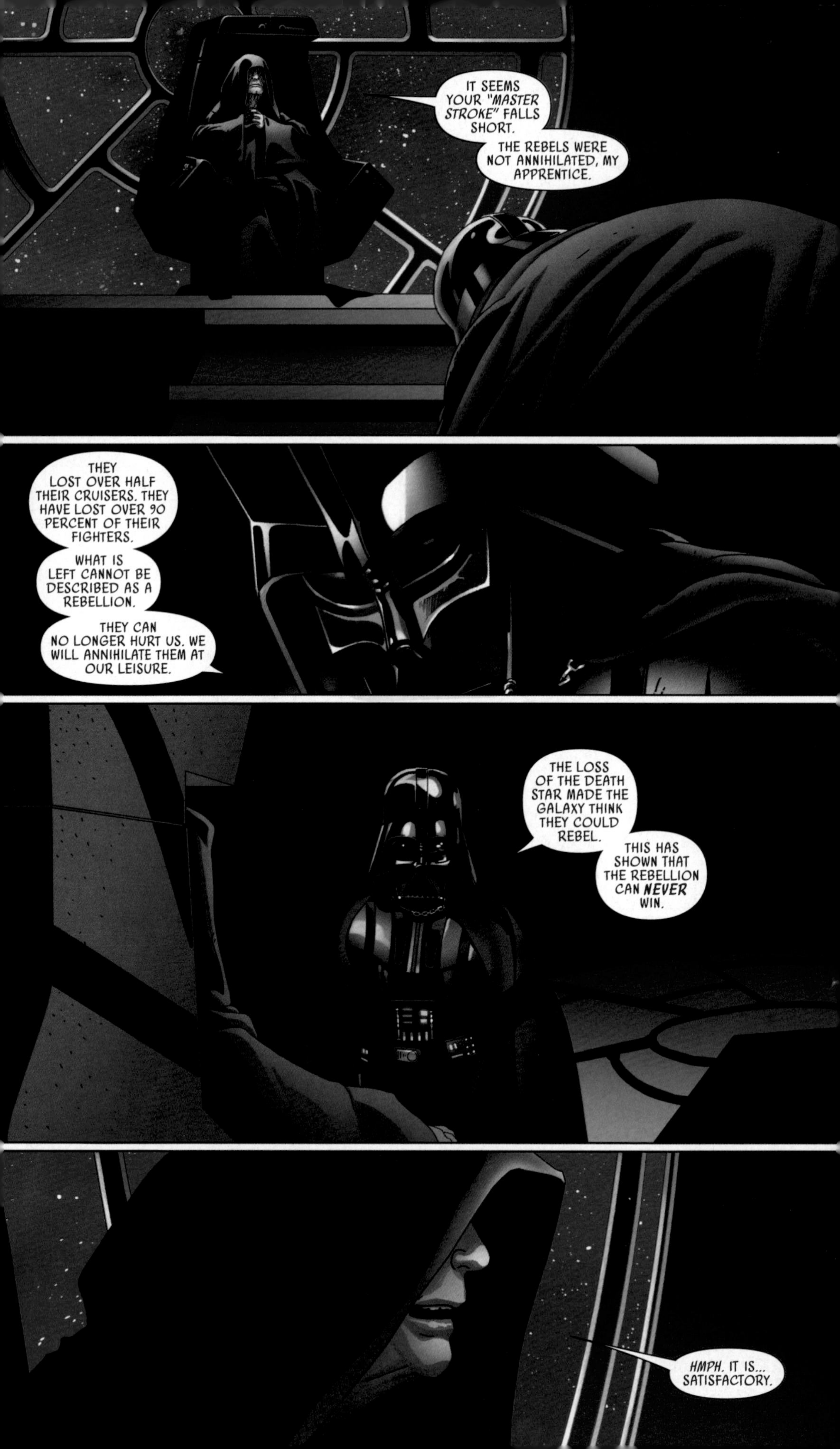

IT SEEMS YOUR "MASTER STROKE" FALLS SHORT.
THE REBELS WERE NOT ANNIHILATED, MY APPRENTICE.
THEY LOST OVER HALF THEIR CRUISERS. THEY HAVE LOST OVER 90 PERCENT OF THEIR FIGHTERS.
WHAT IS LEFT CANNOT BE DESCRIBED AS A REBELLION.
THEY CAN NO LONGER HURT US. WE WILL ANNIHILATE THEM AT OUR LEISURE.
THE LOSS OF THE DEATH STAR MADE THE GALAXY THINK THEY COULD REBEL.
THIS HAS SHOWN THAT THE REBELLION CAN NEVER WIN.
HMPH. IT IS... SATISFACTORY.

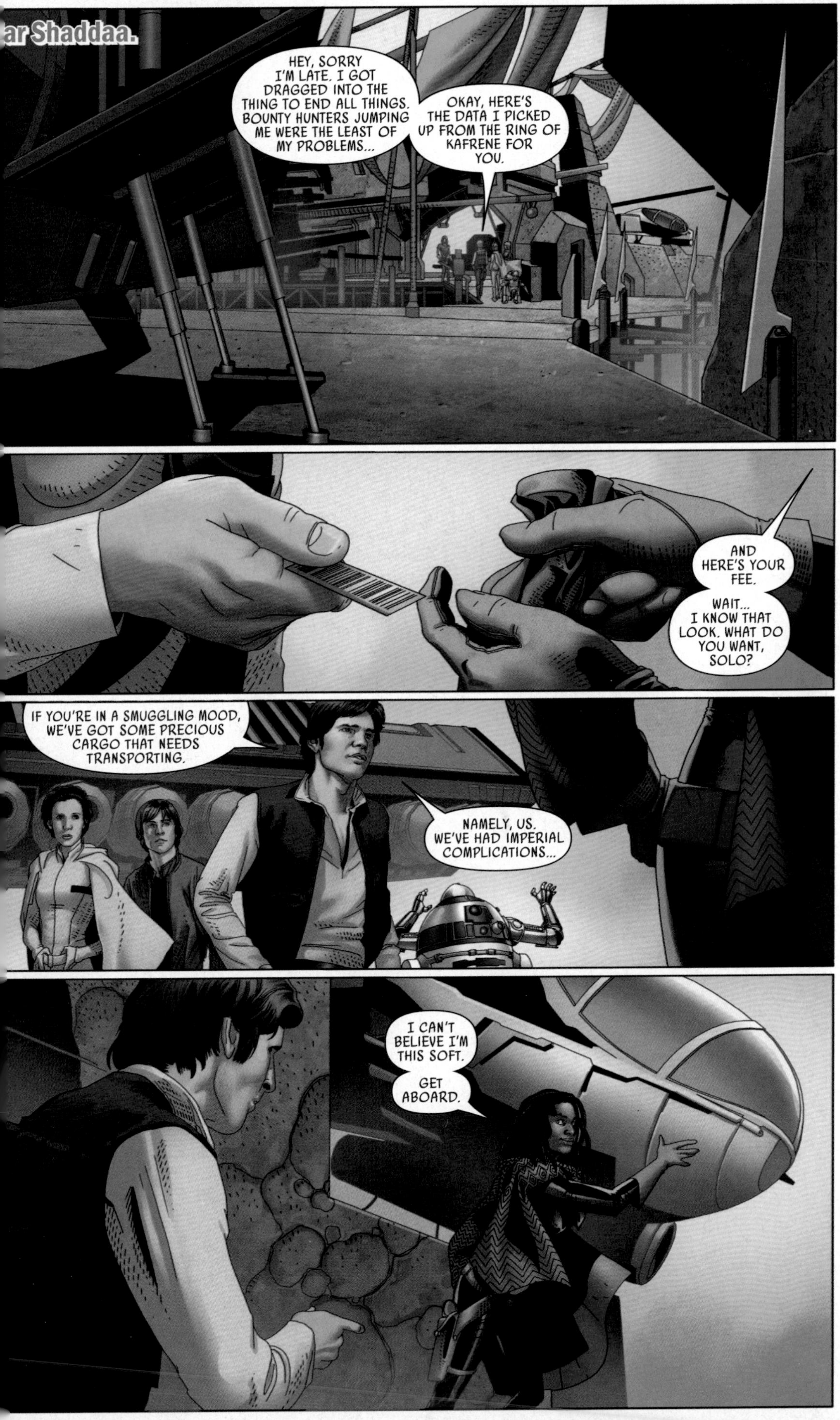
ar Shaddaa.
HEY, SORRY I'M LATE. I GOT DRAGGED INTO THE THING TO END ALL THINGS. BOUNTY HUNTERS JUMPING ME WERE THE LEAST OF MY PROBLEMS...
OKAY, HERE'S THE DATA I PICKED UP FROM THE RING OF KAFRENE FOR YOU.
AND HERE'S YOUR FEE.
WAIT... I KNOW THAT LOOK. WHAT DO YOU WANT, SOLO?
IF YOU'RE IN A SMUGGLING MOOD, WE'VE GOT SOME PRECIOUS CARGO THAT NEEDS TRANSPORTING.
NAMELY, US. WE'VE HAD IMPERIAL COMPLICATIONS...
I CAN'T BELIEVE I'M THIS SOFT.
GET ABOARD.

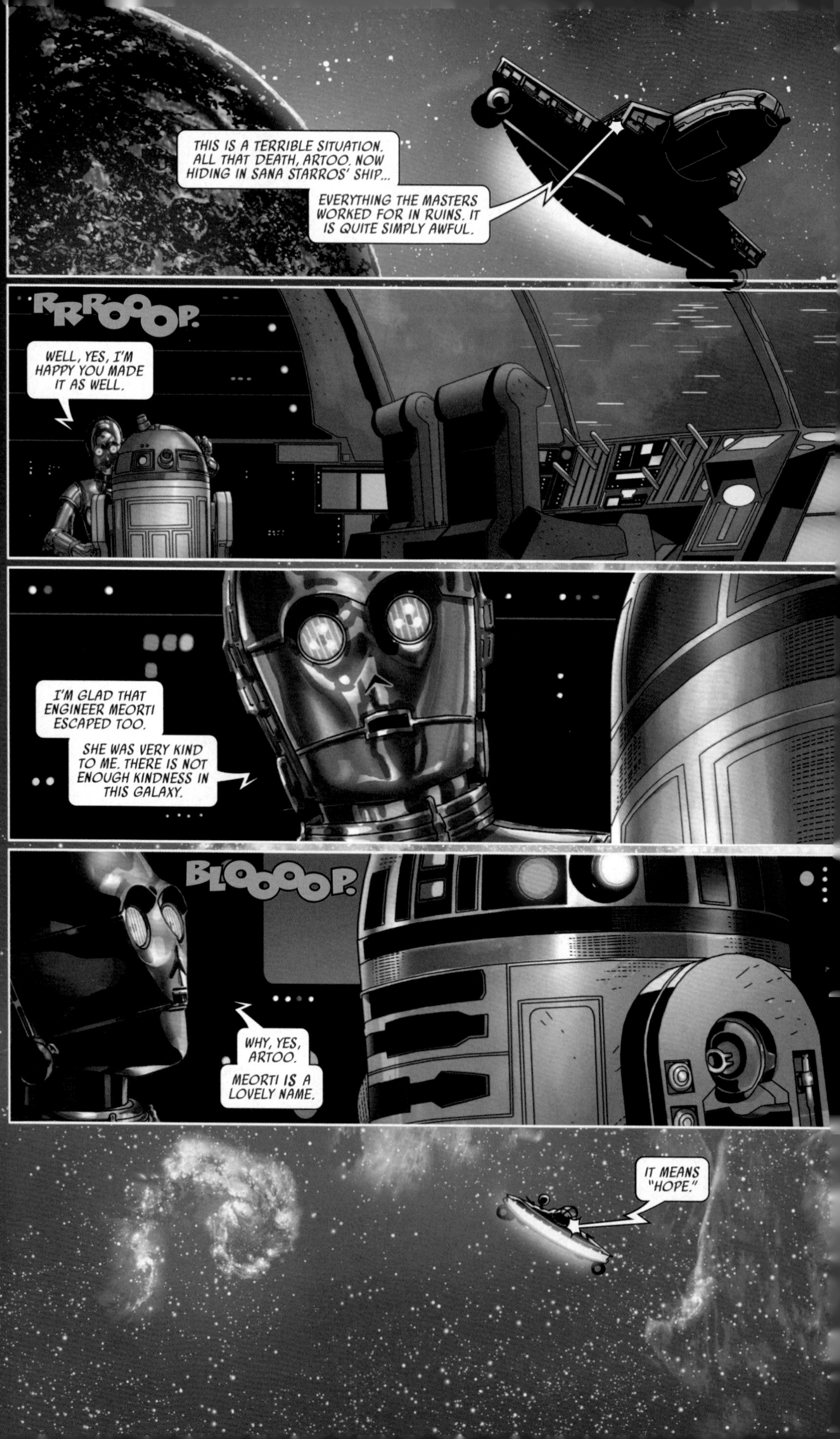
THIS IS A TERRIBLE SITUATION. ALL THAT DEATH, ARTOO. NOW HIDING IN SANA STARROS' SHIP...
EVERYTHING THE MASTERS WORKED FOR IN RUINS. IT IS QUITE SIMPLY AWFUL.
RRROOOP.
WELL, YES, I'M HAPPY YOU MADE IT AS WELL.
I'M GLAD THAT ENGINEER MEORTI ESCAPED TOO.
SHE WAS VERY KIND TO ME. THERE IS NOT ENOUGH KINDNESS IN THIS GALAXY.
BLOOOOP.
WHY, YES, ARTOO.
MEORTI IS A LOVELY NAME.
IT MEANS "HOPE."

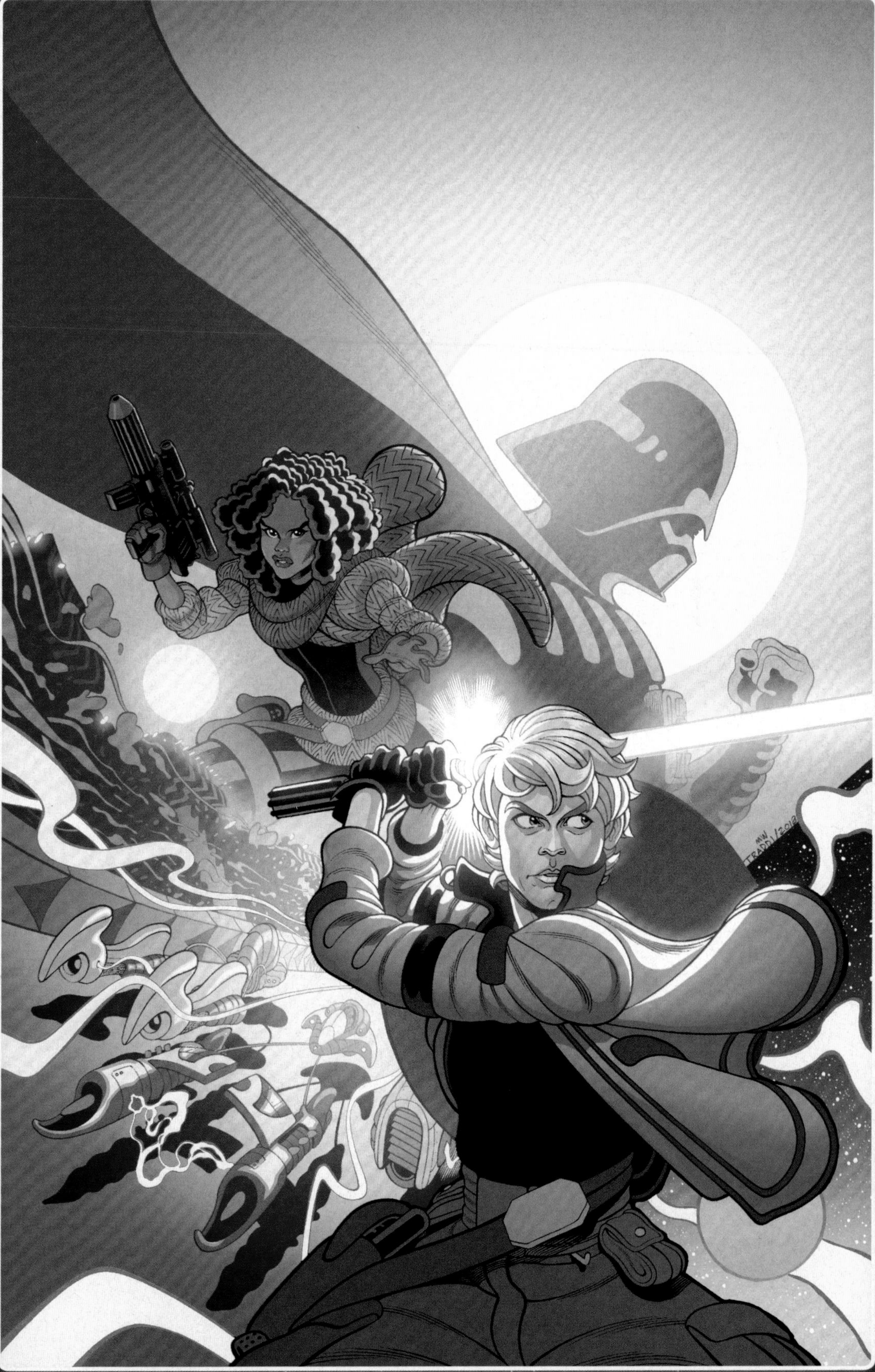

ANNUAL 4

STAR WARS
ANNUAL IV

War consumes the galaxy. The heroic Rebel Alliance has won a major victory against the evil Galactic Empire with the destruction of the dreaded Death Star superweapon.

Now, the Dark Lord of the Sith and the Empire's chief enforcer — DARTH VADER — seeks a means to crush the Rebellion once and for all. Meanwhile, the young hero LUKE SKYWALKER attemps to save it by becoming a Jedi Knight and learning the ways of the Force.

And other factions beyond just the dark and the light seize upon the galaxy's instability. Rogues and smugglers like the infamous SANA STARROS look to profit even on the wildest and mos untamed fringe worlds....

*Note: the events of ANNUAL IV take place before *STAR WARS #8*.

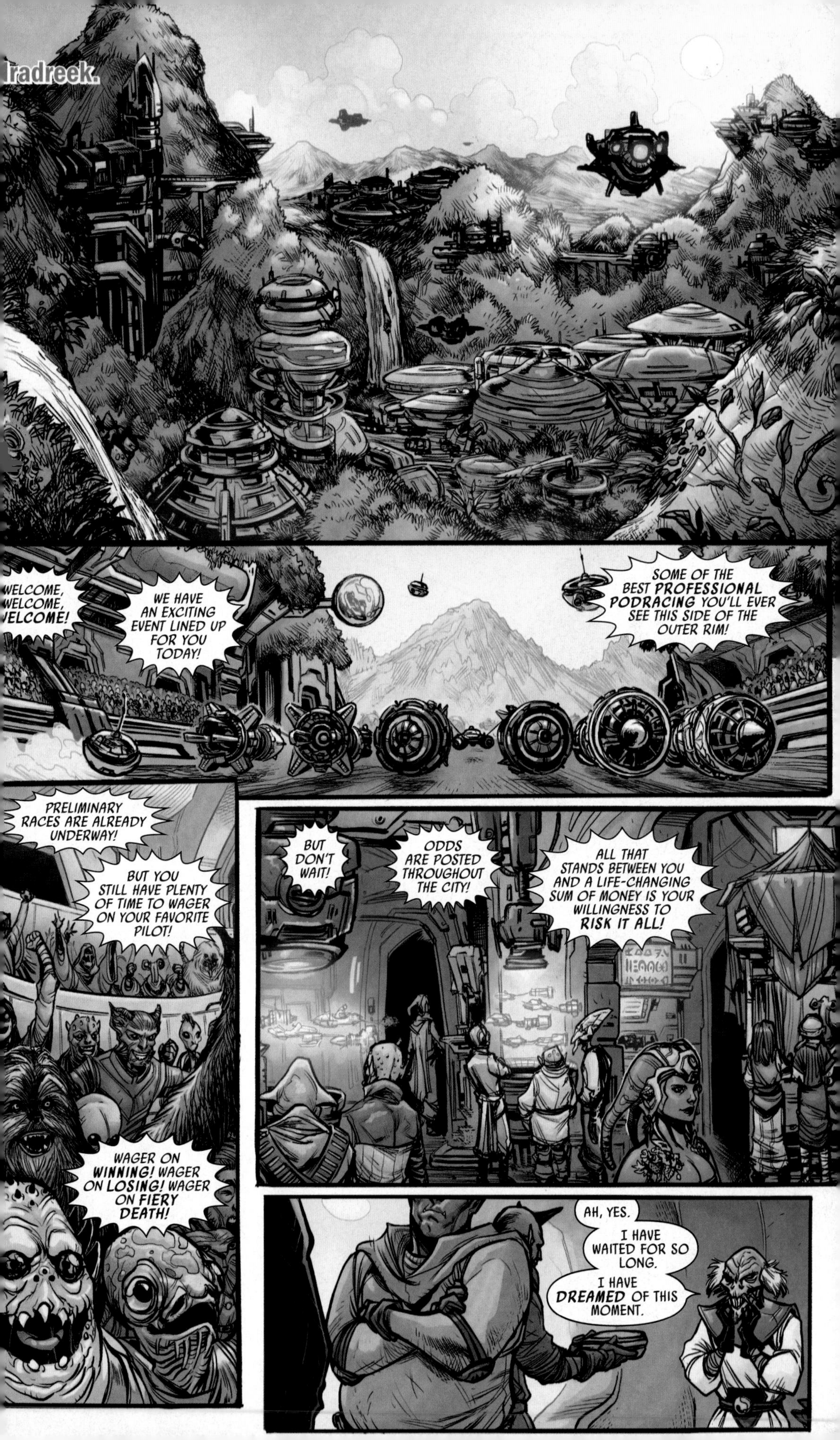
Iradreek.
WELCOME, WELCOME, WELCOME!
WE HAVE AN EXCITING EVENT LINED UP FOR YOU TODAY!
SOME OF THE BEST PROFESSIONAL PODRACING YOU'LL EVER SEE THIS SIDE OF THE OUTER RIM!
PRELIMINARY RACES ARE ALREADY UNDERWAY!
BUT YOU STILL HAVE PLENTY OF TIME TO WAGER ON YOUR FAVORITE PILOT!
WAGER ON WINNING! WAGER ON LOSING! WAGER ON FIERY DEATH!
BUT DON'T WAIT!
ODDS ARE POSTED THROUGHOUT THE CITY!
ALL THAT STANDS BETWEEN YOU AND A LIFE-CHANGING SUM OF MONEY IS YOUR WILLINGNESS TO RISK IT ALL!
AH, YES.
I HAVE WAITED FOR SO LONG.
I HAVE DREAMED OF THIS MOMENT.

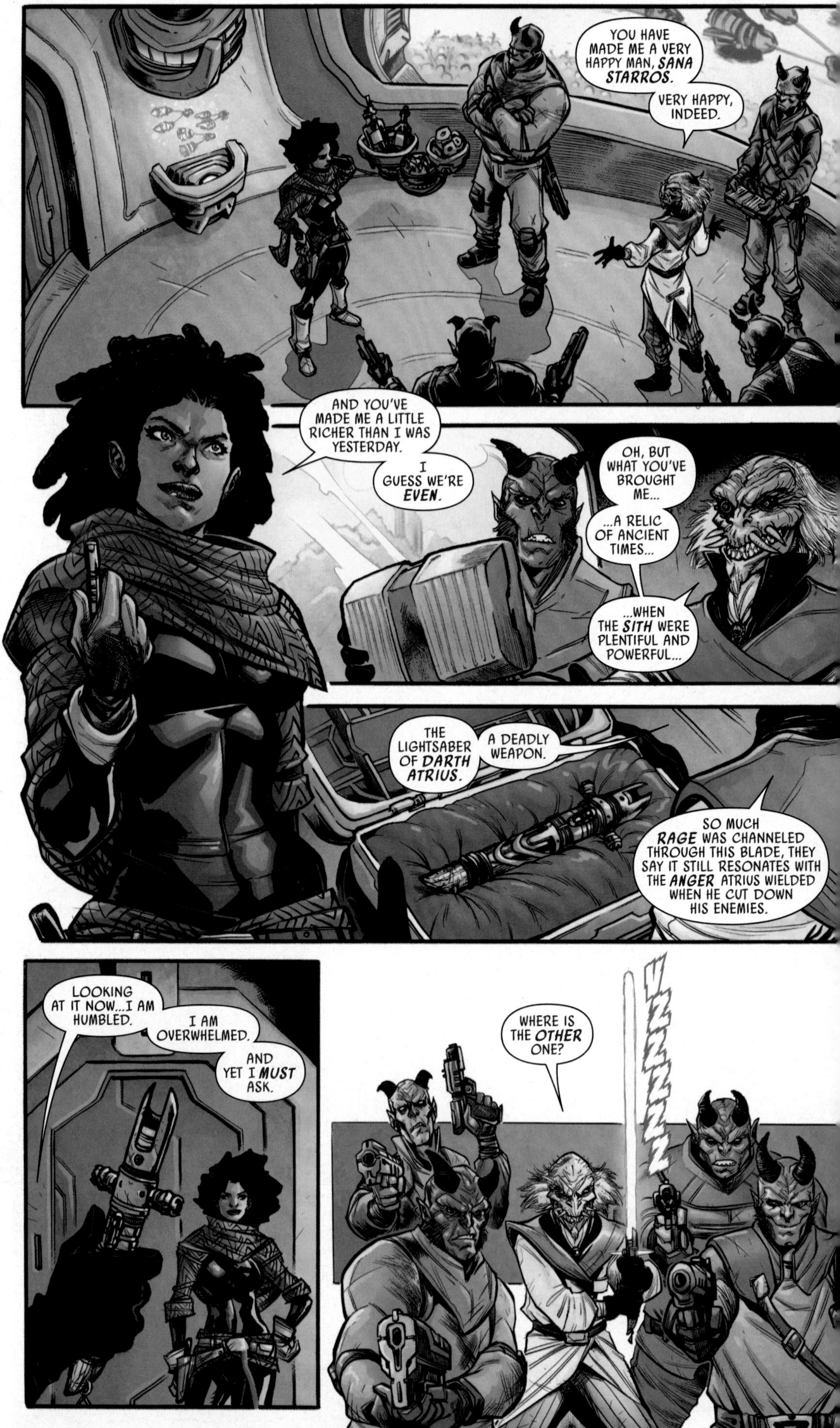

YOU HAVE MADE ME A VERY HAPPY MAN, SANA STARROS.
VERY HAPPY, INDEED.
AND YOU'VE MADE ME A LITTLE RICHER THAN I WAS YESTERDAY.
I GUESS WE'RE EVEN.
OH, BUT WHAT YOU'VE BROUGHT ME...
...A RELIC OF ANCIENT TIMES...
...WHEN THE SITH WERE PLENTIFUL AND POWERFUL...
THE LIGHTSABER OF DARTH ATRIUS.
A DEADLY WEAPON.
SO MUCH RAGE WAS CHANNELED THROUGH THIS BLADE, THEY SAY IT STILL RESONATES WITH THE ANGER ATRIUS WIELDED WHEN HE CUT DOWN HIS ENEMIES.
LOOKING AT IT NOW...I AM HUMBLED.
I AM OVERWHELMED.
AND YET I MUST ASK.
WHERE IS THE OTHER ONE?
VZZZZZZ

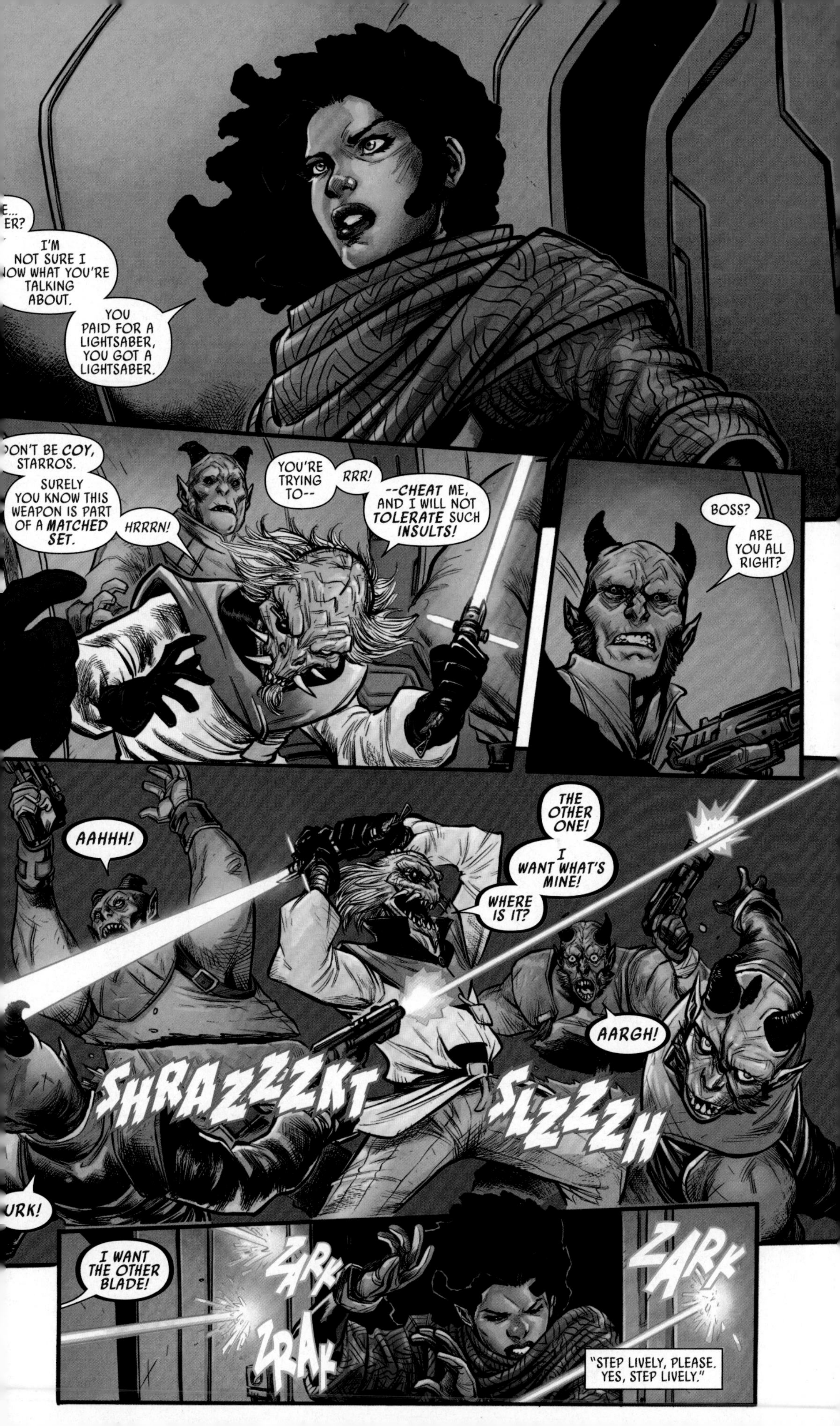
E... ER?
I'M NOT SURE I NOW WHAT YOU'RE TALKING ABOUT.
YOU PAID FOR A LIGHTSABER, YOU GOT A LIGHTSABER.
DON'T BE COY, STARROS.
SURELY YOU KNOW THIS WEAPON IS PART OF A MATCHED SET.
HRRRN!
YOU'RE TRYING TO--
RRR!
--CHEAT ME, AND I WILL NOT TOLERATE SUCH INSULTS!
BOSS?
ARE YOU ALL RIGHT?
AAHHH!
THE OTHER ONE!
I WANT WHAT'S MINE!
WHERE IS IT?
AARGH!
SHRAZZZKT
SIZZZH
URK!
I WANT THE OTHER BLADE!
ZARK
ZARK
ZRAK
"STEP LIVELY, PLEASE. YES, STEP LIVELY."

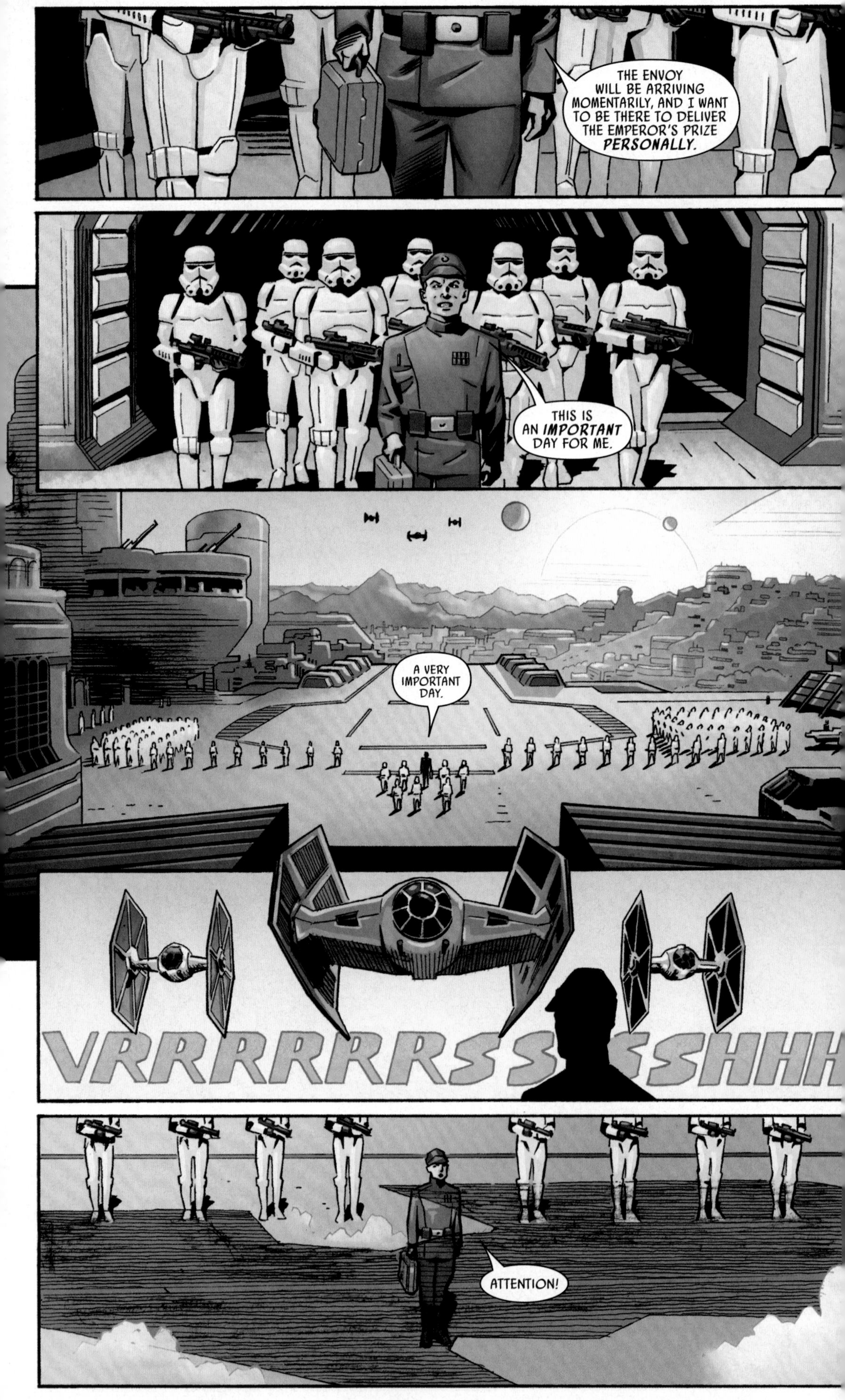
THE ENVOY WILL BE ARRIVING MOMENTARILY, AND I WANT TO BE THERE TO DELIVER THE EMPEROR'S PRIZE *PERSONALLY.*
THIS IS AN *IMPORTANT* DAY FOR ME.
A VERY IMPORTANT DAY.
VRRRRRRSSSSHHH
ATTENTION!

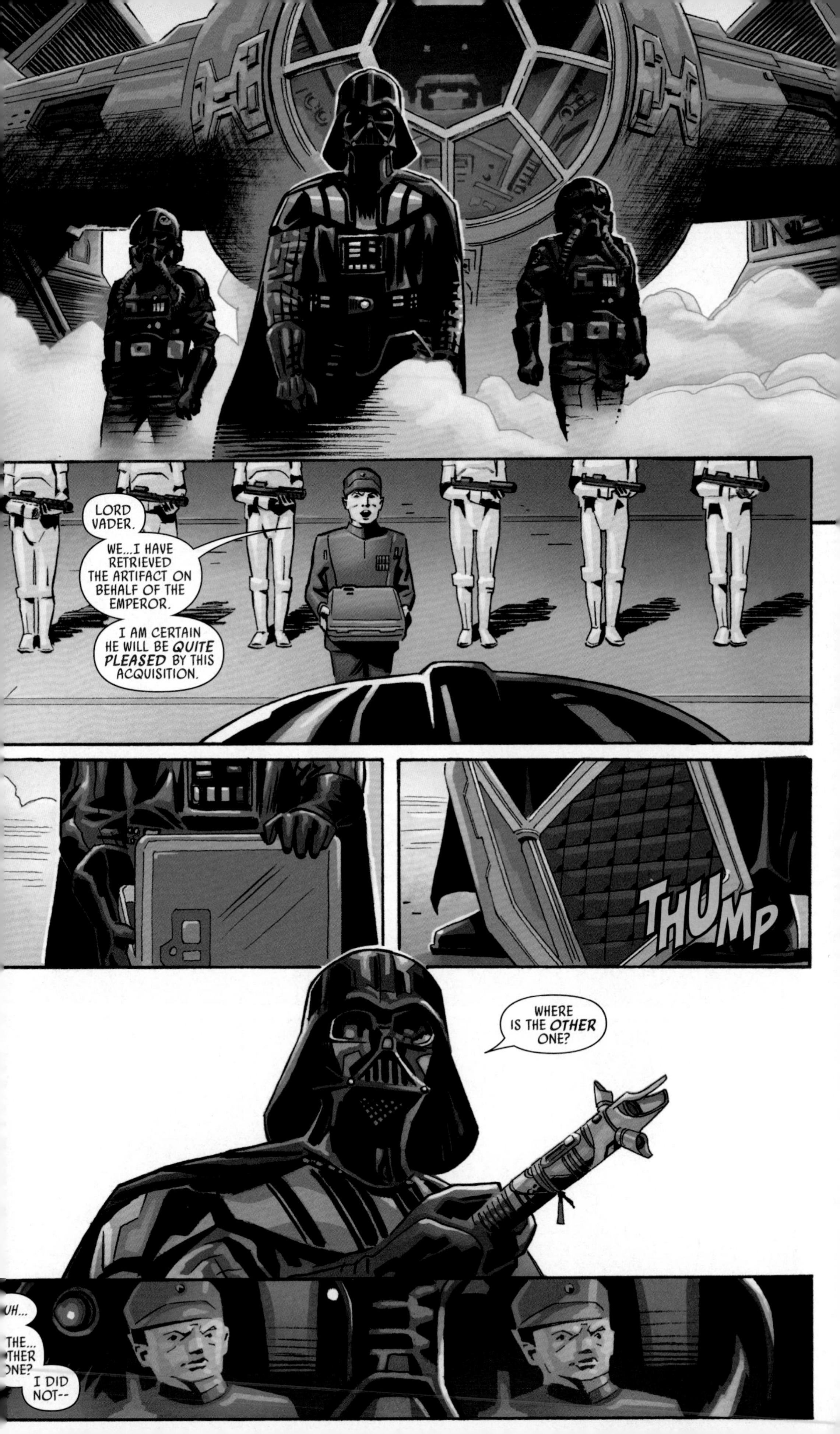
LORD VADER.
WE...I HAVE RETRIEVED THE ARTIFACT ON BEHALF OF THE EMPEROR.
I AM CERTAIN HE WILL BE *QUITE PLEASED* BY THIS ACQUISITION.
THUMP
WHERE IS THE *OTHER* ONE?
UH...
THE... OTHER ONE?
I DID NOT--

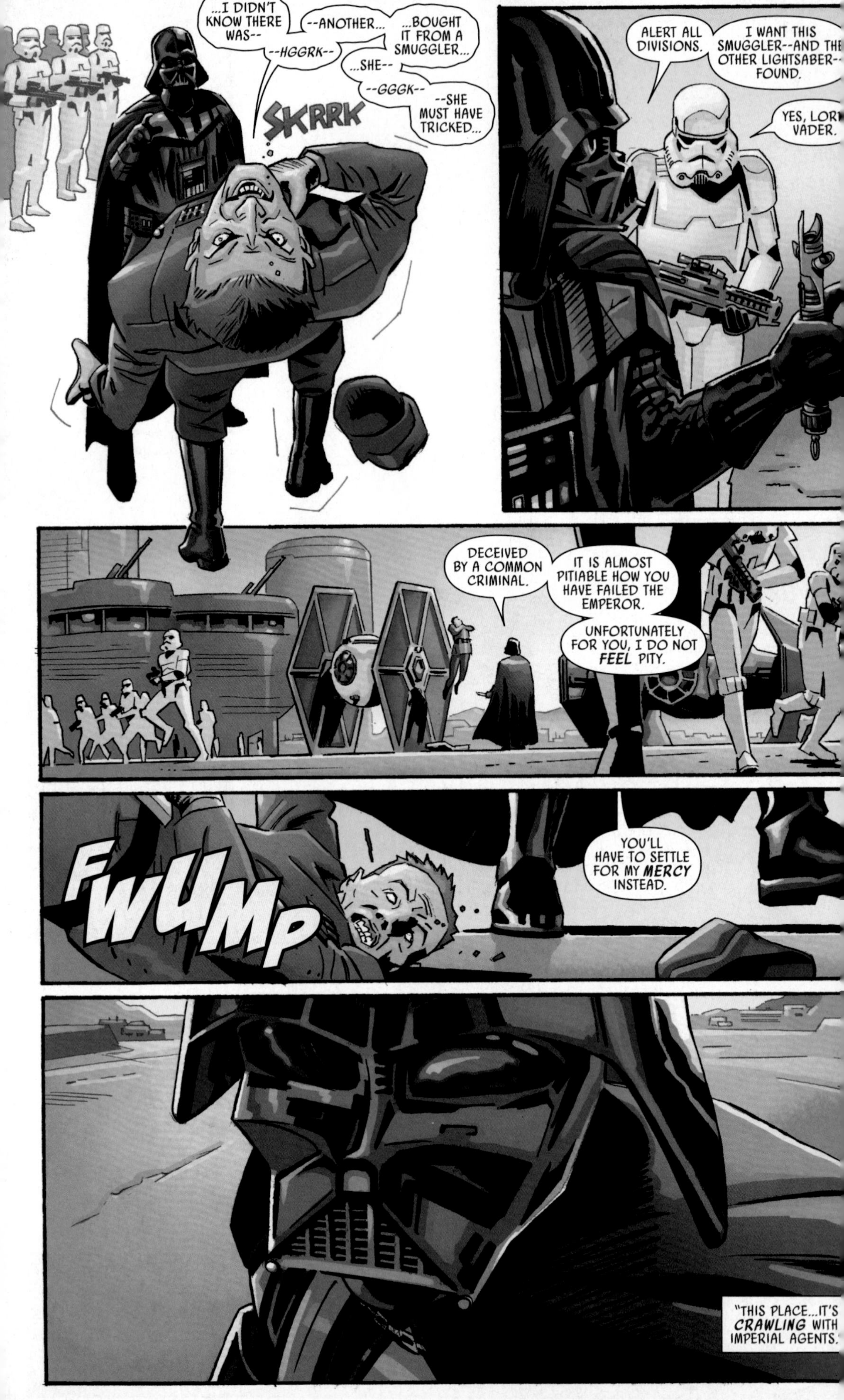

...I DIDN'T KNOW THERE WAS--
--HGGRK--
--ANOTHER...
...BOUGHT IT FROM A SMUGGLER...
...SHE--
--GGGK--
--SHE MUST HAVE TRICKED...
SKRRK
ALERT ALL DIVISIONS.
I WANT THIS SMUGGLER--AND THE OTHER LIGHTSABER--FOUND.
YES, LORD VADER.
DECEIVED BY A COMMON CRIMINAL.
IT IS ALMOST PITIABLE HOW YOU HAVE FAILED THE EMPEROR.
UNFORTUNATELY FOR YOU, I DO NOT FEEL PITY.
FWUMP
YOU'LL HAVE TO SETTLE FOR MY MERCY INSTEAD.
"THIS PLACE...IT'S CRAWLING WITH IMPERIAL AGENTS."

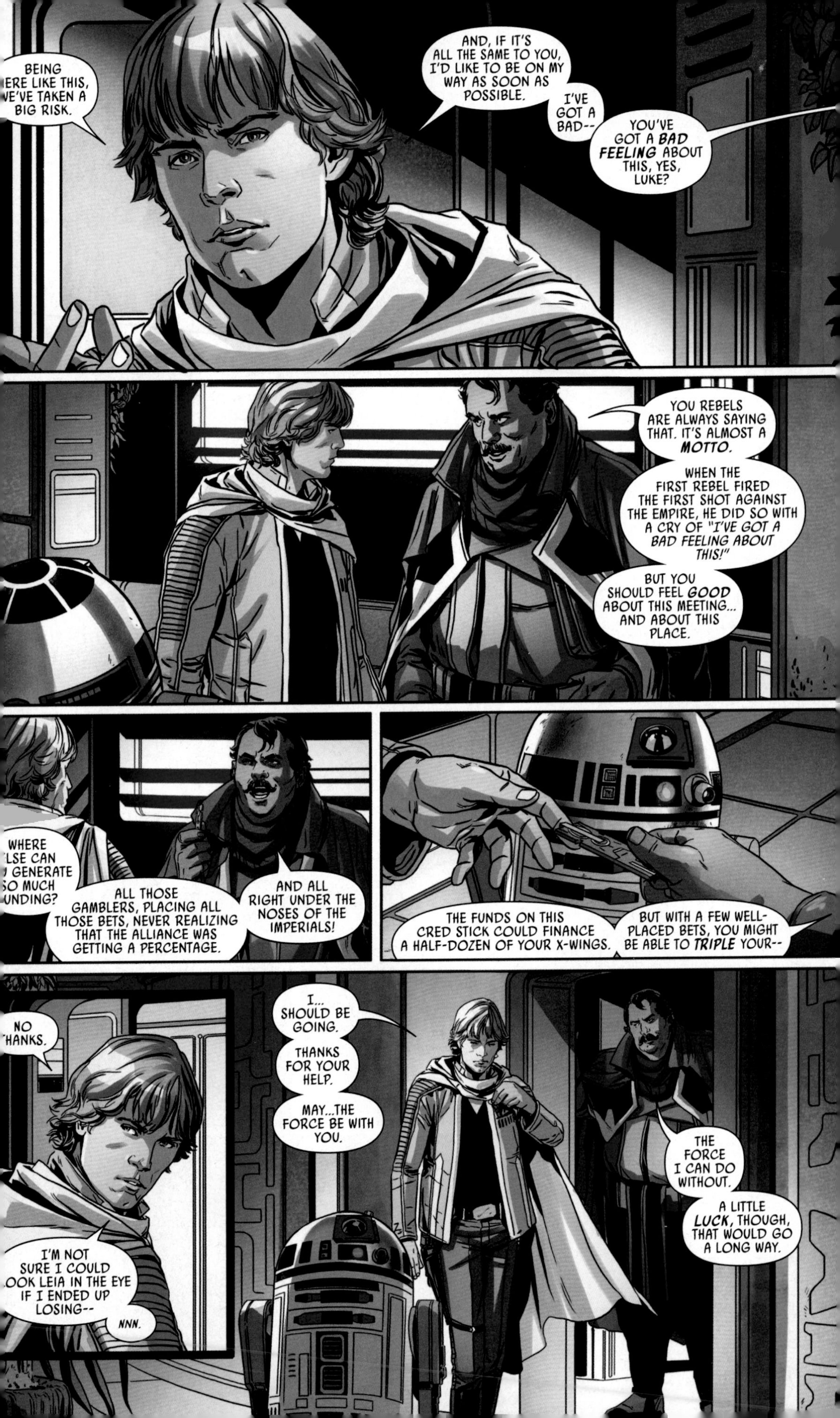
BEING
ERE LIKE THIS,
VE'VE TAKEN A
BIG RISK.
AND, IF IT'S ALL THE SAME TO YOU, I'D LIKE TO BE ON MY WAY AS SOON AS POSSIBLE.
I'VE GOT A BAD--
YOU'VE GOT A BAD FEELING ABOUT THIS, YES, LUKE?
YOU REBELS ARE ALWAYS SAYING THAT. IT'S ALMOST A MOTTO.
WHEN THE FIRST REBEL FIRED THE FIRST SHOT AGAINST THE EMPIRE, HE DID SO WITH A CRY OF "I'VE GOT A BAD FEELING ABOUT THIS!"
BUT YOU SHOULD FEEL GOOD ABOUT THIS MEETING... AND ABOUT THIS PLACE.
WHERE
LSE CAN
GENERATE
SO MUCH
UNDING?
ALL THOSE GAMBLERS, PLACING ALL THOSE BETS, NEVER REALIZING THAT THE ALLIANCE WAS GETTING A PERCENTAGE.
AND ALL RIGHT UNDER THE NOSES OF THE IMPERIALS!
THE FUNDS ON THIS CRED STICK COULD FINANCE A HALF-DOZEN OF YOUR X-WINGS.
BUT WITH A FEW WELL-PLACED BETS, YOU MIGHT BE ABLE TO TRIPLE YOUR--
NO
HANKS.
I'M NOT SURE I COULD
OOK LEIA IN THE EYE
IF I ENDED UP LOSING--
NNN.
I... SHOULD BE GOING.
THANKS FOR YOUR HELP.
MAY...THE FORCE BE WITH YOU.
THE FORCE I CAN DO WITHOUT.
A LITTLE LUCK, THOUGH, THAT WOULD GO A LONG WAY.

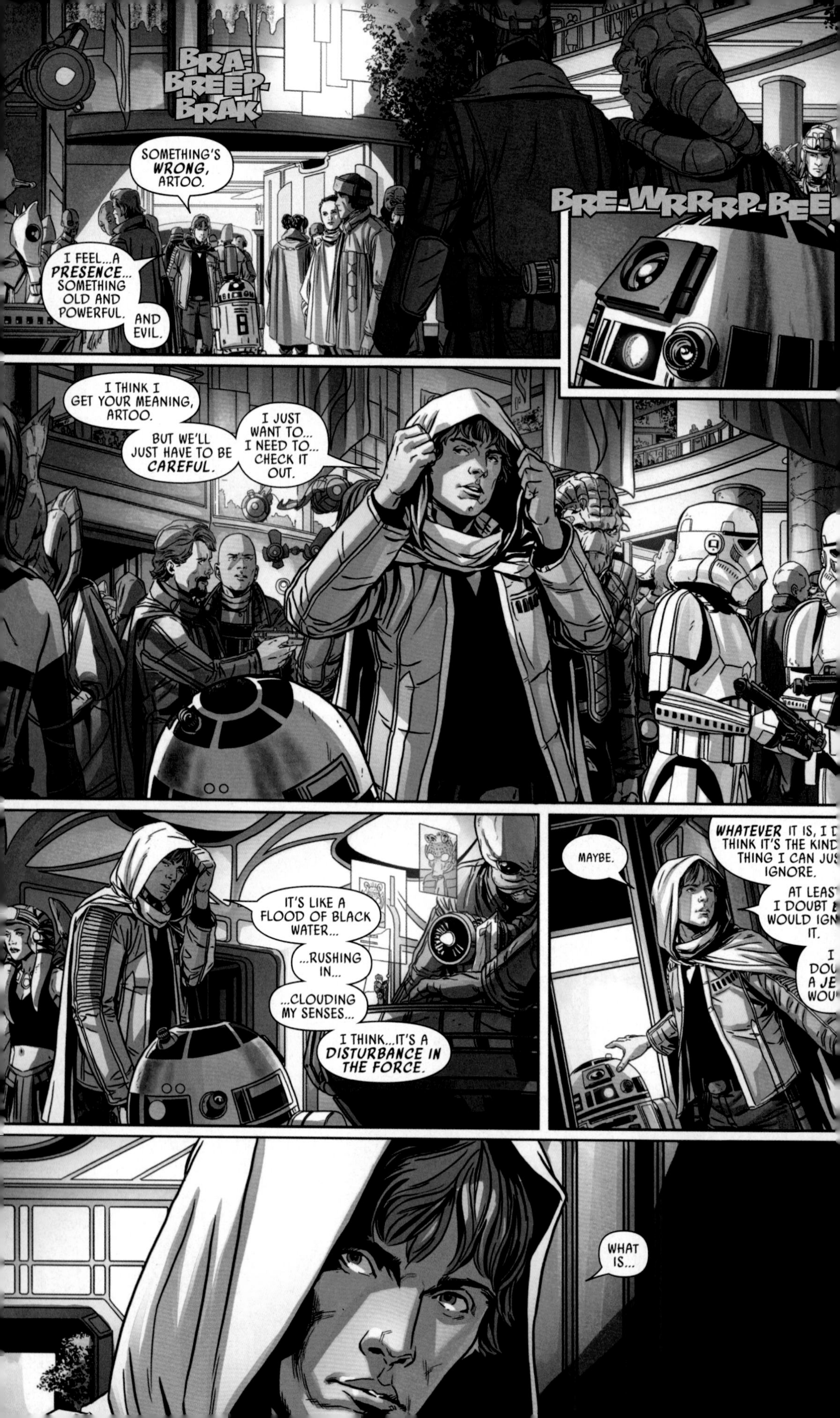
BRA-BREEP-BRAK
SOMETHING'S WRONG, ARTOO.
I FEEL...A PRESENCE... SOMETHING OLD AND POWERFUL.
AND EVIL.
BRE-WRRRRP-BEE
I THINK I GET YOUR MEANING, ARTOO.
BUT WE'LL JUST HAVE TO BE CAREFUL.
I JUST WANT TO... I NEED TO... CHECK IT OUT.
IT'S LIKE A FLOOD OF BLACK WATER...
...RUSHING IN...
...CLOUDING MY SENSES...
I THINK...IT'S A DISTURBANCE IN THE FORCE.
MAYBE.
WHATEVER IT IS, I D THINK IT'S THE KIND THING I CAN JUS IGNORE.
AT LEAST I DOUBT WOULD IGN IT.
WHAT IS...

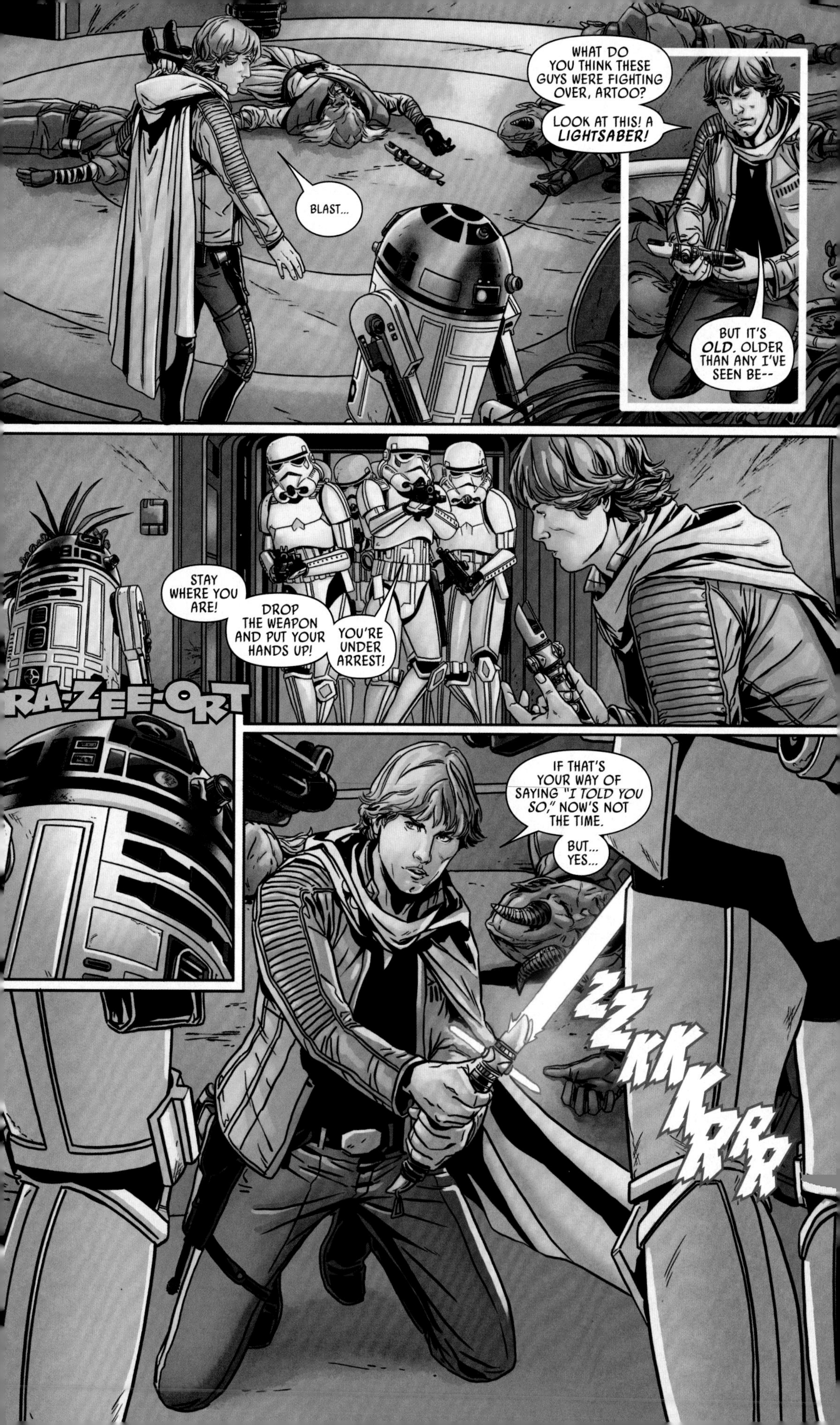
BLAST...
WHAT DO YOU THINK THESE GUYS WERE FIGHTING OVER, ARTOO?
LOOK AT THIS! A LIGHTSABER!
BUT IT'S OLD. OLDER THAN ANY I'VE SEEN BE--
STAY WHERE YOU ARE!
DROP THE WEAPON AND PUT YOUR HANDS UP!
YOU'RE UNDER ARREST!
RA-ZEE-ORT
IF THAT'S YOUR WAY OF SAYING "I TOLD YOU SO," NOW'S NOT THE TIME.
BUT... YES...
ZZKKKRRR

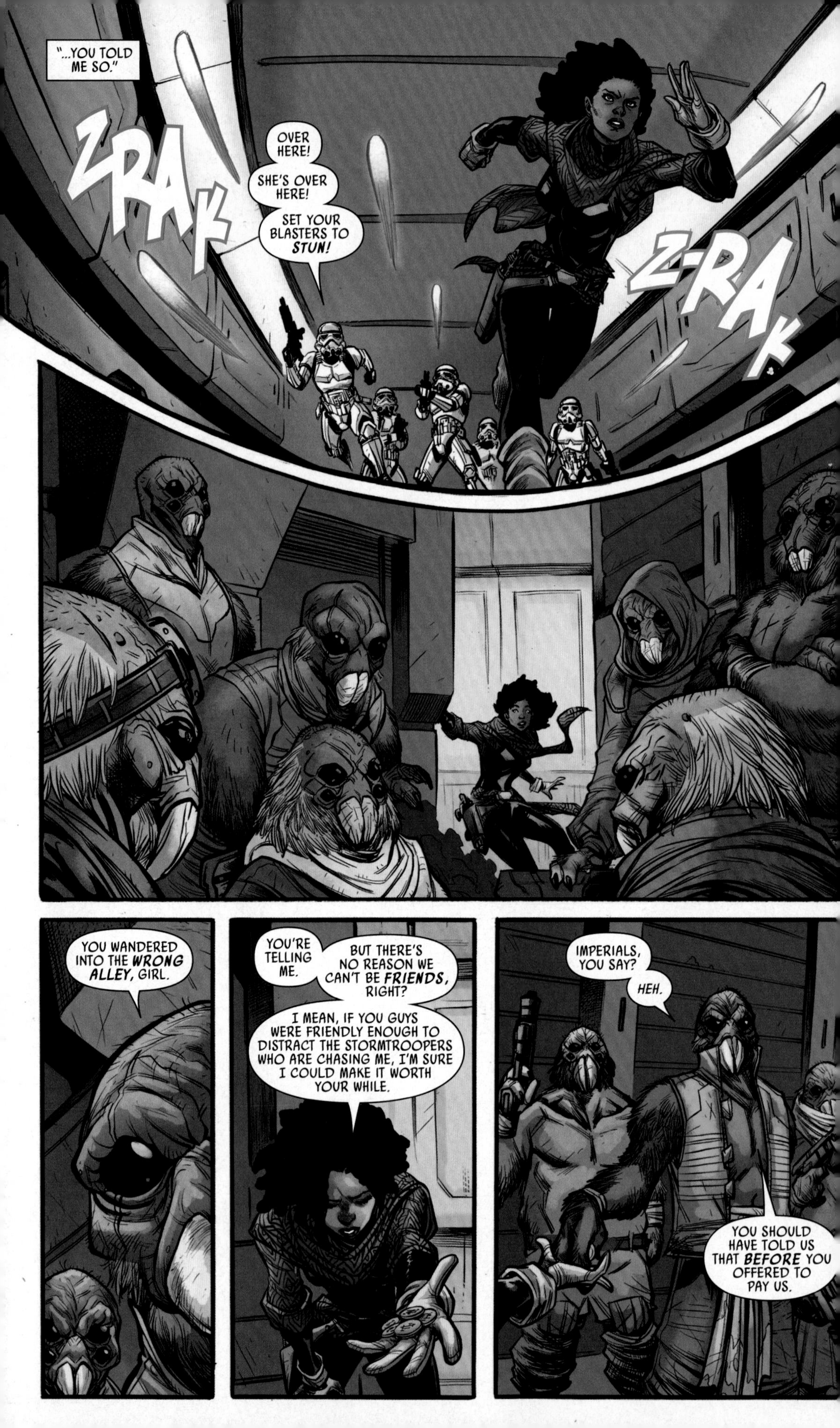
"...YOU TOLD ME SO."
ZRAK
OVER HERE!
SHE'S OVER HERE!
SET YOUR BLASTERS TO STUN!
Z-RAK
YOU WANDERED INTO THE WRONG ALLEY, GIRL.
YOU'RE TELLING ME.
BUT THERE'S NO REASON WE CAN'T BE FRIENDS, RIGHT?
I MEAN, IF YOU GUYS WERE FRIENDLY ENOUGH TO DISTRACT THE STORMTROOPERS WHO ARE CHASING ME, I'M SURE I COULD MAKE IT WORTH YOUR WHILE.
IMPERIALS, YOU SAY?
HEH.
YOU SHOULD HAVE TOLD US THAT BEFORE YOU OFFERED TO PAY US.

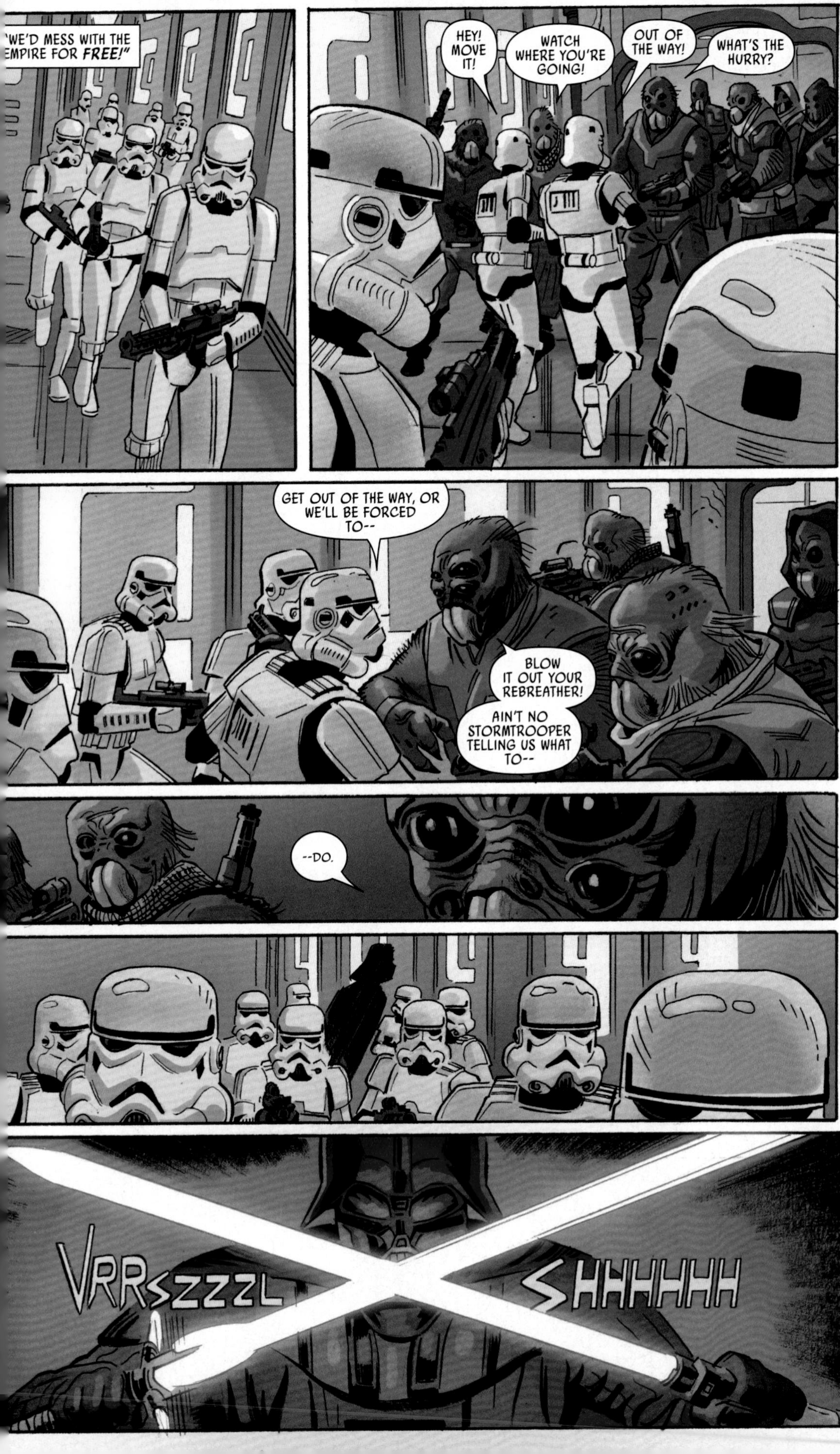
"WE'D MESS WITH THE
EMPIRE FOR FREE!"
HEY! MOVE IT!
WATCH WHERE YOU'RE GOING!
OUT OF THE WAY!
WHAT'S THE HURRY?
GET OUT OF THE WAY, OR WE'LL BE FORCED TO--
BLOW IT OUT YOUR REBREATHER!
AIN'T NO STORMTROOPER TELLING US WHAT TO--
--DO.
VRRSZZZL
SHHHHHH

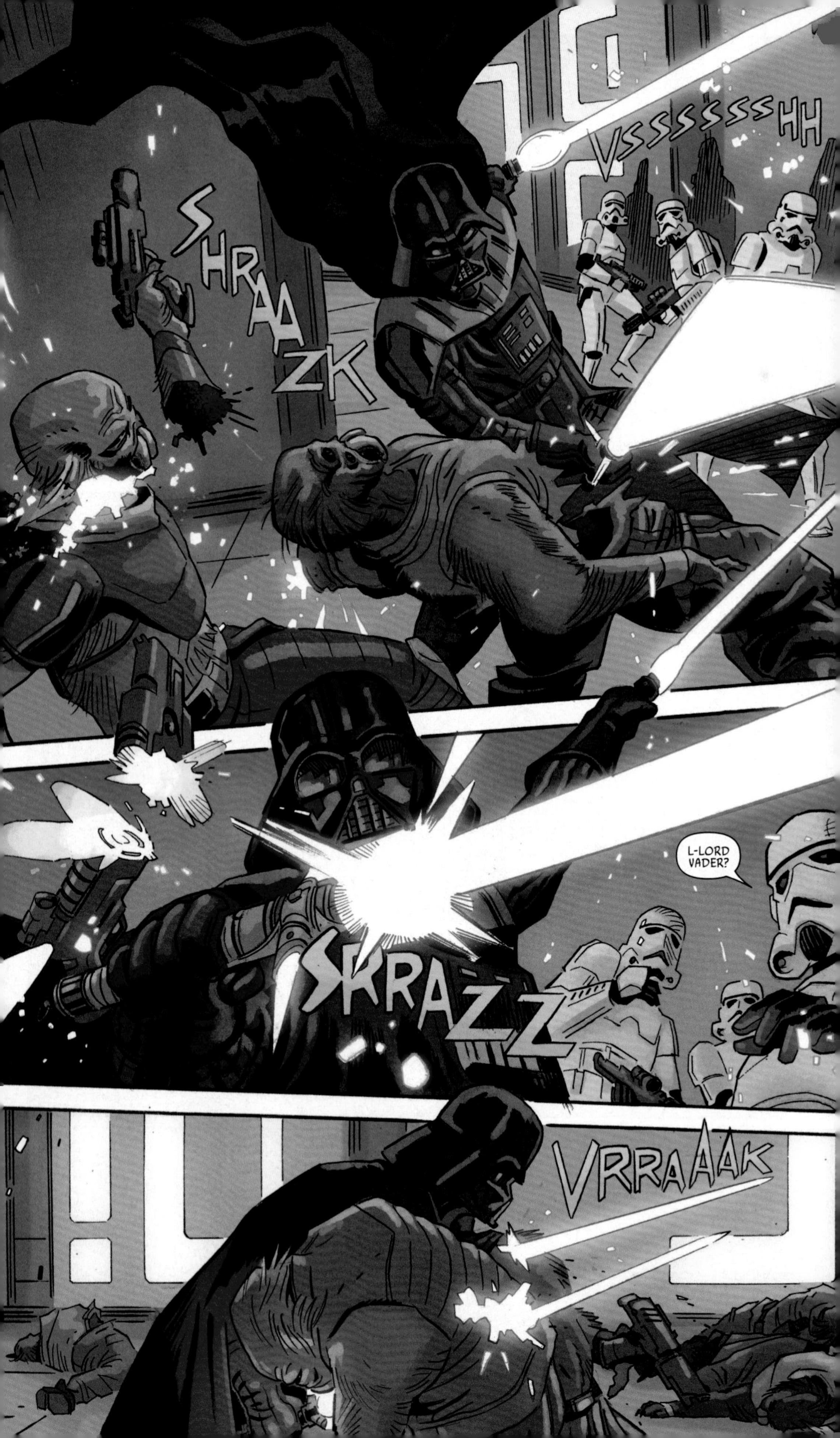
VSSSSSSSHH
SHRAAZK
L-LORD VADER?
SKRAZZ
VRRAAAK

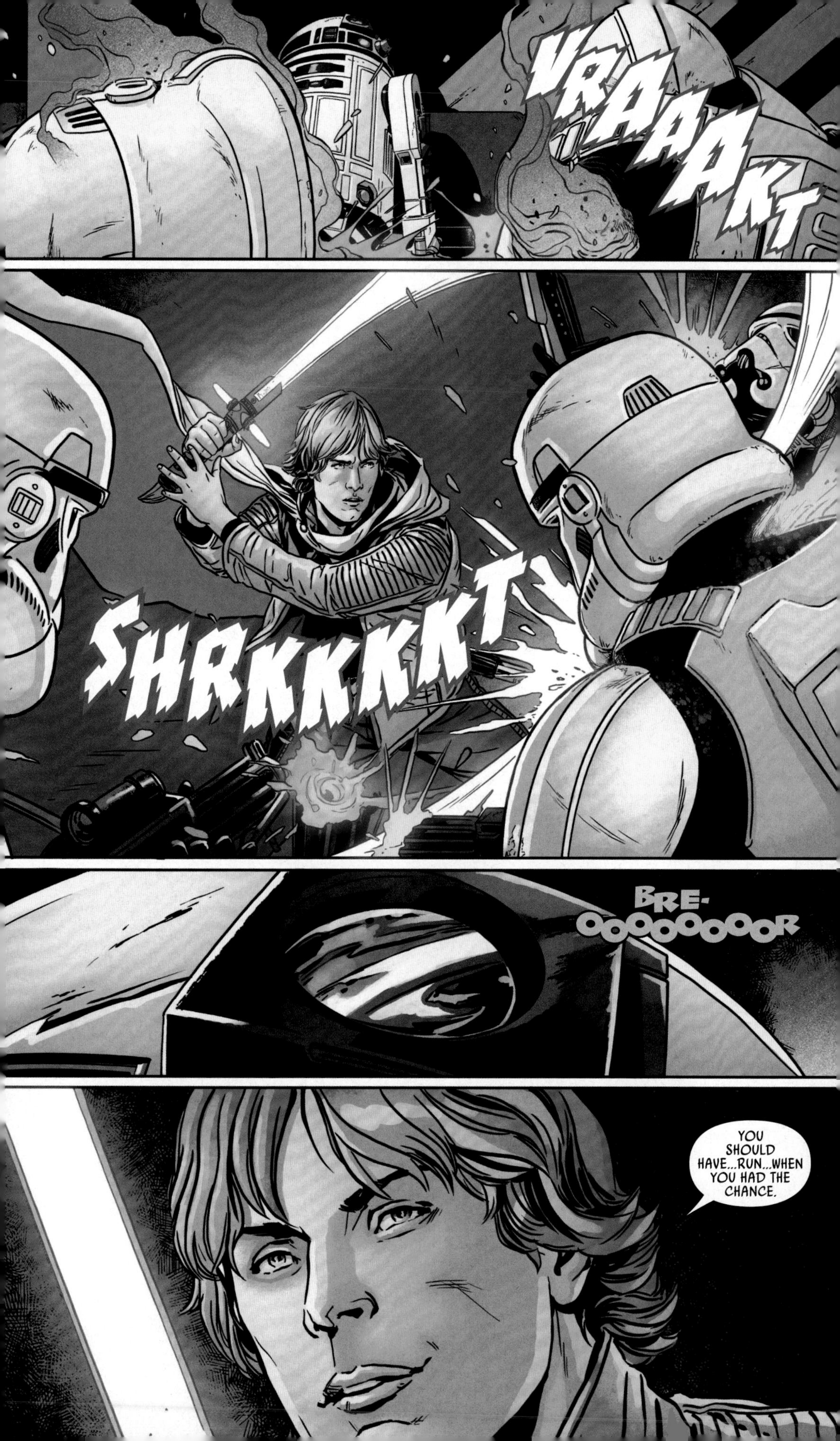
VRAAAAKT
SHRKKKKT
BRE-OOOOOOOOR
YOU SHOULD HAVE...RUN...WHEN YOU HAD THE CHANCE.

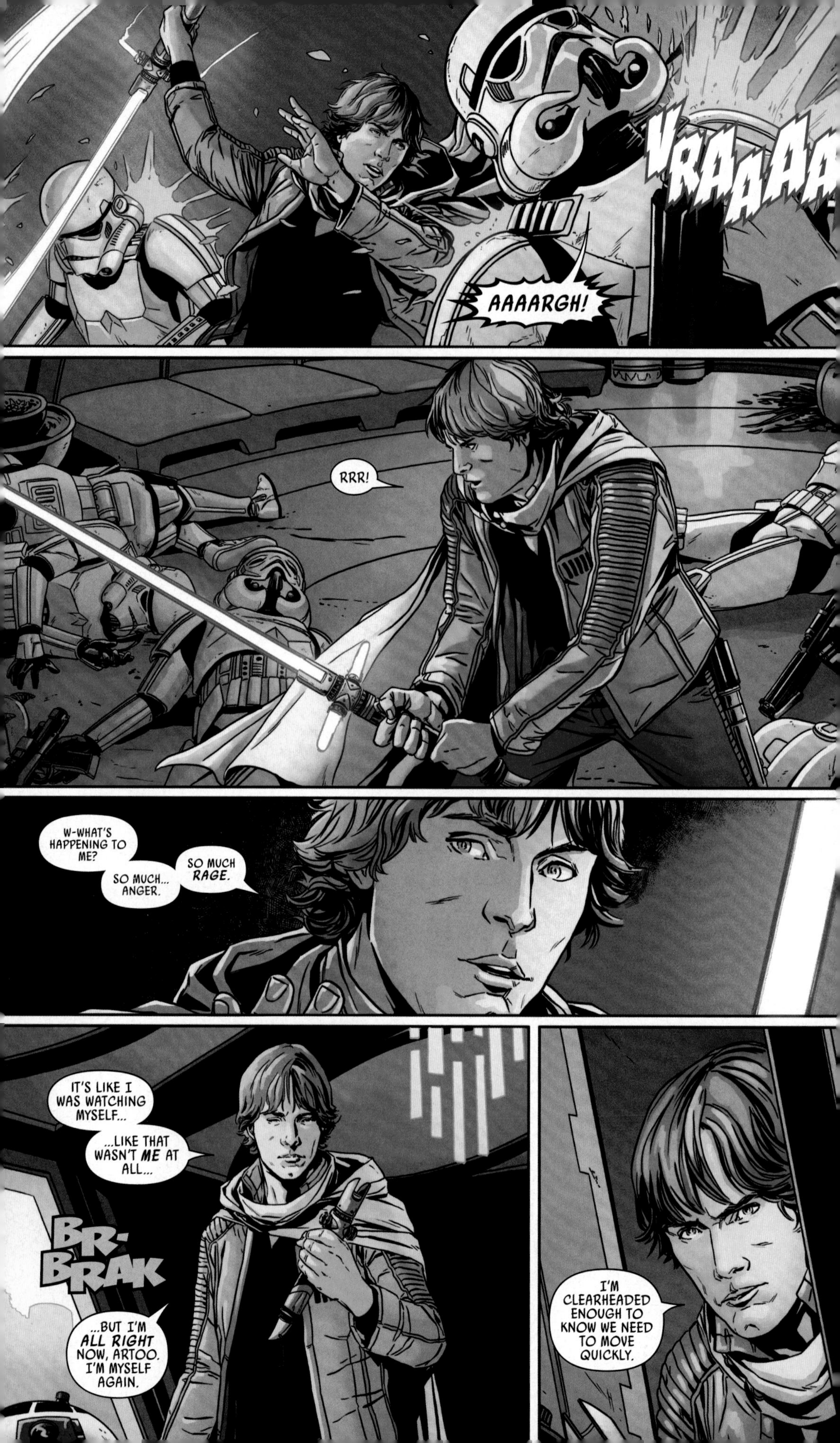
VRAAAA
AAAARGH!
RRR!
W-WHAT'S HAPPENING TO ME?
SO MUCH... ANGER.
SO MUCH RAGE.
IT'S LIKE I WAS WATCHING MYSELF...
...LIKE THAT WASN'T ME AT ALL...
BR-BRAK
...BUT I'M ALL RIGHT NOW, ARTOO. I'M MYSELF AGAIN.
I'M CLEARHEADED ENOUGH TO KNOW WE NEED TO MOVE QUICKLY.

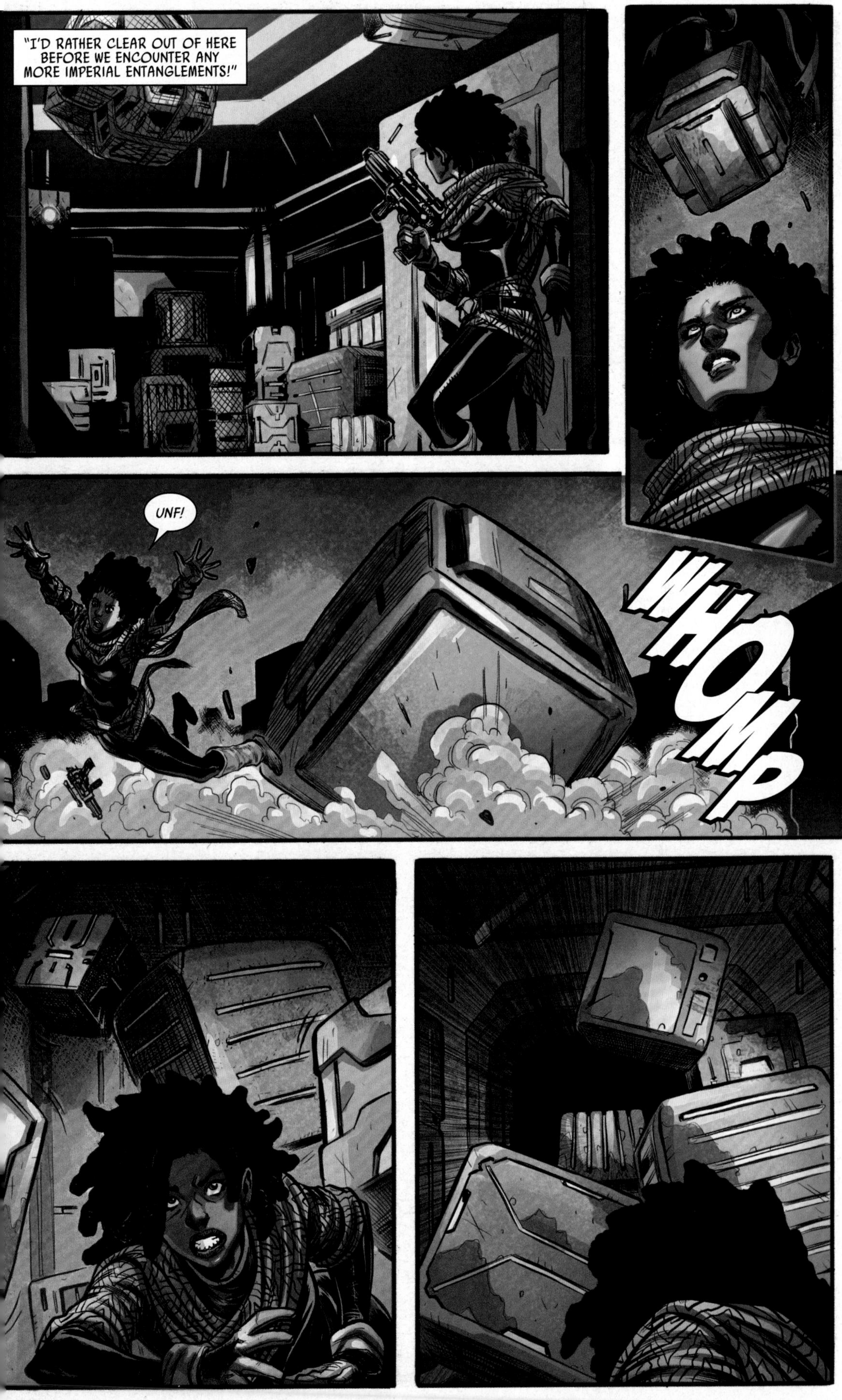
"I'D RATHER CLEAR OUT OF HERE BEFORE WE ENCOUNTER ANY MORE IMPERIAL ENTANGLEMENTS!"
UNF!
WHOMP

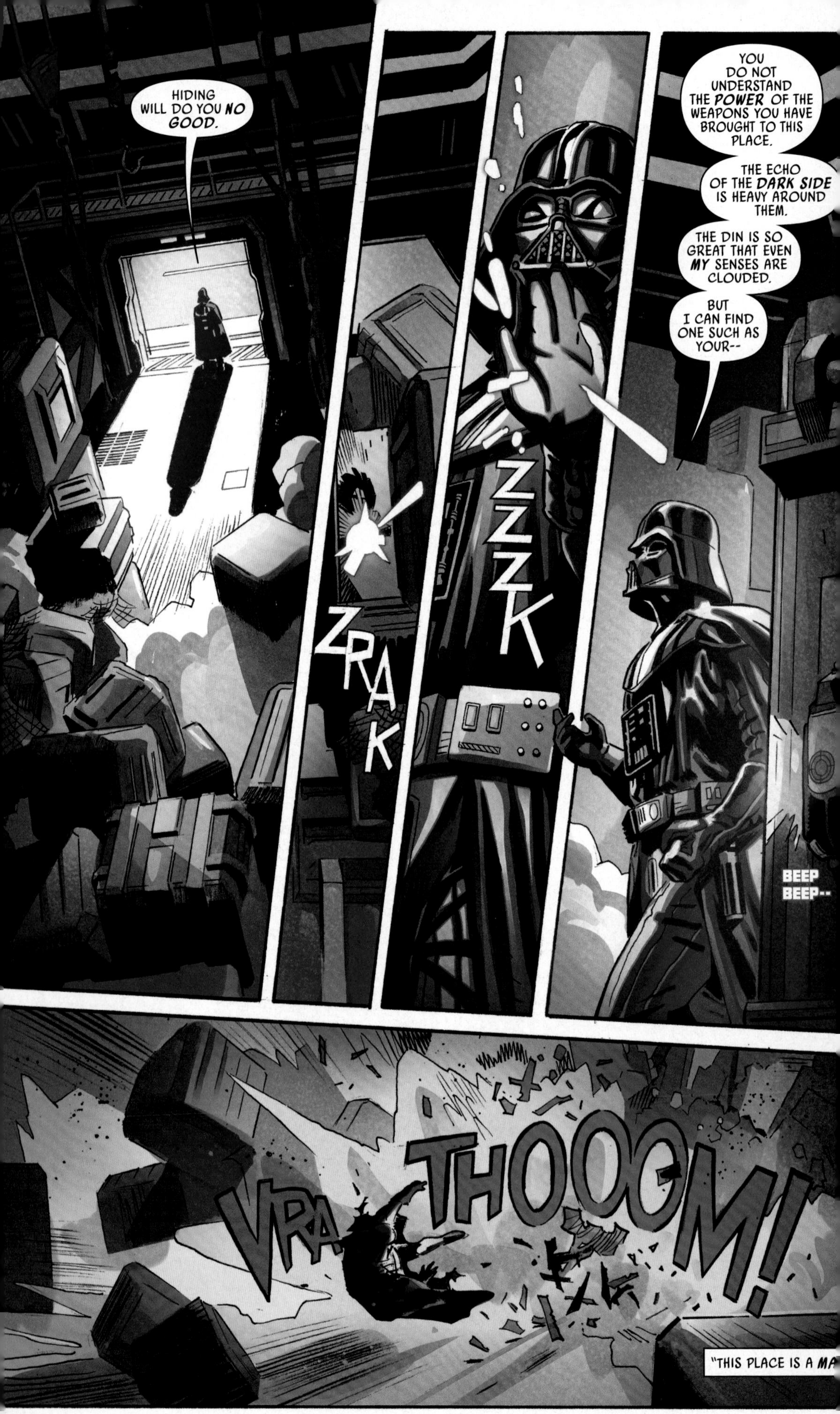
HIDING WILL DO YOU NO GOOD.
ZRAK
ZZZK
YOU DO NOT UNDERSTAND THE POWER OF THE WEAPONS YOU HAVE BROUGHT TO THIS PLACE.
THE ECHO OF THE DARK SIDE IS HEAVY AROUND THEM.
THE DIN IS SO GREAT THAT EVEN MY SENSES ARE CLOUDED.
BUT I CAN FIND ONE SUCH AS YOUR--
BEEP BEEP--
VRA-THOOOM!
"THIS PLACE IS A MA

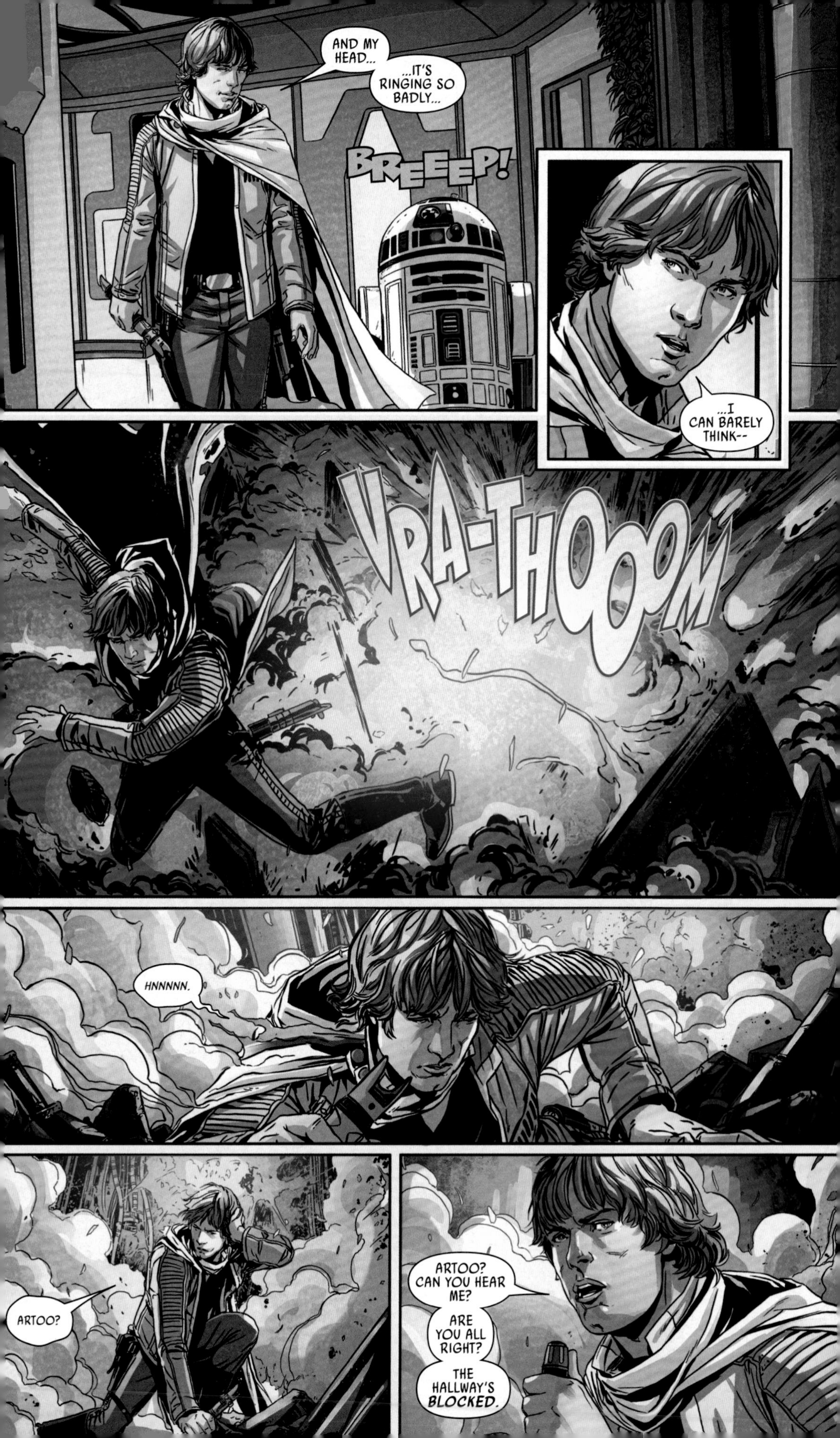
AND MY HEAD...
...IT'S RINGING SO BADLY...
BREEEEP!
...I CAN BARELY THINK--
VRA-THOOOM
HNNNNN.
ARTOO?
ARTOO? CAN YOU HEAR ME?
ARE YOU ALL RIGHT?
THE HALLWAY'S *BLOCKED*.

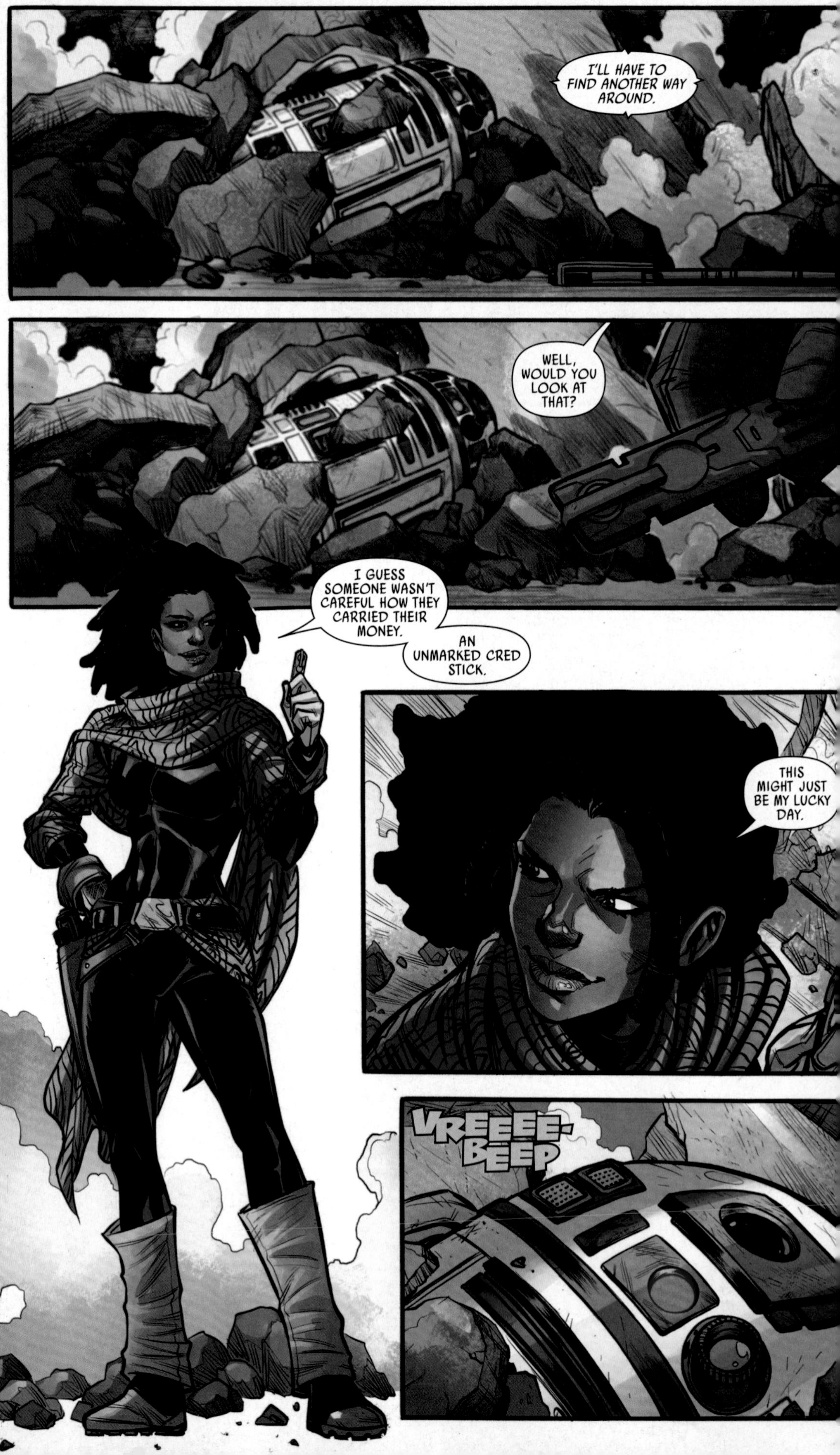
I'LL HAVE TO FIND ANOTHER WAY AROUND.
WELL, WOULD YOU LOOK AT THAT?
I GUESS SOMEONE WASN'T CAREFUL HOW THEY CARRIED THEIR MONEY.
AN UNMARKED CRED STICK.
THIS MIGHT JUST BE MY LUCKY DAY.
VREEEE-BEEP

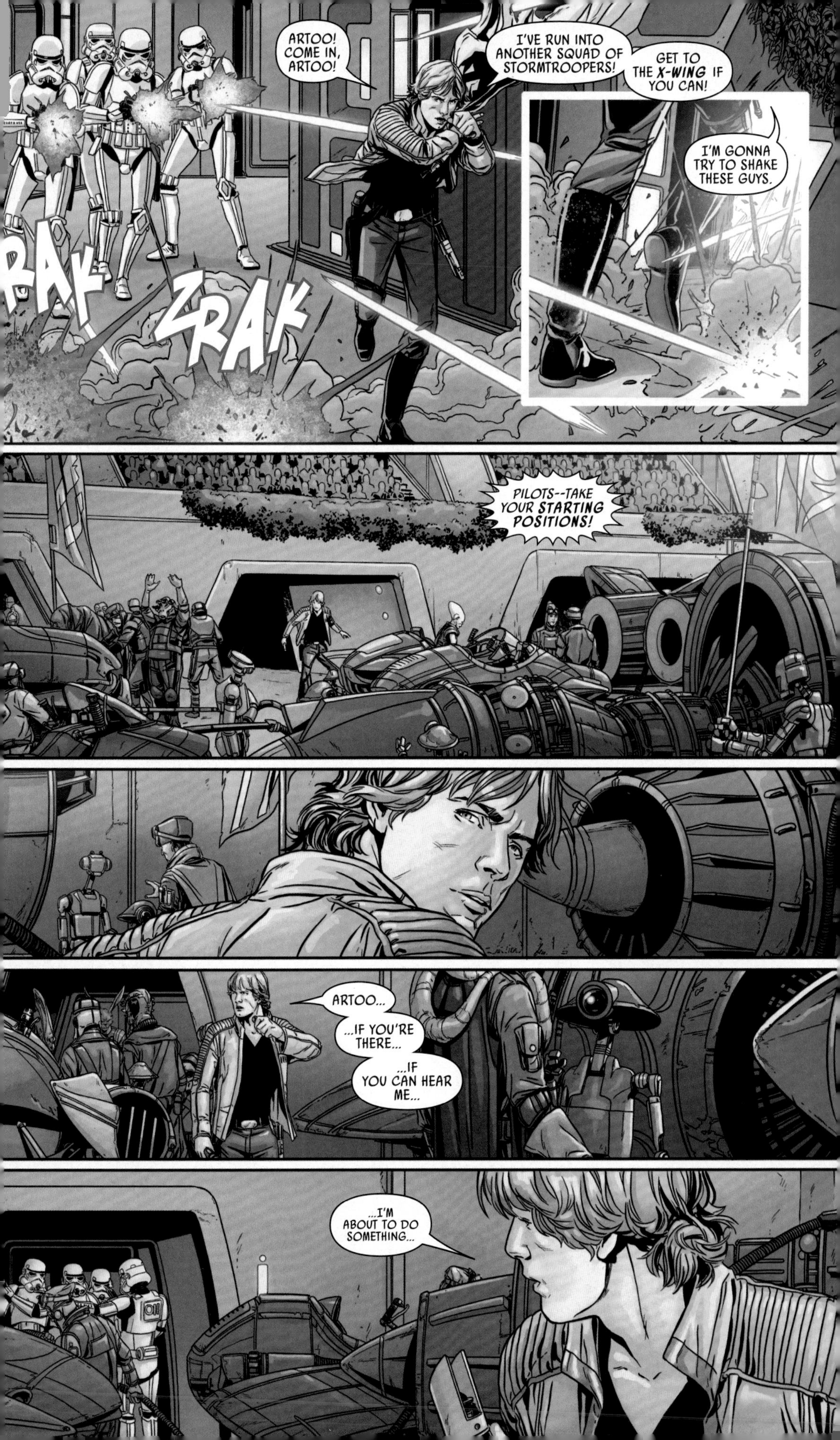
ARTOO! COME IN, ARTOO!
I'VE RUN INTO ANOTHER SQUAD OF STORMTROOPERS!
GET TO THE X-WING IF YOU CAN!
I'M GONNA TRY TO SHAKE THESE GUYS.
RAK
ZRAK
PILOTS--TAKE YOUR STARTING POSITIONS!
ARTOO...
...IF YOU'RE THERE...
...IF YOU CAN HEAR ME...
...I'M ABOUT TO DO SOMETHING...

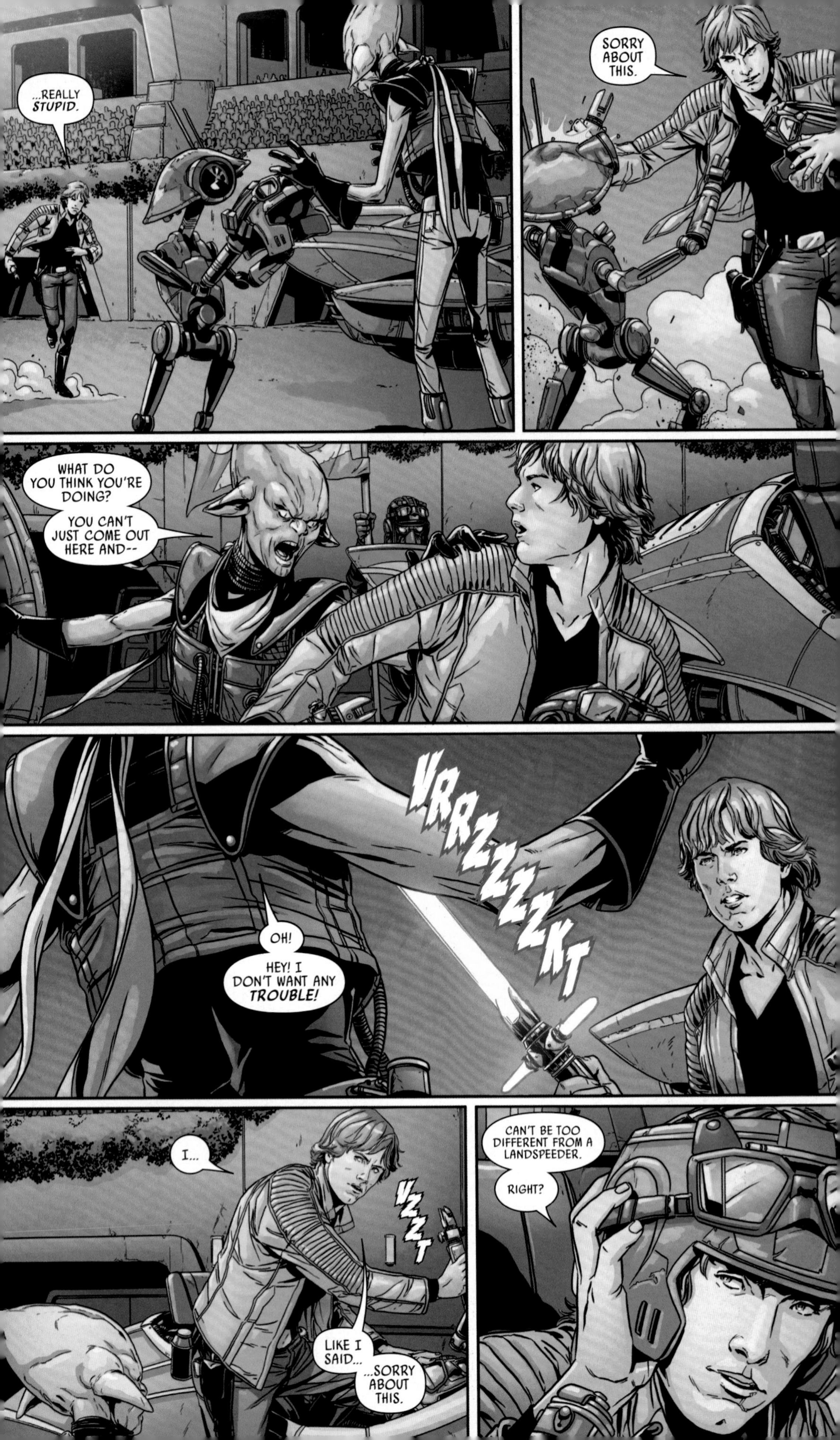
...REALLY *STUPID*.
SORRY ABOUT THIS.
WHAT DO YOU THINK YOU'RE DOING?
YOU CAN'T JUST COME OUT HERE AND--
VRRZZZZZKT
OH!
HEY! I DON'T WANT ANY *TROUBLE!*
I...
VZZT
LIKE I SAID...
...SORRY ABOUT THIS.
CAN'T BE TOO DIFFERENT FROM A LANDSPEEDER.
RIGHT?

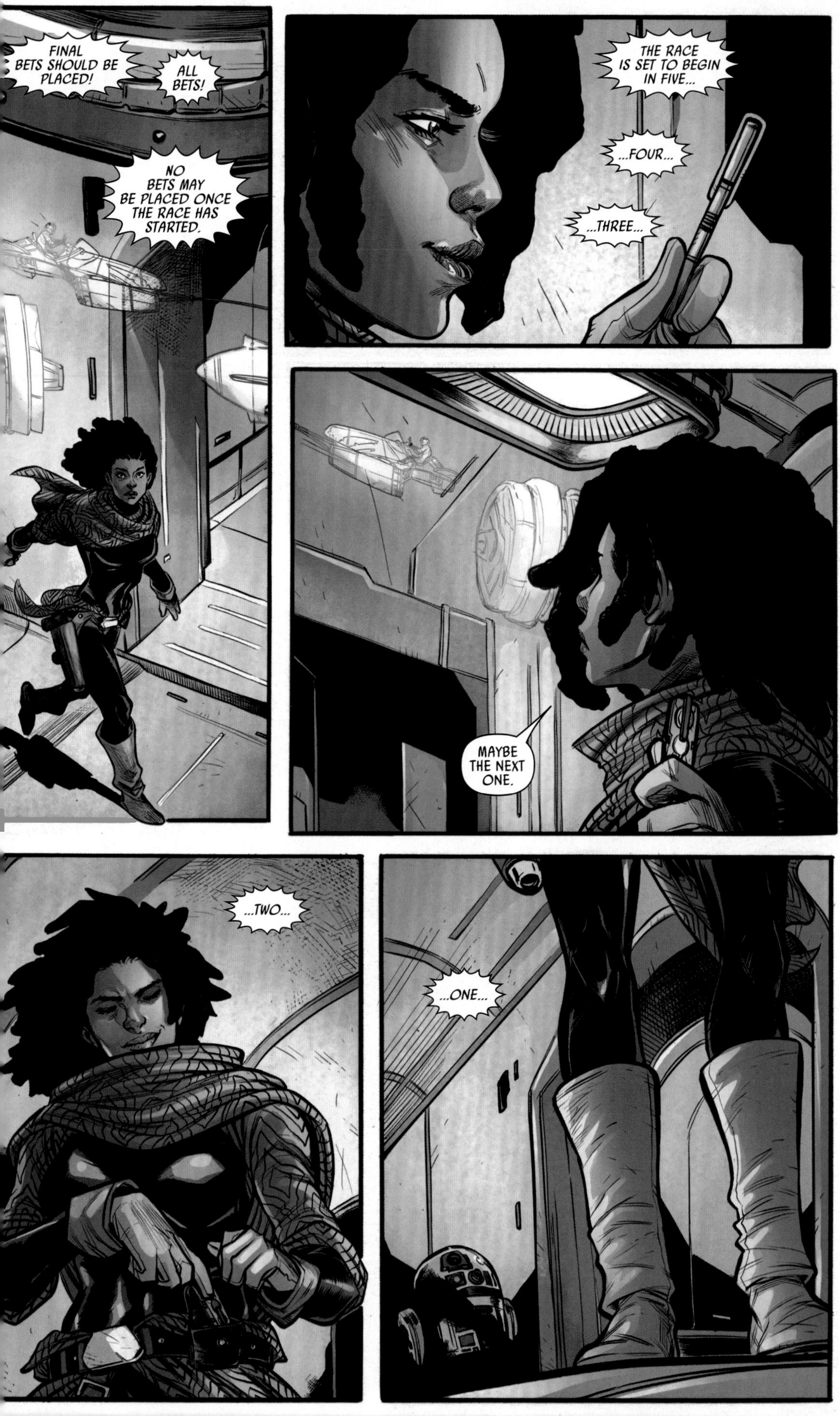
FINAL BETS SHOULD BE PLACED!
ALL BETS!
NO BETS MAY BE PLACED ONCE THE RACE HAS STARTED.
THE RACE IS SET TO BEGIN IN FIVE...
...FOUR...
...THREE...
MAYBE THE NEXT ONE.
...TWO...
...ONE...

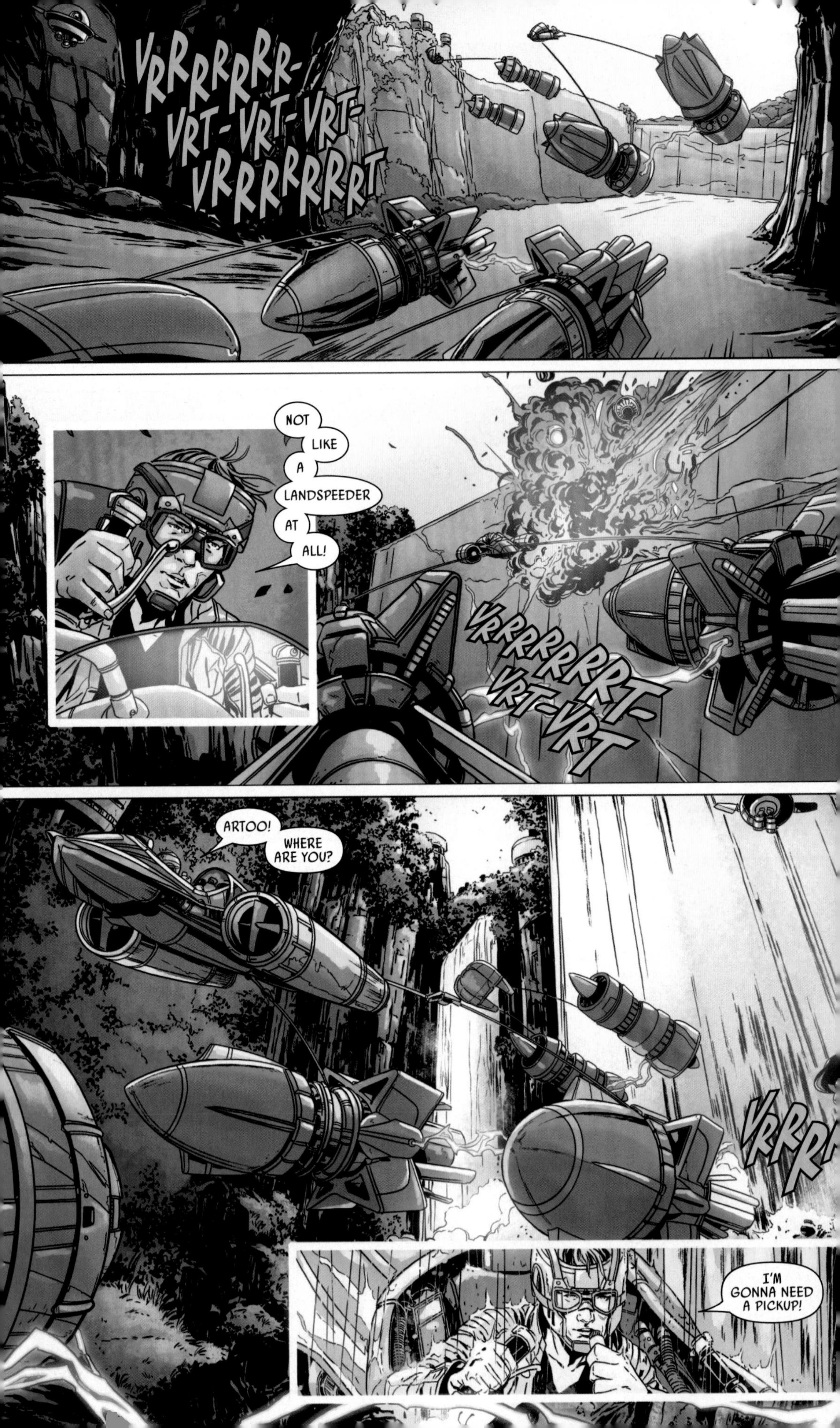
VRRRRRRR-
VRT-VRT-VRT-
VRRRRRRRT
NOT LIKE A LANDSPEEDER AT ALL!
VRRRRRRRRT-
VRT-VRT
ARTOO!
WHERE ARE YOU?
I'M GONNA NEED A PICKUP!

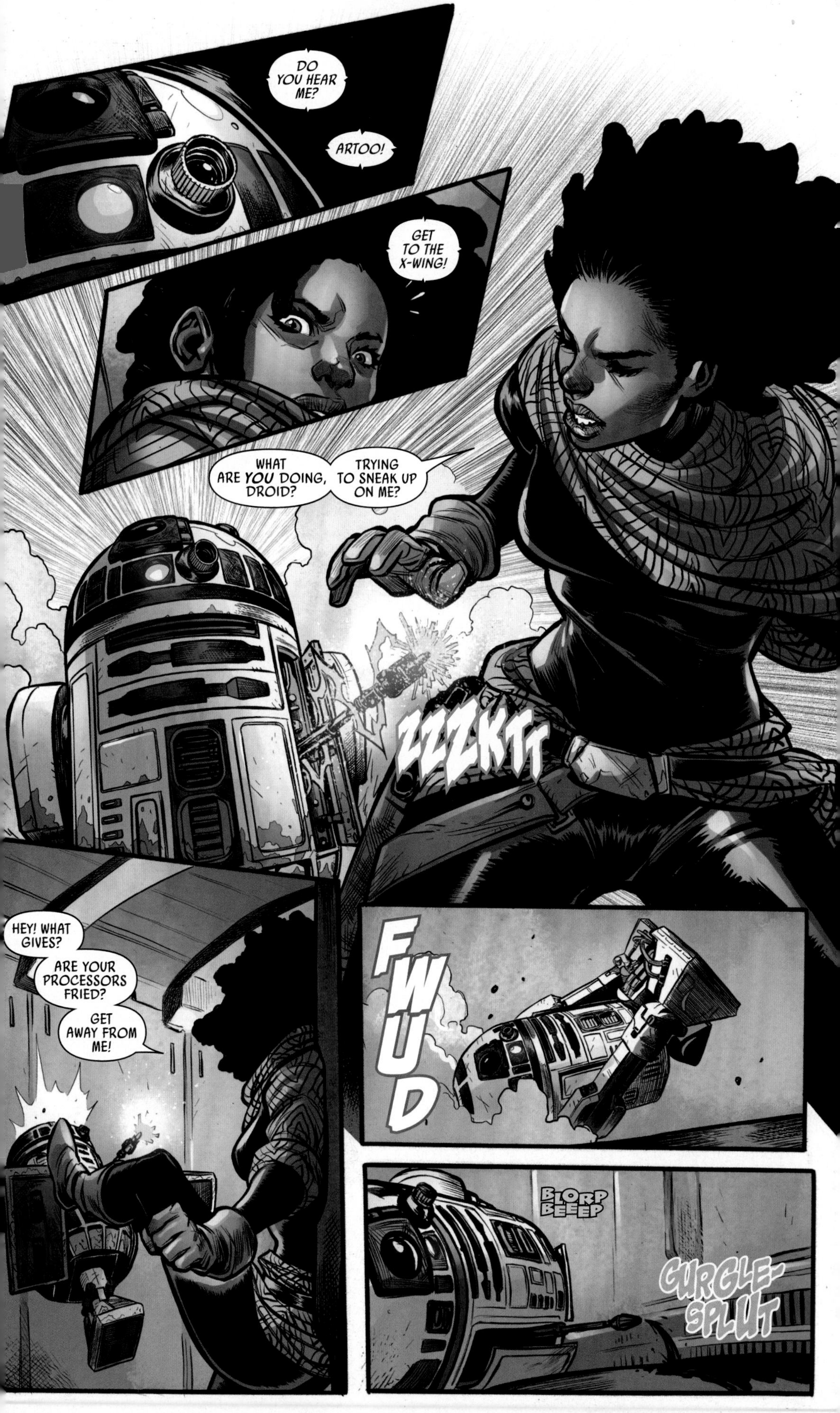

DO YOU HEAR ME?
ARTOO!
GET TO THE X-WING!
WHAT ARE YOU DOING, DROID?
TRYING TO SNEAK UP ON ME?
ZZZKTT
HEY! WHAT GIVES?
ARE YOUR PROCESSORS FRIED?
GET AWAY FROM ME!
FWUD
BLORP BEEEP
GURGLE-SPLUT

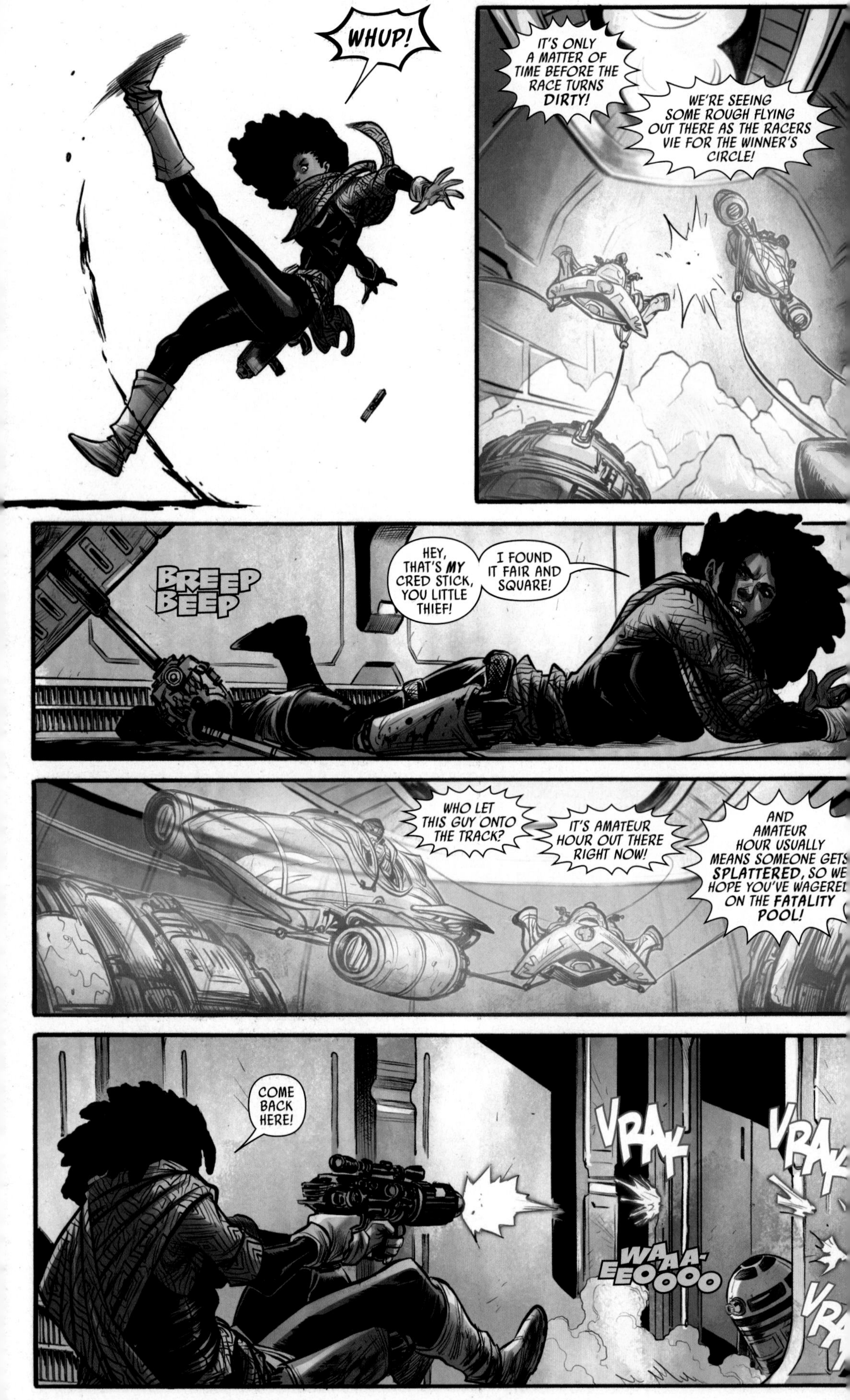
WHUP!
IT'S ONLY A MATTER OF TIME BEFORE THE RACE TURNS DIRTY!
WE'RE SEEING SOME ROUGH FLYING OUT THERE AS THE RACERS VIE FOR THE WINNER'S CIRCLE!
BREEP BEEP
HEY, THAT'S MY CRED STICK, YOU LITTLE THIEF!
I FOUND IT FAIR AND SQUARE!
WHO LET THIS GUY ONTO THE TRACK?
IT'S AMATEUR HOUR OUT THERE RIGHT NOW!
AND AMATEUR HOUR USUALLY MEANS SOMEONE GETS SPLATTERED, SO WE HOPE YOU'VE WAGERED ON THE FATALITY POOL!
COME BACK HERE!
VRAK
VRAK
WAAA-EEOOOO

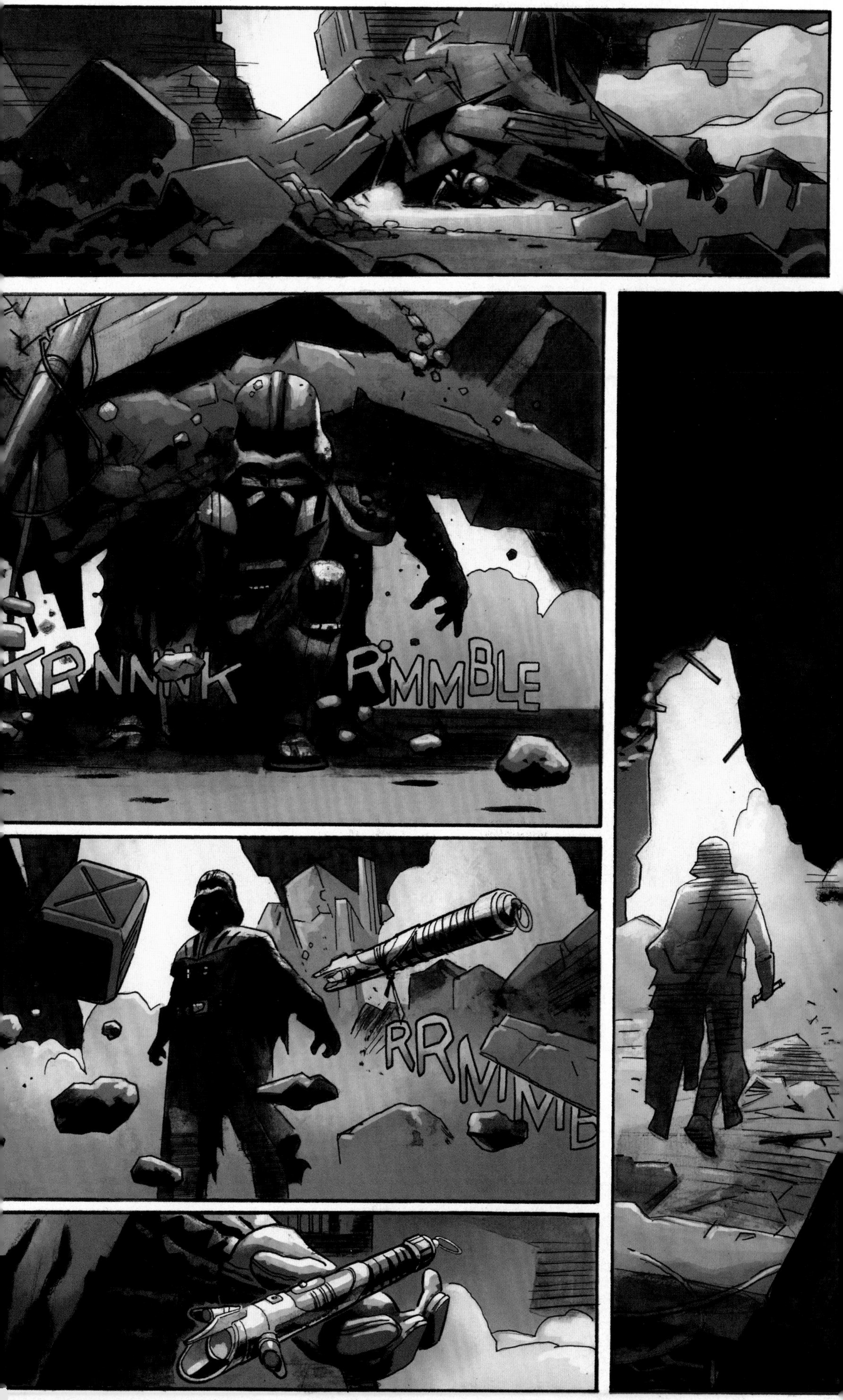

KRNNNK
RMMBLE
RRNNMB

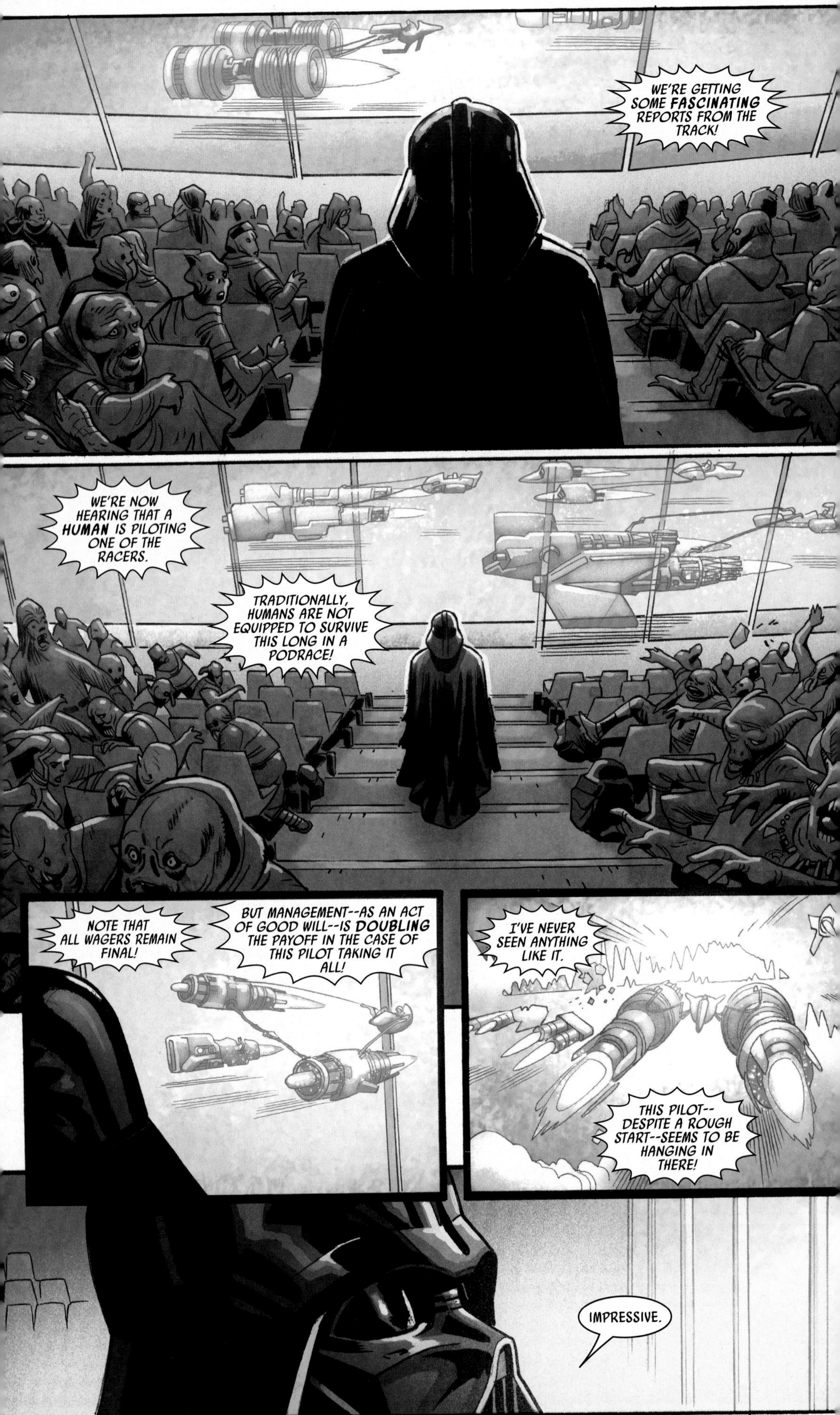
WE'RE GETTING SOME FASCINATING REPORTS FROM THE TRACK!
WE'RE NOW HEARING THAT A HUMAN IS PILOTING ONE OF THE RACERS.
TRADITIONALLY, HUMANS ARE NOT EQUIPPED TO SURVIVE THIS LONG IN A PODRACE!
NOTE THAT ALL WAGERS REMAIN FINAL!
BUT MANAGEMENT--AS AN ACT OF GOOD WILL--IS DOUBLING THE PAYOFF IN THE CASE OF THIS PILOT TAKING IT ALL!
I'VE NEVER SEEN ANYTHING LIKE IT.
THIS PILOT--DESPITE A ROUGH START--SEEMS TO BE HANGING IN THERE!
IMPRESSIVE.

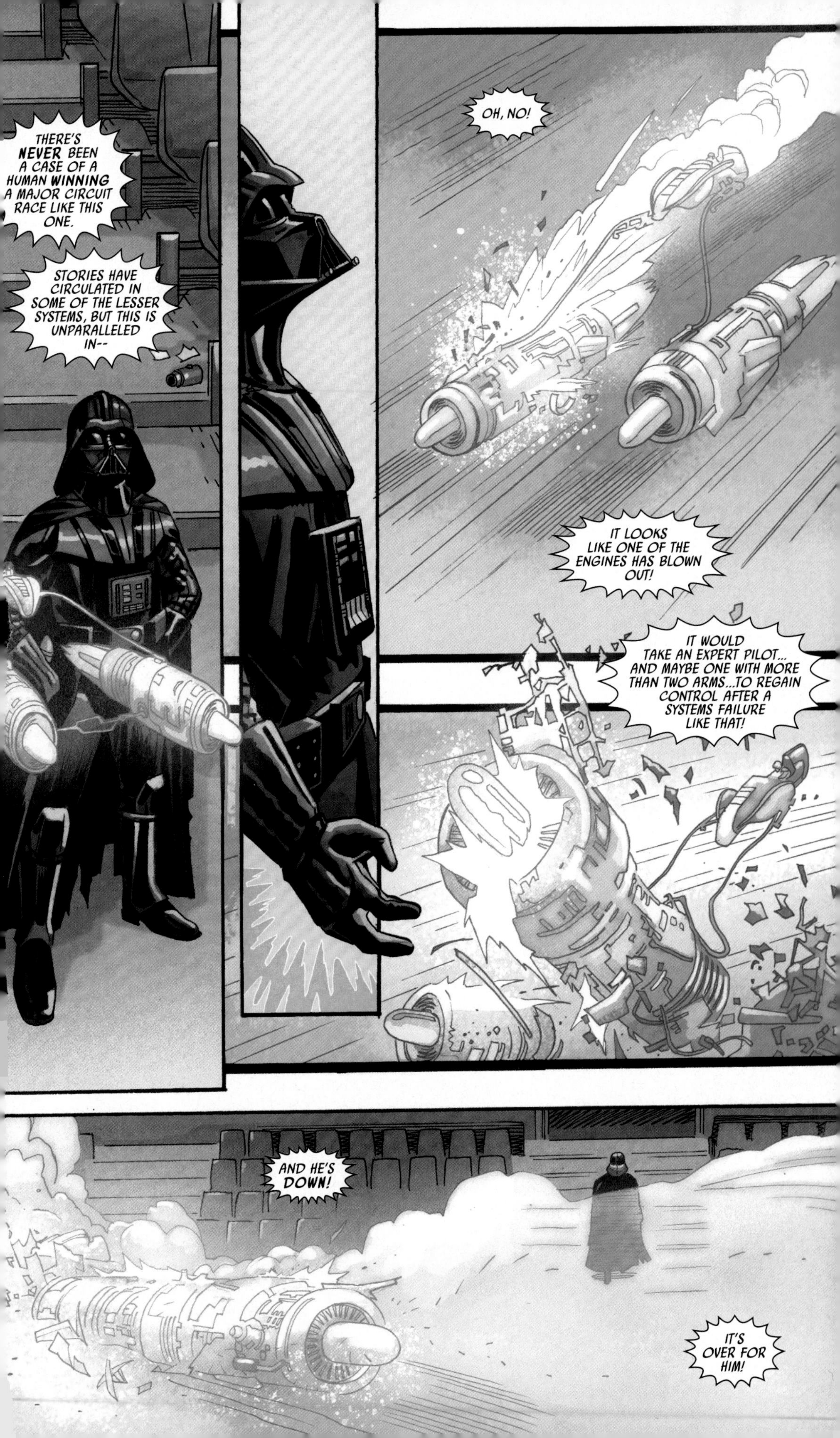

THERE'S NEVER BEEN A CASE OF A HUMAN WINNING A MAJOR CIRCUIT RACE LIKE THIS ONE.
STORIES HAVE CIRCULATED IN SOME OF THE LESSER SYSTEMS, BUT THIS IS UNPARALLELED IN--
OH, NO!
IT LOOKS LIKE ONE OF THE ENGINES HAS BLOWN OUT!
IT WOULD TAKE AN EXPERT PILOT... AND MAYBE ONE WITH MORE THAN TWO ARMS...TO REGAIN CONTROL AFTER A SYSTEMS FAILURE LIKE THAT!
AND HE'S DOWN!
IT'S OVER FOR HIM!

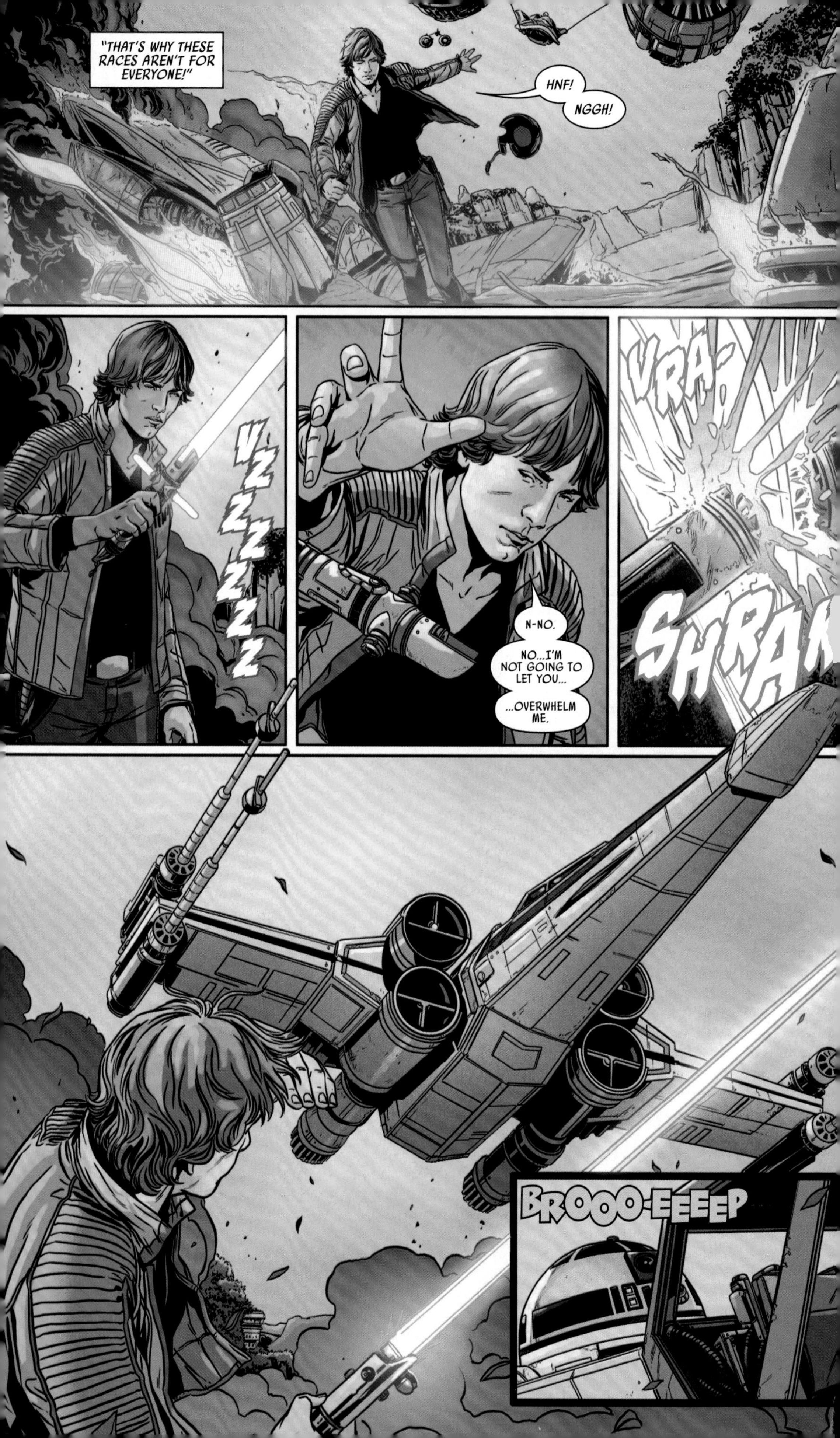
"THAT'S WHY THESE RACES AREN'T FOR EVERYONE!"
HNF!
NGGH!
VZZZZZZZ
N-NO.
NO...I'M NOT GOING TO LET YOU...
...OVERWHELM ME.
VRA-
SHRA
BROOO-EEEEP

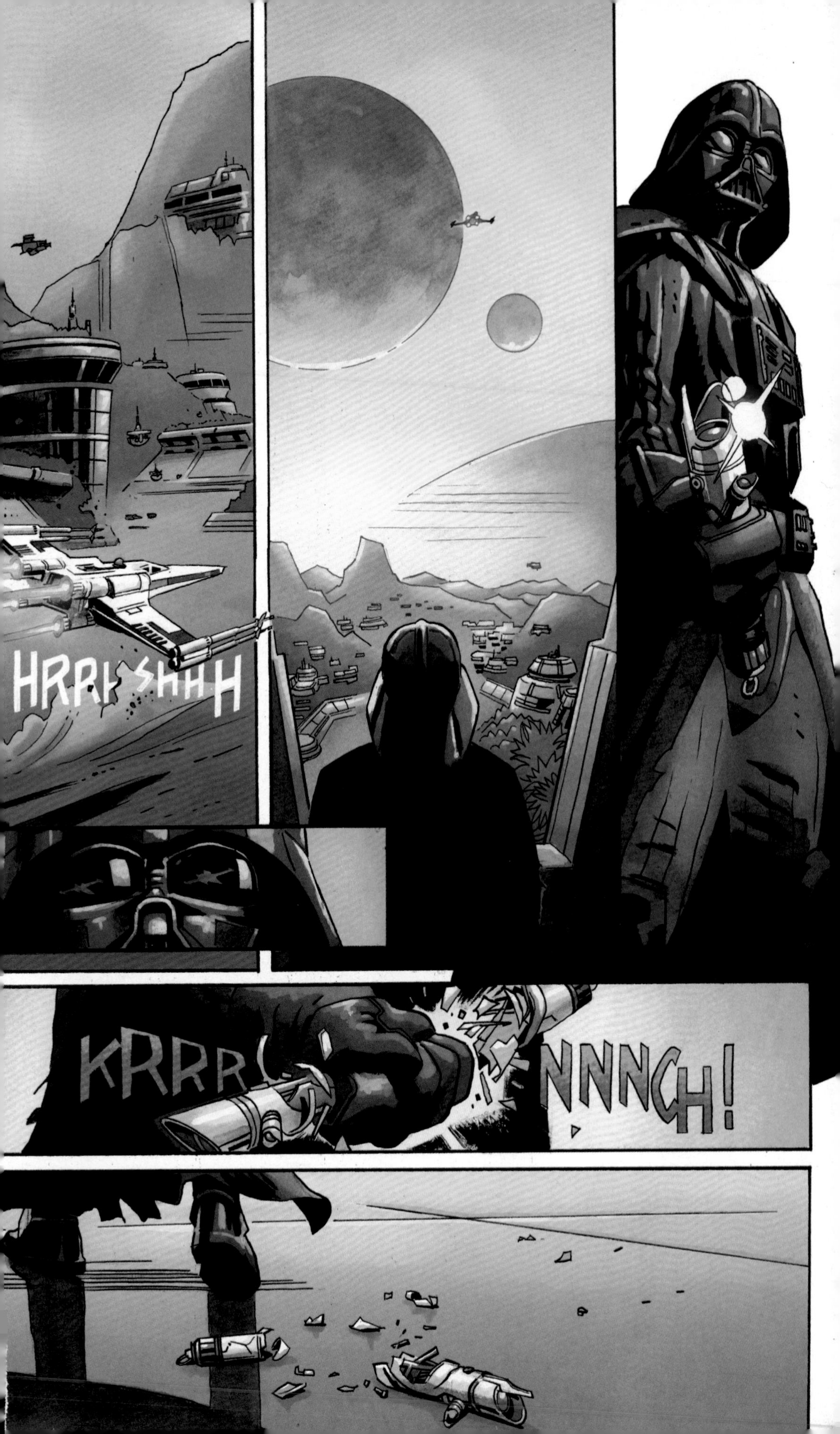
HRRKSHHH
KRRR
NNNCH!

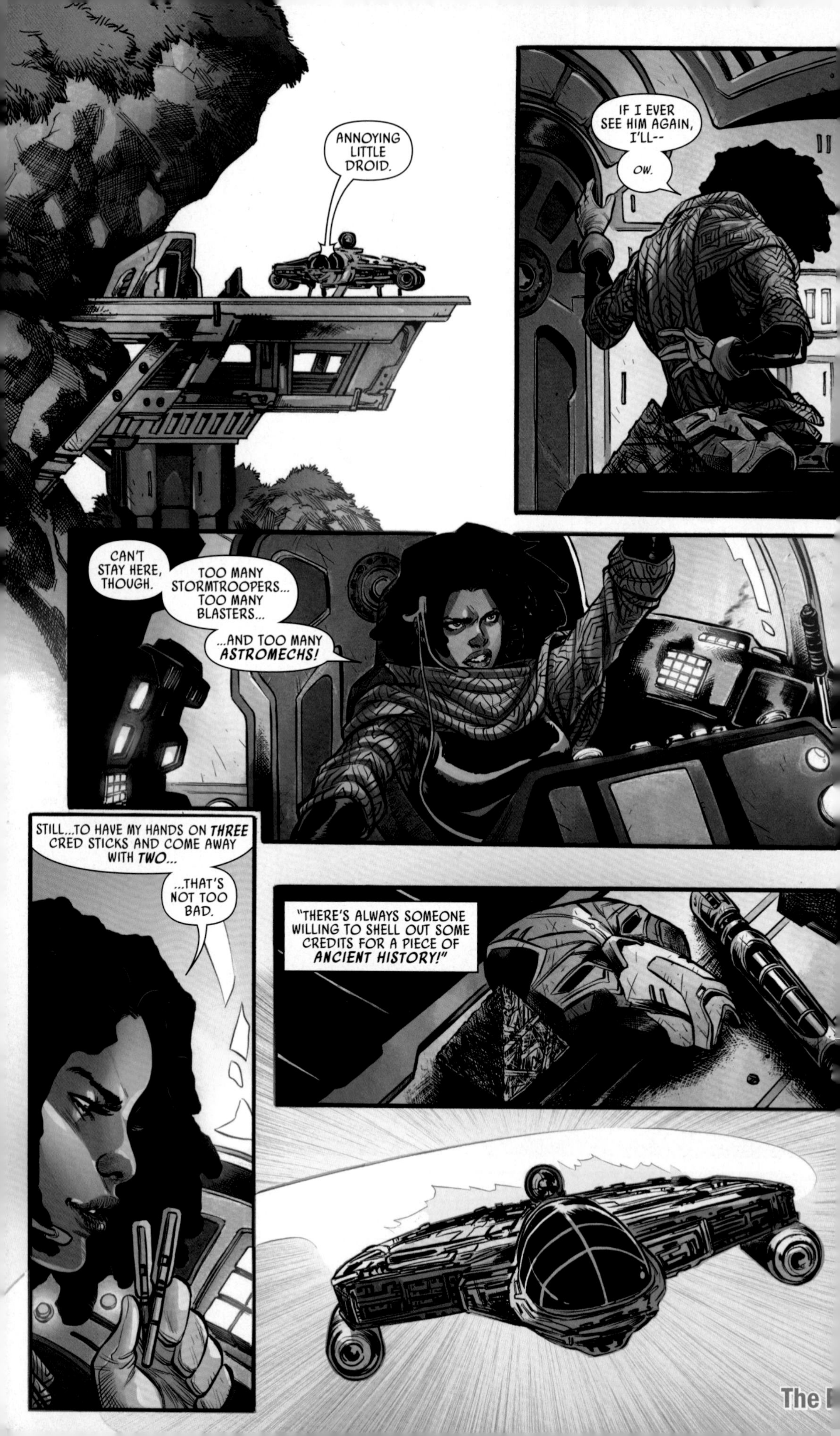
ANNOYING LITTLE DROID.
IF I EVER SEE HIM AGAIN, I'LL--
OW.
CAN'T STAY HERE, THOUGH.
TOO MANY STORMTROOPERS... TOO MANY BLASTERS...
...AND TOO MANY ASTROMECHS!
STILL...TO HAVE MY HANDS ON THREE CRED STICKS AND COME AWAY WITH TWO...
...THAT'S NOT TOO BAD.
"THERE'S ALWAYS SOMEONE WILLING TO SHELL OUT SOME CREDITS FOR A PIECE OF ANCIENT HISTORY!"

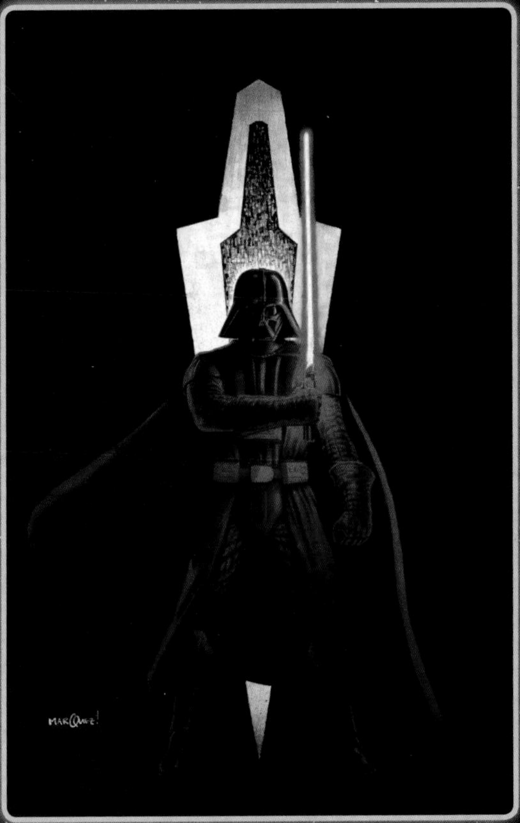

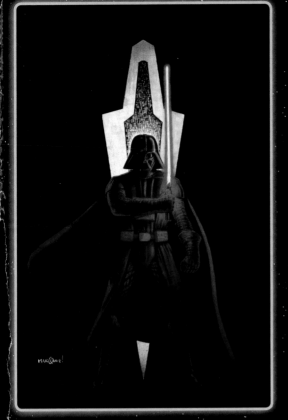

STAR WARS 50 Variant by
DAVID MARQUEZ

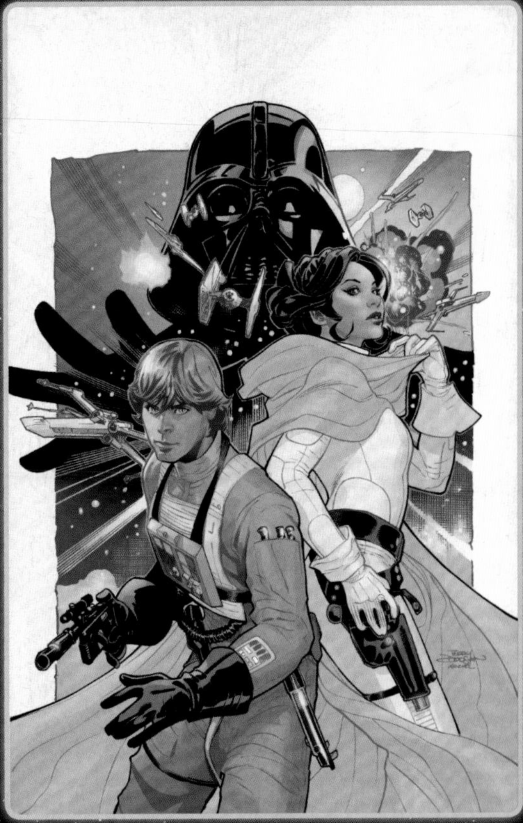

STAR WARS 50 Variant by
TERRY DODSON & RACHEL DODSON

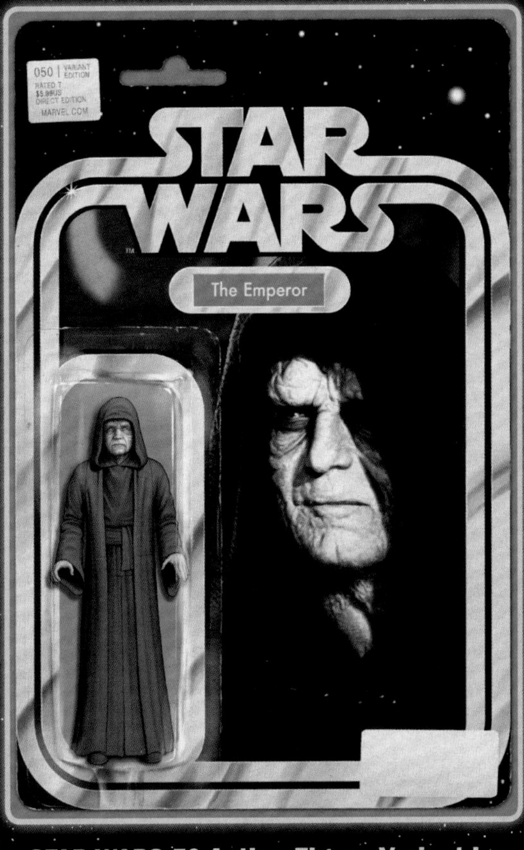
050 | VARIANT EDITION
RATED T
$5.99US
DIRECT EDITION
MARVEL.COM
STAR WARS
The Emperor

STAR WARS 50 Action Figure Variant by
JOHN TYLER CHRISTOPHER

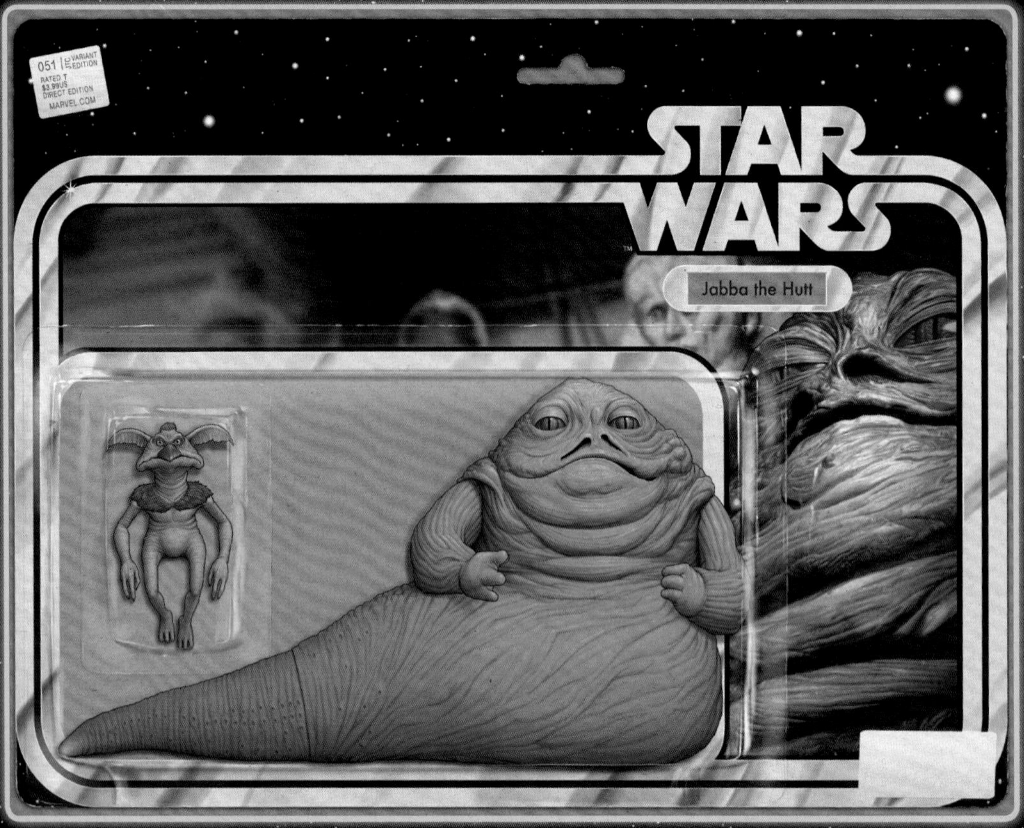
051 | VARIANT EDITION
RATED T
$3.99US
DIRECT EDITION
MARVEL.COM
STAR WARS
Jabba the Hutt

***STAR WARS* 51 Action Figure Variant by**
JOHN TYLER CHRISTOPHER

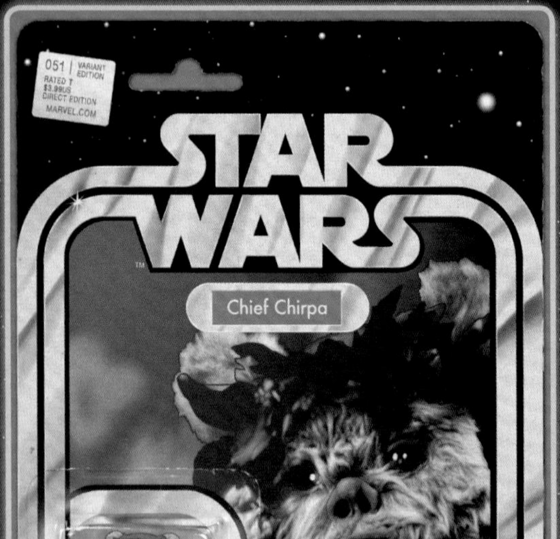
051 | VARIANT EDITION
RATED T
$3.99US
DIRECT EDITION
MARVEL.COM
STAR WARS
Chief Chirpa

***STAR WARS* 51 Action Figure Variant by**
JOHN TYLER CHRISTOPHER

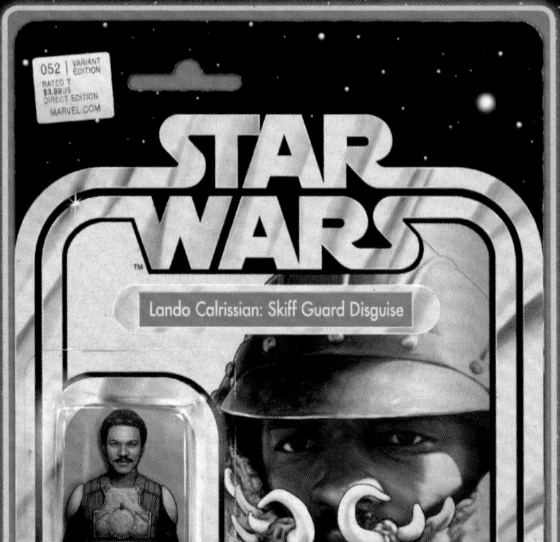
052 | VARIANT EDITION
RATED T
$3.99US
DIRECT EDITION
MARVEL.COM
STAR WARS
Lando Calrissian: Skiff Guard Disguise

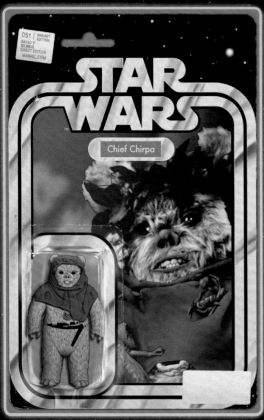

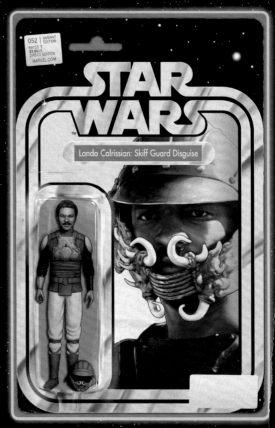

***STAR WARS* 52 Action Figure Variant by**
JOHN TYLER CHRISTOPHER

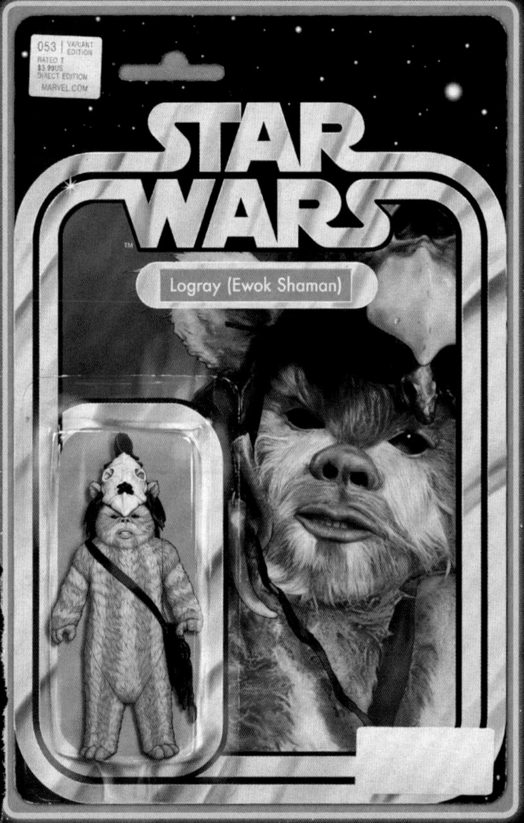
053 | VARIANT EDITION
RATED T
$3.99US
DIRECT EDITION
MARVEL.COM
STAR WARS
Logray (Ewok Shaman)

STAR WARS 53 **Action Figure Variant by**
JOHN TYLER CHRISTOPHER

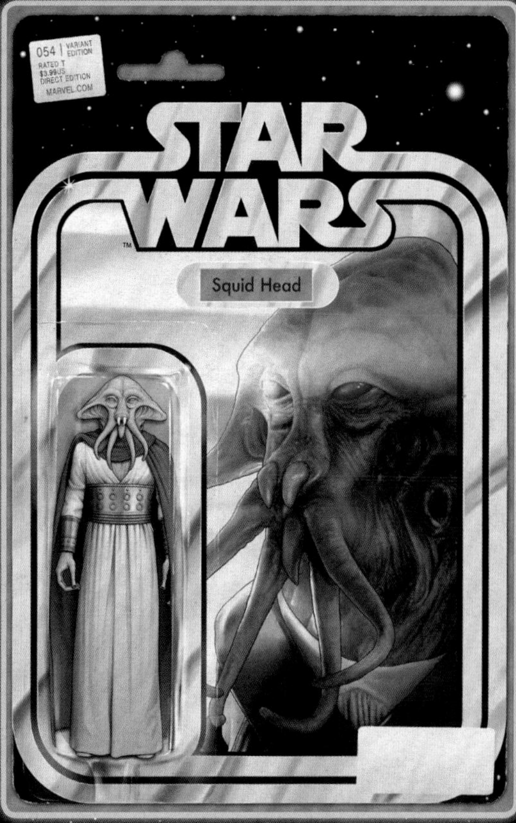
054 | VARIANT EDITION
RATED T
$3.99US
DIRECT EDITION
MARVEL.COM
STAR WARS
Squid Head

STAR WARS 54 **Action Figure Variant by**
JOHN TYLER CHRISTOPHER

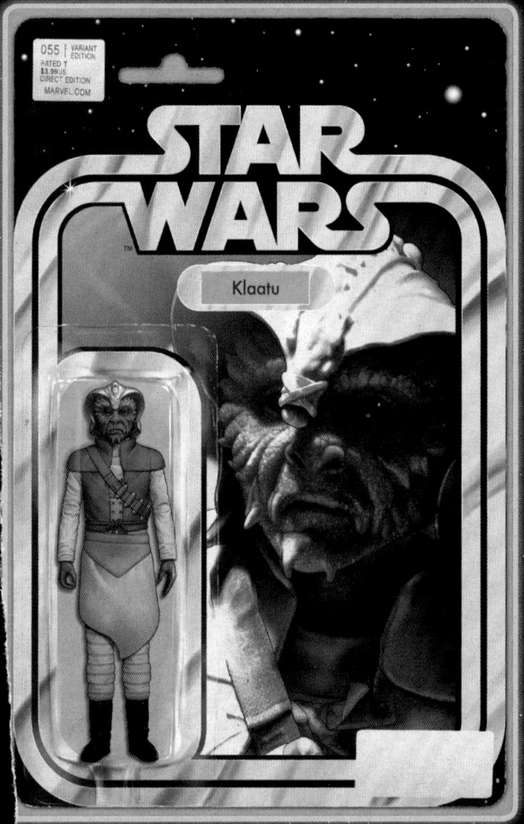
055 | VARIANT EDITION
RATED T
$3.99US
DIRECT EDITION
MARVEL.COM
STAR WARS
Klaatu

STAR WARS 55 **Action Figure Variant by**
JOHN TYLER CHRISTOPHER

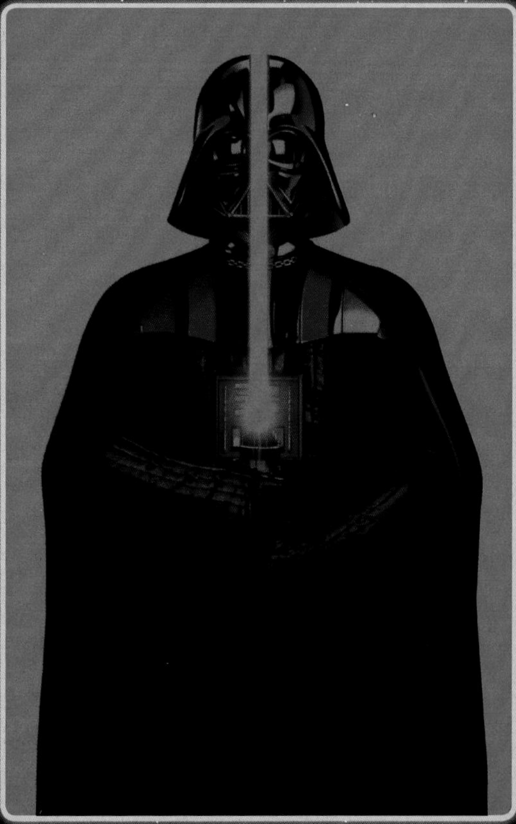

STAR WARS ANNUAL 4 **Variant by**
JOHN TYLER CHRISTOPHER

HAN AND CHEWIE IN A RACE AGAINST TIME, THE EMPIRE AND THE FASTEST SHIPS IN THE GALAXY!

STAR WARS: HAN SOLO HC
978-1302912109

ON SALE NOW
AVAILABLE IN PRINT AND DIGITAL WHEREVER BOOKS ARE SOL

TO FIND A COMIC SHOP NEAR YOU, VISIT COMICSHOPLOCATOR.COM

CHARACTERS YOU KNOW.
STORIES YOU DON'T.

STAR WARS: LANDO TPB
978-0-7851-9319-7 • $16.99

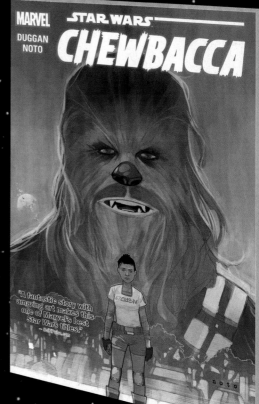

STAR WARS: CHEWBACCA TPB
978-0-7851-9320-3 • $16.99

ON SALE NOW
IN PRINT & DIGITAL WHEREVER BOOKS ARE SOLD.

SENSATIONAL *STAR W*
ARTWORK RETELLING
STORY OF *A NEW HO*

STAR WARS: A NEW HOPE — THE 40TH ANNIVERSARY
978-1302911287

ON SALE NOW
AVAILABLE IN PRINT AND DIGITAL WHEREVER BOOKS

TO FIND A COMIC SHOP NEAR YOU, VISIT COMICSHOPLOCATOR

RETURN TO A GALAXY FAR, FAR AWAY!

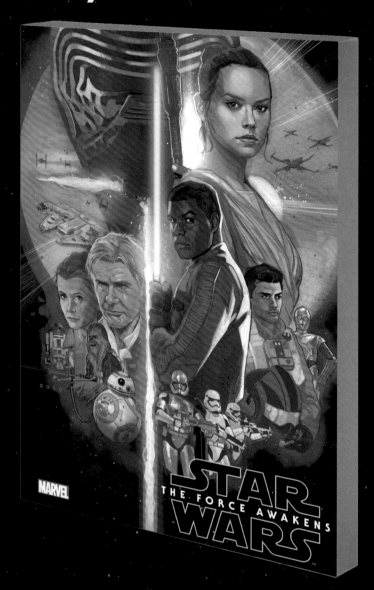

STAR WARS: THE FORCE AWAKENS ADAPTATION TPB
978-1302902032

ON SALE NOW
WHEREVER BOOKS ARE SOLD

TO FIND A COMIC SHOP NEAR YOU, VISIT COMICSHOPLOCATOR.COM

© & TM 2017 LUCASFILM LTD.

YOU LOVE COLORING.
WE KNOW.

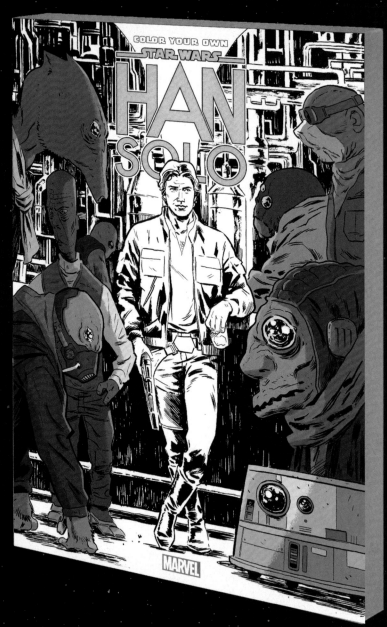

COLOR YOUR OWN *STAR WARS*: HAN SOLO
978-1302912093

ON SALE NOW
AVAILABLE IN PRINT AND DIGITAL WHEREVER BOOKS ARE SOLD

TO FIND A COMIC SHOP NEAR YOU, VISIT COMICSHOPLOCATOR.COM

© & TM 2018 LUCASFILM LTD.